European Financial Reporting

Routledge, in association with the Institute of Chartered Accountants in England and Wales, is pleased to present a major new series in European accounting.

During the last decade many of Europe's largest companies have developed new approaches to financial reporting. In doing so they have sought to explain to the rapidly expanding international investment community not only their own financial results but also the complexities of the business environments in which they operate. Now, with the coming into force throughout the EC of a harmonized accounting framework, the scene is set for European companies to use a common approach to financial reporting. However, despite the moves towards standardization and harmonization, the underlying differences between Europe's various business environments are still far-reaching. Local accounting practices continue to reflect this.

The European Financial Reporting series provides the first detailed, authoritative, country-by-country guides to current accounting and financial reporting practices in Europe. Each volume also includes a comprehensive analysis of the current state of company law, taxation and other matters relevant to business activity.

The series aims to meet the needs of:

- accountants, auditors and other business professionals, including those advising companies operating or intending to operate in the country in question;
- analysts and investors wishing to interpret the financial statements of European companies;
- students of international accounting at universities, business schools and other institutions of higher education.

The series editor **Stuart McLeay** and associate editor **Simon Archer** are Professors, respectively, in the School of Accounting, Banking and Economics at the University of Wales, Bangor and in the Department of Management Studies at the University of Surrey, Guildford. They are both internationally recognized as authorities in the field of financial reporting. In preparing the European Financial Reporting series, the principal editor has assembled a team of authors from among the leading figures in European accounting.

European Financial Reporting

Series editor: Professor Stuart McLeay
Associate editor: Professor Simon Archer

FRANCE
Jean-Claude Scheid and Peter Walton

SPAIN
José A. Gonzalo and José L. Gallizo

IRELAND
Niamh Brennan, Francis J. O'Brien and Aileen Pierce

GREECE
Anthony A. Papas

ITALY
Angelo Riccaboni and Rosanna Ghirri

DENMARK
Merete Christiansen and Jens Elling

GERMANY
Dieter Ordelheide and Dieter Pfaff

PORTUGAL
Leonor Fernandes Ferreira

LUXEMBOURG
Peter Clark

THE NETHERLANDS
Jan Dijksma and Martin Hoogendoorn

BELGIUM
Christian Lefebvre

UNITED KINGDOM
Paul Gordon and Sidney Gray

Germany

Dieter Ordelheide
and
Dieter Pfaff

London and New York

Published
in association with

First published 1994
by Routledge
11 New Fetter Lane, London EC4P 4EE

Simultaneously published in the USA and Canada
by Routledge
29 West 35th Street, New York, NY 10001

Reprinted 1994

Typeset in Times by Solidus (Bristol) Limited
Printed and bound in Great Britain by
Antony Rowe Ltd, Chippenham, Wiltshire

British Library Cataloguing in Publication Data
A catalogue record for this book is available from the British Library

Library of Congress Cataloging in Publication Data
A catalog record for this book is available from the Library of Congress

ISBN 0-415-06775-8

Contents

Figures

Tables

Examples

Series preface

During the last decade many of Europe's largest companies have developed new and innovative approaches to financial reporting. One of their principal aims has been to explain the complexities of the business environments in which they operate to the rapidly expanding international investment community. Indeed, earnings and other reported figures are greatly influenced not only by the divergent account methods adopted in various European countries but also by the specific application of local tax regulations, company laws and employment practices, as well as the considerable diversity of financial and commercial environments in which a European company may operate.

With the coming into force throughout the European Community of a harmonized accounting framework, the scene is now set for European companies to use a common approach to financial reporting. Nevertheless, the EC directives cover only a restricted sub-set of disclosure and measurement issues, and with respect to these, harmonization is sometimes at a fairly superficial level. For example, under the Fourth Directive alone, there are more than thirty optional areas of harmonization which provide for alternative ways of implementing the directive. In spite of this, the immediate impact of the European Commission's actions in the area of financial reporting will be to enhance considerably the level of corporate accountability throughout the EC. At the same time, the latest evidence suggests that International Accounting Standards are assuming an increasingly important role.

As a result, the 1990s will bear witness to an accounting revolution in Europe. In the next few years the extent of financial disclosure will take a quantum leap forward in many countries, particularly with regard to the publication of consolidated financial statements and audit opinions. In some countries the institutional and legal infrastructure of accounting is already undergoing rapid change.

These contemporary changes in European financial reporting are taking place in the context of a rich history of accounting development. Starting with the earliest record-keeping of the ancient Greeks, accounting ideas spread rapidly throughout Europe in the Middle Ages in keeping with the commercialization of the trading ports of the Atlantic and the Mediterranean and Baltic seas. Throughout the entire continent the earliest books of account date back to this period. Subsequently, Napoleonic codification influenced the regulation of business activity throughout a large part of continental Europe, laying the basis for the later introduction of extensive uniformity and national accounting plans. At much the same time the notion of direct accountability to owners and lenders and the establishment of an independent auditing profession occurred as a result of the creation of joint-stock companies during the industrial revolutions which first took place in some of the north European countries.

More recently Europe as a whole has experienced yet another era of cross-fertilization in accounting thought with regard not only to the development of financial accounting standards but also to broader issues such as social accountability. In this respect, the reader who consults the various books in this series will find that remarkable innovations have taken place in some of Europe's smallest countries, such as Greece, Luxembourg, Ireland and Belgium, where the very nature of the society and its economy and the narrowness of the capital market have led to original developments in financial accounting, such as the preparation of ECU accounts, concentration on accounting for financial institutions and investment trusts, innovative voluntary disclosures aimed at international investors and new solutions to the problems of reporting across different languages.

Harmonization may result in a common understanding of the scope of corporate financial reporting in Europe, but there still remain significant differences between Europe's various business environments. The authors of the first twelve volumes in the European Financial Reporting series have produced the most authoritative studies of European accounting to date, which chart the evolution of accounting thought through to its current position. In particular, considerable attention has been paid to the fiscal, legal and financial background, and each book contains a detailed examination of current trends and techniques in accounting practice.

Professor Stuart McLeay
University of Wales, Bangor

Acknowledgements

We are indebted to John Flower, who translated the manuscript and whose comments were a very valuable input. Thomas Schröer, Ray Offord, Ulrich Becker and Christian Leuz critically reviewed the translation. Hanne Böckem, Ulrich Huwald, Nora Müller and Stefan Roth helped with the technical production and did a great job drafting the many tables. We are obliged to all of them. We thank Stuart McLeay and Simon Archer for including the book in the series and Rosemary Nixon of Routledge for her support.

Dieter Ordelheide
Dieter Pfaff

Notes on the authors

Dieter Ordelheide is Professor of Accounting at the J.W. Goethe University, Frankfurt am Main. As a Professor at the European Institute for Advanced Studies in Management (EIASM), Brussels, and a member of the Accounting Advisory Forum of the EC commission, he is also involved in research and the political process of international accounting harmonization.

Dieter Pfaff is currently employed as a lecturer (*Hochschulassistent*) at the J.W. Goethe University, Frankfurt am Main. He is a member of the European Accounting Association and of the editorial management committee of the *European Accounting Review*. His main areas of research are Financial Accounting, Management Accounting and New Institutional Economics.

Introduction

In presenting German financial reporting to the English-speaking accounting community, one of our main aims is to make clear how and why the financial statements of German enterprises differ from those of companies in Britain and the United States, or from financial statements prepared in other countries that use Anglo-American accounting methods. There are many individual differences between German and Anglo-American financial reporting. Taking these differences together, there can be little doubt that financial reporting in Germany is based upon substantially different foundations. Briefly, the German system is distinguished by the following particular characteristics.

Profit as the amount available for distribution. The ascertainment of asset values, or wealth, is subsidiary to the ascertainment of profit. Profit is seen as the amount that can be withdrawn from an enterprise without endangering its capital base, and also as the amount that can be distributed to shareholders and taxed by the state. At least by comparison with Britain and the United States, the role of financial statements in meeting the information needs of interested parties is less important than the periodic measurement of distributable earnings.

A uniform basis for the preparation of financial statements and the taxation of profits. The same fundamental income concept is the basis of the determination of wealth and profits, with respect to both the preparation of financial statements and the computation of tax. In fact, for the vast majority of German enterprises – particularly small and medium-sized firms – the financial statements *are* the tax accounts.

Historical cost accounting, or 'Mark bleibt Mark' *('a mark is still a mark').* Because of the German experience of hyperinflation in the first half of this century, economic policy places great emphasis on monetary stability. The revaluation of assets or the use of inflation accounting techniques would be considered a public admission of inflation; they are not allowed. Profit, both in the financial statements and for taxation, is considered as a money surplus adjusted for timing differences.

Risk-averse profit measurement. Owing to the emphasis on measurement for the purposes of distribution, reported earnings and taxable earnings are measured on a prudential basis. Indeed, reported profit must be almost certain of being realized in cash.

A different approach in the group accounts of international enterprises. Some large enterprises (e.g. Daimler-Benz, Schering) are rather less conservative in their consolidated financial statements, at least by comparison with the strict German rules. This has no effect on profit distribution, since dividends and tax are based on the financial statements of the individual companies. The process is facilitated by the possibility of using in the consolidated accounts options different from those used in the individual accounts. The presentation of the group accounts, in particular the statement of the group's capital, is brought more into line with the conventions of the particular foreign capital market.

A legalistic system of rules. The obligation to prepare accounts, and, in particular, to publish accounts, is an invasion of businessmen's privacy, and, as such, requires the approval of the legislature. There is no accounting standard-setting body recognized by the government. Neither the stock exchange nor the *Institut der Wirtschaftsprüfer* (IdW, the Institute of German Certified Public Accountants) has the power to set standards. The legal rules are comparatively explicit. Additional refinement and interpretation are provided, first, by the courts, particularly the tax courts, and, second, by the 'legal interpretations market', where professional accountants, lawyers, practical businessmen and, not least, academics, offer their services. In this market place the opinions of the Institut der Wirtschaftsprüfer carry special weight. This is particularly the case for the profession; auditors are on safe ground if they follow its opinions.

Differentiation of financial reporting according to legal form, size and branch. Since their liability is limited to the subscribed capital, the financial reporting requirements are stricter for corporations than for other forms of business enterprise. Very large unincorporated enterprises are treated in the same way as corporations, however. For corporations there are three class sizes, each with different requirements concerning auditing and disclosure. There are also different accounting requirements for enterprises in particular sectors (e.g. banking, insurance).

The system of financial reporting is an element of the overall economic system, which, notwithstanding the much-cited globalization of business, still differs markedly from country to country, even within the European Community. Two markets have a particular influence on the development of financial reporting: the capital market and the labour market. Labour markets are national markets. This is also the case, if not to the same extent, with the structure of capital markets. In each country the labour and capital markets are structured differently and, in consequence, financial reporting is different. For example, the way workers are organized in trade unions, how they are represented in business decision-making and what the trade unions consider their self-evident rights, are fundamentally different in Germany as compared with Britain. On the German capital market the various forms of financial instrument have a different importance, compared with, say, the American market (e.g. shares are less important in Germany). The banking systems still differ (all-round banks as opposed to separate commercial and merchant banks); there are differences in the legal position of banks (e.g. as regards proxy voting) and so on. If German enterprises were to adopt Anglo-American-style financial reporting the effect on the labour and capital markets would not be the same as in the United States or Britain. The taxation effects would be different, too. These different effects are already allowed for in the national financial reporting system. It appears that the different structuring of national labour and capital markets, as well as the different relationship between the financial statements and taxation, conditions the various national systems of financial reporting, and vice versa.

The international harmonization of financial reporting is part of the movement towards a world economic system. But we are only at the beginning. In this phase the work of building the overall system is helped by a better understanding of national financial reporting requirements. In this book we present the fundamental features of German financial reporting, making them comprehensible in their context.

The core of the book is Part II, 'Accounting, auditing and financial reporting'. It deals with the objectives of German accounting, the legalistic form of regulation, the rules for keeping the books and for drawing up the inventory (Chapter 6); the annual accounts of the individual enterprise (Chapter 7); the group accounts (Chapter 8); the management report, the legal requirements relating to the interim reports of quoted companies and the special format of accounting for profit per share (Chapter 9), as well as the audit and disclosure regulations (Chapter 10).

We consider financial reporting to be one element in the economy as a whole. Therefore, before this presentation of the individual legal standards, Part I, 'The business environment', gives background information on the country (Chapter 1), the forms of business organization (Chapter 2), the financial markets (Chapter 3) and the labour market (Chapter 4).

On account of the particularly close relationship in Germany between the measurement of profit in the financial statements and the tax computation, Chapter 5 explains the treatment of profits under the German tax regime. Chapter 6, in section 1.3, includes an exposition of the relationship between the financial statements and the tax calculation.

Part III, Appendices, contains practical examples of German financial statements, followed by a glossary and a bibliography.

In a short book it is not possible to deal with all aspects of the German system of financial reporting. Hence the following topics are either not dealt with or are treated only marginally:

1 The special legal standards for particular sectors (banks, insurance companies, savings banks).
2 The special legal standards for particular legal forms of business organization (e.g. co-operatives).
3 Financial reporting for the non-profit-making sector.
4 Detailed aspects of the computation of taxable profit.

Part I
The business environment

1
Germany: the country

1 SOCIETY

1.1 Population

The total population of Germany in October 1990 (the date of the reunification of West and East Germany) was 79.67 million, 63.56 million in the west and 16.11 million in the east. Whereas the population of West Germany had remained almost stationary since the end of the 1960s, that of the former German Democratic Republic had fallen from 18.3 million in 1950 to about 16.6 million in 1989. In West Germany, since 1972, the situation was marked by a decline in numbers of the indigenous population which was only just counterbalanced by net immigration.

The age structure (see Figure 1.1) and the proportion of foreigners are very different in East Germany as compared with West Germany. Overall, East Germany has a much younger population. In West Germany the low proportion of young people under 20 is particularly noteworthy. The proportion of foreigners in West Germany is almost 8 per

Corporate financial reporting in Germany – a profile

Companies
In Germany, the main types of company are the *Aktiengesellschaft*, or AG, which is a corporation with limited liability whose shares (*Aktien*) may be listed on a stock exchange, and the *Gesellschaft mit beschränkter Haftung*, or GmbH, a form of limited liability company whose shares are transferable but cannot be listed on a stock exchange (a large number of important German companies are incorporated as GmbH). In addition, a number of large organizations, such as savings banks, are organized in the form of a co-operative (*eingetragene Genossenschaft*, or eG). A particular characteristic of German business organization is the importance attached to employee participation in the managing board, the *Vorstand* in the case of an AG, or the *Geschäftsführung* in the case of a GmbH.

Accounting
The content and layout of the accounts of all German limited companies are subject to the requirements of the German Commercial Code (*Handelsgesetzbuch*, or HGB) as modified by the 1985 Accounting Directive Law, the *Bilanzrichtliniengesetz*. There is no national accounting standards body in Germany since accounting standards are incorporated in the Commercial Code and the Principles of Regular Accounting (*Grundsätze ordnungsmäßiger Buchführung*), which are subject to legal interpretation (see below). The *Maßgeblichkeitsprinzip*, or Authoritativeness Principle, suggests that financial statements drawn up in accordance with the Principles of Regular Accounting form the authoritative basis for the tax computation. In fact, to take advantage of certain tax concessions such as accelerated depreciation, the financial statements must be prepared using the same method as that used for tax purposes – the so-called Reverse Authoritativeness Principle (*Umgekehrtes Maßgeblichkeitsprinzip*).

Auditing
Auditing is compulsory for all large and medium-sized limited companies, and for large unincorporated enterprises. An audit may be carried out by either an auditing firm or an individual member of the *Institut der Wirtschaftsprüfer* or, in the case of medium-sized companies, by a sworn-in auditor (*vereidigter Buchprüfer*). The auditing profession is self-governing. A detailed written report by the auditor (*Prüfungsbericht*) is required by law, to include an analysis of the accounts, matters influencing the financial situation and any violations of the law by the officers of the company. The precise text of the published audit opinion (*Bestätigungsvermerk*) is set down in law, but should be extended when additional comments are necessary.

Taxation
Corporate income tax, or *Körperschaftsteuer*, is levied at 36 per cent of distributed profits and at 50 per cent of retained profits (a reduction to 45 per cent is planned from 1994 onwards), after deducting a trade tax on earnings, or *Gewerbeertragsteuer*, of about 20 per cent (depending on the location of the company). When a company distributes profits which previously have been taxed at the higher rate, a reduction in the current tax payable may be claimed. Value added tax (*Mehrwertsteuer*, or MWSt) is at a rate of 15 per cent.

Legal system
The highest legislative body is the Federal Parliament, consisting of a lower house, the *Bundestag*, and an upper house, the *Bundesrat*. Germany operates under a system of codified law which includes the Commercial Code. Various laws govern the activities of different types of corporation, including the *Aktiengesetz* with respect to AGs, the *Börsengesetz* on quoted companies and the *Publizitätsgesetz* for large unincorporated enterprises. The tax courts, and especially the Federal Fiscal Court (*Bundesfinanzhof*), are also important in providing interpretations of the law with regard to accounting requirements. As accounting rules are not set out in detail in the law, there is considerable demand for legal interpretations by lawyers, professional accountants and other experts. The *Institut der Wirtschaftsprüfer* also issues expert opinions.

Currency
The currency unit is the ***Deutschmark*** **(DM)**, divided into 100 Pfennig.

Language
The official language is German, and it is a legal requirement that the report and accounts of German companies be prepared in the German language.

Figure 1.1 The age structure of the population

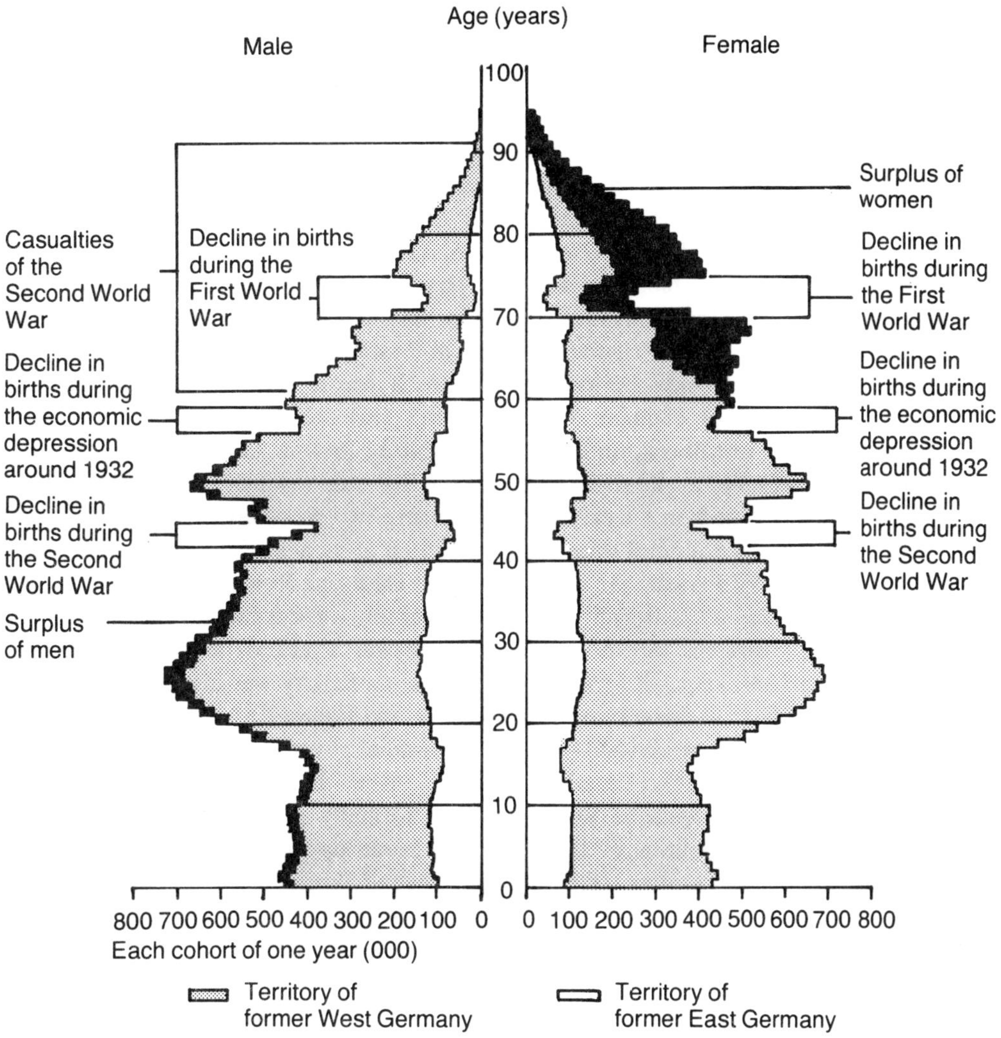

Source: Statistisches Jahrbuch, 1991.

cent, in East Germany it is only 1 per cent. At present every tenth child born in Germany has foreign nationality.

Germany is a comparatively densely populated country. On a land surface (after reunification) of about 357,000 square kilometres, there live, on average, 223 inhabitants per square kilometre. (By contrast the figure for France is about 100 inhabitants per square kilometre.) The position is aggravated by the movement of more and more people from the villages to the cities and conurbations. There has been a consequent increase in land prices and rents in these areas. For example, whereas the average price of building land (all types) in West Germany in 1989 was about DM 89 per square metre, in Munich it was DM 870 and in Stuttgart DM 943.

1.2 The political and legal system

In the course of history Germany has seen many changes in the form of the state, ranging from centralized government to fragmentation into numerous small states. Starting with the Germanic community, based on language rather than territory, there followed various forms of monarchical governments and later the 'Holy Roman Empire of German Nationality', which lasted from 962 until 1806. The successor to the Empire was the German Confederation, established at the Congress of Vienna (1815) by thirty-five crowned heads and four imperial cities. This loose union of states was strongly marked by rivalry between Austria and Prussia. A National Assembly held in Frankfurt in 1848 failed to establish closer links between the states. It was not until the North German Federation (1867–70) of eighteen northern states and the three Hanseatic cities of Hamburg, Bremen and Lübeck, under the leadership of Prussia, that a federal state with a constitutional basis was established. This was the first step towards the Deutsche Reich of 1871, which was based on a treaty between twenty-two crowned heads and the three Hanseatic cities. It was a federal state with a monarch at its head. The German emperor was the current king of Prussia. He represented the Deutsche Reich in international law, he could declare war on its behalf (though the consent of the federal parliament was necessary except when the territory of the empire was attacked) and he could make peace and conclude treaties with foreign states. The monarchy was dissolved at the end of the First World War. A federal republic based on the Weimar constitution was set up; the powers of the state were divided between the federal government and the constituent states. The Weimar Republic lasted until 1933. After the seizure of power by the National Socialists the Deutsche Reich was still formally a republic but in reality a dictatorship. With the abolition of the states that made up the federation, there developed a highly centralized unitary state. After the Second World War the German Federal Republic was founded with the entry into force of the constitutional law in 1949. In all, Germany has only a comparatively recent tradition as a national state.

The German Federal Republic, a member both of NATO and of the European Community, is a social democratic federal state, which, since reunification, consists of sixteen states or *Länder*: Baden-Württemberg, Bayern (Bavaria), Berlin, Brandenburg, Bremen, Hamburg, Hessen (Hesse), Mecklenburg-Vorpommern, Niedersachsen (Lower Saxony), Nordrhein-Westfalen (North Rhine-Westphalia), Rheinland-Pfalz (Rhineland Palatinate), Saarland, Sachsen (Saxony), Sachsen-Anhalt, Schleswig-Holstein and Thüringen (Thuringia). In contrast to the position in a unitary state, the *Länder* are not simply administrative units; they have their own constitution, territory and state powers (legislative, executive and judicial). Admittedly, it is frequently the case that neither the federal government nor the states have exclusive competence. Rather the two sides must work together at the various levels. In fact there is a complex division of competence between the federal government and the states, which may be presented in a simplified fashion as follows:

1. The federal level is, in most areas, responsible for law-making. The highest law-

making body, which has the decisive legislative power, is the Bundestag (Lower Chamber of the federal parliament). The Bundestag consists of representatives of the German people, who are elected in universal, direct, free, equal and secret elections. As a counterweight to the Bundestag stands the Bundesrat (Upper Chamber of the federal parliament) through which the states can participate in the federal law-making and governing process: federal laws that affect the interests of the states can be passed only with the expressed consent of the Bundesrat. The Bundesrat thus embodies the federal system. In the Bundesrat the number of votes each state commands is determined by the size of its population. Each state votes as a bloc.

2. The law-making competences of the federal level of government set the outer limits on its executive competences. The political leadership of the federation is provided by the federal government, whose task includes proposing legislation and issuing regulations. Under the constitution, the federal level is responsible for execution and administration in only a few areas. In general administration is a matter for the states. The federal level has relatively more executive organs in areas where it has responsibility for the whole federal territory. To these belong the highest federal organs, e.g. the *Bundeskanzleramt* (the Federal Chancellor's Office), the *Bundesministerien* (the Federal Ministries), the *Bundesrechnungshof* (the Federal Audit Office) and the so-called federal superior authorities, e.g. the *Bundeskriminalamt* (the Federal Bureau of Criminal Investigation), the *Bundesgesundheitsamt* (the Federal Health Office), the *Bundeskartellamt* (the Federal Monopolies Office), the *Statistisches Bundesamt* (the Federal Statistical Office). In addition there are the federation's own corporations and institutes, such as the *Bundesanstalt für Arbeit* (the Federal Labour Institute) and the *Bundesbank.*

3. The competences in the jurisdiction are particularly closely intertwined between the federation and the states. There is a hierarchy of judical units between the states and the federation. Cases start in the state courts. They end, if as an appeal is lodged, in the federal courts. The five judicial branches, in addition to the constitutional court, are:

1 The regular jurisdiction, divided between the civil and the criminal courts: *Amtsgericht* (the county court), *Landgericht* (the regional court), *Oberlandesgericht* (the superior regional court), *Bundesgerichtshof* (the Federal Court of Appeal).
2 The administrative jurisdiction: *Verwaltungsgericht* (the administrative court), *Oberverwaltungsgericht* (the superior administrative court), *Bundesverwaltungsgericht* (the Federal Administrative Court).
3 The labour jurisdiction: *Arbeitsgericht* (the industrial court), *Landesarbeitsgericht* (the regional industrial court), *Bundesarbeitsgericht* (the Federal Industrial Court).
4 The social jurisdiction: *Sozialgericht* (the social court), *Landessozialgericht* (the regional social court), *Bundessozialgericht* (the Federal Social Court)).
5 The tax jurisdiction (taxation and customs disputes are decided by the tax courts). There are only two bodies: the *Finanzgericht* (the tax court) and *Bundesfinanzhof* (the federal tax court).

In contrast to the courts listed above, the *Bundesverfassungsgericht* (the Federal Constitutional Court) in Karlsruhe is an independent constitutional body. It functions as a court of justice without any courts below it. It is competent to deal only with cases that involve the application of the federal constitution. In a corresponding manner, the state constitutional courts can adjudicate only on matters concerning their own state constitution.

1.3 The educational system

The educational system in West Germany reaches from the *Grundschule* (first four years of compulsory education), through the secondary schools (*Hauptschule*, secondary modern school; *Realschule*, secondary school leading to intermediate qualifications, or *Gymnasium*, secondary school leading to university entry) to the universities, polytechnics and vocational schools (see Figure 1.2). The *Hauptschule* provides a general education as the basis of a practical vocational training. The leaving certificate from a *Realschule* is the qualification for entry to a polytechnic (*Fachhochschule*); the leaving certificate from a *Gymnasium* (known as the *Abitur*) qualifies for university entry. In West Germany a *Gymnasium* education lasts at present for nine years (from the fifth year to the thirteenth); there are proposals to award the *Abitur* certificate earlier, after the twelfth year. Of the working population in 1989, 57.1 per cent had a leaving certificate (or equivalent qualification) from a *Hauptschule*, 24.3 per cent had a certificate from a *Realschule* (or equivalent qualification) and 17.8 per cent had one from a *Gymnasium*. The proportion of women with a leaving certificate from a *Realschule* (30 per cent) is significantly higher than that of men (19.7 per cent).

Of particular interest is the dual system of vocational training. Young people who are following a vocational course (the so-called *Auszubildenden*) receive training not only from their employer (training enterprise) but also, in parallel, from what are called 'vocational schools' (*Berufsschule*). The training provided in the vocational schools covers not only general educational content but also the basic technical theory necessary for the job. The instruction is on a part-time basis involving attendance on one or more days a week. The employer is bound to recognize the time spent at vocational school as working time.

Apart from the initial academic and vocational education, every citizen can choose among a wide range of general and vocational further education opportunities. These are offered by numerous bodies. For further general education, the principal suppliers are the adult educational schools (*Volkshochschulen*); in further vocational training, the employers and companies are clearly the most important. They account for almost half the participants and a third of the time spent in further education and training.

1.4 The social security system

The social security system is made up of four sub-systems:

1 *Worker protection*: the safeguarding of workers by regulations or laws, e.g. on health and safety in the workplace, control of working hours, security of employment (for example, protection from dismissal, provision for young people, working mothers and the handicapped), co-determination, the labour market system (for the last two points, see Chapter 4).
2 *The system of social insurance*: pensions; insurance against sickness, unemployment or accidents; the farmers' old-age pension scheme.

Figure 1.2 The education system

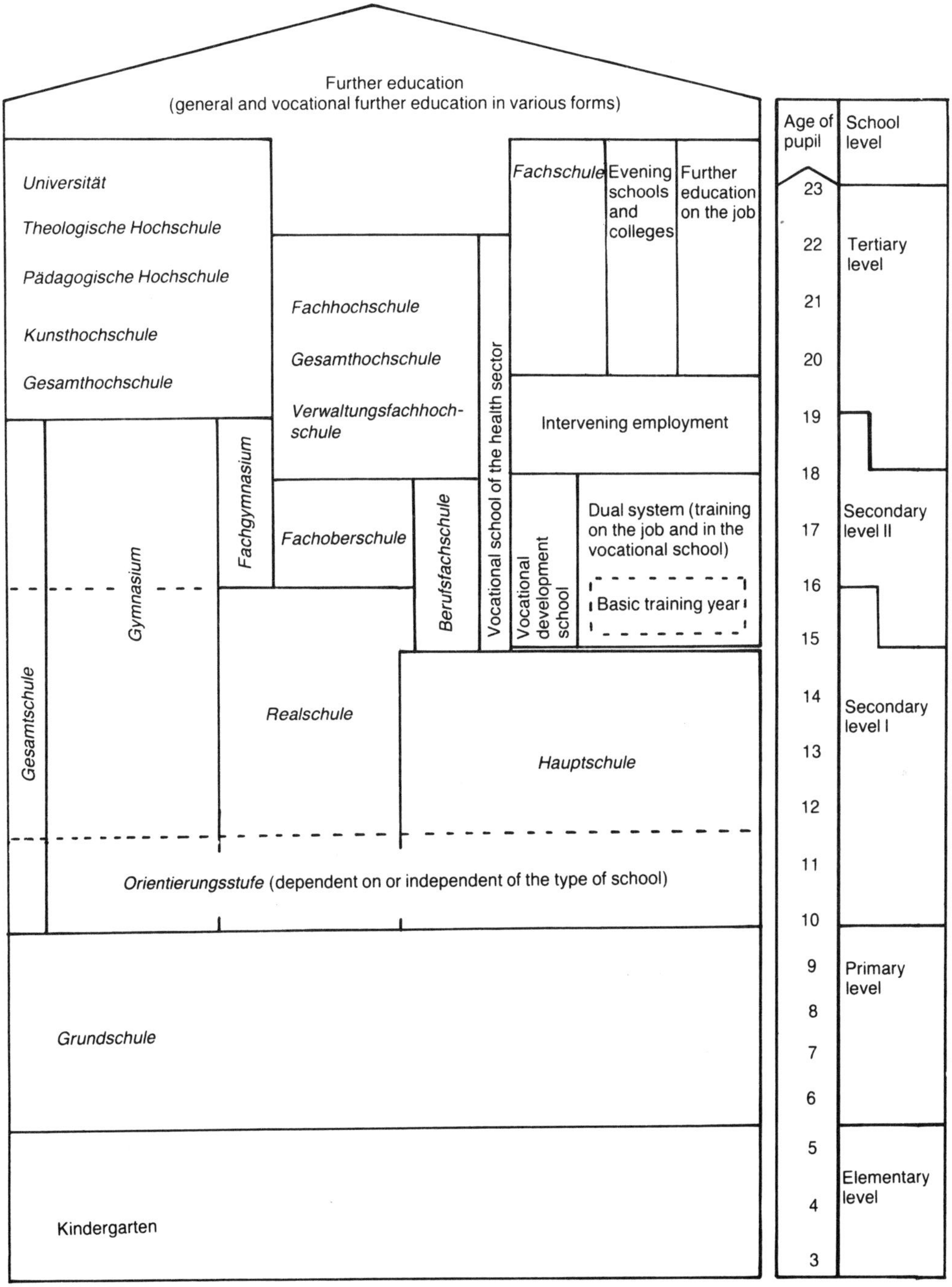

Source: Bundesministerium für Bildung und Wissenschaft (Federal Ministry of Education and Science), *Grund- und Strukturdaten*; table from Hübner and Rohlfs (1991).

3 *The system of social benefits*: social assistance, child allowances, young people's grants, assistance for war victims, rent allowances, training allowances, capital formation, etc.
4 *The employer's contribution*: continuation of wages during illness, company pension schemes, etc.

Table 1.1 shows social expenditure in the former West Germany, both in total and the amounts for the most important areas. It also shows which groups in society bear the cost and to what extent. Two figures are particularly worthy of note: by comparison with other countries the rate of social expenditure (social expenditure as a percentage of gross national product) is high, at almost 30 per cent; and enterprises make a large contribution towards the cost. At 31.7 per cent, enterprises are the largest source of funding, coming even before private households (29 per cent).

Table 1.1 Social expenditure (DM million)

Category	*1975*	*1980*	*1985*	*1990*
Social expenditure total	346,598	478,712	576,076	709,995
of which:				
Pension contributions (*Rentenversicherung*)	101,125	142,585	175,220	215,757
Health insurance (*Krankenversicherung*)	61,142	90,066	114,400	141,670
Accident insurance (*Unfallversicherung*)	7,155	10,019	11,648	13,315
Unemployed insurance (*Arbeitsförderung, Arbeitslosenversicherung*)	18,066	23,098	39,376	49,270
Civil service pensions (*Beamtenpensionen*)	26,016	32,947	36,958	43,282
Old-age allowance for farmers (*Altershilfe für Landwirte*)	1,867	2,773	3,340	4,440
Continued payment of wages (*Entgeltfortzahlung*)	18,490	27,880	25,850	34,000
Child allowances (*Kindergeld*)	14,638	17,609	14,465	14,619
Education allowances (*Erziehungsgeld*)	–	–	–	4,597
Provision for war victims (*Kriegsopferversorgung*)	11,135	13,480	13,474	13,137
Rent allowance (*Wohngeld*)	1,797	2,009	2,714	3,910
Young persons' allowances (*Jugendhilfe*)	4,260	8,098	9,535	13,690
Social assistance (*Sozialhilfe*)	9,218	14,972	22,940	33,750
Social expenditure per head (DM)	5,623	7,779	9,439	11,270
Social expenditure as % of GNP	33.7	32.4	31.4	29.3
Funding of social expenditure, by source (%)				
Firms	30.4	32.1	31.6	31.7
Federal government	24.4	22.4	20.5	19.1
Länder	12.1	11.5	10.9	10.9
Municipalities	7.1	7.2	7.6	8.5
Social insurance	0.3	0.2	0.2	0.3
Private organizations	0.7	0.6	0.6	0.6
Private households	24.9	26.0	28.4	29.0

Source: Bundesministerium für Arbeit und Sozialordnung; Bundesregierung; table from *Institut der Deutschen Wirtschaft*, 1992.
Note: Figures adjusted for transfers between social institutions.

2 THE ECONOMY

2.1 The economic system and economic policy

The economic system of the Federal Republic of Germany is the *Soziale Marktwirtschaft* ('social market economy'). The state is allotted an important regulatory role. It has to set the conditions and the framework of commercial law within which the economic process operates. Among other things, this includes preventing concentrations of firms that would dominate the market. Moreover limits are set to the free market where it would conflict with social concerns, and there is a substantial degree of income redistribution (on this aspect, see the elements of the social security system in section 1.5: rules for the protection of workers, social protection through social insurance, the benefits system and contributions from employers).

Economic policy is based substantially on the Economic Stability and Growth Act of 8 June 1967 (the Stability Act for short). Under this Act the federal and state authorities have to co-ordinate economic and financial measures for maintaining the value of the mark, so as to guarantee stable prices, full employment and balanced external trade, together with reasonable economic growth. There is broad consensus across the parties that the objective of maintaining the value of money should take priority and that, without such stability, the other objectives cannot be realized on a long-term basis.

Those who would like to know more about German economic and monetary policy should consult the annual report of the Council of Economic Advisers (a council of experts for the assessment of overall economic development), and the monthly and annual reports of the Bundesbank. In addition, each year the government presents to parliament an economic report in which it sets out its economic and financial objectives.

2.2 The national income

In 1991 the gross national product (at market prices) of West Germany was DM 2,615 billion and that of East Germany DM 193 billion. In this period GNP per head was DM 12,100 in East Germany, DM 41,100 in West Germany and DM 35,200 in Germany as a whole. Table 1.2 shows the sources and the application of the gross national product. The figures of sources demonstrate the relatively minor importance of agriculture and the prominent role of the service sector. This applies to both East and West Germany. In fact the service sector contributes more than half of gross national product (service industries, trade, transport, state spending, private households). In West Germany almost 53 per cent of GNP flowed into private consumption and about 22 per cent was devoted to gross investment. The net contribution of foreign trade (exports minus imports) was 7.2 per cent. However, in the former German Democratic Republic (East Germany) imports were higher than exports.

The share of wages and salaries in national income has been comparatively stable since the 1970s. About two-thirds of gross output is distributed as wages and salaries, and about one-third comprises profits, interest and other return on capital.

Table 1.2 Sources and application of the national income

Source/application	*Old Länder* DM million	%	*New Länder* DM million	%
Source of national income				
Agriculture, forestry, fishing	32,200	1.3	3,300	1.7
Manufacturing industry	999,800	40.0	67,500	34.1
Commerce and transport	359,200	14.4	33,100	16.7
Service enterprises	771,500	30.9	47,000	23.8
State, private households, private non-profit organizations	335,500	13.4	46,800	23.7
Gross output[1]	2,394,800		173,400	
+ Non-deductible turnover taxes	175,750		8,600	
+ Import duties	28,750		1,000	
= Gross domestic product	2,599,300		183,000	
+ Net income from the rest of the world	15,900		10,100	
= Gross national product	2,615,200		193,100	
Application				
Private consumption	1,379,100	52.7	196,200	101.6
Government expenditure	469,400	17.9	90,200	46.7
Gross investment	578,800	22.2	74,800	38.7
Trade balance	187,900	7.2	−168,100	−87.0

Source: *Statistisches Jahrbuch*, 1992, p. 686; data collected in 1991.
Note:
[1]The total of gross output does not equal the sum of the output of the various sectors because the formula has been reduced by payments for bank services.

2.3 The labour market

Employment. In 1990 the employed population was 37.29 million (of which West Germany 28.43). The analysis of employment by industrial sector is shown in Table 1.3. It shows that the tertiary section (trade, transport, services) dominates also as a source of employment. Manufacturing industry employs almost one-third of the employed population. The number of employed in agriculture and forestry, energy and water supply, and in mining is, by comparison, low. This last point underlines the fact that Germany has few natural resources.

Unemployment. In 1985 at 9.4 per cent unemployment reached its highest level since the 1950s; since then it has declined noticeably. In January 1993 the unemployment rate in West Germany was 7.4 per cent. By comparison, in East Germany employment had collapsed, particularly in manufacturing industry. Here the unemployment rate was 14.7 per cent and would have been much higher but for daily or weekly commuting to West Germany, internal migration to regions in West Germany offering better employment prospects, the return home of foreigners and, above all, the labour market measures, such as early retirement and job creation. There has been very little change over time in the structure of unemployment. The proportion of the unemployed consisting of blue-collar workers is over 60 per cent. Also, 60 per cent of the unemployed have no specific

Table 1.3 The employed population, by economic sectors[1]

					1990			
	1980		*1985*		*West*		*East*[2]	
Employment category/economic sector	*Million*	%	*Million*	%	*Million*	%	*Million*	%
Economically active German residents (*Erwerbstätige Inländer*)	27.06		26.59		28.44		8.92	
Self employed and their family assistants (*Selbständige und mithelfende Familienangehörige*)	3.17		3.03		2.96		0.32	
Employees (*Abhängig Beschäftigte*)	23.90		23.56		25.48		8.60	
Employees in Germany (*Erwerbstätige im Inland*)	26.98		26.49		28.43		8.86	
Agriculture and forestry (*Land- und Forstwirtschaft*)	1.40	5.2	1.20	4.5	0.96	3.4	0.73	8.2
Energy, water supply and mining (*Energie, Wasserversorgung, Bergbau*)	0.49	1.8	0.49	1.9	0.47	1.7	0.37	4.2
Manufacturing industry (*Verarbeitendes Gewerbe*)	9.09	33.7	8.45	31.9	8.94	31.5	2.94	33.2
Construction (*Baugewerbe*)	2.13	7.9	1.86	7.0	1.91	6.7	0.67	7.6
Commerce and transport (*Handel und Verkehr*)	5.03	18.6	4.92	18.6	5.31	18.6	1.45	16.4
Banks and insurance companies (*Kreditinstitute, Versicherungen*)	0.76	2.8	0.79	3.0	0.89	3.1	0.08	0.9
Service enterprises and professions (*Dienstleistungen von Unternehmen und freien Berufen*)	3.22	11.9	3.60	13.6	4.38	15.4	0.61	6.9
State (*Staat*)	3.93	14.6	4.12	15.6	4.30	15.1	1.94	21.8
Private households and private non-profit organizations (*Private Haushalte, private Organisationen ohne Erwerbscharakter*)	0.93	3.5	1.07	4.0	1.26	4.4	0.07	0.8

Source: Statistisches Bundesamt; table from *Institut der Deutschen Wirtschaft*, 1992.
Notes:
[1]Average for the year; figures from the national income statistics.
[2]Figures for East Germany estimated.

occupational training. The most significant change has been a clear increase in long-term unemployment since the 1970s. The proportion of people remaining unemployed for over a year has been rising, from 9.6 per cent in 1975 to 29.7 per cent in 1990. More than half the long-term unemployed have not completed their vocational training.

Wages and working hours. In the private sector, the highest average gross wages were in oil refining (DM 5,940) and in the manufacture of office machinery, data-processing equipment and systems (DM 5,382): see Figure 1.3. Retailing (DM 3,273) and textiles (DM 3,401) paid the lowest average wages.

The average working week in West Germany, as determined by collective agreements, has fallen from 44.6 hours in 1960 to 38.3 hours in 1991. Hours actually worked per employee have fallen even further, from an average of 40.0 to 29.9. In East Germany, collective agreements set the number of weekly hours worked per employee at 41.0 in 1991. The hours actually worked were 27.8 per week. The average holiday entitlement was 30.7 days in West Germany and 25.0 in East Germany.

2.4 Inflation and interest rates

As shown in the survey 'Germany and the European economy' for a long time Germany led the way in price stability. Between 1983 and 1989 the inflation rate according to the national income deflator was kept, for much of the time, under 3 per cent. Since 1990 the price index has risen noticeably, not least because of reunification.

In accordance with the high value attached to price stability in Germany (see also Chapter 3), in recent years the Bundesbank has reacted to developments in prices by raising interest rates. Whereas at the end of the 1980s long-term interest rates were under 7 per cent, in 1990 the yield on fixed-interest investments was, on average, just under 9 per cent.

2.5 External trade

In 1990 Germany was the world's largest exporter. Exports totalled DM 680.7 billion and imports DM 573.4 billion, giving a trade surplus of DM 107.3 billion (West Germany: DM 92.1 billion; East Germany: DM 15.2 billion). Germany's six biggest trading partners are France, Italy, Great Britain, the Netherlands, Belgium and the United States. In both exports and imports, investment goods were predominant. In second place were basic goods and producer goods.

The balance of payments. Table 1.4 presents the balance of payments for selected years; it is clear that the regularly positive trade balance is substantially reduced by transfers and tourism. Moreover there is generally a considerable negative balance on the capital account.

Exchange rates. The priority given to price stability has given rise to the correspondingly strong position of the Deutschmark on the foreign exchanges. As shown in Table 1.5, over time its value has risen against most currencies; particular exceptions are the currencies of Switzerland and Japan.

Figure 1.3 Average gross monthly earnings of employees in industry and commerce (DM 000)

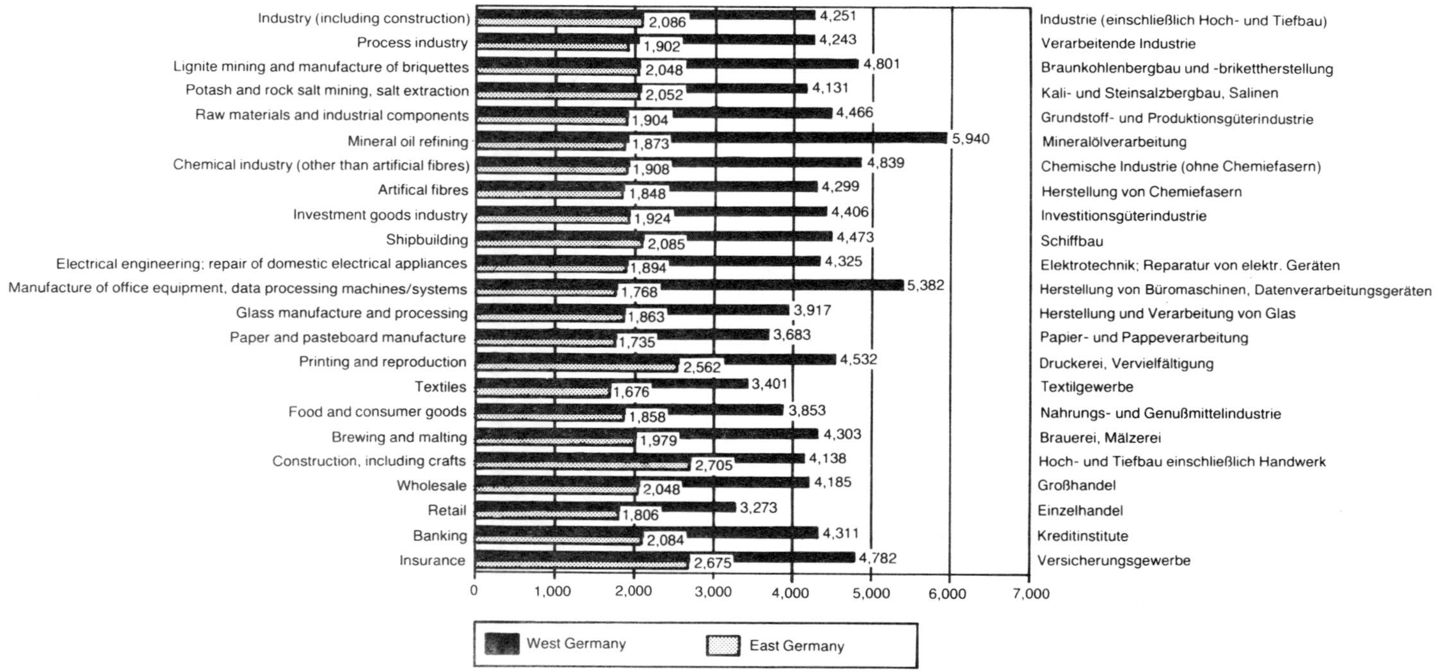

Source: *Statistisches Jahrbuch, 1992*, average for October 1991.

	Germany	European Community
Population	78,780,000	344,735,000
Area (square kilometres)	357,000	2,363,000
GDP per capita (1992)[1]	113.6	100
	Averages 1981 – 1992	
Imports as a % of GDP	26.4%	27.6%
Exports as a % of GDP	30.5%	28.3%
Unemployment rate	5.8%	9.5%
Increase in consumer prices	2.8%	6.3%

Source: EC Commission (*European Economy*, No 50, December 1991)
Note: [1]Estimated GDP at current market prices in ECU, expressed as a percentage of EC average (i.e. EC=100).

Prices and wages

	General inflation[1]		*Consumer prices*[2]	*Labour costs*[3]
	Annual % change	*Index 1980=100*	*Annual % change*	*Annual % change*
1980	4.8	100	5.8	6.6
1981	4.0	104	6.0	4.5
1982	4.4	109	4.7	3.4
1983	3.3	112	3.2	3.4
1984	2.0	114	2.5	3.3
1985	2.2	117	2.1	3.0
1986	3.1	121	-0.2	3.5
1987	2.0	123	0.8	3.0
1988	1.6	125	1.3	3.0
1989	2.6	128	3.1	2.8
1990	3.4	133	2.6	4.2
1991	4.3	138	3.5	6.2
1992	4.5	144	4.2	5.8

Source: EC Commission (*European Economy*, No 50, December 1991)

Notes: [1]Price deflator, gross domestic product at market prices.
[2]Price deflator, private consumption.
[3]Nominal compensation per employee – total economy.

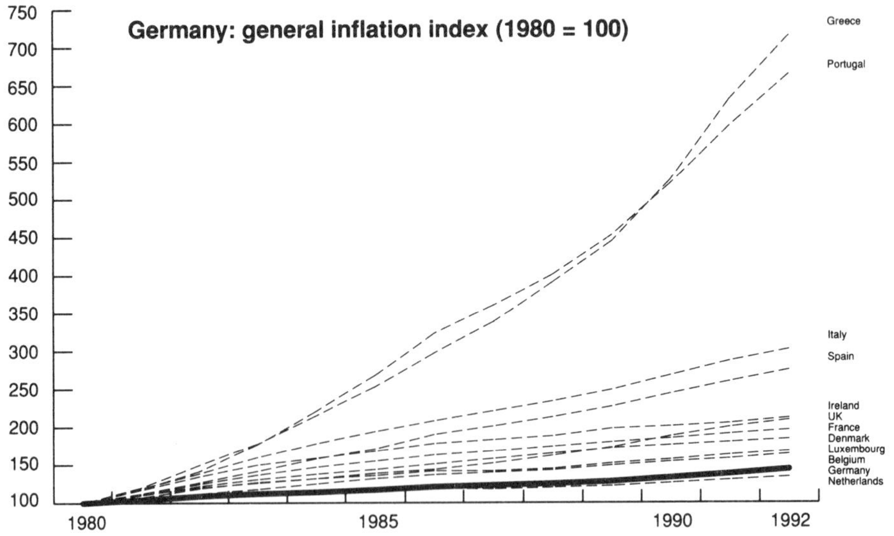

Source: European Economy, No 50, December 1991 (price deflator, gross domestic product at market prices)

Gross Domestic Product per head of population (EC = 100)

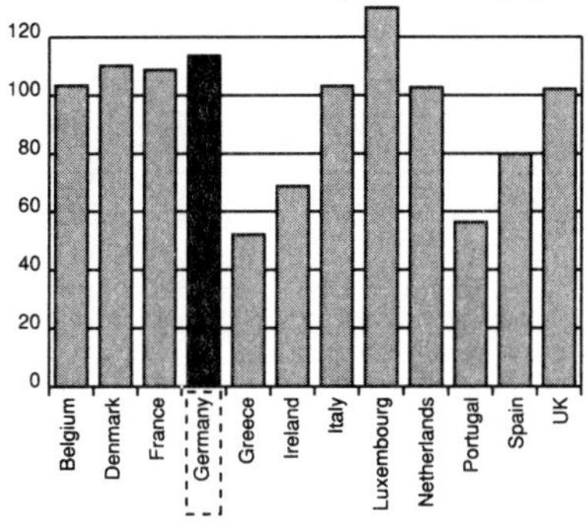

Population (in millions)

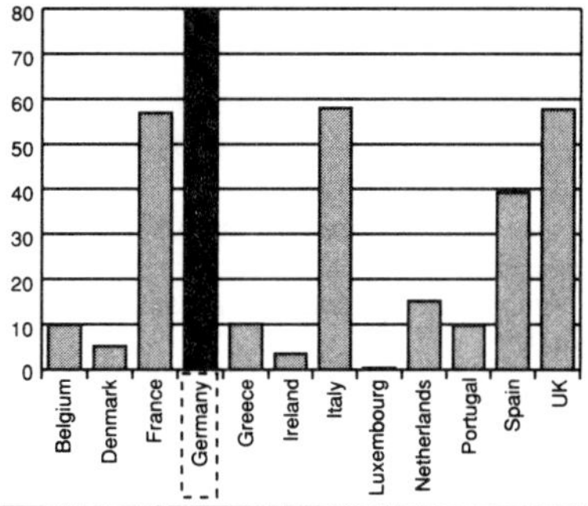

Exchange rates

	Deutschmark/ECU Average rate[1]	*Deutschmark/US$* Average rate[2]
1980	2.52	1.818
1981	2.51	2.260
1982	2.38	2.427
1983	2.27	2.553
1984	2.24	2.846
1985	2.23	2.944
1986	2.13	2.171
1987	2.07	1.797
1988	2.07	1.756
1989	2.07	1.880
1990	2.05	1.616
1991	2.05	1.660
1992[3]	2.03	1.557

Selected exchange rates for the Deutschmark at 31 December 1992

1 ECU	=	DM 1.956
$1	=	DM 1.614
£1	=	DM 2.452
¥100	=	DM 1.296

Sources: 1 EC Commission (*European Economy*, No 50, December 1991);
2 International Monetary Fund (Datastream Economics Codes);
3 Eurostatistic, No 11, 1992.

Variation of the Deutschmark with respect to the ECU (1980 = 100)

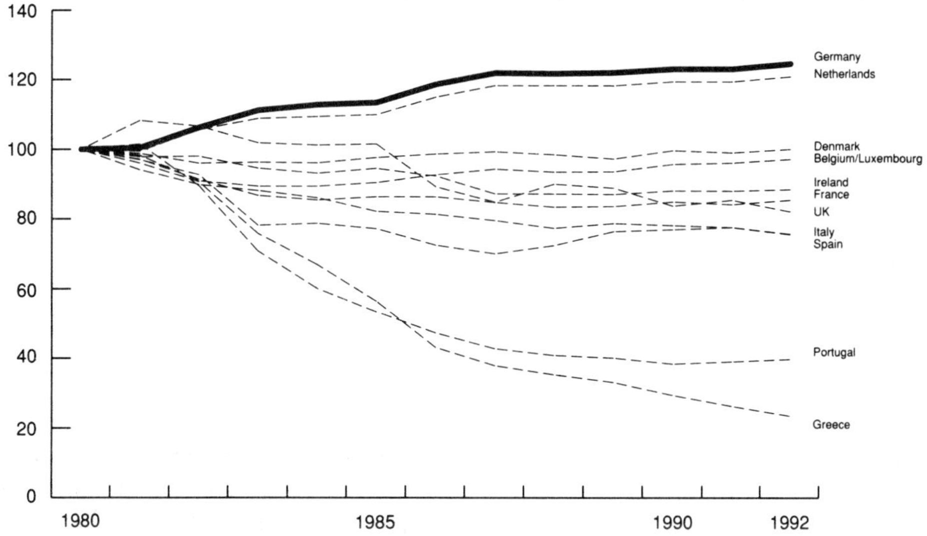

Source: European Economy, No 50, December 1991 (average rate)

Table 1.4 The balance of payments (DM billion)

Measure	*1975*	*1980*	*1985*	*1990*[1]
Trade balance (*Handelsbilanz*)	+37.28	+8.95	+73.35	+105.38
Additions for merchandise movements[2] (*Ergänzungen zum Warenverkehr*)	−1.00	−0.49	−1.34	−0.67
Balance on invisibles (*Dienstleistungsbilanz*)	−8.33	−10.12	+5.40	+8.35
of which:				
Tourism (*Reiseverkehr*)	−14.25	−22.54	−23.73	−30.95
Transfers (*Übertragungen*)	−17.30	−23.47	−29.09	−35.63
of which:				
Migrant workers (*Gastarbeiter*)	−7.90	−7.45	−7.95	−7.35
Current account balance (*Saldo der Leistungsbilanz*)	+10.65	−25.13	+48.33	+77.43
Capital transactions (*Kapitalverkehr*)				
Long-term (*langfristig*)	−18.23	+5.81	−12.87	−68.50
Short-term (*kurzfristig*)	+5.67	−6.21	−41.70	−25.98
Capital account balance (*Saldo der Kapitalbilanz*)	−12.56	−0.40	−54.56	−94.48
Other items[3] (*Restposten der Zahlungsbilanz*)	−0.31	−2.37	+8.08	+28.02
Balancing item (*Ausgleichsposten*)	+5.48	+2.16	−3.10	−5.10
Net balance of payments (*Saldo der Devisenbilanz*)	+3.26	−25.73	−1.26	+5.87

Source: Deutsche Bundesbank; table from *Institut der Deutschen Wirtshaft*, 1992.
Notes:
[1]From July 1990 including the former East German Länder.
[2]Principally warehouse for domestic account.
[3]Net amount of unrecorded items and statistical errors. The principal cause of fluctuation is changes in methods of payment.

2.6 Sectors of the economy

There follows a short survey of the structure of the German economy. Further information can be found in the *Statistical Yearbook*, the annual report of the Council of Economic Advisers, and in the various publications of the Institut der Deutschen Wirtschaft (IW, Institute of German Business) and of the industry associations.

Agriculture, forestry, fishing. A structural change in West German agriculture has been under way for many years. The trend is towards larger production units and a reduction in the number of farms. In 1990 the average farm was just under 19 ha; about half of all farms were under 10 ha. In East Germany most of the former agricultural production collectives have been converted into registered co-operatives. At the same time there has been a marked reduction in the number employed in the sector, as in all sectors of the East German economy.

Industry. Table 1.6 brings together a number of indicators of selected industries. Four industries stand out, on the measures of turnover and employment: mechanical engineering, motor vehicle manufacturing, electrical engineering and chemicals. This finding is also reflected in the list of the twenty largest industrial undertakings (see Table 1.7). Five of the largest are in the motor industry.

The industry with the highest proportion of output exported is the manufacture of office equipment and automatic data-processing equipment (51.1 per cent), but in most other industries the proportion is at least 30 per cent or more. Among the declining sectors are coalmining, steel-making and shipbuilding. Coal is under pressure from cheaper sources of energy (oil, natural gas and nuclear power). In the steel industry there

Table 1.5 The external value of the Deutschmark: (a) equivalent value in other currencies

Year	*USA* *US $1*	*Japan* *¥ 100*	*Switzerland* *Sfr 100*	*Britain* *£1*	*France* *Ffr 100*	*The Netherlands* *Fl 100*	*Italy* *L 1,000*	*For information:* *1 ECU*
1955	4.21	–	98.25	11.74	120.03	110.58	6.70	–
1960	4.17	–	96.56	11.71	85.05	110.59	6.72	–
1965	3.99	–	92.31	11.17	81.50	110.95	6.39	–
1970	3.65	1.02	84.60	8.74	65.97	100.85	5.82	–
1975	2.46	0.83	95.25	5.45	57.41	97.30	3.77	3.05
1980	1.82	0.81	108.48	4.23	43.01	91.46	2.12	2.52
1981	2.26	1.03	115.25	4.56	41.64	90.61	1.99	2.51
1982	2.43	0.98	119.72	4.24	37.00	90.90	1.80	2.38
1983	2.56	1.08	121.61	3.87	33.56	89.50	1.68	2.27
1984	2.85	1.20	121.18	3.79	32.57	88.70	1.62	2.24
1985	2.94	1.24	120.02	3.78	32.76	88.66	1.54	2.23
1986	2.17	1.29	120.92	3.18	31.31	88.64	1.46	2.13
1987	1.80	1.24	120.59	2.94	29.90	88.74	1.39	2.07
1988	1.76	1.37	120.06	3.12	29.48	88.85	1.35	2.07
1989	1.88	1.37	115.04	3.08	29.47	88.65	1.37	2.07
1990	1.62	1.12	116.50	2.88	29.68	88.76	1.35	2.05
1991	1.66	1.23	115.74	2.93	29.41	88.74	1.34	2.05
1992[1]	1.56	1.23	111.13	2.78	29.52	88.80	1.29	–

Source: Deutsche Bundesbank, *Monthly Report*, December 1992.
Note:
[1] Excluding December.

Table 1.5 The external value of the Deutschmark: (b) index of value in relation to other currencies (end 1972 = 100)

Year	*US $*	*¥*	*Sfr*	*£*	*Ffr*	*EMS countries*[1]	*Eighteen industrial countries*	*Real external value*[2]
1973	121.7	106.7	99.7	116.4	105.3	110.6	110.7	109.4
1975	131.3	126.3	88.1	138.8	109.8	121.0	119.2	103.4
1980	177.6	130.5	77.4	179.2	146.5	164.4	151.5	100.2
1981	143.1	102.1	73.0	166.2	151.4	166.8	143.1	90.6
1982	132.9	107.2	70.1	178.3	170.4	182.7	150.4	92.0
1983	126.5	97.4	69.0	195.5	187.8	198.0	155.9	92.5
1984	113.6	87.4	69.3	199.6	193.4	203.1	153.8	88.0
1985	110.3	84.8	70.0	200.0	192.3	205.4	154.0	85.5
1986	149.0	81.1	69.5	238.5	201.2	219.4	168.2	90.7
1987	179.5	84.2	69.6	257.2	210.7	228.9	178.9	94.0
1988	183.8	76.4	69.9	242.2	213.7	228.6	177.4	91.4
1989	171.6	76.8	73.0	246.0	213.7	228.2	175.7	89.0
1990	199.9	93.7	72.1	263.1	212.3	230.9	185.5	91.8
1991	194.9	85.0	72.5	258.5	214.2	230.9	183.1	89.6
1992[3]	207.1	85.3	75.5	273.1	213.4	235.4	188.1	92.2[4]

Source: Deutsche Bundesbank, *Monthly Report*, December 1992.
Notes:
[1] Over the whole period including the same currencies as in Table 1.5(a), i.e. Italy and Great Britain, but not Greece.
[2] How much the Deutschmark would buy in eighteen industrialized countries.
[3] Excluding December.
[4] Provisional figure.

Table 1.6 Indicators for selected industries[1]

Industry	Enterprises No.	Enterprises %[2]	Employment (000s)	Employment %[2]	Turnover DM billion	Turnover %[2]	Export ratio[3]
Mining	273	0.6	173.2	2.3	27.70	1.5	7.3
Iron and steel	161	0.3	178.5	2.4	49.58	2.7	33.3
Mechanical engineering	6,062	13.0	1,075.4	14.5	210.21	11.5	44.1
Motor vehicles	2,609	5.6	889.9	12.0	254.35	13.9	45.4
Electrical engineering	3,924	8.4	1,036.3	14.0	201.75	11.1	30.2
Precision engineering	1,363	2.9	144.2	1.9	23.48	1.3	37.4
Metalworking	2,561	5.5	334.4	4.5	64.04	3.5	26.0
Chemicals	1,601	3.4	592.4	8.0	195.67	10.7	42.0
Office machines and automatic data processing equipment	188	0.4	83.7	1.1	19.33	1.1	51.1
Textiles	1,503	3.2	209.5	2.8	41.29	2.3	28.7
Clothing	2,074	4.4	164.1	2.2	26.78	1.5	20.2
Food	4,524	9.7	462.5	6.2	182.73	10.0	9.0

Source: *Institut der Deutschen Wirtschaft*, 1991.
Notes:
[1] Provisional figures for West Germany, 1990.
[2] Percentage of industry as a whole.
[3] Share of exports in total turnover.

Table 1.7 The largest industrial undertakings

Industrial enterprise	*Turnover (DM million)*	*Employment (000s)*
Daimler-Benz	85,500	376.7
Volkswagen	68,061	268.7
Siemens	63,185	373.0
Veba	54,591	106.0
BASF	46,623	134.7
Hoechst	44,862	172.9
RWE	44,235	97.6
Bayer	41,643	171.0
Thyssen	36,185	149.6
Bosch	31,824	179.6
BMW	27,178	70.9
Mannesmann	23,943	124.0
Adam Opel	23,708	57.4
Ruhrkohle	22,921	119.5
Ford	20,754	50.1
Metallgesellschaft	19,827	32.2
Viag	19,423	55.8
Preussag	19,046	72.3
MAN	18,937	66.6
Krupp	15,570	58.9

Source: *Frankfurter Allgemeine Zeitung*, figures for 1990.
Note: As a rule, the figures are consolidated.

has been a shift from the production of basic steel to high-quality special steels. The shipbuilding industry, once very busy, faces stiff price competition from the Far East, particularly Japan and Korea.

West Germany is still a favoured recipient of foreign investment. According to a survey by Prognos (Basel, 1990), high taxes and production costs and the short working week are regarded as a disadvantage but have little impact on the generally very favourable picture. They are outweighed by considerations such as high purchasing power, social and political stability, the efficiency of the infrastructure and the quality of labour.

Crafts. Craft industry is of considerable importance. It accounts for one in four enterprises, trains one in three apprentices and employs one in six workers. The average size of firm is, however, quite small: 6.7 workers.

Construction. Construction accounts for around 12 per cent of GNP and for about 60 per cent of total capital investment. Almost 7 per cent of the working population are employed directly in construction.

The service sector. Services constitute the dominant sector of the economy. They produce more than half the national income and employ the most workers. Although the trend in turnover and in employment is upward, the number of enterprises has been going down steadily for many years not only in commerce but also in banking and insurance. The end of this process of concentration is not yet in sight. Table 1.8 presents the largest commercial enterprises, banks and insurance companies.

Table 1.8 The largest service organizations:
(a) commercial concerns

Company	*Turnover (DM million)*	*Employment (000s)*
Tengelmann	42,218	167.0
Metro	40,925[1]	–
Rewe	36,200	120.0
Edeka	32,000[2]	–
Aldi	19,800[2]	–
Stinnes	16,427	24.3
Otto-Versand	16,100[2]	35.0
Franz Haniel	15,152	27.6
Asko	15,065	54.9
Karstadt	15,033	71.0
Spar	14,801	–
Schickedanz	14,800	–
Thyssen Handel	12,777	24.3
Klöckner	9,854	8.3
Toepfer	8,800	0.8
Brenninkmeyer	8,200[2]	–
Raab Karcher	8,176	15.3
Aral	6,026	0.9
Hertie	5,900	24.2
Bay Wa	5,734	11.1

Source: *Frankfurter Allgemeine Zeitung*, figures for 1990.
Notes:
[1]Including Massa and Kaufhof.
[2]Estimate.

Table 1.8 The largest service organizations: (b) banks

Bank	*Total assets and commitments (DM million)*	*Employment (000s)*
Deutsche Bank	404,700	68.6
Dresdner Bank	286,951	42.2
Westdeutsche Landesbank	250,899	8.3
Commerzbank	215,954	28.2
DG Bank	214,931	10.7
Bayerische Vereinsbank	207,423	20.2
Bayerische Hypotheken- und Wechselbank	176,036	14.4
Bayerische Landesbank	174,100	4.4
Kreditanstalt für Wiederaufbau	137,223	1.0
Norddeutsche Landesbank	127,842	6.1

Source: as Table 1.8(a).

Table 1.8 The largest service organizations: (c) insurance companies

Company	*Premium income (DM million)*	*Employment (000s)*
Allianz	38,275	56.2
Münchener Rückversicherung	12,652	1.8
Colonia	9,596	12.0
Gerling	8,170[1]	9.4
Aachener und Münchener	7,800[2]	10.0
Victoria	5,640	9.2
R+V Versicherung	5,338	9.6
SR Beteiligung	5,302	7.5
Vereinte Versicherung	4,232	8.5
HDI	4,045	3.5

Source: as Table 1.8(a).
Notes:
[1] Estimate.
[2] Not consolidated.

2.7 Summary

The most important characteristics of the German economy may be summarized as follows:

1 The social aspect of the market economy which finds expression in numerous protective rules, social insurance provisions, social security benefits to those in need and a range of contributions from employers.
2 The priority given to price stability, based on the Stability Act of 1967.
3 The dominant position of the service sector: in terms of both its contribution to GNP and its importance for employment.
4 The high proportion of output in many enterprises and sectors that goes for export.

2

Forms of business organization and corporate governance

1 STRUCTURAL DIFFERENCES BETWEEN THE VARIOUS FORMS OF BUSINESS ORGANIZATION

In principle, the owners of an enterprise are free to decide how their enterprise is to be structured and how the drawing rights are to be fixed and allocated (freedom of contract). However, on occasions, there are legal conditions. These may be either mandatory laws or avoidable provisions, i.e. they apply in so far as the enterprise's basic contract or constitution does not provide otherwise.

The legal forms under which, normally, business may be carried out in Germany are presented in Table 2.1: the German names are given in column 1. Certain specialized forms are not included: co-ownership of ships (the *Partenreederei*), the mutual insurance society (*Versicherungsverein auf Gegenseitigkeit*) and public-sector enterprises under private law (*öffentliche Betriebe in privatrechtlicher Form*). In the other columns of Table 2.1 various characteristics are presented. The differences relating to the regulation of the accounts, of the distribution of profit and of reporting are not listed; these are dealt with in detail in Part II.

As shown in Table 2.1, there are five general forms of business organization:

1 Sole proprietorship (*Einzelunternehmung*).
2 Civil law partnership (*Gesellschaft bürgerlichen Rechts*).
3 Commercial partnership (*Personenhandelsgesellschaft*).
4 Corporation (*Kapitalgesellschaft*).
5 Registered co-operative (*eingetragene Genossenschaft*).

Table 2.1 Forms of business organization and their characteristics

Business form	*Is the enterprise a legal person?*	*Is the enterprise entered in the commercial register?*	*Is liability limited to the capital contribution?*	*Can the enterprise own property?*	*Who has the authority to manage?*	*Formal bodies of the enterprise*	*Is the enterprise a taxable entity?*
Sole proprietor	No	Yes	No	No	The sole proprietor	Not regulated by law	No
Civil law partnership	No	No	No	No	The partners	Not regulated by law	No
Commercial partnerships:							
• *offene Handelsgesellschaft* (OHG, general partnership)	No	Yes	No	Yes	The partners	Not regulated by law	Partly (not ESt/VSt)
• *Kommanditgesellschaft* (KG, limited partnership)	No	Yes	Only the liability of the *Kommanditisten* (limited partners) is limited	Yes	The *Komplementär* (the general partner)	Not regulated by law	Partly (not ESt/VSt)
• GmbH & Co. KG	No	Yes	Yes	Yes	The manager of the GmbH	Not regulated by law	Partly (not ESt/VSt)
Corporations:							
• *Aktiengesellschaft* (AG, joint stock corporation)	Yes	Yes	Yes	Yes	The executive board	The executive board; supervisory board; general meeting	Yes
• *Kommanditgesellschaft auf Aktien* (KGaA, limited partnership with shares)	Yes	Yes	Only the liability of the *Kommanditisten* (limited partners) is limited	Yes	The executive board	The executive board; supervisory board; general meeting	Yes
• *Gesellschaft mit beschränkter Haftung* (GmbH, limited liability company)	Yes	Yes	Yes	Yes	The executive board	The manager(s); (supervisory board); shareholders' meeting	Yes
Eingetragene Genossenschaft (eG, registered co-operative)	Yes	Yes	Yes	Yes	The executive board	The manager; supervisory board; general meeting	Yes

Notes: ESt Einkommensteuer (income tax). VSt Vermögensteuer (assets tax).

The first two forms are not legal persons; they exist only through the persons who constitute the enterprise – in the first case, a single person; in the second, two or more natural or legal persons. The law does not recognize the enterprise as separate from the person who is conducting it. The fourth form (the *Kapitalgesellschaft*) is, in law, a corporation; it is a legal person separate from the natural persons who are involved in the enterprise (the shareholders or managers). The third form (*Personenhandelsgesellschaft*) lies somewhat between these two extremes: for some purposes the law recognizes the enterprise as a separate entity, but for others it also considers the natural persons involved, notably in respect of their liability for the enterprise's debts. The fifth form (*Genossenschaft*) is also in law a corporation but differs from corporations of the fourth type in its aims and in the manner in which economic benefits are passed to the owners.

The sole proprietorship (*Einzelunternehmung*) has no separate legal identity. It is the property of a single individual, who manages the enterprise and who is responsible for its liabilities to the limits of his entire wealth (his private assets as well as the business assets). As a general rule, the enterprise is registered in the commercial register (*Handelsregister*). Taxes are levied on the individual, not the enterprise.

The civil law partnership (*Gesellschaft bürgerlichen Rechts*) is a contractual association between two or more natural or legal persons. The contract takes no special form; it can be oral. The partnership is not registered in the commercial register. The business assets belong to the partners jointly. They are liable to the extent of all their assets; natural persons are also liable to the extent of their private assets. The management function accrues to all partners jointly and profits are shared equally among the partners, unless the partnership contract provides otherwise. This legal form is found principally among professional firms (lawyers, doctors), in cartel arrangements, profit-pooling agreements, property management companies and casual ventures (consortia for the issue of securities or for the financing of large projects, joint ventures for carrying out building projects). They also serve as a means of setting up sub-partnerships, that is, participation in part of another person's enterprise.

The various types of commercial partnership (*Personenhandelsgesellschaften*) are not strictly separate legal persons – for example, they cannot exist independently of their partners – but they can participate on their own in legal proceedings under the firm name (e.g. they can acquire rights, incur liabilities, sue and be sued). The enterprise's assets belong to the partners jointly. The company is listed in the commercial register. *Vermögensteuer* (VSt, assets tax) and *Einkommensteuer* (ESt, income tax) are levied on the partners. It is otherwise with *Gewerbesteuer* (GewSt, trade tax), *Grundsteuer* (GrSt, real property tax) and taxes on transactions and consumption (*Verkehr- und Verbrauchssteuern*), where the enterprise is liable for the tax.

In the *offene Handelsgesellschaft* (OHG, general partnership) all partners have unlimited direct liability, in principle, for the debts of the firm. All partners are authorized and obliged to participate in the management of the firm, but the partnership contract may provide for individual partners to be excluded from management. The sharing of profits is governed by § 121 (German laws are made up of paragraphs, denoted by the symbol §) of the *Handelsgesetzbuch* (HGB, Commercial Code), unless the partnership contract specifies otherwise: each partner is credited with 4 per cent on his capital account, the remainder to be divided equally. In general, this legal rule is overridden by the partnership contract. In practice, profits and losses are divided according to capital shares, taking into account not only the fixed capital contribution but also the associated risk relating to the personal property of each partner. Managing partners normally receive a salary for their activities, which under commercial law is a deduction from the profits that are shared among the partners. For tax purposes, however, the salary and the share of profits are part of the partner's income.

The *Kommanditgesellschaft* (KG, limited partnership) differs from the general partnership principally in that, in addition to the personally liable general partners (the *Komplementäre*), there are limited partners (called the *Kommanditisten*) whose liability is limited to the capital contribution recorded in the commercial register. Where this capital contribution has not been fully paid, they are liable with their private assets for the unpaid amount. Limited partners act as financiers; they do not participate in management, unless the partnership contract provides otherwise. Before profits may be distributed to the limited partners, their capital contribution must have been fully paid in.

A special form of the limited partnership is the *Kapitalgesellschaft & Co. KG*, commonly denoted by the legal form of GmbH & Co. KG. In this limited partnership, the general partner (there is usually only one) is a limited liability company, normally a GmbH (see below), on account of this form's greater flexibility in company law. Frequently the shareholders of the GmbH are also the limited partners in the KG. Because of the exclusion of personal liability, the GmbH & Co. KG in matters of legal liability is similar to a corporation. The reason for the relative popularity of this legal form is the combination of completely limited liability with tax treatment as a limited partnership. In corporations retained profits are taxed at 50 per cent (corporation tax). In limited partnerships the rate of the tax on profits (income tax) depends on the level of the personal income. On account of this and other taxation differences, which are not dealt with further here, the legal form of GmbH & Co. KG can be more advantageous than that of a limited liability company.

Corporations (*Kapitalgesellschaften*) have their own legal personality: they are themselves the subject of rights and duties; their existence is independent of their shareholders. They are recorded in the commercial register. They own property, which is the backing for their debts. The owners of the company are liable only to the extent of their capital contribution, except in the special case where the shareholder is another corporation (see below on groups). The management of the company is the responsibility of the organs specified in the law, not of the shareholders. However, natural persons can be shareholders and organs of the company. The sharing-out of profit is based on capital contributions, as these determine the level of risk assumed. In taxation matters the corporation is itself liable for tax on profits (known as *Körperschaftsteuer*, or KSt for short: corporation tax) and for the *Vermögensteuer* (or VSt for short: assets tax). Distributed profits are subject to personal income tax in the hands of individual shareholders, but the corporation tax paid by the company (which is at a lower rate for distributed profits) may be deducted from the personal income tax payable, so finally distributed profits are subject only to the personal income tax of the shareholders (see Chapter 5, section 2.4).

Gesellschaft mit beschränkter Haftung (GmbH, limited liability company). Indispensable bodies are the managers and the general meeting. When the company's articles of association or the law (here the co-determination law – see Chapter 4) so provides, there is also a supervisory board. The managers are responsible for the day-to-day running of the company. In a few cases, prescribed by law, the general meeting is competent. The general meeting formally adopts the annual accounts, decides on the allocation of profits, appoints and dismisses the managers, and controls and supervises the management. The supervisory board's role is similar to that of the equivalent body in the joint stock corporation (see below). The shareholders are entitled to the entire annual profit after taking account of the profit or loss brought forward. Part of the profit can be excluded from distribution either by a provision in the company's articles or by a decision of the general meeting. The shares of the GmbH are transferable, but there is no organized capital market. In contrast to joint stock corporations, many of the law's provisions may be modified by the company's constitution, and protection for minority shareholders is weaker.

Aktiengesellschaft (AG, joint stock corporation). The executive board consists of one or more persons, who are appointed by the supervisory board for a maximum of five years. Reappointment is permitted. In enterprises to which the co-determination law applies the executive board must include a director of labour relations. The executive board is responsible for the management of the corporation, independently and on its own responsibility. It is not bound to accept instructions from the supervisory board or from the general meeting, unless the corporation's constitution provides that the agreement of the supervisory board is required for certain, particularly important, acts. In addition its powers may be limited in the case of what are known as 'contractual groups' (see below, section 3). The director of labour relations is responsible for matters concerning employees: remuneration, recruitment, training, social facilities.

The members of the supervisory board are appointed by the general meeting for a maximum of four years; they supervise the work of the executive board, which must report at least quarterly on planned activities, and on the profitability and progress of the enterprise. Members of the executive board may not be members of the supervisory board of the same corporation. The supervisory board may consist of no fewer than three and no more than twenty-one members. In the case of enterprises to which the *Betriebsverfassungsgesetz* (BetrVG, Industrial Constitution Act) applies (see Chapter 4), a third of the members must be elected by the employees. Special rules apply to enterprises which are subject to the *Montan* Co-determination Act or extended participation (see Chapter 4).

Under § 119 (1) of the *Aktiengesetz* (AktG, Joint Stock Corporation Act), the general meeting has particular responsibility for the appointment of the supervisory board (with the exception of the employee representatives), the allocation of the *Bilanzgewinn* (see Chapter 6, section 1.1), the formal approval of the decisions of the members of the executive board and of the supervisory board, the appointment of auditors (including auditors for special investigations), any changes in the corporation's constitution, increases and reductions in capital, and ultimately the liquidation of the company. The general meeting has no direct influence over the day-to-day management of the corporation.

The shares (*Aktien*) of the AG may be traded and quoted on organized capital markets. This makes the AG the appropriate legal form for enterprises that are dependent on their ability to raise large sums of money in anonymous capital markets.

German shares are generally bearer and not registered shares.

Kommanditgesellschaft auf Aktien (KGaA, limited partnership with shares). This is a legal person, which differs from an AG in that it has two types of members. The limited shareholders hold the equity in the form of their shares, and are liable for the debts only to the extent of their capital contribution. In addition there is at least one member who is personally liable and who is comparable to the *Komplementär* of a KG. The KGaA is very rare.

Eingetragene Genossenschaft (eG, registered co-operative). The special features of co-operatives lie in their objectives and, consequently, in the way in which economic benefits are passed on to the members. In corporations and commercial partnerships the members own a share of the enterprise's capital, and their legal rights depend on the number of shares they own. They receive economic benefits in the form of dividends, and, where appropriate, in the form of increases in the value of their shares. By contrast, co-operatives usually operate on a mutual basis for the benefit of the enterprises of their members. The number of shares a member holds is a secondary consideration. Each member has only a single vote in the members' meeting, the *Generalversammlung* (general meeting), as it is termed, like the members of, say, a sports club. The economic benefits can consist of:

1 Access to certain resources which it would not be economic for a single individual to acquire (*producer co-operatives*), for example a large wine press in a wine growers' co-operative.
2 Combining the buying power of small craftsmen, shopkeepers or farmers, so as to improve their purchasing conditions by placing larger orders (*purchasing co-operatives*).
3 Joint marketing of products so as to reduce transaction costs (*commercial co-operatives*).

In Germany credit co-operatives (*Volksbanken* and the *Raiffeisenkassen*) are of particular importance. Co-operatives are recorded in a special register, known as the *Genossenschaftsregister.* Like corporations, they are legal persons and are administered by a management board, which is overseen by a supervisory board. Also, as in corporations, liability for the organization's debts is limited to the sum of its assets (limited liability).

2 INCIDENCE AND IMPORTANCE OF THE VARIOUS FORMS OF BUSINESS ORGANIZATION

Table 2.2 presents information on the various legal forms of business organization: columns 2 and 3 show the number of enterprises (in absolute numbers and in percentage terms); columns 4 and 5 deal with the number of workers (the percentage figures in column 5 show the share of the global labour market taken by each type of business form); column 6, workers per enterprise, shows the average size of the different business forms. The data are taken from the latest labour statistics for the former West German state; no figures are yet available for the whole of Germany.

Table 2.3 shows the turnover of the different business forms (in absolute and

Table 2.2 Statistics on the number of enterprises and of employees

1	*2*	*3*	*4*	*5*	*6 = 4 ÷ 2*
	Enterprises		*Employees*		*Employees per enterprise*
Business form	*No.*	*%*	*No.*	*%*	*(No.)*
Einzelkaufmann (sole proprietorship)	1,622,481	77.34	6,071,114	27.70	3.74
BGB-Gesellschaft (civil law partnership)	136,711	6.52	831,570	3.79	6.08
Commercial partnerships:					
• *offene Handelsgesellschaft* (OHG, general partnership) } • *Kommanditgesellschaft* (KG, limited partnership) }	52,871	2.52	1,526,877	6.97	28.88
• GmbH & Co. KG	49,030	2.34	2,996,819	13.67	61.12
Corporations:					
• *Aktiengesellschaft* (AG, joint stock corporation) } • *Kommanditgesellschaft auf Aktien* (KGaA, limited partnership with shares) }	2,780	0.13	3,177,099	14.50	1,142.84
• *Gesellschaft mit beschränkter Haftung* (GmbH, limited liability company)	219,665	10.47	5,671,070	25.88	25.82
Eingetragene Genossenschaft (eG, registered co-operative)	7,022	0.33	264,538	1.21	37.67
Others	7,230	0.35	1,377,552	6.28	190.53
Total	2,097,790	100.0	21,916,639	100.0	10.45

Source: Wöhe (1990: 335).
Note: The figures are for the former West Germany and West Berlin, 1987.

percentage terms) according to the turnover tax statistics for 1986. There is a difference in the relative importance of the various business forms in the market for goods and services by comparison with the labour market: in the supply of goods and services sole proprietors are less important than corporations. Table 2.4 presents statistics on capital employed, for AGs and GmbHs. Statistics for all forms of business organization, comparable with those presented in Table 2.2 and 2.3, do not exist. The statistics are analysed by size of company (measured by the amount of subscribed capital): the number of companies in each size class and the global amount of subscribed capital (in absolute terms and in percentage), and the average amount of subscribed capital per company. It is clear that, on the measure of total subscribed capital, the GmbHs, as a group, are significantly larger than the AGs (total subscribed capital of DM 147 billion, as against DM 116 billion); that, in terms of number of companies, the smaller companies predominate, particularly among the GmbHs; and that, as measured in terms of subscribed capital, it is the larger companies that dominate, both among the AGs (57.6 per cent) and the GmbHs (63.5 per cent).

3 GROUPS

Individual, legally independent, enterprises can come together in economic units. Such economic combinations (combines, working agreements, consortia, joint ventures, cartels, groups of companies, mergers) are the rule rather than the exception in the German economic system. Economically the most important type is the group of affiliated companies (*Konzerne*). Groups are combinations of legally independent companies, set up under a unified management, on a permanent business basis. In this section, only groups of subordinate companies will be dealt with, as in Germany only this type of group is required to prepare consolidated accounts. The most common way of forming a group of subordinate companies is by one enterprise owning a share of the capital of another enterprise (*de facto* group, *faktischer Konzern*). The connection can be strengthened through enterprise contracts (control contracts, profit-ceding contracts, company leasing or company cession contracts). Through these contracts *de facto* groups become contractual groups (*Vertragskonzerne*), which are bound by legal requirements that are stricter than those upon *de facto* groups. A further connection arises through the personal obligations which, normally, follow the investment in the capital of another company and which, as a rule, take the form of the management of the parent undertaking being represented on the supervisory board of the subsidiary.

In Germany there is a Group Governance Law (*Konzernverfassungsrecht*), on which the proposal for a European constitution for groups (the proposed Ninth Directive) is based. In this, and in the rules of the HGB (Commercial Code) relating to consolidated accounts (see Chapter 8), are set out certain obligations of the individual enterprises, particularly those of the organs of the parent undertaking. The group itself is not a legal person. The detailed obligations are:

1 Obligation to provide information on the existence of connections between enterprises in the notes on the annual report and the obligation to record enterprise contracts in the commercial register.

Table 2.3 Taxable turnover (global per taxpayer), analysed by legal form of business

Business form (1)	*Global taxable turnover*		*Taxpayer*		*Turnover per taxpayer*
	DM million (2)	% (3)	*No.* (4)	% (5)	*DM million* (6)
Sole proprietors	748,591	14.9	1,545,264	73.4	0.48
Commercial partnerships:					
• *offene Handelsgesellschaft* (OHG)	342,897	6.8	173,294	8.2	1.97
• *Kommanditgesellschaft* (KG) } • GmbH & Co. KG }	1,204,775	23.9	85,219	4.1	14.1
Corporations:					
• *Aktiengesellschaft* (AG) } • *Kommanditgesellschaft auf Aktien* (KGaA) }	1,017,320	20.2	1,717	0.1	592.50
• Gesellschaft mit beschränkter Haftung (GmbH)	1,466,155	29.1	263,341	12.5	5.57
Registered co-operatives	87,572	1.7	6,106	0.3	14.34
Others	170,464	3.4	29,033	1.4	5.87
Total	5,037,774	100.0	2,103,974	100.0	2.40

Source: Statistisches Bundesamt, Fachserie 14, *Finanzen und Steuern*, Reihe 8, *Umsatzteuer 1990*.
Note: The figures are for the former West Germany and West Berlin.

Table 2.4 Statistics on AGs and GmbHs: numbers and subscribed capital

Size band: amount of subscribed capital (DM)	*AGs*					*GmbHs*				
			Subscribed capital					*Subscribed capital*		
	Corporations		*Global amount*		*Average amount per corporation*	*Companies*		*Global amount*		*Average amount per company*
	No.	*%*	*(DM million)*	*%*	*(DM million)*	*No.*	*%*	*(DM million)*	*%*	*(DM million)*
(1)	*(2)*	*(3)*	*(4)*	*(5)*	*(6)*	*(7)*	*(8)*	*(9)*	*(10)*	*(11)*
Up to 50,000						248,685	71.8	11,922	8.1	0.05
50,000–100,000	396	18.1	127	0.1	0.32	23,721	6.9	1,464	1.0	0.06
100,000–1 million						61,373	17.7	13,110	8.9	0.21
1 million–10 million	809	36.9	3,105	2.7	3.84	10,376	3.0	27,301	18.5	2.63
10 million–100 million	748	34.1	24,734	21.2	33.07					
100 million–250 million	146	6.7	21,399	18.4	146.57	2,216	0.6	93,625	63.5	42.25
Over 250 million	91	4.2	67,033	57.6	736.63					
Total	2,190	100.0	116,398	100.0	53.15	346,371	100.0	147,422	100.0	0.43

Source: Wöhe (1990: 341).
Note: The figures are for the former West Germany and West Berlin, 1986.

2 Obligations concerning the preparation, audit and publication of accounts (see Chapter 8).
3 Obligations in respect of subsidiary enterprises and their minority shareholders and creditors:

(a) Reasonable treatment of these shareholders in the conclusion of contracts ceding control and contracts ceding profits.
(b) Liability for the debts of the subsidiary enterprise in the case of a control contract and compensation for possible losses in the case of profit-ceding contracts and liabilities for the debts in the case of a *de facto* group if the ruling enterprise were to misuse its position.
(c) The *Abhängigkeitsbericht*, or dependence report, as it is called, of a subsidiary enterprise, which deals with measures the enterprise has taken at the instigation or in the interests of the controlling enterprise or of an enterprise that is closely related.
(d) The obligation to compensate for any economic loss suffered by the subsidiary enterprise as a result of such transactions.
(e) The obligation of the subsidiary enterprise to comply with instructions when a control contract exists, and to cede its profit when a profit-ceding contract exists.

The aim of the Group Governance Law is to reduce the particular risks to which shareholders, creditors and workers are exposed on account of the structure of the group. In economic terms, reducing these risks should make the capital and labour markets more efficient.

An indication of the significance of groups is the frequency of majority shareholdings. A 1983 study that involved a random sample of 210 joint stock corporations (the total population of active joint stock corporations was 2,109) investigated whether they held a majority stake in another enterprise or whether another enterprise owned a majority stake in them (see Table 2.5). A joint stock corporation that met either of the two

Table 2.5 Extent of group integration of joint stock corporations (%)

Size band[1]	*'50%+' corporations*	*Other corporations: Public*	*Hybrid*	*Private*	*Total*
Under 1	9	0.5	0.5	8.6	18.6
1–10	27.1	3.4	–	7.1	37.6
10–50	26.2	1.4	0.5	1.0	29.1
50–100	5.7	–	–	–	5.7
100–250	3.8	1.0	–	0.5	5.2[2]
Over 250	3.8	–	–	–	3.8
		6.2[2]	1.0	17.2	
Total	75.6		24.4		100.0

Source: Ordelheide (1986: 295).
Notes:
[1]Subscribed capital (DM million).
[2]Differences are due to rounding.

conditions was termed a '50 per cent-plus' corporation. The proportion of '50 per cent plus' corporations was 75.7 per cent (a confidence interval of ± 7.7 per cent at 99 per cent). In the sample, the subscribed capital of the '50 per cent plus' corporations was 93 per cent of the total subscribed capital. By comparison with preceding years, the trend was upward.

The non-'50 per cent plus' corporations belonged, with few exceptions, to the two smallest size bands. However, even in the size band of less than DM 10 million subscribed capital, the proportion of '50 per cent plus' corporation was almost double that of the others. Thus the smaller joint stock corporations are often part of a group. The proportion of non-'50 per cent plus' corporations owned by the state was relatively high. The proportion of subsidiary companies that were bound by a control contract or a profit-ceding contract was about 30 per cent.

GmbHs too are frequently part of a group. In 1979 there were 5,600 companies with a subscribed capital of over DM 500,000 out of the total of 220,000 such companies. Of these 5,600 companies (whose subscribed capital make up 90 per cent of the total subscribed capital of all companies), 40 per cent were under the decisive influence of another enterprise (Hansen 1980). However, these figures are only to a limited extent comparable with those for joint stock corporations. On the one hand, parent undertakings are not included. On the other, decisive influence can occur without a majority stake.

To summarize, the AG as an independent economic enterprise belongs to the past, and the larger and medium-size GmbHs appear to be following the same road.

3
Finance and capital markets

1 THE FINANCIAL STUCTURE OF INDUSTRY

The sources of finance available to German enterprises are summarized in Table 3.1: column 1 lists the sources, columns 2–5 indicate the quantitative importance of these sources for the large corporations. The figures show that, as far as the large corporations are concerned, *equity financing* (including retained profits), at 25.3 per cent of the total, is not the prime source of finance. This finding is not limited to large corporations. According to a survey by the Bundesbank in 1992, the equity ratio (i.e. the ratio of equity to all sources of finance) for all forms of business was nearly 26 per cent. Unfortunately, there are no comparable figures for other countries. The latest comparative data available to the authors concern the equity ratio for manufacturing industry. This table makes it clear that German manufacturing enterprises are characterized by a relatively low provision of equity (30.3 per cent). By comparison, manufacturing enterprises in Britain and the United States reveal a much higher ratio, at 47.6 per cent and 40.2 per cent respectively. However, in looking at the figures, two factors should be taken into account. First, they are aggregate figures: the actual equity ratio varies a good deal from industry to industry and from firm to firm. Second, differences between countries in accounting and tax law, as well as in the conventions and standards of the accountancy profession, can influence the level of reported equity and may account for part of the difference. The magnitude of these influences is difficult to estimate, but should be considerable. For example, Perlitz *et al.* 1985, using a simulation model based on similar accounting rules and practices, conclude that, after adjustment, the equity ratios of German and British enterprises are not substantially different.

The equity capital of German enterprises has essentially the same characteristics as in other countries. The liability of the equity holder for the claims of creditors depends on

Table 3.1 The financial structure and sources of finance of large corporations

1	*DM million* 2	*DM million* 3	*DM million* 4	% 5
I *Equity*			187,041.7	25.3
1 Subscribed capital		86,932.2		(11.7)
of which: ordinary shares	52,419.7			
preference shares	2,206.5			
2 Participation certificates deposits of personally liable members		2,000.1		(0.3)
3 Capital reserve		32,186.7		(4.4)
4 Profit reserves		56,061.6		(7.6)
5 Unappropriated profit (net of losses)		9,861.1		(1.3)
II *Special item with a reserve component*			17,246.9	2.3
III *Income subsidies received*[1]			13,330.4	1.8
IV *Provisions*			220,465.8	29.8
of which: provisions for pensions and similar commitments	98,559.6			
V *Liabilities*			295,183.7	39.9
of which payable within one year	154,827.0			
1 Loans		1,390.0		(0.2)
of which payable after five years	632.0			
2 Liabilities to banks		79,947.3		(10.8)
of which payable after five years	35,472.3			
3 Payments received on account of orders		58,777.8		(7.9)
of which payable after five years	383.6			
4 Liabilities to suppliers		46,483.3		(6.3)
of which payable after five years	108.9			
5 Bills of exchange		4,019.2		(0.5)
of which payable after five years	26.9			
6 Liabilities to associated companies		40,192.6		(5.5)
of which payable after five years	7,431.9			
7 Liabilities to affiliated companies		6,722.4		(0.9)
of which payable after five years	403.2			
8 Liabilities to members (only in GmbHs)		19,424.5		(2.6)
of which payable after five years	3,686.2			
9 Other liabilities		38,226.6		(5.2)
of which payable after five years	5,351.7			
VI *Accruals and deferred income*			6,286.4	0.9
Balance sheet total (sources of finance)			739,554.9	

Source: Statistisches Bundesamt (ed.), Fachserie 2, *Unternehmen und Arbeitsstätten*, Reihe 2.1, *Abschlüsse von Kapitalgesellschaften 1988*, Stuttgart 1991; own calculation.
Note: Data from 1,078 large corporations, 1988, excluding finance and insurance companies: corporations that exceeded for a reporting period two of following three limits: total assets of DM 15.5 million, turnover of DM 100 million, 250 employees.
[1] A special feature of municipal enterprises; the entitlement to the revenue subsidies depends on the general conditions of delivery; the subsidies can be booked as deferred income in the balance sheet and a certain percentage credited to the profit and loss account each year.

the legal form of the enterprise: it is limited to his capital contribution (shareholders of a GmbH or an AG or the limited partner of a KG), or it extends additionally to his personal wealth (sole proprietor, partner in a civil law partnership or an OHG, or the general partner of a KG): see Chapter 2, section 1. The varying extent of liability is usually matched by corresponding variations in the degree of control. Whereas investors whose liability extends to their private wealth generally participate in the management of

Table 3.2 Equity ratios: international comparisons

Country	*1970*	*1975*	*1980*	*1987*	*1988*	*1989*	*1990*
Germany[1]	35.7	32.6	30.5	32.2[2]	30.5	30.4	30.3
Denmark	–	40.2	30.5	41.8	42.0	42.1	41.9
France	35.0	30.2	31.9[2]	36.2	37.8	40.8	–
UK	47.4	47.6	47.8	47.1	47.5	44.3	47.6
Netherlands[1]	–	–	42.6	44.4	44.4	–	–
Austria[1]	–	27.0	21.7	20.1[3]	–	–	–
Japan	18.2[4]	16.8	21.9	29.4	30.1	31.0	–
United States[1]	53.8	53.7	49.8	42.7	42.0	40.5	40.2

Source: OECD; US Department of Commerce; Federal Statistical Office; calculations of the Institut der Deutschen Wirtschaft, table from *Institut der Deutschen Wirtschaft*, 1993.
Notes: As a percentage of balance sheet total.
[1]Excluding provisions.
[2]Break in continuity of series.
[3]1985.
[4]Excluding pension provisions.

the firm, such is not the case with shareholders of large corporations or the limited partners in limited partnerships. In many small corporations the majority shareholder is also the general manager. A special situation exists with regard to large joint stock corporations, whose shares are widely owned. Here the shareholders' ability to control the enterprise is very limited. It can be exercised only through the use of their votes on important matters (e.g. an increase in capital or the allocation of profits). The position is made worse by the fact that most small shareholders do not themselves vote in the general meeting but allow the bank with which they have deposited their shares to vote on their behalf (proxy voting).

The limited influence of small shareholders on the policy of the enterprise is in marked contrast to the high liquidity of the variable income securities of joint stock corporations. If they are unhappy with the business strategy the shareholders of a quoted joint stock corporation can sell their bearer shares, at no great transaction cost, on the secondary market (stock exchange). Together with preference shares and subscription rights, bearer shares are the most widely traded form of variable income security on the eight German stock exchanges (Frankfurt am Main, Düsseldorf, Hamburg, Munich, Berlin, Hanover, Stuttgart and Bremen; there are plans for further stock exchanges in the former East Germany). Shares in a GmbH cannot be traded on a stock exchange. On the other hand, various intermediate financing instruments issued by joint stock corporations may be traded, such as participating bonds, convertible bonds and option bonds. The option right can be separated from the option bond and traded on the stock exchange as a warrant in its own right.

Private shareholding is not very widespread. Quoting figures for West Germany, whereas at the start of the 1970s 28 per cent of all shareholdings were in the hands of private householders, by early 1991 the proportion had fallen to 17 per cent. Today it is businesses, with 42 per cent, that hold by far the largest part. Other shareholders included foreign investors (14 per cent), insurance companies (12 per cent), credit institutions (10 per cent) and the state (5 per cent) (see *Die Bank* 1, 1992, p. 62).

Self-financing is very important – more significant than equity financing. For example, provisions represent almost 30 per cent of the sources of finance (see Table 3.1). The scope for creating provisions is dealt with more fully in Chapter 7, section 4.2.

Debt (loan capital) is the most prominent source of finance. The importance of loan capital is clear from Table 3.1; for the larger corporations debt finance constitutes 39.9 per cent of the balance sheet total. Within this category, bank credit (10.8 per cent) stands out. Also important are customers (7.9 per cent), suppliers (6.3 per cent) and associated companies (5.4 per cent).

The granting of *bank credit* generally depends on the availability of security (for example, real property or stocks that may be pledged as security). A source of finance that has become more important in recent years is *Schuldscheindarlehen* (borrowers' note loans) which are shown in Table 3.1 under 'Other liabilities'. Note loans are typically long-term large-scale loans (the minimum amount is DM 100,000) made available by financial institutions through the banking system (not through the stock exchange). The insurance companies, particularly life assurance companies, play a prominent role as

Table 3.3 Government financial aid: (a) public credit programmes – a selection

Programme	*Interest rates (%)*	*Amount of aid paid (%)*	*Maximum period in years (repayment holiday in brackets)*	*Maximum amount of finance or credit (per project)*
European Recovery Programme credits				
Business start-up programme	8.5	100	10/15 (2)	DM 300,000
Regional programme	8.5	100	10/15 (2)	DM 300,000
Location programme	8.5	100	10/15 (2)	DM 200,000
Investment in sewage disposal, clean air, waste disposal	8.0	100	10/15 (2)	–
Energy programme	8.0	100	10/15 (2)	DM 3 million
Creation of additional training places	8.5	100	10/15 (2)	DM 30,000 per place
Press programme (small and medium-size publishers)	8.5	100	10/15 (2)	DM 500,000
Inland navigation (individuals and small shipowners)	8.5	100	10/15 (2)	60% of total cost
Ports (businesses in seaports)	8.5	100	12 (2)	
Delivery of capital goods to developing countries (ERP/KfW):				
(a) Class II countries	9.75	100	10	Max. DM 170 million
(b) Class III countries	9.20	100	5	
Kreditanstalt für Wiederaufbau				
Small and medium-size business programme	8.25	96	10 (2)	DM 10 million
Special credits	Capital market rates		10 (2)	–
Environment programme	7.25	96	10 (2)	DM 10 million

Note: The figures are for the former West Germany as at the beginning of November 1991.

purchasers of such notes. The contract for the note does not have to follow any particular legal formalities.

A form of financing now practically extinct is the *corporate bond*, which, being quoted on the stock exchange, is available to non-bank investors, especially small investors. At the end of 1989 the market value of this type of security in the jurisdiction of the Bundesbank represented only 0.10 per cent of the total credit granted by the banks to the non-financial sectors.

Other credit instruments traded on German stock exchanges are the loans of credit institutions (mortgage bonds, local authority bonds, other bonds), and government funds (e.g. central government loans, state government loans, local authority loans, loans of the German Federal Railways).

In addition to the above sources of finance, it is possible to claim *financial support from the government*, subject to set conditions. Government help extends from promoting exports (e.g. through the guarantees of the *Hermes Kreditversicherung AG*) to assistance in setting up new enterprises, including aid for projects which strengthen the regional economy and for the encouragement of research, development and innovation. Table 3.3 lists some examples. The financial contributions mainly take the form of tax concessions (e.g. accelerated depreciation, see Chapter 7, section 5.5), investment grants

Table 3.3 Government financial aid: (b) other important measures – a selection

Programme	*Promoted projects*	*Level of finance (maximum)*
Regional development		
Federal and provincial government investment grants to firms in designated development areas under the Regional Economic Structure Improvement programme	Setting up of enterprises and acquisition of closed down firms or of firms threatened with closure	12%, 15% or 18%
	Expansion investment	12% or 15%
	Reconversion/rationalization	10%
	Creation of new high-grade jobs	DM 15,000 or DM 20,000 per job
Support for research, development and innovation		
Support of projects by the Ministry of Research and Technology in the form of grants (in exceptional cases public orders)	Research and development plans in certain specialized sectors	As a rule 50%
Co-operation in research between industry and science (subsidies)	Employment of young scientists in research and development, particularly in key technologies	DM 33,750 in the first year; DM 30,000 in the second year and DM 26,250 in the third year for a maximum of six scientists (ending on 31 December 1991)
Programme for the technology of microsystems (for firms with an annual turnover of less than DM 1 billion; of which at least DM 100,000 is in products in which information technology is applied)	Development of miniaturized and intelligent systems which can be employed in a decentralized way, including the necessary tasks relating to qualifications, organization, marketing and management	40% of the qualifying incurred costs in the so-called advance phase and the development phase, to a maximum DM 400,000 or, in certain cases, DM 800,000 (of which a maximum of DM 50,000 in the advance phase)

Source: Industriekreditbank AG – Deutsche Industriebank (ed.): *IKB Mitteilungen 3/1991*, pp. 32ff.
Note: Position as at the beginning of November 1991.

which do not have to be repaid, or loans on terms a good deal more favourable then the financial markets can offer.

Financial help in the form of tax concessions has a direct impact on the legal financial statements of the enterprise. Thus most of the opportunities for accelerated depreciation in the tax computation may be taken only if such special write-offs are also included in the financial statements. (For details see Chapter 6, section 1.3.2, which also explains the 'justification' for this procedure.)

When equity and debt financing are considered side by side, two characteristics of the way German business is financed become apparent: the relatively large share of debt in the capital structure, and the very considerable importance of banks and other investment institutions in debt financing.

2 THE IMPORTANCE OF BANKS AND INSURANCE COMPANIES

Before dealing with the system of financial intermediaries in detail, a brief word on the supervisory system and the association system in Germany is in order. Important supervisory bodies are the *Bundesaufsichsamt für das Kreditwesen* (the Federal Banking Supervisory Board), the *Bundes- und Landesaufsichtsbehörden* (the federal and regional supervisory bodies), the *Bundesaufsichtsamt für das Versicherungswesen* (the Federal Supervisory Office for Insurance) and the *Bundeskartellamt* (the Federal Monopolies Commission). Their function is to enforce and monitor the working of the laws and basic principles laid down by the state to regulate the business activities, the assumed risks and the competitive actions of the institutions within their purview. By contrast, the purpose of the industry-based associations is to represent the interests of their members in relation to the state and the public. These associations include the *Bundesverband Deutscher Banken eV* (the Confederation of German Banks) in Cologne, the *Deutscher Sparkassen- und Giroverband eV* (the German Savings Bank Association), the *Deutsche Genossenschafts- und Raiffeisenverband* (the German Association of Co-operatives), and the *Gesamtverband der Deutschen Versicherungswirtschaft* (the German Insurance Association), all in Bonn. Many financial intermediaries play no part in the commercial banking system – for example, building societies, investment trusts, deposit banks, guarantee banks, insurance companies, pension funds, property funds, leasing and factoring companies. In the following section, of the financial intermediaries, only the commercial banks and insurance companies are dealt with, on account of their outstanding importance in the financing of business.

Characteristic of the banking system and, beyond it, of the entire German financial system is the dominant role of the *Universalbanken* (universal banks). The term refers to a type of bank which, in contrast to the specialized banks that are common in other countries, in principle undertakes all forms of banking activity – not only deposit and giro business but other forms of business as well, such as credit, discounts, securities, deposits of securities, investments, the floating of loans and guarantees. Of the approximately 4,000 commercial banks in Germany, well over 90 per cent are run as universal banks. To this category belong the private commercial banks as well as the co-operative banks and the publicly owned credit institutions (savings banks and state-owned clearing banks).

Table 3.4 shows the different categories of banks by volume of business at the end of 1990. The category with the largest turnover is the savings banks (including the state-owned clearing banks) with 35.1 per cent of the total assets of the banking sector. Savings banks are publicly owned legal bodies which come under the jurisdiction of, and whose deposits are guaranteed by, the local authority in which they operate (province, country, region, town and municipality). The so-called 'free' savings banks are an exception (for example, the *Hamburger Sparkasse* and the *Frankfurter Sparkasse von 1822*), which can be private bodies (for example, a foundation or a registered association). The giro centres are the central credit institutions of public savings banks.

The second largest group are the private universal banks, the *Kreditbanken* (credit banks), with a 26.9 per cent share of total business volume. They are not publicly owned. The credit banks comprise:

1 The three large banks (*Deutsche Bank AG*, *Dresdner Bank AG* and *Commerzbank AG*, all of them joint stock corporations as regards their legal form).
2 The regional and other commercial banks, which all take the legal form of a corporation and which, in many respects, come a close second to the large banks (for example the *Bank für Gemeinwirtschaft* (BfG-Bank), *Berliner Handelsgesellschaft-*

Table 3.4 Categories of banks and their business volume

	Volume of business[1]	
Category of bank	*DM billion*	*% of total of all categories*
Universal banks	4,060.1	77.4
• Credit banks	1,408.9	26.9
Large banks	(468.6)	(8.9)
Regional and other commercial banks	(801.4)	(15.3)
Branches of foreign banks	(76.3)	(1.5)
Private bankers	(62.7)	(1.2)
• Savings bank sector	1,842.6	35.1
Giro centres (including Deutsche Girozentrale)	(761.8)	(14.5)
Savings banks	(1,080.9)	(20.6)
• Co-operative sector	808.6	15.4
Central institutions of credit co-operatives (including Deutsche Genossenschaftsbank)	(216.7)	(4.1)
Credit co-operatives	(591.9)	(11.3)
Specialized banks	1,183.7	22.6
• Mortgage banks	611.2	11.7
Private mortgage banks	(456.7)	(8.7)
Publicly owned mortgage banks	(154.5)	(3.0)
• Credit institutions with special functions	499.6	9.5
• Postal giro transfer offices and postal savings banks	72.9	1.4
Total, all categories[2]	5,243.8	100.0

Source: Deutsche Bundesbank, *Monthly Report*, March 1991.
Notes: Figures as of 31 December 1990.
[1]The total of the balance sheet plus the following items: withdrawals in course of collection, endorsement liability on rediscounted bills, bills sent for collection before maturity.
[2]The total of institutions included in the banking statistics (except building societies). Differences are due to rounding.

Frankfurter Bank (BHF-Bank) and the *Bayerische Vereinsbank*).

3 The private bankers, who take the legal form of a sole proprietor or a partnership, whose activities are partially confined to a particular region or locality and are mostly specialized (for example *Trinkaus & Burkhardt*; *Sal. Oppenheim jr. & Cie*, *Schröder Münchmeyer Hengst & Co.*).

The third category of universal bank is the co-operative banks (*Volksbanken, Spar- und Darlehnskassen*) and the central institutions of the credit co-operatives (for example, the *Deutsche Genossenschaftsbank* (DG-Bank), with a 15.4 per cent share of total business volume. Since the activities of co-operatives are essentially to serve the interests of their members, in principle the borrowers must be members of the co-operative.

In contrast to the types of banks mentioned so far, the field of activity of the *Spezialbanken* (special banks) is limited by law. The most important are the mortgage banks (both private and publicly owned mortgage banks) with 13.9 per cent of total business volume. They finance their lending to private and public property owners primarily by issuing their own bonds (both private mortgage bonds and municipal bonds) and by taking on long-term loans. To this category also belong the postal giro transfer offices and the postal savings banks. The credit institutions with special functions have been set up at the instigation of the state or through the finance sector's own initiative. Examples are the *Kreditanstalt für Wiederaufbau* (Reconstruction Loan Corporation), which was originally set up to finance the reconstruction of Germany and nowadays specializes in long-term export finance and the granting of credit to developing countries, and the *Industriekreditbank AG* (Industrial Credit Bank), which grants long-term loans to private industry.

Not represented in Table 3.4 is the Bundesbank, the central bank, which occupies a special position as the leading institution in the German banking system. The Bundesbank is a federal public-law body, with a nominal capital of DM 290 million, which belongs to the Federal government. It is located in Frankfurt am Main. Attached to the Bundesbank are nine *Landeszentralbanken* (regional central banks). The organs of the Bundesbank are the *Zentralbankrat* (the Central Bank Council), the *Direktorium* (directorate) and the boards of the regional central banks. The Central Bank Council is the highest organ of the Bundesbank and is made up of the president and vice-president of the Bundesbank, the other members of the directorate and the presidents of the *Landeszentralbanken* (the regional central banks). It meets, as a rule, once a fortnight and determines the bank's monetary and credit policy. The directorate is responsible for the execution of the resolutions of the Central Bank Council and manages and administers the bank. The regional central banks effect business with the *Länder* in which they are located, dealing both with the public authorities and with the credit institutions.

The task of the Bundesbank is to regulate the money supply and the volume of lending in the economy, with the aim of protecting the currency, that is, maintaining price stability at home and the value of the Deutschmark abroad. In addition, it is responsible for the settlement of payment transactions between banks both within Germany and with foreign countries. In order to strengthen the Bundesbank's hand in its mission of protecting the currency, German law has made it independent of the government. In addition, although the Bundesbank is legally obliged to support the government's general economic policy, the obligation is subject to the specific condition that this should not lead the bank to neglect its proper task of safeguarding the currency. In fulfilling this task the Bundesbank benefits from the breadth of German banks' business and their importance in the country's financial system. As the Bundesbank has itself said, the business activities of the banks offer an almost 'universal' starting point for the monetary control of the entire financial system, because there is little need to anticipate much in the way of evasive reactions by the non-bank institutions in the sector of the credit market which is outside the banking system (see *Sonderdruck der Deutschen Bundesbank* No. 7, fifth edition, February 1989, p. 42). The only significant exceptions derive from the foreign financial connections of German enterprises.

Second only to the banks as investing institutions are the private insurance companies, particularly in the financing of German businesses. They channel funds, especially from private households, into construction, manufacturing industry, the state and the banking system. The investment policies of the insurance companies are governed by legal and supervisory rules which focus mainly on investment principles and categories. On 1 January 1991 a modification of the investment rules of the Supervisory Office for Insurance came into force, expanding the range of permitted investment. Among other changes, the upper limit for participating investments in enterprises was raised to 30 per cent of the subscribed capital of the enterprise concerned. Table 3.5 presents an overview of the total investments of the insurance industry, analysed by type of investment. It shows that for years registered bonds, notes and loans have been the clear investment favourite of the insurance industry. In 1990 they made up 45.7 per cent of total investments. In second place, with 27.2 per cent (1990), come fixed-interest securities and shares. The fastest-growing categories in 1990 were the registered debt of the federal and state governments and deposits (fixed-term and savings deposits). Participating investments also increased considerably, by 36.5 per cent, to reach DM 38,328 million in 1990.

Table 3.5 Total investments of the insurance industry[1]

	1980		*1985*		*1990*	
Type of investment	*DM million*	%	*DM million*	%	*DM million*	%
Land	27,360	9.8	37,176	8.0	44,706	6.2
Mortgages	43,249	15.5	67,370	14.5	85,032	11.9
Registered bonds and loans	120,560	43.3	193,241	41.5	326,057	45.7
Securities and shares	71,482	25.6	144,844	31.1	193,977	27.2
Loans and advances on insurance certificates	3,391	1.2	6,779	1.5	9,680	1.3
Participations	5,630	2.0	9,015	1.9	38,328	5.4
Registered debt of the federal and regional governments	4,025	1.5	3,151	0.7	9,575	1.3
Fixed-term, time and savings deposits	3,055	1.1	3,716	0.8	6,904	1.0
Total	278,752	100	465,292	100	714,259	100

Source: Bundesaufsichtsamt für das Versicherungswesen (Federal Supervisory Office for Insurance).
Note:
[1] Analysed by type of investment and percentage share (balance sheet values).

To summarize, the banks and the other investing institutions, in particular the private insurance companies, play a central role in the economy. Moreover the importance of the banks for enterprises in the non-financial sector is reinforced by the following consideration.

In Germany proxy voting has been in existence for over a century, with the consequence that the influence of banks in the annual meetings of shareholders has become considerable. According to a survey in the mid-1970s of sixteen large German joint stock corporations without a principal shareholder, over 90 per cent of attendance at shareholders' meetings was accounted for by the proxy votes of banks and investment companies (BMF 1979: 113, 438 ff.). In addition, banks and insurance companies possess, *in their own right,* large blocks of shares in commercial and industrial companies in various sectors of industry (BMF 1979: 407). But, as the banks often act as suppliers of credit to enterprises, in addition to managing both the deposited shares of their clients and their own shareholdings, the danger is that banks might act in their own interest and not in that of the small shareholders. Ceteris paribus, a conservative calculation of profits or a modest dividend increases the funds available for creditors and may motivate the shareholders to take a close interest in the efficient management of the enterprise, on account of their greater capital accumulation (the incentive function of capital maintenance). This in turn reduces the risk to creditors.

The weight of banks' presence at the shareholders' meeting combines with a strong showing by the representatives of banks on the supervisory boards. This gives the banks opportunities of influencing the business policy and, in particular, the financial policy of the company. Since over 90 per cent of all AGs (as measured by nominal share capital) are members of a group, and as a considerable proportion of GmbHs also belong to groups, either as holding companies or as subsidiary companies (see Chapter 2, section 3), it is often sufficient to be represented on the supervisory board of a large holding company in order to have a voice formulating the policy of many group companies. Such influence can also work to the advantage of shareholders and management, notwithstanding the concentration of power in the hands of the banks. For example, as part of their role on supervisory boards, lending institutions perform with great professional competence many tasks in the fields of management consultancy and financial advice that would otherwise prove expensive.

4

Co-determination and the labour market

1 Co-determination at macro-economic and industry level
2 Co-determination at the level of the enterprise
3 Co-determination at plant and shop-floor level

A characteristic of the German economic system is the great importance attached to employees and their representatives. There are five levels at which employees or their representatives can participate in decisions that affect their working life and other parts of the business sector:

1 Macro-economic level.
2 Industry level.
3 Enterprise level.
4 Plant level.
5 Shop-floor level.

1 CO-DETERMINATION AT MACRO-ECONOMIC AND INDUSTRY LEVEL

Employees' influence is embodied mainly in the unions. German trade unions are voluntary, private-law associations of employees which have the aim of collectively protecting their members' interests, independently and at a supra-plant level. The trade union movement is comprised of sixteen predominantly *industry-wide individual unions*, such as IG Metall (the engineering workers' union); IG Chemie, Papier, Keramik (the chemicals, paper and pottery trade union); Gewerkschaft Öffentliche Dienste, Transport und Verkehr (ÖTV, the public services and transport workers' union), together with their umbrella organization, the Deutscher Gewerkschaftsbund (DGB, German Trade Union Federation); the Deutsche Angestellten Gewerkschaft (DAG, German Salaried Employees' Union) and the Deutscher Beamtenbund (German Public Service Federation). The model of a small number of industry-wide unions dates from the days of the

Weimar Republic, when the principle of organizing the economy on an industry basis prevailed in the transformation of the individual craft unions into industrial unions.

The membership of the DGB in the period 1970–89, both in numbers and as a percentage of all employees, is given in Table 4.1. This shows that the percentage of employees organized in the DGB (i.e. excluding the Salaried Employees' Union and the Public Service Federation) has remained constant at a little over 30 per cent. Not least because of this relatively high density of membership, the influence of the trade unions in politics, particularly on economic and social policy, is considerable. Representatives of individual trade unions or of the DGB are commonly found in the most important political bodies, above all in the federal and provincial legislatures. Positions in government have frequently been occupied by trade union officials. Moreover from 1967 the trade unions were party to the so-called *konzertierte Aktion* (concerted action). The members of the concerted action were the federal Minister of Economics as chairman, ten to twelve authorized representatives of employers' associations and trade unions, members of the Council of Economic Experts and of the Bundesbank, and the federal Ministers of Finance and Labour. The aim of the regular meetings was to co-ordinate through the exchange of information the government's economic policy and the decision-making of the independent groups. The concerted action was terminated in 1977, during the dispute over co-determination.

The principal concern of the trade unions is the negotiation with the employers' associations of improvements in conditions of employment, especially in wages and working hours. Usually the negotiations are carried out at industry level. Only occasionally does a trade union negotiate with an individual enterprise. Individual employees cannot be parties to a collective agreement, so a trade union must always be involved.

In the negotiations between trade unions and employers' associations the basic principle of free collective bargaining (*Tarifautonomie*) applies. Hence the parties do not take orders from the government but decide on the terms of the collective agreement between themselves. If the negotiations fail, the next step involves a conciliation procedure, in which an independent third party tries to get the parties to agree. If the attempt is unsuccessful, the only way to resolve the dispute is through industrial action;

Table 4.1 Number of employees and membership of the German Trade Union Federation

1	*2*	*3*	*4*	*5*
Year	*Working population (000s)*	*Employees (000s)*	*Membership (000s)*	*Col. 4 as a % of col. 3*
1970	26,668	22,246	6,713	30.2
1975	26,110	22,467	7,365	32.8
1980	27,059	23,897	7,883	33.0
1985	26,626	23,491	7,719	32.9
1990	29,334	25,910	7,938	30.6

Source: Kittner (1991: 88) and *Institut der Deutschen Wirtschaft*, 1992.
Note: Figures are from the sample census in the former West Germany.

the trade unions have the right to strike, and the employers the right of lock-out (suspension of employment contracts or mass dismissals, in order to force the employees to accept the employer's offer). That, in the past, there have been relatively few strikes and lock-outs, speaks for the predominance of economic calculations by both parties over purely class warfare considerations.

In law, the collective agreements negotiated by the trade unions and the employers apply only to members of trade unions. In practice the collectively agreed conditions are applied to all employees, whether or not they belong to a trade union.

Among the factors the trade unions take into account in preparing their claims, apart from the increase in productivity and the rate of inflation, are the profits reported by companies in their industry. If the profitability of the industry is healthy, the trade unions want their members to benefit – the so-called 'redistribution bonus'. Moreover, high profits can stimulate union demands for so-called 'voluntary' fringe benefits. As a result, it seems, managements are inclined to build up hidden current value reserves (see Chapter 7, section 8) and to report conservatively calculated profits. Especially with respect to large undertakings, accounting policy is often also part of pay rate policy. Moreover the government, for reasons of economic policy, particularly with a view to maintaining price stability, has an interest in ensuring that wage claims are based on reasonably certain profits and not on an over-optimistic view of the net worth, financial and income position.

2 CO-DETERMINATION AT THE LEVEL OF THE ENTERPRISE

Employees participate in the decisions of certain enterprises through their representatives on the supervisory board and through the industrial relations director on the executive board. Whether co-determination applies at all, and, if so, under what law, depends on the legal form, the number of employees, and the objects and aims of the business (see Table 4.2).

The *Montan-Mitbestimmungsgesetz* of 1951 (*Montan* Co-determination Act) applies, principally, to AGs and GmbHs with over 1,000 employees in coal, iron and steel (the *Montan* or extractive industries). It provides that half the members of the supervisory board are to be appointed by the shareholders (at the shareholders' meeting), and the other half are appointed by the employees (joint or equal co-determination). Some of the employee representatives can be drawn from outside the business, e.g. from the staff of the trade union. To avoid deadlock, the two sides jointly elect an additional, neutral member. On the executive board the employees are represented by the industrial relations director, who is a full member of the board and is responsible for personnel and social matters.

AGs and GmbHs in industries other than coal and iron and steel that regularly employ more than 2,000 people are subject to the *Mitbestimmungsgesetz* of 1976 (MitbestG, Co-determination Act). Under its terms, employees are entitled to half the seats on the supervisory board, as under the *Montan-Mitbestimmungsgesetz*. But in contrast to the *Montan* Act it is a requirement that the employees' representatives should include a managerial employee of the company. The equal representation is further weakened by the double voting rights of the chairman, who regularly comes from the shareholders'

Table 4.2 Co-determination laws

<table>
<tr><th rowspan="3">Legal form</th><th colspan="6">No. of employees</th></tr>
<tr><th rowspan="2">Under 500</th><th rowspan="2">500–1,000</th><th colspan="2">1,001–2,000</th><th colspan="2">2,001 and over</th></tr>
<tr><th>Montan</th><th>Other</th><th>Montan</th><th>Other</th></tr>
<tr><td>AG</td><td></td><td></td><td></td><td></td><td></td><td></td></tr>
<tr><td>Family enterprise</td><td>–</td><td rowspan="2">BetrVG 52</td><td rowspan="2">Montan-MitbestG</td><td rowspan="2">BetrVG 52</td><td rowspan="2">Montan-MitbestG</td><td rowspan="2">MitbestG</td></tr>
<tr><td>Others</td><td>BetrVG 52</td></tr>
<tr><td>KGaA</td><td></td><td></td><td></td><td></td><td></td><td></td></tr>
<tr><td>Family enterprise</td><td>–</td><td rowspan="2">BetrVG 52</td><td rowspan="2">BetrVG 52[1]</td><td rowspan="2">BetrVG 52</td><td rowspan="2">MitbestG[1]</td><td rowspan="2">MitbestG</td></tr>
<tr><td>Others</td><td>BetrVG 52</td></tr>
<tr><td>GmbH</td><td>–</td><td>BetrVG 52</td><td>Montan-MitbestG</td><td>BetrVG 52</td><td>Montan-MitbestG</td><td>MitbestG</td></tr>
<tr><td>eG</td><td>–</td><td>BetrVG 52</td><td>n.a.[2]</td><td>BetrVG 52</td><td>n.a.[2]</td><td>MitbestG</td></tr>
</table>

Source: Wächter (1983: 64).
Notes:
[1]No cases known.
[2]Does not exist (not possible).
Not considered: exclusion from co-determination in organizations concerned with influencing opinion, e.g. the press, politics, churches.

side. The MitbestG of 1976 also provides for an industrial relations director, but, in contrast to the position under the *Montan* Co-determination Act, this director can be appointed or dismissed against the votes of the employee representatives on the supervisory board.

The *Betriebsverfassungsgesetz* of 1952 (BetrVG, Industrial Constitution Act) applies to all corporations and co-operatives with more than 500 employees which are not covered by the *Montan-Mitbestimmungsgesetz* or the MitbestG of 1976. It also applies to AGs with less than 500 employees that are not family enterprises. Under the BetrVG, one-third of the places on the supervisory board must be filled by employees. The appointment of an industrial relations director on the managing board is not required.

All three co-determination laws follow the common principle that co-determination should not be achieved through the creation of additional bodies specially for the employees but should be integral to those bodies which were formerly the preserve of the shareholders – on the supervisory board through the employees' representatives, on the managing board through the industrial relations director. Co-determination therefore depends on the rights and duties of these regular bodies of the company.

The *executive board* (the *Vorstand* of an AG or the *Geschäftsführung* of a GmbH) of a corporation consists, as a rule, of a number of people who bear the main responsibility for the management of the business. Under section 77 of the *Aktiengesetz* (AktG, Joint Stock Corporation Act) the several members of the executive board are only authorized to carry out this management role collectively, as a body. In this regard the industrial relations director has the same rights and duties as any other member of the board. In practice, however, the responsibilities are commonly shared out, and the individual board member can act relatively independently in the field of responsibility allocated to him. Usually the industrial relations director is responsible for personnel and welfare matters; he may also be allocated responsibilities in other areas.

The *supervisory board* (*Aufsichtsrat*) of an AG appoints the members of the executive board for a maximum period of five years and oversees their activities. In the exercise of its supervisory function it has various rights to information. Furthermore the articles of association or the supervisory board itself can prescribe that certain transactions (for example, investments or borrowings above a certain amount, the setting up or closing down of branches) require its approval. It must also approve the annual accounts and the proposed appropriation of profits, unless, with the agreement of the executive board, this responsibility is given to the general shareholders' meeting. However, empirical studies have shown that it is exceptional for the shareholders' meeting to be responsible for approving the accounts. Consequently the members of the supervisory board can influence the company's accounting policies and the proposed distribution of profits. Hence in the literature it is sometimes argued that co-determination has led to an increase in the degree of self-financing (through retained profits) among larger companies that are subject to the various participation laws (see Wächter 1983). The presumption is that the employees, like the company's bank, which often has a seat on the supervisory board, have an interest in a high level of self-financing. The banks for their part are bound to be anxious to reduce their credit risk; for the employees it is a question of influencing decisions that could affect employment. Regardless of whether the hypothesis is true of any individual case, it may be stated in general that the two-tier system, with its division of management (the executive board) and supervision (the supervisory board), coupled with the representation of banks and employees (co-determination) on the supervisory board, tends to encourage rather than otherwise the ploughing of profits back into the business.

3 CO-DETERMINATION AT PLANT AND SHOP-FLOOR LEVEL

At the plant level, the most important institution concerned with participation is the *Betriebsrat* (workers' council), which is elected by the employees of the plant. Further co-determination bodies are the *Wirtschaftsausschuß* (economic council) and the jointly elected *Einigungsstelle* (conciliation board). The rights and functions of these bodies are set out in detail in the BetrVG of 1972. (The BetrVG of 1952 was comprehensively modified by the BetrVG of 1972. Only the provisions relating to the representation of workers on the supervisory board (see section 2 above) remain in force, and they are thus still referred to as the BetrVG of 1952.) The BetrVG 1972 applies to all *Betriebe* (plants) with, as a rule, five permanent workers. *Betrieb* is a legal term defining an organizational unit that pursues its aims through the use of labour; a manufacturing plant would be an example but there are also *Betriebe* that provide services: administrative offices, shops, theatres, pharmacies and hospitals.

Other differences from co-determination at the company level concern the legal form and the subject matter of the co-determination.

1 At company level, through their representatives on the supervisory board and managing board, the employees participate in the decision-making process which was formerly governed solely by the shareholders; the legal structure of the undertaking remains unchanged. The representatives of the employees and of the shareholders sit with identical rights and duties in an organ of the company, the supervisory board, and decide *jointly.* At plant level, the management and the workers' council meet as *opposing parties.* If they cannot come to an agreement on a particular question, the matter must be referred to the conciliation board, or, if need be, to the labour court.
2 Co-determination within the supervisory board is concerned primarily with company-wide economic *decisions* (e.g. investment and finance plans, the distribution of profits). By comparison the workers' council has certain *rights,* essentially in personnel and social matters: participation rights (to information, to put its views, to instruction and to advice) and co-determination rights (of veto, of approval and of acting on its own initiative). Social matters include, for example, the setting of working hours, questions of the plant's wage structure, the prevention of accidents, and the design, layout and management of social facilities (crèche, canteen, sports club, etc.). Personnel matters include manpower planning, training, hiring and firing. In economic matters, the economic council, which must be formed from the workers' council in enterprises with more than 100 employees, has only rights of instruction and advice. The management must give the economic council and the workers' council a full explanation of the annual accounts immediately following the completion of the statutory audit. Generally it is agreed that the tax computation should be presented at the same time, in cases where it differs significantly from the financial statements. Because of this requirement to inform the economic council, even enterprises that are not subject to the legal provisions relating to compulsory disclosure and participation at the company level are obliged to give the employees' representatives information about the enterprise's net worth, financial position and results. If it is felt that reporting relatively high profits might prompt calls for greater welfare and other types of provision from the workers' council, and could undermine the management's case against such demands, it is clear that here too the reporting of fairly modest profits serves to dampen down over-hasty claims on the resources of the business.

Co-determination at shop-floor level is governed in a basic fashion by § 90 of the 1952 BetrVG, which deals with the organization of the workplace, the working environment and the flow of work. In contrast to participation at plant level, there are no detailed implementing provisions in the Act. For a fuller understanding of German accounting requirements it is unnecessary to consider participation at shop-floor level further.

5 Taxation

In Germany there is a close connection between the reporting of assets, liabilities, provisions and profits in the annual accounts and in the tax accounts. The great majority of enterprises are small businesses (see Table 2.2), which are either not obliged to publish accounts or do not in fact publish even when there is a legal obligation. In order to minimize costs, these enterprises, as a rule, compute only one figure for profit, and that according to the tax rules, with the aim of reducing the tax burden or at least postponing it.

With the enterprises that publish accounts and, in particular, with those that are quoted on the stock exchange, there is a more or less significant difference between the profits reported in the annual accounts and the profits computed for taxation. Nevertheless there are numerous bridges between the two systems (see Chapter 6, section 1.3). The following introduction to the tax system, and the taxation of enterprises, thus serves indirectly to build a better understanding of financial reporting.

1 THE TAX SYSTEM

Germany, like other industrial nations, is a tax state. In contrast to the Middle Ages, when taxes made up only a small part of the state's revenue, today they are the most important source of revenue, before social security contributions. The share of GNP taken by taxes and social security contributions together came to 40.6 per cent in 1990. Germany was somewhat below the European average (see Table 5.1). In Germany taxes alone represented 22.7 per cent of GNP in 1990 (see Table 5.2). At present there are about fifty different taxes. The most important are listed in Table 5.2.

Ertragsteuern (earnings taxes) are those levied on business profits:

1 *Einkommensteuer* (ESt, income tax) on natural persons who are either self-employed or partners in a firm.
2 *Kapitalertragsteuer* (KapESt, withholding tax), taxes on interest and income from the profits of legal persons which are treated as part of income tax.
3 *Körperschaftsteuer* (KSt, corporation tax) on legal persons.
4 *Gewerbeertragsteuer* (GewErtSt, trade tax on earnings), which is levied by municipalities on the profits of domestic businesses (*Gewerbebetrieben*). Basically, the businesses that are subject to this tax are in effect all enterprises except the self-employed (doctors, lawyers, business consultants, etc.), and those in agriculture, forestry and private property management.

Lohnsteuer (LSt, salary tax) is a tax on the income of employees: workers, staff, officials, etc. In Table 5.2 income tax and salary tax include the *Kirchensteuer* (church tithe) which is paid as a percentage (about 9 per cent) of income or salary tax.

Substanzsteuern (capital taxes) are based on the gross or net values of assets, which are the expression of business capacity. They include:

1 *Vermögensteuer* (VSt, assets tax): in simplified terms, this is levied on the total assets of all legal and natural persons who are subject to income tax or corporation tax.
2 *Grundsteuer* (GrSt, real property tax): this is levied on real property, including agricultural land and woodland.
3 *Gewerbekapitalsteuer* (GewKapSt, trading capital tax): it is levied on the value of domestic businesses (*Gewerbebetriebe*).

Table 5.1 Taxes and social security contributions as a percentage of GNP/GDP

Sweden	57.0
Denmark	52.3
The Netherlands	46.5
France	44.9
Belgium	42.9
Luxembourg	42.0
Ireland	41.9
Greece	41.4
West Germany	40.6
Italy	40.4
UK	36.3
Portugal	35.4
Spain	34.3

Source: OECD; IW Cologne.
Note: Figures as at 1990, except Portugal (1988) and Spain (1989); some estimated.

Table 5.2 Yield of the main German taxes[1]

	1986		*1990*	
Tax	*DM million*	%	*DM million*	%
Taxes on profit	97,492	21.55	110,418	20.08
Income tax	29,881	6.61	36,519	6.64
Withholding tax	8,121	1.79	10,832	1.97
Corporation tax	32,301	7.14	30,090	5.47
Trade tax on earnings[2]	27,189	6.01	32,977	6.00
Salary tax	152,233	33.65	177,590	32.31
Taxes on capital	18,721	4.14	23,898	4.35
Assets tax	4,396	0.97	6,333	1.15
Real property tax	7,637	1.69	8,724	1.59
Trading capital tax[2]	4,798	1.06	5,819	1.06
Inheritance tax/Gift tax	1,890	0.42	3,022	0.55
Taxes on transactions	127,823	28.25	166,399	30.27
Turnover tax (VAT)	111,139	24.56	147,585	26.85
Real property transfer tax	3,151	0.70	4,198	0.76
Insurance tax	2,578	0.57	4,432	0.81
Bills of exchange tax	366	0.08	291	0.05
Motor vehicle tax	9,356	2.07	8,314	1.52
Share transfer tax	1,233	0.27	1,579	0.28
Taxes on consumption	52,348	11.57	66,698	12.14
Customs duties	5,239	1.16	7,163	1.30
Tobacco tax	14,480	3.20	17,402	3.17
Coffee tax	1,657	0.37	1,928	0.35
Alcoholic spirits tax	4,065	0.89	4,229	0.77
Beer tax	1,263	0.28	1,355	0.25
Oil and petrol tax	25,644	5.67	34,621	6.30
Other taxes	3,819	0.84	4,665	0.85
Total yield	452,436	100.0	549,668	100.0
Gross national product	1,949,000		2,425,000	
Proportion of tax		23.21		22.66

Source: *Statistisches Jahrbuch, 1991*, pp. 500, 638.
Notes:
[1]There are no separate statistics for the trade tax on earnings and the trading capital tax.
[2]The figures are based on the official data for the total of these two taxes and on an unpublished survey of the German association of municipalities, which found that the breakdown in 1990 was 85% for trading capital tax and 15% for trade tax on earnings. In the absence of other figures, the same percentages have been used for 1986.

4 *Erbschaft-/Schenkungsteuer* (ErbSt, inheritance tax/gift tax): the tax is levied on assets transferred from one person to another on death or through a gift.

Verkehrsteuern (transaction taxes) are levied on transactions irrespective of whether or not they are profitable for the parties concerned. They include:

1 *Mehrwertsteuer* (MWSt, value-added tax) on sales of goods within the country and as *Einfuhrumsatzsteuer* (import turnover tax) on imports.

2 *Grunderwerbsteuer* (GrESt, real property transfer tax), levied on the acquisition of undeveloped land, of developed land, of inheritable building rights and buildings on third-party land.
3 *Versicherungsteuer* (insurance tax), levied on the premiums on insurance policies.
4 *Wechselsteuer* (tax on drafts and bills of exchange), levied on bills of exchange when they are brought into circulation.
5 *Kapitalverkehrsteuer* (KVSt, capital transfer tax), levied on the issue of shares in joint stock corporations and limited liability companies (*Gesellschaftsteuer*) and on the transfer of shares and bonds that are already in circulation (*Börsenumsatzsteuer*). These taxes were abolished in 1991 and 1992 in order to make the German capital market more attractive to investors.

The *Kraftfahrzeugsteuer* (KraftSt, motor vehicle tax) is levied on the operation of motor vehicles. It can be considered as a form of assets tax or, if the use of the vehicle is treated as consumption, as a form of consumption tax.

Verbrauchsteuern (consumption taxes) are levied on the consumption of certain goods (coffee, alcoholic spirits, etc.). In order to limit the cost of collection, they are levied on the enterprises that market the goods or use them themselves. Over time, these taxes have come to be understood as taxes on production, given the way in which they are collected.

At present the two main taxes, salary tax and turnover tax, account for just under 60 per cent of the total. If the profit taxes are added, they make up almost 80 per cent. The proportion of income and profit taxes (salary tax and profit taxes) fell between 1986 and 1990 from 55.20 per cent to 52.39 per cent. This was the result of a tax reform which had as its objective the reduction of the tax burden on these sources of revenue. The above figures refer only to the former West Germany. It is to be expected that, for the reunited Germany, the share of profit taxes will fall during a transitional period.

2 THE TAXATION OF THE ENTERPRISE'S EARNINGS

2.1 Types of earnings taxation

The profits of enterprises are subject to the following types of tax:

1 Income tax (*Einkommensteuer*).
2 Corporation tax (*Körperschaftsteuer*).
3 Trade tax on earnings (*Gewerbeertragsteuer*).

As income tax and corporation tax are alternatives, dependent on the legal form of the business, enterprise profits are subject either to income tax plus trade tax on earnings or corporation tax plus trade tax on earnings.

Income tax and corporation tax are levied on a uniform basis and at a uniform rate throughout Germany. The level of trade tax on earnings is set partly by the municipality in which the enterprise is located.

The bases of assessment for the three taxes are different definitions of earnings or profit. Furthermore none of the three concepts of profit is identical with what is understood as profit in economic theory or in commercial accounting. There are common features in the different concepts of profit but they are not identical.

Nor are the rates of the three taxes the same. The rate of income tax increases with the level of income (see Figure 5.1). The rate of corporation tax is 36 per cent of distributed profits and, normally, 50 per cent of retained profits. The government is planning to reduce the rates for retained profits to 45 per cent. The rate of trade tax on earnings is around 20 per cent of the business's profit, depending on the municipality in which it is located. In appraising these rates it is important to note that the amount of trade tax on earnings (in contrast to the position with income tax and corporation tax) is deductible from its own basis in calculating taxable profit. The effective tax (s_e) for trade tax on earnings is thus lower than the nominal rate (s_n): $s_e = s_n/(1 + s_n)$. For example, a nominal tax rate of 25 per cent would be equal to an effective rate of 20 per cent. In addition, the extent to which taxes are mutually deductible in calculating taxable profit is of considerable importance in assessing the tax burden. The trade tax on earnings is deductible from profits for income and corporation tax, but not vice versa.

2.2 Income tax

In the German system, as regards taxes on profits, the enterprise, as an organization, is not the ultimate object of taxation. Taking the entire life of the enterprise into consider-

Figure 5.1 Income tax scale

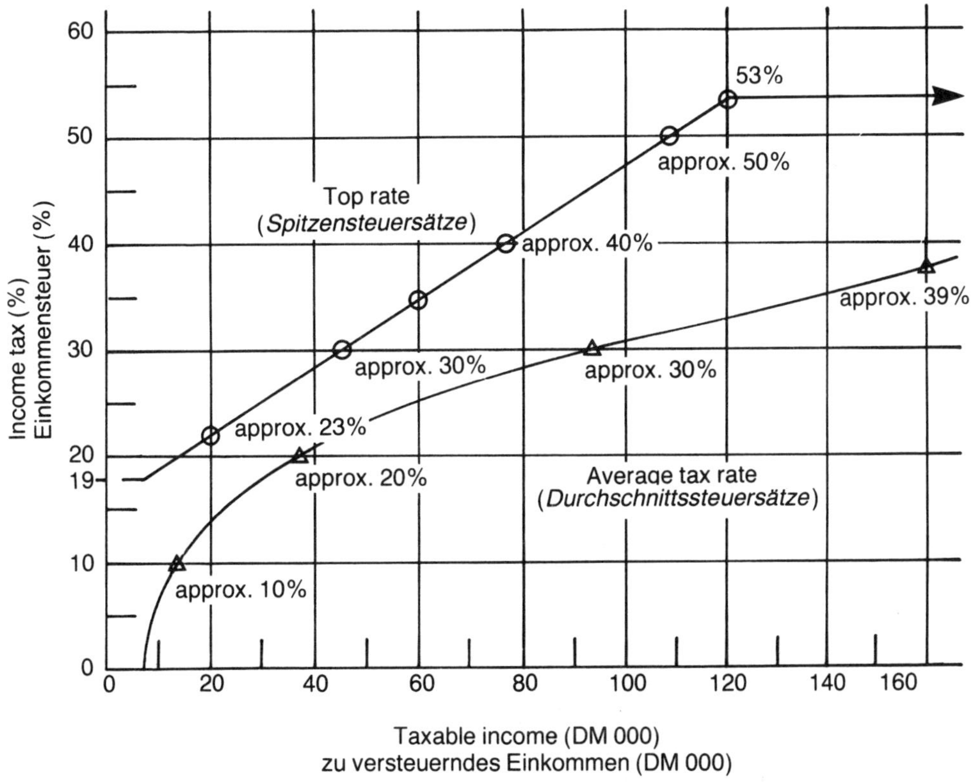

Source: Rose (1989: 26).

ation, only the returns to the owners are liable to tax. If the owner of an enterprise is itself an enterprise, then ultimately the private owners of the parent enterprise are liable to tax. In order to understand the taxation of enterprise profits, at least a broad outline of income taxation must first be sketched in. In Germany income tax law distinguishes between:

1 *Unlimited tax liability.* This applies mainly to natural persons who are resident in Germany and who are liable to tax on their world income.
2 *Limited tax liability.* This concerns natural persons who are not resident or domiciled in Germany, who are liable to tax on their German income.
3 *Extended limited tax liability.* This applies, in certain circumstances, to emigrants from Germany, who are liable to tax on an extended definition of German income. This rule is intended to reduce the incentive to change one's residence to a country with a lower rate of tax or to have no formal place of residence.

There has been long-running technical debate in the public finance literature about the basis on which taxable income should be calculated (see Neumark 1947). At the time when the present income tax system was evolving, around the turn of the century, there were two opposing theories.

The *Quellentheorie* (source theory), propounded by the Prussian financial expert Fuisting (1902), held that income should be subject to tax only if it was received by the taxpayer from a continuing source that was laid down in the law. Occasional revenue from the disposal of fixed assets, donations, inheritances and speculative profits should not be regarded as components of income. The Prussian income tax of 1891 was based on Fuisting's *Quellentheorie.* However, Prussia broke with the pure *Quellentheorie,* as early as 1916, followed even more decisively by the whole of Germany in 1920.

The opposing theory is known as the *Reinvermögenszugangstheorie* (increase in net assets theory); it was developed by Schanz (1896). Income is the increase in net assets between the beginning and end of the accounting period, including all occasional receipts. Schanz's theory influenced the determination of income primarily in France and, to a lesser extent, in Germany.

Germany currently has a mixed system. The basis of assessment for income tax, according to the law, is the income that the taxpayer has received in the accounting year. Taxable income is the total of seven components of income (classes of revenue; see Table 5.3). Certain deductions may be made from this total, on general economic and social grounds (e.g. foreign taxes and retirement bonuses). In the classification of the classes of revenue traces can still be discerned of classical economic theory, where income is made up of returns from the factors of labour (revenue from employment and self-employment), land (revenue from agriculture and forestry, and from rents and leases) and capital.

In Table 5.3 the first three components of income are described as profits. However, these are profits only in the sense of an increase in net assets, when the taxpayer is obliged, under tax law, to maintain books of account. Small enterprises, particularly in agriculture and forestry, and the self-employed may calculate their profits in a simplified fashion, principally on the basis of the cash surplus.

The next four components (Table 5.3, 4–7) are described as surpluses. They are the

Table 5.3 Components of income (classes of revenue) according to the Income Tax Act (EStG)

A **Profits**

1 *Agriculture and forestry*
Profits from agriculture and forestry, including ancillary activities (dairies, distilleries); viticulture, cultivation of fruit and vegetables, animal breeding, cattle farming; hunting

2 *Business*
Profits (or share of profits) of a sole proprietor, of a partner in a general partnership, of a general partner in a limited partnership, including profits from the disposal of shares in enterprises; profits from the disposal of substantial holdings (more than 1%) in corporations, if held for more than five years

3 *Self-employment*
Revenue from professional activities, from other independent work, e.g. executor, fund trustee, member of a supervisory board; profits from the disposal of assets used in self-employed activity

B **Surpluses**

4 *Dependent employment*
Wages, salaries, gratuities, profits, bonuses and other benefits related to activity (employment) in an enterprise, in the government sector or other organizations; pensions, including survivor pensions, and other receipts arising from former employment relationships

5 *Capital assets*
Income from capital assets, if not considered as revenue under (2) or (6), in particular: distributed profits of corporations and co-operatives, interest and discount on loans, interest on insurance bonds

6 *Rents and leases*
Surpluses from rental and leasehold contracts, including fictional surpluses such as the implied rent of a flat in one's own house

7 *Other revenues*
Regular income from life annuities, from certain maintenance payments, irregular income from certain speculative transactions, damages and office holders' emoluments

surplus of income (money and benefits in kind) over certain outlays, the income-related expenses (*Werbungskosten*). Income-related expenses are expenses that are incurred in acquiring, securing and maintaining the income. They are made up principally of money outlays, e.g. expenditure on the journey between home and work in the case of revenue from employment, or mortgage interest payments in the case of revenue from rents and leases. However, allocated costs are also included in income-related expenses, particularly in calculating income from rents and leases, e.g. depreciation of buildings. Nevertheless, in the calculation of income for the surpluses (Table 5.3, 4–7) there is only a partial application of the matching and accruals principles, in contrast to the position for the profits (Table 5.3, 1–3).

The determination of income according to its different components makes possible not only the use of different methods of calculating income but also the application of differential tax-free allowances and limits or of different rules for offsetting prior-period losses.

The income tax payable is calculated by applying to the taxable income a rate of tax depending on the level of income. Figure 5.1 shows the rate of tax as a function of income. The first DM 5,616 of taxable income is tax-free. On taxable income between DM 5,616 and DM 8,153 the tax rate is 19 per cent. The higher levels of income are subject to progressively higher rates of tax: the curve in Figure 5.1 gives a simplified impression of the marginal tax rates for the different bands of taxable income. Taxable income over DM 120,042 is subject to a level tax rate of 53 per cent. The German government is planning to reduce the rate to 47 per cent. The tax burden for each income level can be read from the curve for the average rate of tax. The government is planning to change the formula.

2.3 Income tax and the sole proprietor

A sole proprietor earns income (in the sense of the Income Tax Act, or EStG) from his business when his activity:

1 Is economically independent, i.e. he alone enjoys the profit or suffers the loss.
2 Is a continuing one, i.e. there is at least the intention of repeating it in the next financial year.
3 Has an objective of making profits.
4 Contributes to general economic activity, i.e. the output is not restricted to a specific number of people.

In practice the definition of a sole proprietor in tax law is frequently the same as in commercial law (see Chapter 2, section 1).

The business profit of a sole proprietor who, under tax law, is obliged to keep books of account, is defined as follows:

  the net assets of the business at the end of the business year
− the net assets of the business at the end of the previous business year
\+ withdrawals of capital by the owner
− capital contributions of the owner
= business profit

The following problems arise with this definition:

1 What may or must be included in the account as assets or liabilities?
2 How may or must these assets and liabilities be valued?
3 What is the boundary between the business area and the private area?

The first two problems may be most conveniently dealt with when the calculation of profit under commercial law is discussed (see Chapter 7, sections 4–5). A fundamental problem in the calculation of profit is where to draw the boundary between the business and private domains of the businessman. The calculation of profit is based solely on the business assets. Corrections are made for changes in assets that arise from transfers between the two domains (contributions and withdrawals of capital). Since in the case of a sole proprietor the business assets belong not to the business as an entity but rather to the owner of the business (see Chapter 2, section 1), when a balance sheet is drawn up of the total assets of the sole proprietor a distinction has to be drawn between the business assets and the private assets. Particular problems arise with assets whose allocation has still to be decided (e.g. an undeveloped building plot which could be used for an extension of the business or which could be sold privately) and with assets that can have both a business and a private use. In Germany there are many rules and an extensive jurisdiction that deal with these problems. They are not dealt with here, as it would involve too detailed a consideration of tax law.

In commercial law the distinction between business and private assets is irrelevant for questions of liability, since the sole proprietor is also liable with his private fortune. Hence the annual accounts of such businesses need to be interpreted with care. By contrast, corporations are not permitted to transfer assets from the business to the shareholders for no consideration, as that would reduce the value of the assets available for repaying debts.

In contrast to the position with corporations and partnerships, a sole proprietor cannot transfer assets at a favourable price by concluding a contract between himself and the business (e.g. for a purchase, rent, a loan or consultancy). Contracts between a sole proprietor and his business are not recognized in the *Bürgerliches Gesetzbuch* (BGB § 181 - German Civil Code) on account of the lack of legal autonomy. In respect of this point the businessman and his business are not separate legal entities.

2.4 Taxation of the profits of corporations and co-operatives

Since 1920 businesses that have their own legal personality (corporations and co-operatives) have been separately liable to tax on their profits. This tax is called corporation tax. The assessment base for corporation tax is defined as follows:

business net assets at the end of the business year
− business net assets at the end of the previous business year
+ distributions of profit and returns of capital
− contributions of capital and other contributions from the shareholders
= profits subject to corporation tax

For the determination of net assets, substantially the same rules apply as for sole proprietors. In drawing the boundary between the enterprise and the private domain of the shareholders, however, the problems are rather different. As legal persons these enterprises own their own assets, which legally are quite distinct from those of the shareholders. The transfer of assets between the enterprise and the shareholders through legal transactions is possible, provided that the terms of the transaction correspond to those which the enterprise would enter into with a third party. If such is not the case, the terms are reinterpreted (revised) in the calculation of assets and profits for tax purposes.

When a shareholder or a member of his family receives such a benefit, it is treated as a 'hidden distribution of profit' (*verdeckte Gewinnausschüttung*). The amount of the benefit is added to the company's taxable profits and taxed at the rate (36 per cent) set for distributed profits.

If, on the other hand, the benefit flows from the shareholder to the company, the transaction is treated as a hidden contribution of capital (*verdeckte Kapitaleinlage*). Of particular significance is the reclassification of shareholders' loans as equity. Such loans create a tax advantage, because the interest on the loan is a tax-deductible expense. In simplified terms, this can lead to tax savings, so long as the profits are not distributable, when the tax paid by a shareholder on his interest earnings is lower than the tax paid by the company on its retained profits.

The principles underlying the distinction between the company's domain and the shareholders' domain are clear, but their application is not easy in practice. Thus a considerable volume of jurisprudence has arisen in this area of taxation too.

The avoidance of double taxation of the profits of corporations (first at the level of the enterprise and second as dividends in the hands of shareholders) is a theme that has been long debated, and not only in Germany. Before the tax reforms of 1977 the profits of corporations, when distributed as dividends, were liable to income tax in the hands of shareholders and were thus taxed twice. However, in 1977 an imputation system was introduced, with the effect that, ultimately, the profits of corporations are taxed only as the personal income of shareholders, being subject to personal income tax. This system has had a lasting influence on the nature of the equity in the balance sheet; in view of the importance of this item, a brief outline of the system will be given, in which a distinction will be drawn between the taxation of the company and the taxation of the shareholders.

The taxation of the corporation. The corporation's profits, to the extent that they are retained, are subject to corporation tax at a rate of 50 per cent (called the tariff rate charge or tax rate burden). Because of tax exemptions and reductions granted on political grounds, the tax charge for parts of the profit may vary between 0 per cent and 50 per cent. Frequently there are reserves consisting of earlier profits which have borne a tax charge of 56 per cent.

It is therefore necessary to differentiate retained profits and reserves according to the rate of tax that they have borne, because when they are distributed they must bear a uniform rate of tax of 36 per cent. When the enterprise distributes profits which have already been taxed at more than 36 per cent, it can claim a reduction in its current tax bill or even a tax refund. Conversely, additional tax is payable on distribution when the profits originally bore tax at less than 36 per cent. The enterprise suffers tax at the normal rate of 50 per cent only as long as it retains the profits. Conversely when it has received fiscal advantages in the form of tax rates below 36 per cent, these benefits are claimed back if the profits are distributed. Behind this is the political idea that in return for tax relief at the expense of the community, granted as it often is to encourage investment, the enterprise should forgo dividends and the shareholders should abstain from consumption to the extent of the tax saved. The state stipulates, through this rule, as an implicit price for the tax saving, that the tax saved should be ploughed back into the enterprise.

In order to be able to ascertain the amount of corporation tax to be paid or refunded, following a distribution of profits, it is necessary to have a system for the permanent recording of the retained profits available for distribution. The profits carried forward are currently classified in four separate reserves: EK 56, EK 50, EK 36 and EK 0. (EK, *Eigenkapital* (equity); EK 56: 56 per cent tax paid.) This is to avoid having to create a separate reserve for each possible tax rate. When the profit to be retained has borne tax at one of these rates, the after-tax amount is allocated to the appropriate reserve, e.g. profits that have borne tax at the standard rate of 50 per cent are allocated to the EK 50 reserve. If the element of profit has borne tax at a rate that is not exactly equal to any of the four specified rates, it is divided between two reserves: for example, if it has borne tax at 24 per cent, the after-tax retained amount (76 per cent) is divided between EK 0 and EK 36. The division is done in such a way that, if the profit were to be distributed from these two reserves, and the amount of the tax burden is ascertained at 36 per cent, the outcome would be the identical tax payments or refunds that would occur if a special reserve of 24 per cent had been set up.

There is still a problem regarding the sequence with which reserves are used for the distribution of profit. The basic rule is that EK 56 is distributed first and, when that reserve is exhausted, EK 50 is distributed, etc. This rule corresponds to what the enterprise would normally want to do in order to maximize tax refunds and minimize additional tax payments.

In the balance sheet the different classes of reserve are summarized under the heading 'Profit reserves' (*Gewinnrücklagen*). When these reserves are taken into account in analysing the return on capital or the debt/equity ratio, the evaluation will be different, depending on whether the total figure for profit reserves conceals an EK 50 or an EK 0. However, there is no obligation to disclose this difference either in the balance sheet or in the notes.

The taxation of the shareholder. When profits are retained, the corresponding corporation tax is levied only on the company, normally at a rate of 50 per cent, but at a lower rate when there are tax concessions. The profits do not affect the income of the shareholder as long as they remain with the company. Nor is the increased capital value of the shares arising from the retained profits treated as part of the shareholder's income. However, the retained profits have already borne the company's corporation tax. Only when this increased capital value is realized through the disposal of the shares on the market is there an increase in the taxable income of the shareholder, subject to further conditions. There is an exception when the shareholder is itself an enterprise and such a close economic relationship exists between the two enterprises that, for tax purposes, their profits can be aggregated. This relationship is regarded as a fiscal unit for corporation tax purposes (*Organschaft*, interlocking relationship). (On this point see section 2.7 below.)

When the profits are distributed they bear corporation tax of 36 per cent. If distribution is out of equity which has been subject to different tax rates, the tax burden is adjusted to 36 per cent at the corporation level (see above, 'The taxation of the corporation'). The remaining 64 per cent is termed a gross cash dividend. From this 64 per cent withholding tax of 25 per cent is deducted by the company and paid to the fiscal authorities as the shareholder's income tax deducted at source. The shareholder thus receives a net cash dividend of 48 per cent of the profit (64 per cent minus 25 per cent of 64 per cent), so that he has suffered tax at an effective rate of 52 per cent prior to receiving the refund from the tax authorities. The amount of tax reclaimable by the shareholder depends on his personal tax rate based on his total income.

Table 5.4 shows how the shareholder's tax liability is calculated in respect of a corporation's pre-tax profit of DM 100,000. The result is that the shareholder receives DM 48,000 from the enterprise and DM 15,153 from the fiscal authorities, a total of DM 63,153. This is exactly the amount that he would retain if the enterprise were to pay him the full amount of DM 100,000, which would be liable to income tax in his hands. Thus it

Table 5.4 Dividend taxation on the shareholder (DM)

	Gross cash dividend (64%)	64,000
+	The shareholder's claim on the imputed corporation tax paid by the corporation. This benefit is considered to be part of the shareholder's income (36%)	36,000
=	Taxable income	100,000
−	Deductible expenses and tax allowance, say	400
=	Income from capital assets (see Table 5.3); this is part of the individual's total taxable income	99,600
	German income tax, calculated on the basis of his total income (see Figure 5.1)	36,847
−	Imputation of the withholding tax paid over by the corporation to the fiscal authorities	16,000
−	Claim on the imputed corporation tax paid by the corporation	36,000
	Shareholder's claim on the fiscal authorities for a tax refund	−15,153

Source: Jacobs (1988: 134).

is clear that, over the lifetime of the enterprise, the corporation tax paid is the anticipated income tax of the shareholder. To this extent the various legal forms (sole proprietor, partnerships and corporations) are neutral for tax purposes. What is certainly not compensated for is the loss of interest the shareholder suffers when profits are retained, arising from the delay in reclaiming the tax paid against his personal income, which may not occur until many years later. Owing to the widespread policy of retaining a proportion of profits, especially on the part of corporations run by management rather than by the owners, the holder of shares in a German corporation suffers interest losses if his personal income tax rate is lower than the corporate tax rate on retained profits.

In the above analysis it is assumed that the owner holds the shares as part of his personal wealth. If, on the other hand, they are part of the business assets of an enterprise, then the dividends are counted not as revenue from capital assets but as income from a business (see Table 5.3). This has the result that:

1 The dividend is treated as the income of the shareholder as from the date of the resolution of the general meeting and not merely from the date of the dividend payment. If there is a profit and loss transfer agreement (*Gewinn- und Verlustübernahme-Vertrag*), the balance sheet date is the date for the recognition of revenue in the hands of the shareholder.
2 The deductible expenses and tax-free allowances (see Table 5.4: DM 400) do not apply or take on other values.
3 Above all, falls in the shares' value can be taken into account in the calculation of income. Increases in value, arising, for example, from the retention of profits, have no effect here, since, under German law, both for the balance sheet and for the computation of taxable income, the upper limit on the value is set by the historical cost (see Chapter 7, section 5.1.2). The use of the equity method to value the shareholding is permitted neither in the financial statements nor in the tax accounts.

2.5 Income tax for commercial partnerships

With general partnerships (OHG) and limited partnerships (KG), which on account of their line of business are liable to tax on their profits, the income tax liability falls not on the firm but exclusively on its owners. The shares in the profits arising from the firm's activities are attributed, generally as income from business, directly to the partners' taxable income.

Owing to the hybrid position of commercial partnerships between the civil law partnership and the corporation (see Chapter 2, section 1), the kind of taxation that should be applied to them has been a controversial issue for decades now and has been changed frequently. For a long time the 'bundle' principle (*Bilanzbündeltheorie*) was dominant. Each partner was treated for income tax purposes as a joint proprietor (*Mitunternehmer*). The balance sheet of the firm was conceived as a 'bundle' of the balance sheets of the individual partners. This had not inconsiderable consequences. For example, legal contracts between a partner and the firm, which in this form of business organization are legally permissible (in contrast to the position of sole proprietors), were ignored for tax purposes.

However, recent judgements of the Federal Fiscal Court (*Bundesfinanzhof*) have tended to accept the idea that the firm itself should be recognized to a certain extent for tax purposes. As a result the partners' income is determined in two stages.

First stage. First, the profit of the commercial partnerships is determined according to general taxation principles for the calculation of profits. Since this form of company may own property on its own account, all economic goods that are in its legal or economic ownership are considered to be part of its business assets. At this stage there is no fundamental problem in separating the private assets of the partners and the assets of the business. Legal transactions between the firm and the partners are accepted for tax purposes as well. As with transactions with third parties, the cost and revenue of these transactions affect the profits of the firm and hence those of all the partners. However, the firm itself is not subject to tax on the profits calculated in this way. The profits are allocated to the various partners on the basis of the rules for sharing profit, laid down in the partnership agreement.

Second stage. The income of each partner from the business is now calculated separately. To the share of profit determined at the first stage are added profits that the partner has made from services rendered to the firm or from making available to the firm economic goods that are part of his private property. These assets are termed special business property (*Sonderbetriebsvermögen*). The determination of profit is arrived at for each partner separately, but following the same general principles as for the first stage.

It has been proposed that, for transactions between the partner and the firm, the same principles should be followed as are used for the consolidated accounts of corporations. This would mean, for example, in the case of a sale by a partner to the firm, that the profit made by the partner would not be treated as realized until the firm has itself realized the profit by means of a sale to a third party. It would also mean that debts between the partner and the firm would be set off in the consolidation. However, this approach has not yet been accepted by the courts. The profit made by a partner on a sale to the firm is added to his taxable income in the second stage. In the case of debts owed by the firm to the partner, which are included in the partner's special business property, the general principles relating to the reduction in value of bad and doubtful debts are applicable. This can have the effect that, when the firm does badly, the partner suffers a fall in income from two sources.

At the second stage the same problem arises concerning the separation of the partner's business property and his private property that has already been considered in the case of the sole proprietor (see section 2.3 above).

The income from business calculated in this way is included, together with other possible components of income, in the total income of the partner. The rate of tax (see Figure 5.1) is determined not on the basis of the income of the commercial partnership but separately for each partner on the basis of his total income.

2.6 Trade tax on earnings

The trade tax (*Gewerbesteuer*) is made up of the trade tax on earnings (GewErtSt, *Gewerbeertragsteuer*) and the trading capital tax (GewKapSt, *Gewerbekapitalsteuer*). The trade tax is levied not on the partners but on the enterprise. However, only enterprises that are business entities are subject to trade tax. Corporations and co-operatives are automatically considered to be business entities by virtue of their legal form. Sole proprietors and commercial partnerships are business entities when they are engaged in business activity. Business activity has already been defined at the beginning of section 2.3 above.

As the taxable entity for trade tax is the enterprise, the tax paid is not taken into account in determining the income tax of the partner. The position with corporation tax is different. Trade tax is additional to corporation tax and income tax. For this reason, trade tax paid is treated as a deduction from taxable income in the determination of profit for corporation tax, but not vice versa.

The trade tax goes primarily collected to the municipality. However, the yield is shared with the federal and state governments. Since one enterprise can carry on business in several municipalities and, also, the trade tax is understood to be a compensation for the charges caused by the enterprise, it is laid down how and in what way the tax is shared between municipalities. The tax revenue is shared between all the municipalities in which a part of the enterprise (a *Betriebsstätte*, a (permanent) establishment) operates. Examples of establishments are the head office, factories, branches, warehouses and retail outlets. To go further into how the division is arrived at would involve the reader in too much detail.

The trade tax on earnings is levied on a particular measure of profit, called the *Gewerbeertrag* (business profit). The starting point for the determination of business profit is the income for income tax or corporation tax purposes, with certain modifications, not dealt with here. To this are added back certain amounts which are customarily allowed as deductions from taxable income. On the other hand, certain amounts are deducted.

The additions consist primarily of expenses relating to certain forms of debt capital. A prominent example, expressed in simple terms, is the adding back of half the interest paid on long-term debt capital, known as *Dauerschuldzinsen* (interest on permanent debt).

Payments made by the enterprise to sleeping partners are also added back. In law, sleeping partners are lenders, with the characteristic that they receive, instead of a fixed rate of interest, a return that is dependent on the level of profits. The business profit is thus, by comparison with profit for income tax purposes, more a measure of the profit earned on the total capital, that is, on the total assets of the enterprise.

Deductions are made, above all, for the share of the profits of the enterprises that is included in the profits of the assessed enterprise. The aim is to avoid double liability to trade tax on earnings and to exclude foreign enterprises from the system. The trade tax is thus, contrary to the position with income tax, restricted to domestic income.

The calculation of trade tax on earnings is shown in Table 5.5.

The basic federal rate is set by law and is uniform across the whole country (at the time of writing it is 5 per cent). The municipal percentage is fixed by the municipality: it may range between 150 per cent and 650 per cent. Some municipalities seek to attract industry by setting a low rate. When calculating the effective tax rate, it has to be taken into account that the trade tax on earnings is deductible from its own taxable base, from which the trade tax on earnings is calculated.

Table 5.5 Determination of trade tax on earnings: an example (DM)

	Calculation	*Example*
	Business profit (after trade tax on earnings)	386,000
	Tax-free allowance (not for an AG, GmbH or Gen (*Genossenschaft*))	36,000
=	Adjusted business profit	350,000
×	Basic federal rate (5%)	0.05
=	Tentative tax	17,500
×	Municipal percentage (300%)	×3
=	Trade tax on earnings	52,500

2.7 Earnings taxation for groups

In previous sections it has been observed more than once that special rules apply when the owner of an enterprise is itself an enterprise. Moreover, as demonstrated in Chapter 2, section 3, this is frequently the rule with corporations.

The difficulty with the taxation of the profits of groups lies in the fact that in economic terms the companies in the group are not independent of each other. This can lead to a situation where the individual profits of the companies are not a meaningful indication of their economic performance. Transactions can be effected, on terms beneficial to the group as a whole, that the individual company itself would never have effected, or at least not on the same terms, had it been acting as an economically independent company operating in its own interests. This applies especially, but not exclusively, to transactions between group companies. In this situation, basing tax on the company's profit would be contrary to the fundamental principle that tax should be based on economic capacity. In addition, a further fundamental principle would be infringed: the equal treatment of economic subjects in matters of taxation. The principle would be infringed because the profits of a group company which include profits on transactions with another group company manifest a risk structure different from that of an economically independent company. When an economically independent company sells an asset, the profit is no longer vulnerable to production and marketing risks once the asset has been delivered. When the goods are delivered to a subsidiary company, all that happens is that the risks take on a different form; they become investment risks. These risks also occur even when sales within the group are made on market terms. When the profits of the individual group companies form the basis of taxation, then the profits being taxed are riskier, in respect of their definitive confirmation through cash receipts, than those of an economically independent enterprise. There are two ways of trying to resolve this problem.

According to the *principle of the fictional legal entity*, all the group companies are treated as constituting a single legal entity. One profit is then determined for the group as a whole. Intra-group profits are eliminated. Profits are realized only on transactions with enterprises that do not belong to the group. This is the preferred solution for the preparation of the group's financial statements (see Chapter 8). German tax law has not followed this route. Consolidated profits are not the basis of income tax, corporation tax or trade tax on earnings.

According to *the principle of fictional economic independence* (the arm's-length principle), the profits of the separate companies are restated as if the group company had acted in its dealings as an economically independent enterprise. In particular transfer prices for inter-company deliveries and services are corrected if they are not market prices. In Germany the taxation of the companies in a group has followed this route. However, it should be noted that, here, only the risks relating to the transfer of assets between group companies which are not in accordance with market conditions are covered. The additional risks relating to the intra-group profit which were considered above are not eliminated, since intra-group profits are still subject to tax. Profit is realized at the boundary of the individual company and not solely at the boundary of the group.

The problem of the group is, however, taken into account in a second way. Under certain conditions, surpluses generated by one group company can be matched with the deficits of another group company. Thus only the balance of profits is liable to tax. This arrangement is known as a fiscal unit for corporation tax purposes (*Organschaft*). It exists both for income/corporation tax and for trade tax on earnings.

A necessary condition for the existence of a fiscal unit, for corporation tax and for trade tax on earnings alike, is that a domestic corporation, known as the *Organgesellschaft* (dependent company), is integrated financially, organizationally and economically within another enterprise, called the *Organträger* (dominant company). The dominant company may be a sole proprietor, a partnership or a corporation. Financial integration is established only when the dominant company controls, directly or indirectly, a majority of the votes. The precondition for organizational integration is that the dominant company can influence the management of the dependent company directly through a control contract and not just through the usual channels (shareholders' meeting, supervisory board). Economic integration is deemed to exist when, for example, the dominant company undertakes the marketing or finance functions of the dependent company.

A fiscal unit for corporation tax purposes is subject to the further condition that both companies must have concluded a profit and loss sharing agreement for at least five years which obliges the dependent company to transfer its profits to the dominant company, and the dominant company to make up the losses of the dependent company.

If these and other conditions are fulfilled, the profit or loss of the dependent company is added to the profit or loss of the dominant company, in the period it arises. The dependent company is then not liable to corporation tax.

The fiscal unit for trade tax on earnings is essentially subject only to the conditions of financial, organizational and economic integration. The trade earnings of the dependent company are calculated according to the procedure shown above. In this calculation intra-group profits are not eliminated. Components of profit that are included in the calculation of the business profit of both companies are taken out of the calculation once. The dependent company's business profit is then added to that of the dominant company, and trade tax on earnings is levied on the latter in the way described above.

Part II

Accounting, auditing and financial reporting

6

An introduction to financial reporting in Germany

1 THE ROLE OF THE FINANCIAL STATEMENTS

1.1 The regulation of profit distribution

The legal rules relating to financial statements – with the exception of the rules concerning the consolidation procedures for group accounts – serve to determine the profit as the amount available for distribution (*Gewinnverteilungsfunktion*, distribution function). This means, in the first place, that the profits calculated according to the law are the basis on which the distributable profits are shared out among those entitled to them – shareholders (owners), etc. For example, in the case of general partnerships and limited partnerships the HGB stipulates what share of the year's profit (established from the financial statement) each partner is entitled to (HGB §§ 120 f., §§ 167 f.). In addition, it lays down the maximum that a partner may withdraw from the firm: he may withdraw up to 4 per cent of his capital share without the agreement of the other partners and, provided that no harm is inflicted on the firm, he can, in addition, demand the rest of his share of the year's profits (HGB, § 122). The limited partner of a limited partnership, who, in contrast to the general partner, is liable only to the extent of his contribution, has no right of withdrawal, other than a claim on the payment of his share of the profits.

Second, for enterprises, where only the company's assets, and not the private assets of the owners, are available for the payment of creditors, the role of the distribution function is to limit to 'a reasonable level' the creditors' risk of not receiving their entitlement of interest and repayment of capital. On account of historical experience (fraudulent promotions, company collapses), and in view of the importance of credit financing and banks in the German economic system (see Chapter 3), the protection of creditors is one of the primary aims of company law. This protection is also the object of a number of other provisions, the most significant of which are described below. They concern restrictions on the appropriation of profits, a prohibition on the refund of capital contributions, limitations on the acquisition of own shares and a ban on absolving anyone from the obligation to contribute.

The prohibition on absolving anyone from the obligation to contribute (GmbHG §§ 9, 9a, 9b, 19 (2); AktG §§ 36a, 54, 65 f.) compels the shareholder to make the capital contributions that he has promised in a declaration to the companies' registry. Furthermore the capital contributions may not be refunded to the shareholder (prohibition of any refund of capital contributions, in GmbHG § 30(1), and AktG § 57). Payments by the company for the acquisition of its own shares are not considered to be refunds of contributions. Such a purchase is permitted only under conditions that are defined by law (limitation on the acquisition of own shares).

A GmbH may acquire its own shares only when:

1 All capital contributions on these shares have been fully paid (GmbHG § 33 (1)), and
2 The payment can be made from assets that are surplus to the assets representing the amount of the company's subscribed capital, and the company can set up a reserve for its own shares in the amount of the acquisition costs without reducing its share capital and special reserves as fixed either by law or in its statute (GmbHG § 33 (2)). This reserve is not allowed for distribution to the shareholders.

In contrast to the position with a GmbH, an AG may acquire its own shares only when additionally at least one of the following conditions is fulfilled:

1 To prevent serious harm to the company.
2 To provide shares for employees of the company.
3 To compensate shareholders.
4 When the acquisition is costless.
5 In the context of a universal succession.
6 As part of a reduction of capital (AktG § 71 (1)).

In all other circumstances the acquisition of own shares is forbidden. The total nominal value of own shares acquired under points 1, 2 and 3 above may not, when added to the own shares which the company already possesses, exceed 10 per cent of the share capital. In addition the corporation must set up a reserve for own shares, without reducing its share capital or capital reserve (AktG § 71 (2)).

The regulation of the appropriation of profits is simple in the case of a GmbH; for an AG, by comparison, it is rather complicated. The shareholders of the GmbH adopt the financial statements and determine the appropriation of the results (GmbHG § 42a (2), § 46 No. 1). In principle they may claim the year's profit, increased by any profits brought forward and reduced by any losses brought forward (GmbHG § 29 (1)). In the resolution relating to the appropriation of profits the shareholders may, unless the company's articles provide otherwise, transfer any amount to reserves or carry it forward as unappropriated profits. Thus the company's shareholders have the sole competence as regards the distribution and retention of profits, which can, if need be, be limited by the company's articles of association.

By contrast, the rights of stockholders of a joint stock corporation are limited both by the law and by the powers of the executive board and the supervisory board. The corporation is obliged (AktG § 150) to build up from its profits a legal reserve in the balance sheet. To this legal reserve are transferred, among other amounts, 5 per cent of the year's profits (reduced by any losses brought forward) until the sum of the legal reserve and the capital reserve reaches 10 per cent of the share capital (or any higher percentage specified in the company's statutes). The year's profit (after transfer to the legal profit reserve (*gesetzliche Rücklage*) is then the basis for distribution according to the provisions of AktG § 58 (see Figure 6.1), which distinguishes, at first, between two cases:

1 If the stockholders' meeting adopts the annual accounts – as is the case when the executive board and the supervisory board so resolve or when the supervisory board has not approved the accounts – then the executive board and the supervisory board have no powers over the appropriation of profits (AktG § 58 (1)). However, in that case, the articles can specify the part of the year's profit that should be transferred to other (not legal) profit reserves. But the amount of the year's profits that may be retained on the basis of such a provision is limited to half.
2 Usually, however, the executive and the supervisory boards adopt the annual accounts. Without asking the stockholders they can retain part (no more than half) of the profits for the purposes of financing of the corporation (AktG § 58 (2)). But this

Figure 6.1 Appropriation of profit according to AktG § 58

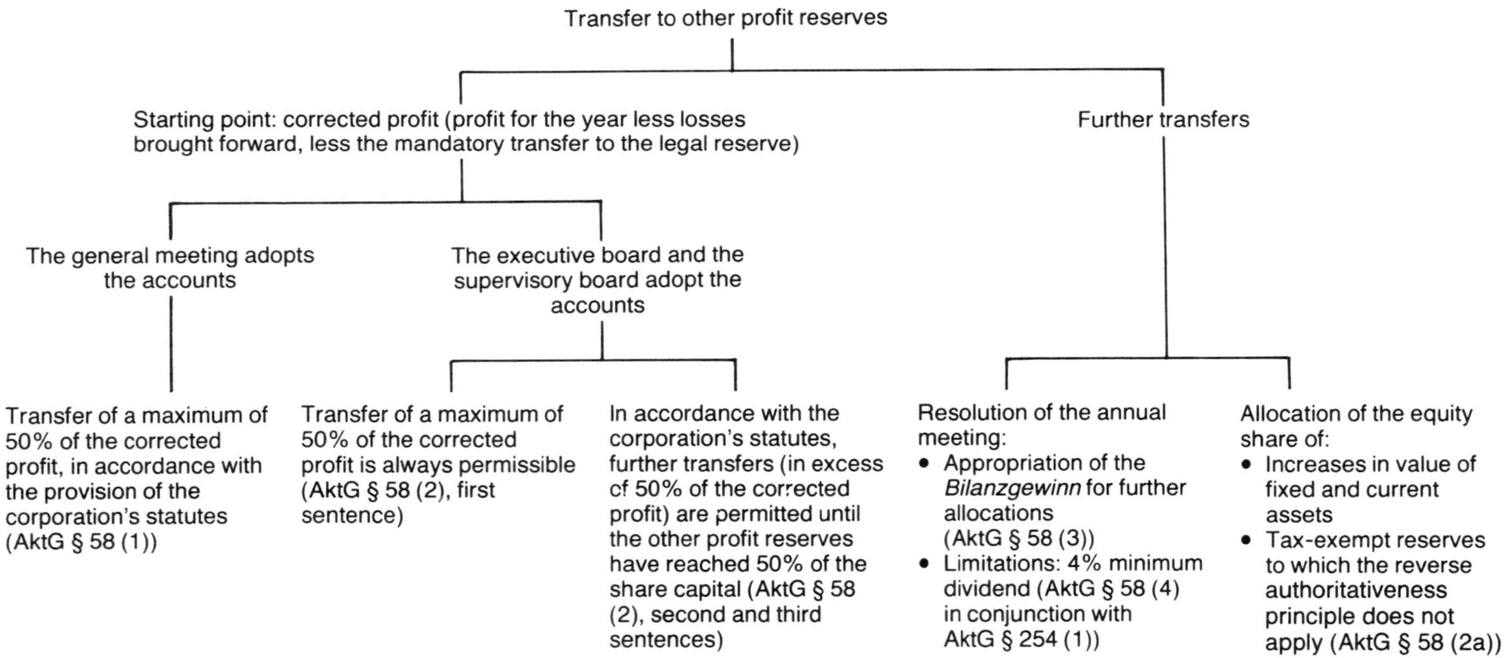

Source: Coenenberg (1992).

argument can be turned on its head. If the articles of association are silent on the matter, the shareholders have access to virtually 50 per cent of the profit disclosed. This too may be a remarkable incentive to prudent accounting for joint stock corporations.

By means of a special provision in the articles, the management may be authorized to transfer up to 100 per cent of the year's profits to profit reserves. However, any provision in the corporation's articles has no effect when the other profit reserves exceed half the subscribed capital. Where the employees and banks are represented on the supervisory board there is a tendency to use the opportunities to retain profits provided by the law (see Chapters 3 and 4).

Once the possibilities arising from either the provisions of the articles of association or the powers of the management of transferring part of the year's profits to profit reserves have been utilized, the stockholders' meeting can resolve that, from the remaining profits (the *Bilanzgewinn*, or balance sheet profit), further amounts should be transferred to profit reserves. The rest will be distributed as dividends, or carried forward as profit (AktG § 58 (3) in connection with § 174). This means it is at the discretion of the shareholders to distribute it as part of dividends in the next year.

The general meeting's voice in the way the other profit reserves are used is also very limited. Only the body that adopted the accounts can decide to distribute them to shareholders. When, as is often the case, the accounts are adopted by the executive board and the supervisory board, the general meeting cannot decide to pay a dividend out of the other profit reserves. The general meeting has only the right to convert the other profit reserves into capital by way of a capital increase from internal funds. Hence only the body that adopted the accounts can authorize distributions from the other profit reserves.

The marked emphasis on capital maintenance which is evident in the rules outlined above, as it is in other regulations relating to the financial statements, has not gone unchallenged in the discussions of professional lawyers and business economists. For example, in the debate about reform of the profit appropriation provisions in company law the different positions were made very clear.

According to the reasons given in justification when the Joint Stock Corporation Act was proposed in 1965, the AktG represents an attempt by the government to strike a reasonable balance between the concern of the stockholders for dividends and the interest of the executive board and the supervisory board in retention. That there is a conflict of interest is conventional wisdom in the literature. Whereas it is assumed that the executive board and the supervisory board have a continuing commitment to keep the enterprise a going concern, the stockholders' preference for distributions is justified by the opportunity of investing the dividends outside the enterprise, perhaps more profitably.

German legislation has, over the years, resolved the problem of conflicting interests in the appropriation of profits in widely differing ways. In the HGB of 1897 the stockholders' meeting alone was responsible for adopting the annual accounts and the appropriation of profits. On the other hand, under the AktG of 1937 the management adopted the annual accounts in the normal way. Coupled with this, the management had the right to create profit reserves, with no restriction on allocations to reserves specified in the law.

> Advocates of the present rules stress the compromise that underlies the solution: On the one hand, it cannot be contested that the stockholder has a claim on the profits that his money has earned. It seems not to be acceptable to take from him the decision on whether he wants the profits to remain in the enterprise. On the other hand, there can be no mistaking that the creation of reserves is a business decision and thus the responsibility of the executive board, as the governing body, and the supervisory board, as the controlling and counselling organ of the company.
>
> (Wilhelmi 1965: 154)

However, critics argue that insufficient weight has been attached to the interests of stockholders. The distribution of the profits that have been earned is seen as the natural recompense for the contribution of capital. The view is legitimized by the thesis that the investor's pursuit of his private interests furthers the aims of society as regards the creation and distribution of wealth. In pursuing his own interests the shareholder is presumed to invest his capital where it brings him the highest return. The task of co-ordination is assigned to market forces: the reporting of profits and losses, it is argued, induces operators in the economy to act in the most efficient way; there is no perceived difference between persons and corporations. Like the capital of the sole proprietor, the stockholder's property is said to fulfil the capital directing function described above.

German law has not as yet come round to the view that the interests of shareholders are paramount. As the regulations on worker participation indicate, it relies more on a stakeholder perspective, which entails balancing the interests of stockholders, creditors and employees.

1.2 The regulation of information

After the determination of profit to be distributed the principal function of the annual accounts is to disclose information about the economic position of the enterprise (information function). The information is addressed, in particular, to the needs of the following users:

1 The management.
2 The shareholders.
3 The creditors.
4 The employees and their organizations.

1.2.1 The enterprise's management

The annual balancing of the books compels the management to keep itself informed about the economic position of the enterprise. Should it become clear that the position has deteriorated to the extent that half the capital stock has been lost, the managing director of a GmbH must summon a shareholders' meeting (GmbHG § 49 (3)). The same rule applies to the executive board of a joint stock corporation in respect of its subscribed capital (AktG § 92 (1)). The obligation to call a shareholders' meeting arises not only when the capital loss is established in the annual accounts or the interim accounts, but also, it is generally accepted, at other times when such a loss is evident to anyone competent to judge. But this means that the enterprise's management is obliged to consult and evaluate the accounting record on a continuous basis. In this way, potential dangers are to be recognized as early as possible and corrective action taken. The accounting rules are in harmony with this objective in that they contribute to a rather cautious statement of the financial position.

1.2.2 Shareholders

The information function of the annual accounts in respect of shareholders depends very much on the legal form of the enterprise. In the case of a *sole proprietor* and *commercial partnerships*, reference can be made essentially to the need for the management to inform itself, since, where the partners are liable for the firms' debts with their private fortune, they also generally form the management. Normal business transactions are effected by the executive partners, but exceptional transactions are decided by all partners together (HGB §§ 116 (2), 164). For these purposes, the partners require a degree of disclosure base that goes well beyond the annual accounts.

The situation is similar with the *smaller GmbHs.* According to the usual articles of association the managing director is responsible for the day-to-day running of the business, and the shareholders are responsible for all further decisions, in particular for the direction of business strategy. They keep an eye on what is happening in the enterprise and, when necessary, intervene to correct matters. The accounts presented by the managing director are an important instrument but are not in themselves sufficient either as a means of control or for the purpose of deciding broader policy.

For the stockholder in a *public corporation*, the balance of forces is different: at best, the relationship with the management and with the enterprise as a whole is distant. In consequence, the annual accounts represent one of the few opportunities, along with comment in the newspapers and the professional press, to gain an insight into the present position and future development of the enterprise. The information can be used in decisions on the sale or purchase of shares, the monitoring and control of management and how to vote at the general meeting. The stockholder's most direct influence is the right to cast his vote at the general meeting, particularly in relation to such matters as:

1 Appointment of the members of the supervisory board.
2 The appropriation of profits.
3 Discharging the executive board and the supervisory board from responsibility.
4 The appointment of the auditors.
5 Changing the articles of association.
6 An increase or reduction in the equity.
7 The liquidation of the company.

The shareholders' meeting can decide on management matters only when so asked by the executive board.

The annual report and accounts constitute the most important source of information on which to base the exercise of the vote, along with the management report and the supporting documents for the resolutions on discharge and profit appropriation.

However, the information they convey loses much of its significance for the individual stockholder if he assigns his vote to the bank at which he has deposited his shares (proxy voting). The relevance of the annual accounts to stock exchange transactions, the purchase and sale of shares, seems to be limited as well. The lengthy procedure for drawing up, auditing and certifying accounts, which can take up to nine months, often means that the information comes too late to influence decisions to buy or sell, even when given in advance on a voluntary basis. Hence other sources of information assume greater importance, such as, interim reports, brokers' circulars and articles in the financial press.

1.2.3 Creditors

Another aspect of the information function of the annual accounts is to aid the decision of potential creditors in granting or withholding credit. For example, under article 18 of the *Kreditwesengesetz* (KWG, German Banking Act), credit institutions have to require any client business to which they have extended loans totalling more than DM 100,000 to disclose its financial position, in particular through the production of annual accounts. The Bundesbank normally insists on seeing the annual accounts of anyone accepting bills of exchange which have been offered to it by credit institutions. The Bundesbank relies on article 19 of the *Bundesbankgesetz* (Federal Bank Act), which provides that it may only purchase such bills which are backed by three solvent acceptance houses.

The banks have an interest beyond the requirements of the law in the presentation of financial statements by their debtors. For example, analysis of the annual accounts is an important way of estimating whether the debt is likely to be serviced in an orderly manner. This applies especially to smaller firms because of the higher transaction costs which would otherwise have to be borne by the banking sector in being represented on the supervisory boards of a large number of smaller firms. In addition, when assessing the credit standing of the borrower, attention is paid to the maintenance of certain ratios relating to the capital structure. For example, insurance companies are obliged, following a ruling of the *Bundesaufsichtsamt für das Versicherungswesen* (Federal Office of Insurance Supervision) to observe the following provisions, among others, when granting loans:

1 The ratio of equity capital to debt capital should not be lower than 1:2.
2 Assets that have been committed on a long-term basis should be financed by long-term capital.
3 The current assets that are realizable in the short run should amount to at least 50 per cent of the sum of the current liabilities and provisions.
4 There should be no losses reported or expected.

In spite of the close connection between the granting of credit and the annual accounts, this is by no means the only source of information. In the case of large credits, the lender frequently stipulates the right to further information and to a say in decisions concerning the borrower. With joint stock corporations there is the possibility of exercising influence through representation on the supervisory board (see Chapter 3 for details).

1.2.4 Employees

For employees, the extent of disclosure in the annual accounts is important at three levels:

1 At the industry level, to determine the element of redistribution in the wage negotiations.
2 At the enterprise level, to support the monitoring function of the employee representatives on the supervisory board.
3 At plant level, to guide the co-determination policy of the workers' council.

These functions are described in detail in Chapter 4.

In addition to meeting the specific information needs of each of these groups, the presentation of the accounts fulfils an important documentation role for all concerned. The provisions in the HGB relating to the drawing up and maintenance of books of account, inventories, annual accounts and other records are meant to ensure that documents are available in the event of potential conflicts of interest (for example, to establish the value of the assets in the event of bankruptcy), preventing the appropriation of assets to the detriment of shareholders, creditors, employees or even the state.

In general it is true to say that, in Germany, disclosure for investment purposes in the annual accounts takes second place to their role in determining the distribution of profits. As indicated above, the reasons lie principally in the fact that the parties who have a vital interest in an enterprise (major shareholders, creditors and employees) do not rely solely on the information in the annual accounts when making decisions, but have access to inside information by institutional means, e.g. via the supervisory board and the workers' council.

1.3 The relationship between the financial statements and the tax computation

The calculation of the profit in the financial statements and the computation of taxable profit are interconnected. There is nothing peculiar to Germany in this. It is reasonable to assume that, in other countries too, the accounts of the legal entities are drawn up with a view to minimizing the tax burden. When, in international circles, German accounts are said to be more tax-oriented, the reference is being made to the particularly close relationship because of the 'reverse authoritativeness principle' and the special role of the *Bundesfinanzhof* (BFH, Federal Fiscal Court). Moreover, in Germany there is a distinction between the consolidated accounts and those of the individual enterprise. As was shown in Chapter 5, the taxation of a group of enterprises is based on the accounts of the individual enterprises that make up the group; thus the close relationship between the calculation of profits in the financial statements and the computation of taxable profit applies mainly at the level of the individual enterprise. In the following outline, the accounts of the individual company are considered first.

1.3.1 The 'authoritativeness principle' (*Maßgeblichkeit*)

The relationship between the financial statements and the tax computation is characterized by the 'authoritativeness principle' (*Maßgeblichkeitsprinzip*) and the 'reverse authoritativeness principle' (*umgekehrte Maßgeblichkeit*). The authoritativeness principle means that the financial statements, drawn up in accordance with the *Grundsätze ordnungsmäßiger Buchführung* (GoB, principles of regular accounting) form the authoritative basis for the tax computation. The computation of taxable profits must be based on the assets (and liabilities) reported in the financial statements according to GoB. This means, first, that only the basic principles carry authority for tax purposes, not every detailed rule. Second, the application of the basic principles is not theoretical (called the 'abstract authoritativeness' principle). Where the authoritativeness principle is applicable, the specific values from the financial statements must be used in the tax computation (the formal or concrete authoritativeness principle).

This principle was introduced in the independent states of Bremen and Saxony before the formation of the unified German state in 1871. If the question is asked how it has managed to survive into the present, part of the answer lies in the similar functions of the two calculations. The accounting rules of the HGB have as their aim the reporting of a profit that can be distributed to the owners. For the purposes of calculating taxable profit, a calculation should also be made of an amount that can be withdrawn. Normally it is in the interests of both the owner and the state that the source of income should be maintained. Hence it is likely that both will agree on a conservative reckoning of profit which may be expected, with a high degree of probability, to materialize in cash. Their close interrelationship is also justified by the fact that it serves to simplify accounting. Those parts of the two calculations (the financial statements and the tax computations) that are identical need not be recorded twice. Third, the net assets increase theory of income, developed by Schanz (see Chapter 5, section 2.2) corresponded, both in structure and in content, with the calculation of profit in the financial statements. Moreover in France, where the net assets increase theory has assumed considerable significance, there is a close relationship between the calculation of profit for both commercial and tax purposes.

Admittedly, since the beginnings of the debate on accounting theory at the turn of the century it has often been objected that the authoritativeness theory disregards the current value of the assets. Supporters of this point of view, *ältere Bilanzstatiker* (early representatives of current value-accounting at the beginning of the century), have never been able to assert themselves to the same extent as, for example, in Britain. However, the argument can be turned round. In Germany it has never been possible to move towards the aim of disclosing information on the current value of assets because of the existence of the authoritativeness principle.

From a current standpoint the authoritativeness principle has further aspects that are worthy of consideration. It has the effect of a constraint on the fiscal authorities, in the sense that they do not change the definition of income for short-term fiscal reasons. They are tied to the commercial concept of income. A further effect of the authoritativeness principle is that it encourages a high quality of debate about accounting matters in Germany. When controversial questions of financial reporting are settled by the courts, it is almost exclusively the tax courts that are involved: in the first instance the fiscal courts

(*Finanzgerichte*) and, on appeal, the *Bundesfinanzhof* (BFH, Federal Fiscal Court). Since, however, the tax computation is based on the financial statements, the tax courts promulgate far-reaching interpretations of the commercial principles of regular accounting. In practice, the clarification of many basic, but also specific, controversies relating to financial reporting is largely the task of the fiscal jurisdiction.

1.3.2 The 'reverse authoritativeness principle' (*umgekehrte Maßgeblichkeit*)

By the 'reverse authoritativeness principle' is understood that the tax computation has a retroactive effect on the financial statements. First, this is a deliberately planned effect of the authoritativeness principle. Because of it, in the preparation of the financial statements, the taxpayer takes into account the taxation consequences and inclines towards a conservative calculation of profit. The goal of tax minimization thus determines the content of the financial statements – but, at first, only within the constraints of the HGB rules. A condition of this *voluntary* reverse authoritativeness principle is that the HGB permits some choice and that there are no tax rules that prescribe a different treatment.

In addition, legislation requires the reverse authoritativeness principle to be applied in other cases. Under EStG § 5 (1), sentence 2, the taxpayer may avail himself of options offered under the tax laws only if his financial statements are in agreement (*forced* reverse authoritativeness principle). Such options exist for all taxation reliefs on depreciation and for tax-exempt reserves allowed on political grounds, for example accelerated depreciation on investment in the former East German *Länder* or for environmental protection (see Chapter 7, section 5.5.3). The tax concessions can be taken up only if the depreciation charge or the tax-exempt reserve is also recorded in the financial statements. Special regulations (for sole proprietors and partnerships under HGB § 254, and for corporations under HGB § 279 (2)) ensure that this treatment, which runs counter to the GoB, is permissible in the financial statements.

One of the reasons for the reverse authoritativeness principle is presumably that the law in this way obliges taxpayers to reinvest the tax benefits in the business and not distribute them (see the corresponding presentation of incentive tax rates for corporation tax in Chapter 5). As far as sole proprietors and partnerships are concerned this argument is unconvincing, since they may withdraw capital at will. Conversely, as regards corporations, the objective of investment in the enterprise could be achieved equally well if they were obliged to create a non-distributable reserve in the balance sheet to the corresponding amount. Another argument is that smaller enterprises were meant to be able to limit themselves to one calculation. For this it would have been sufficient merely to admit the option of a single calculation but not to prescribe it. Further, the option could have been limited to companies that are not obliged to file accounts, or, at least, quoted companies could have been excluded. As a counter to this not unjustified criticism of the forced reverse authoritativeness principle, it is pointed out that enterprises are obliged to report in the notes on the accounts the amount of depreciation charges and write-backs allowed on taxation grounds only. However, this rule applies only to corporations, and only to the annual depreciation charge. The brought and carried forward figures are not given. Managers seem to be in favour of the forced reverse authoritativeness principle because its additional options facilitate income smoothing and dividend policy. This may be particularly the case with joint stock corporations, whose shareholders can normally insist on the distribution of up to 50 per cent of the profits. On the other hand joint stock corporations which operate on an international scale soon begin to feel the disadvantages of the misinformation due to the forced reverse authoritativeness principle. Hence a number of them exclude it from their group accounts.

1.3.3 The uncoupling of group accounts

The authoritativeness principle and the reverse authoritativeness principle need not have the same effect on the consolidated accounts as they have on the accounts of the individual enterprise. Under German law the consolidated accounts must be drawn up in accordance with the HGB principles that apply to the parent undertaking (see Chapter 8, section 5). That means that the consolidated accounts too must be prepared according to German accounting principles, which are based on prudence. However, there is no commitment to the specific values in the individual accounts. These can be departed from in drawing up the consolidated accounts without incurring any direct consequences as regards tax. Moreover the statutory pressure of the reverse authoritativeness principle embodied in EStG § 5 (1), second sentence, applies only to the accounts of the individual enterprise. Thus there is no need for consolidated accounts to be tax-driven. Some groups take full advantage of this opportunity, particularly those which are quoted on foreign stock exchanges. Particularly in the first year of listing, this can lead, to a not inconsiderable increase in equity, as was the case, for example, with Schering AG when it was first quoted on the London stock exchange in 1986, or with Daimler-Benz AG adapting to more international accounting standards in 1990.

If, nevertheless, numerous groups also use tax-driven values in their consolidated accounts, then it is mainly for the following reasons. In the first place, it is expensive to run two accounting systems side by side. Second, possible capital market and labour market effects may persuade management to eschew a different approach in the consolidated accounts. If a higher profit is shown in the consolidated accounts than in the individual accounts, it may induce the absentee owners and the trade unions to demand higher dividends or higher wages and social benefits. The enterprise's management, which, as a rule, prefers self-financing through retained profits, is able to avoid any discussion on this matter by using tax-driven values. In addition the banks have their own good reasons for encouraging the quiet retention of profits.

2 A LEGALISTIC SYSTEM

2.1 The regulation of accounting by law

In Germany decisions on accounting rules are traditionally understood not as a technical matter on which a group of accounting experts should be competent, but as an issue of policy, decisions on which should have a relatively broad social basis and be enacted by due process of law. Hence, in Germany, accounting rules are legal provisions.

The political importance attached to the matter may also be seen from the fact that, despite specific proposals, no council of accounting experts, endowed with the necessary authority, which could establish accounting rules in individual cases, has yet been set up. Even the stock exchange regulatory bodies have no competence to issue accounting regulations for quoted companies. Such regulations – for example, those relating to interim reports (see Chapter 9, section 2) – are instead enshrined in law, such as the *Börsengesetz* (BörsG, Stock Exchange Act) and the *Börsenzulassungsverordnung* (BörsZulV, Stock Exchange Listing Requirements Order).

The new law relating to the accounts of corporations is formally, in the first stage, European law, and only in the second stage German law. The provisions of the Fourth, Seventh and Eighth Directives have been incorporated into the HGB. As, however, European law provides for national options in crucial areas, and, in other respects has been gently assimilated to German law, the traditional way of thinking still dominates, particularly in all rules relating to the ascertainment of the profit of the individual enterprise. On the other hand, in the areas of classification and consolidated accounts the existing law has been heavily influenced by ideas that had no place in the old legislation. In some cases, admittedly, these innovations are not mandatory, but are options which it is open to the enterprise to takeup, e.g. the classification of the profit and loss account according to the cost of sales–accounting format.

With the implementation of the EC directives there was, at the same time, a reform of accounting law relating to enterprises other than corporations. Although this was not a requirement of the directives, it was a way of bringing in European law, particularly for consolidated accounts. By contrast, all the rules concerning the measurement of the profit of the individual, unincorporated enterprise follow the German tradition, i.e. they require the maintenance of the enterprise through a conservative presentation of profit, even more so than the rules that apply to corporations.

2.2 The historical development of accounting law

An affinity can still be detected between German accounting law and that of other continental countries, such as France and Italy; it is grounded in their common legal and cultural history. The starting point of German accounting law is generally considered to be the Ordonnance de Commerce (1673) of the Frenchman, Jacques Savary, and the commentary, *Le Parfait Negociant* (1675), written by him.

German commercial law was first codified on a comprehensive basis by the Prussian general Act of 1794, based closely on the Code Savary, which contained exhaustive provisions on the duty to maintain accounts. Admittedly an inventory and a balance sheet were mentioned only in the case of bankruptcy. However, the Act included provisions (partly based on *Le Parfait Negociant*) for the valuation of assets in the case when there was no specific term in the business agreement. The valuation rules that were laid down in the Act would be described today as the historical cost method, the principle of lower value and systematic depreciation. The valuation rules in the European Community's directives thus perpetuate the continental European tradition of the seventeenth and eighteenth centuries, albeit with subsequent overlays provided by the national states.

The development of the country's own distinct accounting law was closely bound up with the movement towards a German national state. It culminated in the *Allgemeines Deutsches Handelsgesetzbuch* of 1861 (ADHGB, General German Commercial Code), which came into force in Prussia that year and in Austria the following year. Businessmen were now obliged to draw up an inventory and a balance sheet. In the matter of valuation there was a break with Savary's tradition, for, in drawing up the inventory and the balance sheet, all assets and liabilities were to be stated at the values which were attributable to them at the time of the stocktaking. The term 'attributed value' (*beizulegender Wert*) was understood to be primarily the current value at the balance sheet date.

However, with accelerating industralization there developed, in addition to the ADHGB, the corporate governance law relating to the AGs which included the accounting law for this legal form. In the debate that accompanied the amendment of the AG Act in 1870 the new trend was already clear. On the one hand, many were sceptical about the distribution of profit before the liquidation of the AG, because such profits were seen as not definitive. On the other hand, however, it became progressively clearer that, with the involvement of smaller, anonymous shareholders, it was no longer possible to wait upon the liquidation of the AG for the distribution of profits. There was also a debate about the need to reduce the risks to creditors by limiting dividends to profits that were virtually assured. There was, however, a delay in coming to the logical conclusion that it should be obligatory to determine profits on a basis of prudence. Partly on account of this, problems ensued. Between 1871 and 1873 the number of AGs increased fivefold, reflecting increased industrialization and the associated demand for capital. Unscrupulous company promoters made themselves rich by overvaluing the assets that contributed to newly formed companies.

This was the background to the amendment of the AG Act in 1884. Acquisition cost and production cost were established by law as the upper limit for the value of the fixed assets, at least, as a means of reducing the risk of overvaluations and of the distribution of still uncertain profits. The foundations of accounting law, which still apply today, were laid down following very protracted and thorough deliberations, the results of which were noted in other European countries, particularly in France.

These valuation rules were not generally held at the time to apply to other forms of business organization, for which the authoritative rules were those of the ADHGB. The new Commercial Code of 1897 brought the fundamental innovation that assets must be valued according to *Grundsätze ordnungsmäßiger Buchführung* (GoB). It was believed that these principles could be derived inductively, from the practice of honest businessmen. Since the GoB were not comprehensively detailed in the Act, accounting law became more flexible. At the same time legal loopholes in the law were closed, for there was a legal requirement to follow the GoB in the accounts.

In succeeding decades theoretical discussion flourished. In particular, the foundations of different procedures for inflation accounting were established. Revaluation techniques, the most prominent of which was Fritz Schmidt's *Organische Tageswertbilanz* (organic current value balance sheet), failed to be adopted by the authorities as part of accounting law. Instead, the law relating to corporate governance was refined and developed. In particular, law relating to the accounts of AGs now incorporated regulations on the format of the balance sheet and profit and loss account, on the audit obligation and on special disclosure requirements.

In the AG Regulation of 1931 and the new AktG of 1937 the historical cost system of accounting was refined. A distinction was drawn, in valuation, between fixed assets in the narrow sense (land, buildings, machinery, plant and equipment), other fixed assets (concessions, patents, participating interests and other investments) and current assets. It became illegal to capitalize formation expenses and capital issue costs, as well as self-produced goodwill.

The AktG of 1965 halted the trend towards ever more cautious valuation. The calls of small shareholders for dividends were endorsed in that the scope for creating hidden reserves by means of the valuation process was cut back. In addition, for the first time, it became compulsory to prepare group accounts (see Chapter 8, section 1.1).

In 1969 stricter accounting rules for large enterprises in the form of sole proprietors, commercial partnerships and GmbHs were brought in (*Publizitätsgesetz*, or Disclosure Act – PublG for short), with requirements broadly similar to those upon AGs.

The basis of current accounting law is Book III of the HGB, in particular §§ 238–63. Its regulations apply to all enterprises unless they are overruled by particular enactments. For:

1 Enterprises taking certain legal forms,
2 Large enterprises as defined in the PublG,
3 Enterprises in particular industrial and commercial sectors,
4 Quoted enterprises, and
5 Public enterprises

there are special rules, which are to be found in a large number of Acts. Figure 6.2 presents a survey of the system of accounting law as it affects financial statements.

2.3 Legal interpretations

Laws are a good way of giving democratic legitimacy to regulation but they are relatively inflexible and unspecific. German law lays down the important principles; many points of detail, such as foreign currency translation, and accounting for leasing and government grants, are not regulated explicitly. Furthermore, regulation by law would make the resolution of new problems more difficult, since decades normally pass before there is a reform of the law. Nevertheless, the German system does provide the necessary detail and flexibility. They are assured by the system of legal interpretations.

First, legal interpretations clarify the meaning of rules that are an explicit part of the law, for example the definition of production cost that is to be found in HGB § 255. In addition, rules are established concerning accounting problems that are not explicitly dealt with in the law, such as foreign currency translation (see Chapter 7, section 5.7.2). Solutions to problems of this nature are evolved through judicial interpretation of the principles enunciated in the law. On one hand, the existing and generally accepted understanding of these principles limits the range of possible solutions. On the other, consensus settles on a single solution, or a small number of solutions, thus enhancing the content of the principles and confirming the existing understanding or modifying it, as the case may be. Finally, legal interpretation includes the adaptation of the law to newly emerging conditions; legal interpretation also encompasses continued development.

Figure 6.2 Summary of German accounting law: (a) regulations applicable to all enterprises. Sources of law are abbreviated as follows in Fig. 6.2(a)–(d):

AktG	*Aktiengesetz* (Joint Stock Corporation Act)
BBankG	*Bundesbankgesetz* (Federal Bank Act)
BundesbahnG	*Bundesbahngesetz* (Federal Railway Act)
BHO	*Bundeshaushaltsordnung* (Federal Budgetary Regulations)
BörsG	*Börsengesetz* (Stock Exchange Act)
BörsZulV	*Börsenzulassungsverordnung* (Ordinance regulating Stock Exchange Listings)
GenG	*Genossenschaftsgesetz* (Co-operative Associations Act)
GmbHG	*Gesetz betreffend die Gesellschaften mit beschränkter Haftung* (Act concerning Limited Liability Companies)
HGB	*Handelsgesetzbuch* (Commercial Code)
HGrG	*Haushaltsgrundsätzegesetz* (Budgetary Principles Act)
PostVerfG	*Postverfassungsgesetz* (Act concerning the Constitution of the Federal Post Office)
PublG	*Publizitätsgesetz* (Disclosure Act)
VAG	*Versicherungsaufsichtsgesetz* (Act concerning the Supervision of Insurance Enterprises)
VuReV	*Verordnung über die Rechnungslegung von Versicherungsgesellschaften* (Ordinance regulating the Financial Reporting of Insurance Businesses)

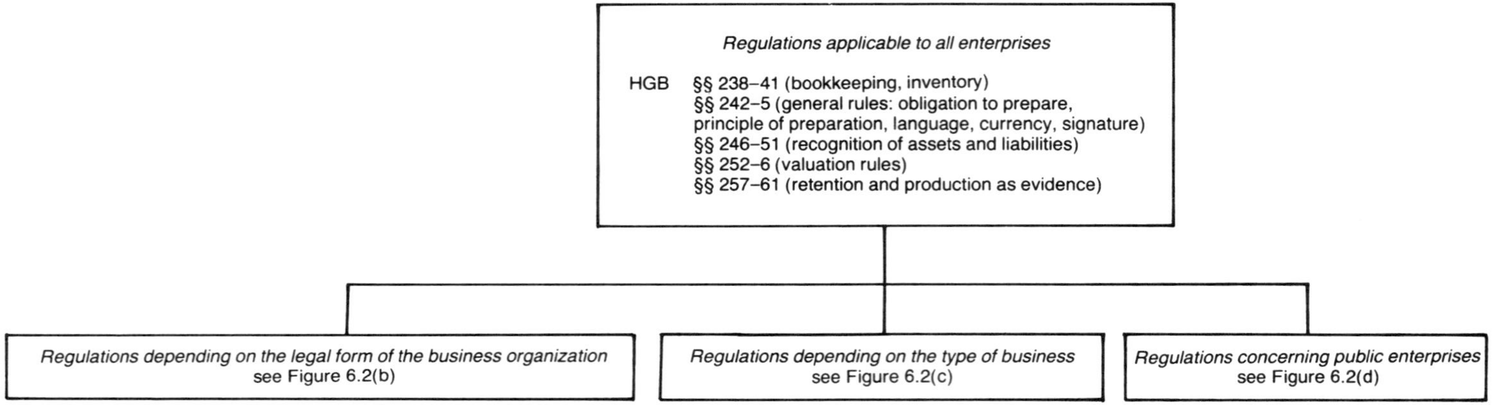

Figure 6.2 Summary of German accounting law: (b) regulations depending on the legal form of the business organization

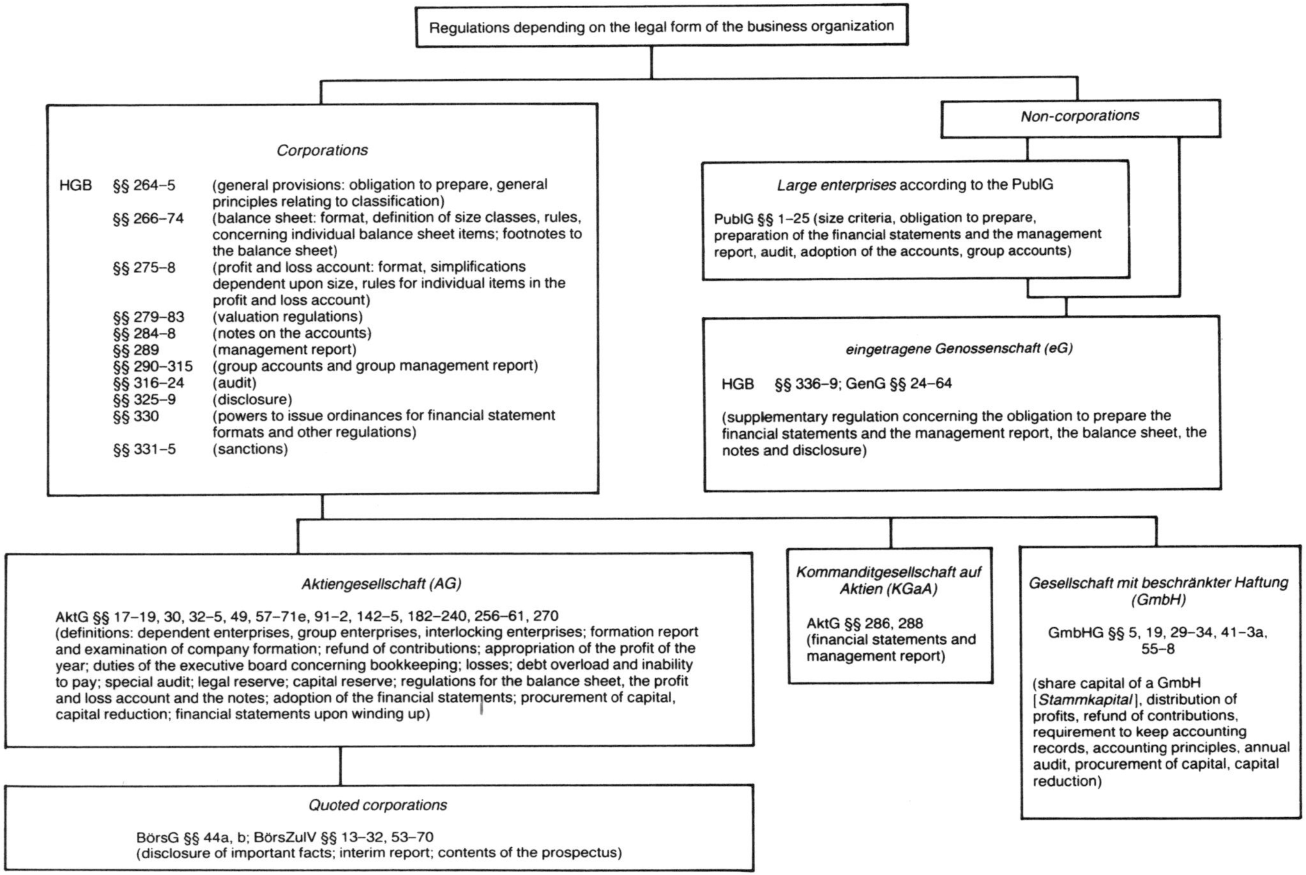

Figure 6.2 Summary of German accounting law: (c) regulations depending on the type of business activity

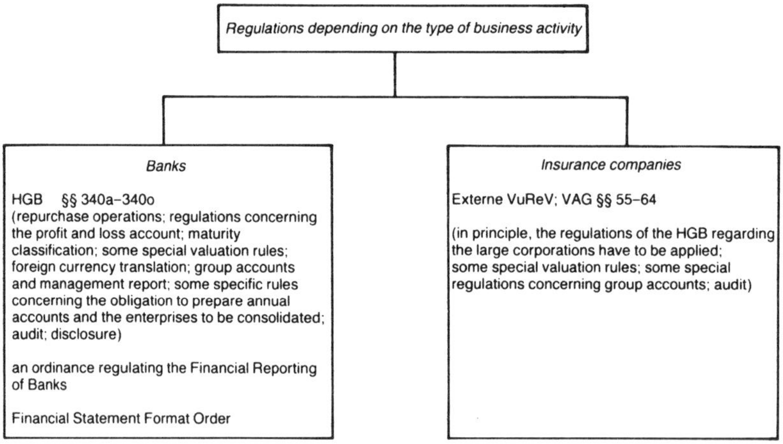

Figure 6.2 Summary of German accounting law: (d) regulations concerning public enterprises

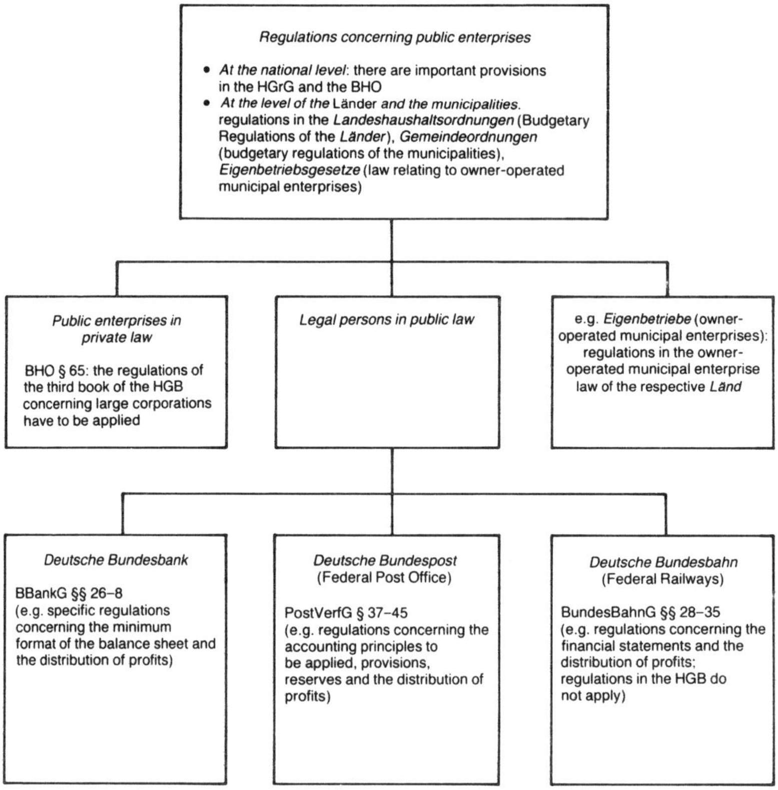

Under the heading of legal interpretation, three intertwined strands can be identified:

1 The market for legal interpretations.
2 The opinions of associations and professional organizations.
3 Judge-made law.

2.3.1 The market for legal interpretations

Legalistic regulation soon provokes the criticism of bureaucratic rule-making. Closer examination reveals that German accounting law is a matter of subtle interplay between the bureaucracy and the market. Commentary by experts on the law is largely organized as an information market. The sellers in this market are not only lawyers (barristers and judges as in their published writings) but also, particularly in the case of accounting law, *Wirtschaftsprüfer*, experts from business and the public sector, and, last but not least, academics such as professors of accounting. The direct buyers are the publishers of widely read specialist journals such as *Der Betrieb*, *Der Betriebs-Berater*, *Deutsche Steuerzeitung*, *Finanzrundschau*, *GmbH-Rundschau*, *Steuer und Wirtschaft*, *Steuerliche Betriebsprüfung* and *Die Wirtschaftsprüfung*; there are also the book publishers, particularly those which specialize in very comprehensive commentaries on accounting law. The indirect consumers of this output are business and other organizations as well as the information producers themselves. The size of the market is substantial (see, for example, the *Beck HdR-Literaturdienst*, which lists the references in the field of financial accounting, updated annually).

A collective product of this information market is the professional reputation of authors and editors, which helps them in other markets. This applies particularly to firms of accountants. Their representatives are also active in the market for legal interpretations because such activity demonstrates their competence and hence improves their chances of attracting audit and consultancy work. Many commentaries on accounting law are edited and written by members of the larger accountancy firms.

2.3.2 Opinions of associations and professional organizations

A second sub-system consists of the recommendations and expert opinions that are developed and issued by the relevant committee of the *Institut der Wirtschaftsprüfer* (IdW). They are not legally binding, even on members of the Institute. However, the risk of being accused in court of professional malpractice is a good deal higher if the auditor has certified a balance sheet that conflicts with one of these opinions. The opinions and recommendations of the IdW that are currently in issue are given in Table 6.1.

Apart from the *Institut der Wirtschaftsprüfer* there are some other institutions whose statements have some bearing in practice. The wide-ranging recommendations of the 'external enterprise accounting' working party of the *Schmalenbach-Gesellschaft/ Deutsche Gesellschaft für Betriebswirtschaft* (Schmalenbach Society and German Association for Business Economics) have grown in practical importance in recent years. Those which have appeared are listed in Table 6.2. In addition the professional associations of certain industries, such as the economic committee of the Chemical Industry Association, from time to time, put out statements on accounting matters which are of practical relevance, especially within the industry concerned.

Table 6.1 Opinions and recommendations of the IdW

Expert opinions of the IdW

1/1937 i.d.F. 1990
Mandatory Audit and Fraud
Der Wirtschaftstreuhänder, 1937, p. 97; with supplementary notes, see WPg 1982, p. 94; FN 1982, p. 55

1/1953 i.d.F. 1990
Publication of the Audited Financial Statements and Management Reports
WPg 1953, p. 333; FN 1953, p. 49

1/1988
Principles of Proper Conduct in the Auditing of Financial Statements
WPg 1989, p. 9; FN 1989, p. 1

2/1988
Principles of Proper Reporting of the Results of the Audit of Financial Statements
WPg 1989, p. 20; FN 1989, p. 9

3/1988
Principles of the Audit Opinion
WPg 1989, p. 27; FN 1989, p. 14

Recommendations of the main technical committee of the IdW

5/1952
Risks Associated with Participation in Joint Ventures and the Audit Opinion
WPg 1952, p. 217; FN 1952, p. 35

1/1960 i.d.F. 1990 (1990 version)
On the Interpretation of the Audit Requirements of §§ 3 and 4 of the Capital Increases Act
WPg 1960, p. 163; FN 1960, p. 20; with supplementary notes, see WPg 1982, p. 94; FN 1982, p. 55

2/1966
Exposition of the Principles of the Collaboration of Members of the Institute with the Internal Audit. (Joint statement of the IdW and the Institute of Internal Auditors.)
WPg 1966, p. 646; FN 1966, p. 122

1/1969
The Treatment of the Employer's Social Security Contributions in the Disclosure of the Gross Remuneration of Members of the Executive Board
WPg 1969, p. 180; FN 1969, p. 36

1/1972 i.d.F. 1990
On the Audit of the Financial Statements of Commercial Partnerships and Sole Proprietors under the PublG
WPg 1972, p. 75; FN 1972, p. 15

2/1973 i.d.F. 1990
Provisions for the Cost of Preparing and Auditing the Financial Statements under HGB § 249 (1)
WPg 1973, p. 503; WPg 1975, p. 147; FN 1973, p. 117; FN 1975, p. 18; with supplementary notes, see WPg 1982, p. 407; FN 1982, p. 213

1/1975 i.d.F. 1990
On the Treatment in the Annual Accounts of the Equalization Levy under the Third Electricity Generation Act
WPg 1975, p. 555; FN 1975, p. 135; with supplementary notes, see WPg 1982, p. 94; FN 1982, p. 55

2/1975
Taking Account of Capital Maintenance in Determining the Annual Profit
WPg 1975, p. 614; FN 1975, p. 173

1/1976
On the Annual Accounts of Commercial Partnerships
WPg 1976, p. 114; FN 1976, p. 41

2/1976 i.d.F. 1990
On the Legal Reporting Requirements Relating to the Declarations to be Made to the Creditor of a Third Party
WPg 1976, p. 528; FN 1976, p. 215

2/1977 i.d.F. 1990
On the Effects on the Financial Statements of the Reform of Corporation Tax
WPg 1977, p. 463; WPg 1980, p. 80; FN 1977, p. 265; FN 1980, p. 4

1/1978 i.d.F. 1990
The Cash Flow Statement as a Supplement to the Annual Accounts
WPg 1978, p. 207; FN 1978, p. 99

1/1981 i.d.F. 1990
Sampling for Stocktaking in the Annual Accounts
WPg 1990, p. 649; FN 1990, p. 329
2/1981
Audit Working Papers
WPg 1982, p. 44; FN 1982, p. 4
1/1983
On the Reversal of the Dependence Assumption in AktG § 17 (2)
WPg 1983, p. 429; FN 1983, p. 218
2/1983
Basic Principles in the Valuation of Enterprises
WPg 1983, p. 468; FN 1983, p. 218
1/1984 i.d.F. 1990
Accounting for Contributions, with Special Reference to the Treatment of Government Subsidies
WPg 1984, p. 612; FN 1984, p. 362
1/1985 i.d.F. 1990
The Treatment of Turnover Tax in the Annual Accounts
WPg 1985, p. 257; FN 1985, p. 161
1/1986
Accounting for Zero Coupon Bonds
WPg 1986, p. 248; FN 1986, p. 140
1/1988
The Use of Sampling Methods in the Audit of the Annual Accounts
WPg 1988, p. 240; FN 1988, p. 105
2/1988
Pension Obligations in the Annual Accounts
WPg 1988, p. 403; FN 1988, p. 219
3/1988
Uniform Valuation Methods in Group Accounts
WPg 1988, p. 484; FN 1988, p. 258
4/1988
Group Accounts with Differing Balance Sheet Dates
WPg 1988, p. 682; FN 1988, p. 337
5/1988
Comparative Figures in the Annual Accounts of the Enterprise and of the Group, including their Audit
WPg 1989, p. 42; FN 1989, p. 21
6/1988
The Audit of Fusions (legal merger with one legal entity disappearing) under AktG § 340b (4)
WPg 1989, p. 42; FN 1989, p. 22
1/1989
Leases in the Accounts of the Lessor
WPg 1989, p. 625; FN 1989, p. 333
1/1990
The Taking of a Physical Inventory in the Light of Different Inventory Methods
WPg 1990, p. 143; FN 1990, p. 61
2/1990
Valuation of Enterprises in the GDR; Application of the Basic Principles
WPg 1990, p. 403; FN 1990, p. 216a–d
3/1990
The Audit Opinion on the Opening Deutschmark Balance Sheet in the GDR
WPg 1990, p. 574; FN 1990, p. 286a
1/1991
Accounting for an Interest in a Commercial Partnership in the Accounts of a Corporation
WPg 1991, p. 334; FN 1991, p. 181
2/1991
The Modification of the Annual Accounts and the Adaptation of the Annual Accounts for Tax Reasons
WPg 1992, p. 89; FN 1992, p. 1
3/1991
On the Preparation and Audit of the Report on the Connection with Related Enterprises (Dependence Report under AktG § 312)
WPg 1992, p. 91; FN 1992, p. 3

Tables 6.1 Continued

4/1991
On the Person of the Supplementary Auditor in the Supplementary Audit of the Opening Deutschmark Balance Sheet of Enterprises Owned by Treuhand
WPg 1992, p. 94; FN 1992, p. 5
5/1991
On the Capitalization of Production Cost
WPg 1992, p. 94; FN 1992, p. 6
In 1991 the HFA issued 13 opinions on the law on accounting by companies in the former East Germany. Besides the HFA, the BFA (*Bankenfachausschuß*, technical committee for accounting by banks), the VFA (*Versicherungsfachausschuß*, technical committee for accounting by insurance companies), the KFA (*Fachausschuß für Kommunales Prüfungswesen*, technical committee for municipal auditing), the KHFA (*Krankenhausfachausschuß*, technical committee for accounting by hospitals), the WFA (*Wohnungswirtschaftlicher Fachausschuß*, technical committee for accounting in the building industry), the AKW (*Arbeitskreis Weltbilanz*, working group on the consolidated accounts (global accounts)) and the SABI (*Sonderausschuß Bilanzrichtliniengesetz*, special committee on the Accounting Directives Law) have issued numerous pronouncements which are not mentioned here.

Note:
FN *Fachnachrichten* series published by the IdW. HFA *Hauptfachausschuß* (main technical committee) of the IdW. WPg *Die Wirtschaftsprüfung*. The opinions and recommendations of the IdW are published only in German.

Table 6.2 Recommendations of the *Schmalenbach-Gesellschaft/Deutsche Gesellschaft für Betriebswirtschaft* working party on external enterprise accounting

Earnings per Share (*Zeitschrift für betriebswirtschaftliche Forschung*, February 1988, pp. 138–48)[1]
The Preparation of Consolidated Accounts (see Busse von Colbe *et al.* 1989)[1]
Interim Reports under the new Law relating to Quoted Businesses (see Busse von Colbe and Reinhard 1989)[2]
Earnings according to the DVFA/SG Method: joint recommendation with the DVFA Commission on the Methodology of the Financial Analysis (see Busse von Colbe *et al.* 1991)[3]

Notes:
[1] Published in German only.
[2] Partly in English.
[3] Published in German and English.

2.3.3 Judge-made law

The judges, particularly those of the higher courts, give binding interpretations of the law, based on the prior professional debate. In doing so they pass judgement on the professional arguments. If the commercial accounting law is relevant for lawsuits between legal persons under civil law and if the amount in litigation is higher than DM10,000, then the competent court in the first instance is the *Landgericht* (regional court); on appeal, the *Oberlandesgericht* (intermediate court of appeal); and, ultimately, the *Bundesgerichtshof* (Federal Supreme Court). However, these courts rarely pass important judgements in accounting matters. Considerably more important are the tax courts: in the first instance the *Finanzgericht* (fiscal court) and then the highest court, the *Bundes-*

finanzhof (BFH, Federal Fiscal Court). The importance of the tax courts in commercial accounting matters arises, in the first place, from the fact that numerous small and medium-sized enterprises normally prepare only one set of accounts for both taxation and financial reporting purposes. Second, the taxation courts also interpret the GoB of the HGB, for, according to EStG § 5 (1), the taxable profit must be determined according to the GoB of the HGB, unless the latter conflict with specific taxation rules. Hence, the decisions of the taxation courts and, in particular, the decisions on basic points of the BFH are of considerable importance for financial reporting, even though they refer to tax cases. As the BFH hands down a considerable number of decisions in accounting matters each year, a large reserve or reservoir of judgements on numerous individual questions relating to the determination of profit for financial reporting purposes has been built up.

3 BOOKKEEPING, CHARTS OF ACCOUNTS AND STOCKTAKING

Every business is obliged to maintain books of account and to record in them business transactions and assets in accordance with GoB (HGB § 238). The GoB may be categorized as:

1 Principles of regular bookkeeping (*Grundsätze ordnungsmäßiger Buchführung*) as narrowly defined.
2 Principles of regular stocktaking (*Grundsätze ordnungsmäßiger Inventur*).
3 Principles of regular financial reporting (*Grundsätze ordnungsmäßiger Bilanzierung*).

3.1 Bookkeeping rules and GoB (as narrowly defined)

Arising from the professional debate, the following GoB (as narrowly defined) have become accepted as conventions. Some are also mentioned in HGB §§ 238 f.:

1 *The principles of accuracy and objectivity.* The documentary evidence of the business transaction must accord with the underlying facts. When the business transaction is recorded in the books of account, the information contained in the documentary evidence must not be falsified.
2 *The principle of clarity.* All necessary records and entries in the books must be clearly and openly written in according to a prescribed system that enables an entry to be reproduced later. This implies, among other things, a sufficiently detailed chart of accounts, unambiguous specification of the business transaction, the recording of the date, the account number and the voucher number of every entry.
3 *The principle of completeness.* All business transactions must be fully and comprehensively recorded.
4 *The principle of consistency.* In principle, the structure of the accounts, in particular the chart of accounts, must be retained over time; any deviation means that information should be given on the reason for the inconsistency.
5 *The principle of security.* All entries must be made within the customary time limit.

Table 6.3 Recommendations of professional organizations and associations on EDP bookkeeping

Fachausschuss für moderne Abrechnungssysteme des IdW (technical committee of the IdW for EDP accounting systems)

1/1972
The Regularity and Audit of an External EDP Bookkeeping System
WPg 1972, p. 534; 1982, p. 96
1/1974
The Audit of EDP Bookkeeping Systems
WPg 1974, p. 83; 1977, p. 433; 1979, p. 16
1/1975
On the Interpretation of GoB in the Use of EDP Systems in Accounting
WPg 1975, p. 555; 1982, p. 96
1/1978
EDP as a Bookkeeping Aid
WPg 1978, p. 208
1/1979
The Data Protection Act and the Audit of Annual Accounts
WPg 1979, p. 440

Ausschuss für wirtschaftliche Verwaltung (committee for efficient administration)

Manual on the Preparation of Documentation of EDP Bookkeeping Procedures

Note: The recommendations are published in German only.

The content and date of subsequent alterations must be capable of being established. The books must be kept using a living language.

6 *The principle of verifiability.* No entry may be made without documentary evidence.
7 *The principle of auditability.* It must be possible for an expert third party within a reasonable time to gain from the books an insight into the business transactions and position of the enterprise.
8 *The principle of economy.* The cost of providing the information required must not be out of proportion to its value.

Of particular importance has been the development in the course of the professional debate of concrete rules for EDP bookkeeping, especially as the legal rules in this area are very broad and general. Note should be taken of the recommendations of professional organizations and associations listed in Table 6.3.

3.2 Charts of accounts

German accounting usage distinguishes between two technical terms, both of which can be translated as 'chart of accounts':

1 *Kontenrahmen* ('accounts framework'), which is an outline chart of accounts developed for companies in a particular sector of industry or commerce.
2 *Kontenplan* ('accounts plan'), which is the detailed chart of accounts developed by a business for its own use. In principle the *Kontenplan* of the enterprise should be based on the *Kontenrahmen* of the industry to which it belongs.

The *Kontenrahmen* consists of:

1 A classification system for the accounts.
2 The definition of the contents of the groups of accounts within the classification system.
3 A numbering system for the accounts.

In Germany (in contrast to the position in France) the chart of accounts does not include rules for asset recognition and valuation.

On the basis of the *Kontenrahmen* of its economic sector the individual enterprise is free to develop a *Kontenplan* to meet its own requirements. The *Kontenplan* contains all the accounts that are employed in the bookkeeping of the enterprise.

The *Kontenrahmen* and the *Kontenplan* are organized on the decimal system. They comprise ten classes of accounts, beginning with 0 and ending with 9. Each account class is divided into ten account groups, each account group into ten account types and each account type into ten sub-accounts (see Table 6.4). Further subdivision is possible, as required, by the addition of further digits to the account number.

The definition of the contents of the accounts is part of the *Kontenplan*. The definitions are devised so that there is no overlapping in the contents of the accounts in a

Table 6.4 The construction of a *Kontenrahmen*: an example

Account class	0	Intangible and tangible fixed assets		
	00	Unpaid calls on capital		
	01	Expenses for the start-up and expansion of the business		
Account group	. . .			
	05	Land, land rights and buildings, including buildings on third-party land		
Account type		050	Undeveloped land	
		051	Land with buildings	
Sub-account			0511	With own buildings
			0519	With third-party buildings

Table 6.5 Gemeinschaftskontenrahmen of the industry

Account class	
0	Fixed assets and long-term capital
1	Financial current assets and current liabilities
2	Other expenses and revenues (not related to the achievement of the objective of the business)
3	Stocks (raw materials and supplies)
4	Categories of cost
5 6	Reserved for the business's own cost accounts
7	Stocks of work in progress and finished goods
8	Operating revenue (turnover and variations in stocks)
9	Closing accounts

Table 6.6(a) Simplified *Industriekontenrahmen* (IKR) for account classes 0–9

Balance sheet accounts				
Asset accounts			*Equity and liability accounts*	
Class 0	*Class 1*	*Class 2*	*Class 3*	*Class 4*
Intangible and tangible fixed assets	*Financial assets*	*Current assets and pre-paid expenses*	*Equity and provisions*	*Liabilities and deferred income*
00 Subscribed capital unpaid 01 Start-up and business expansion expenses 02 Concessions, industrial and similar rights and assets and licences in such rights and assets 03 Goodwill 04 Down payments on intangible fixed assets 05 Land, land rights and buildings, including buildings on third-party land 07 Technical equipment and machinery 08 Other equipment, plant and office equipment 09 Payments on account and tangible assets under construction	11 Shares in affiliated enterprises 12 Loans to affiliated enterprises 13 Participations 14 Loans to enterprises in which participations are held 15 Long-term investments 16 Other loans (other financial assets)	20 Raw materials and supplies 21 Work in progress 22 Finished goods and merchandise 23 Down payments on stock 24 Trade receivables 25 Receivables from affiliated enterprises and enterprises in which participations are held 26 Other assets 27 Marketable securities 28 Cheques, cash in hand, central bank and postal giro balances, bank balances 29 Pre-paid expenses	30 Subscribed capital 31 Capital reserve 32 Profit reserves 33 Appropriation of profit 34 Net income/net loss for the year 35 Special item with reserve constituent 36 Valuation adjustment 37 Provision for pensions and similar obligations 38 Tax provisions 39 Other provisions	41 Loans 42 Liabilities to bank 43 Down payments on orders 44 Trade payables 45 Liabilities on bills accepted and drawn 46 Payables to affiliated enterprises 47 Payables to enterprises in which participations are held 48 Other liabilities 49 Deferred income

Accounts of the profit and loss account			*Accounts for opening and for closing*	*Accounts of cost accounting and results accounting*
Revenues	*Expenses*		*Final accounts*	
Class 5	*Class 6*	*Class 7*	*Class 8*	*Class 9*
Revenue	*Operating expenses*	*Other expenses*	*Statement of operating results*	*Cost accounting and results accounts*
50 Sales 52 Increase or decrease in finished goods inventories and work in progress 53 Own work capitalized 54 Other operating revenue 55 Revenue from participations 56 Revenue from other investments and long-term loans 57 Other interest and similar revenue 58 Extraordinary revenue 59 Revenue from transfer of losses	60 Cost of raw materials, consumables, supplies and of purchased merchandise 61 Cost of purchased services 62 Wages 63 Salaries 64 Social security and other pension costs 65 Depreciation 66 Other personnel expenses 67 Expenses for the utilization of rights and services 68 Expenses for communication (documentation, IT, travelling, advertising) 69 Expenses for contributions, etc., valuation adjustments and expenses unrelated to accounting period	70 Company taxes 71–3 Other expenses 74 Amortization of financial assets and investments classified as current assets and losses attributable to respective disposals 75 Interest and similar expenses 76 Extraordinary expense 77 Taxes on income 78 Other taxes 79 Expenses from profit transfer agreements	80 Opening/closing 81 Cost of production 82 Selling expenses 83 Cost of general administration 84 Other operating expenses 85 Adjustment accounts to revenue of account class 5 86 Adjustment accounts to expenses of account class 6 87 Adjustment accounts to expenses of account class 7 88 Statement of short-term operating results 89 Intra-year accruals	90 Enterprise-specific accruals 91 Cost accounting adjustments 92 Cost types and result types 93 Cost centre 94 Cost objective 95 Finished goods 96 Internal supplies and services and their costs 97 Cost of sales 98 Sales results 99 Profit disclosed

Table 6.6(b) Vereinfachter Industriekontenrahmen für die Kontenklassen 0 bis 9

Konten des Bilanzbereichs (Beständerechnung)				
Aktivkonten			*Passivkonten*	
Klasse 0	*Klasse 1*	*Klasse 2*	*Klasse 3*	*Klasse 4*
Immaterielle Vermögensgegenstände und Sachanlagen	*Finanzanlagen*	*Umlaufvermögen und aktive Rechnungsabgrenzung*	*Eigenkapital und Rückstellungen*	*Verbindlichkeiten und passive Rechnungsabgrenzung*
00 Ausstehende Einlagen 01 Aufwendungen für die Ingangsetzung und Erweiterung des Geschäftsbetriebs 02 Konzessionen, gewerbliche Schutzrechte und ähnliche Rechte und Werte sowie Lizenzen an solchen Rechten und Werten 03 Geschäfts- oder Firmenwert 04 Geleistete Anzahlungen auf immaterielle Vermögensgegenstände 05 Grundstücke, grundstücksgleiche Rechte und Bauten einschließlich der Bauten auf fremden Grundstücken 07 Technische Anlagen und Maschinen 08 Andere Anlagen, Betriebs- und Geschäftsausstattung 09 Geleistete Anzahlungen und Anlagen im Bau	11 Anteile an verbundenen Unternehmen 12 Ausleihungen an verbundene Unternehmen 13 Beteiligungen 14 Ausleihungen an Unternehmen, mit denen ein Beteiligungsverhältnis besteht 15 Wertpapiere des Anlagevermögens 16 Sonstige Ausleihungen (Sonstige Finanzanlagen)	20 Roh-, Hilfs- und Betriebsstoffe 21 Unfertige Erzeugnisse, unfertige Leistungen 22 Fertige Erzeugnisse und Waren 23 Geleistete Anzahlungen auf Vorräte 24 Forderungen aus Lieferungen und Leistungen 25 Forderungen gegen verbundene Unternehmen und gegen Unternehmen, mit denen ein Beteiligungsverhältnis besteht 26 Sonstige Vermögensgegenstände 27 Wertpapiere 28 Flüssige Mittel 29 Aktive Rechnungsabgrenzung	30 Kapitalkonto/ Gezeichnetes Kapital 31 Kapitalrücklage 32 Gewinnrücklagen 33 Ergebnisverwendung 34 Jahresüberschuß/ Jahresfehlbetrag 35 Sonderposten mit Rücklageanteil 36 Wertberichtigungen 37 Rückstellungen für Pensionen und ähnliche Verpflichtungen 38 Steuerrückstellungen 39 Sonstige Rückstellungen	41 Anleihen 42 Verbindlichkeiten gegenüber Kreditinstituten 43 Erhaltene Anzahlungen auf Bestellungen 44 Verbindlichkeiten aus Lieferungen und Leistungen 45 Wechselverbindlichkeiten 46 Verbindlichkeiten gegenüber verbundenen Unternehmen 47 Verbindlichkeiten gegenüber Unternehmen, mit denen ein Beteiligungsverhältnis besteht 48 Sonstige Verbindlichkeiten 49 Passive Rechnungsabgrenzung

Konten des Ergebnisbereichs (Erfolgsrechnung)			*Konten für Eröffnung und Abschluß*	*Konten der Kosten- und Leistungsrechung*
Erträge	*Aufwendungen*		*Abschlußrechnung*	
Klasse 5	*Klasse 6*	*Klasse 7*	*Klasse 8*	*Klasse 9*
Erträge	*Betriebliche Aufwendungen*	*Weitere Aufwendungen*	*Ergebnisrechnung*	*Kosten- und Leistungsrechnung (KLR)*
50 Umsatzerlöse 52 Erhöhung oder Verminderung des Bestandes an unfertigen und fertigen Erzeugnissen 53 Andere aktivierte Eigenleistungen 54 Sonstige betriebliche Erträge 55 Erträge aus Beteiligungen 56 Erträge aus anderen Wertpapieren und Ausleihungen des Finanzanlagevermögens 57 Sonstige Zinsen und ähnliche Erträge 58 Außerordentliche Erträge 59 Erträge aus Verlustübernahme	60 Aufwendungen für Roh-, Hilfs- und Betriebsstoffe und für bezogene Waren 61 Aufwendungen für bezogene Leistungen 62 Löhne 63 Gehälter 64 Soziale Abgaben und Aufwendungen für Altersversorgung und für Unterstützung 65 Abschreibungen 66 Sonstige Personalaufwendungen 67 Aufwendungen für die Inanspruchnahme von Rechten und Diensten 68 Aufwendungen für Kommunikation (Dokumentation, Informatik, Reisen, Werbung) 69 Aufwendungen für Beiträge und Sonstiges sowie Wertkorrekturen und periodenfremde Aufwendungen	70 Betriebliche Steuern 71–3 Sonstige Aufwendungen 74 Abschreibungen auf Finanzanlagen und auf Wertpapiere des Umlaufvermögens und Verluste aus entsprechenden Abgängen 75 Zinsen und ähnliche Aufwendungen 76 Außerordentliche Aufwendungen 77 Steuern vom Einkommen und Ertrag 78 Sonstige Steuern 79 Aufwendungen aus Gewinnabführungsverträgen	80 Eröffnung/Abschluß 81 Herstellungskosten 82 Vertriebskosten 83 Allgemeine Verwaltungskosten 84 Sonstige betriebliche Aufwendungen 85 Korrekturkonten zu den Erträgen der Kontenklasse 5 86 Korrekturkonten zu den Aufwendungen der Kontenklasse 6 87 Korrekturkonten zu den Aufwendungen der Kontenklasse 7 88 Kurzfristige Erfolgsrechnung (KER) 89 Innerjährige Rechnungsabgrenzung	90 Unternehmensbezogene Abgrenzungen 91 Kostenrechnerische Korrekturen 92 Kostenarten und Leistungsarten 93 Kostenstellen 94 Kostenträger 95 Fertige Erzeugnisse 96 Interne Lieferungen und Leistungen sowie deren Kosten 97 Umsatzkosten 98 Umsatzleistungen 99 Ergebnisausweis

particular area and the content of a subordinate account does not exceed that of its superior account.

The earliest works on charts of accounts began to appear around the turn of the century. The first comprehensive system was developed by Schär in 1911. The leading authority was Schmalenbach's *The Kontenrahmen*, which appeared in 1927. In 1937 a mandatory *Kontenrahmen*, based closely on the Schmalenbach chart, was issued for use by German industry. The individual economic sectors were required to work out their own *Kontenrahmen* based on it.

Since 1945 *Kontenrahmen* have ceased to be mandatory. They are now the responsibility of trade associations, which recommend them to their members, principally with the object of facilitating inter-firm comparisons within sectors of industry. In order to prevent the *Kontenrahmen* of different sectors from diverging too far, the *Bundesverband der Deutschen Industrie* (BDI, Association of German Industry) in 1951 issued a Common Framework of Accounts for Industry (*Gemeinschaftskontenrahmen der Industrie*, GKR) and recommended it to member firms. Its account classes are shown in Table 6.5. Their sequence follows that of the production process. The classes from 0 to 9 reflect the process of acquiring and exploiting resources (investment, production, sales). A bookkeeping system based on the GKR constitutes a unified system. The financial accounts and the management accounts form a single system; the two sets of accounts cannot be balanced separately.

A tendency for accounting practices in different industries to diverge since 1951 has led to revision of the GKR. In 1971 the BDI issued the Industry Accounting Framework (*Industriekontenrahmen*, IKR). Following the transformation wrought by the Fourth EC Directive in 1985 it was adapted to the new accounting regulations. Table 6.6 presents a shortened version of the latest revision of the IKR. The IKR is no longer based on the stages of the production process, but rather follows what is known as the dual system. It incorporates a strict division between the financial accounts (account classes 0 to 7) which flow into the annual accounts (account class 8), and the management and cost accounts (account class 9). Account classes 0 to 4 are based on the classification system for the balance sheet of corporations (see Chapter 7, section 3.1), and account classes 5 to 7 follow the classification system of the profit and loss account, using the total cost method (see Chapter 7, section 3.2.1).

In 1964 the Union Européenne des Experts Comptables Economiques et Financiers (UEC) published a proposal for a European chart of accounts, based on the classification of the annual accounts. However, efforts to achieve a uniform European chart of accounts have since petered out.

3.3 Stocktaking and simplified valuation procedures

When starting a business the owner has to prepare a list of all its assets and liabilities, then value them. This procedure must be repeated at the end of each financial year. The list of assets and liabilities is known as the inventory; in Germany it has a very broad meaning, since it includes all assets and liabilities.

It is not essential for the inventory to be taken at the balance sheet date; the operation can be spread over the whole year (continuous inventory). Moreover, since 1977 it has

Table 6.7 Official recommendations on sample-based valuation

Hauptfachausschuss der Wirtschaftprüfer
Statement 1/1981, *Sampling Methods for Year-end Stocktaking* (WPg 1981), pp. 479–91

Arbeitsgemeinschaft für wirtschaftliche Verwaltung eV (AWV)
The Rationalization of Stocktaking (Wiesbaden, 1976)
Technical Information: Stocktaking in an Automated Warehouse (Eschborn, 1977)
Technical Information: Sequence Test for the Stocktaking of Non-valued Items in an Automated Warehouse (Eschborn, 1980)
Technical Information: Permanent Inventory with Sampling (Eschborn, 1982)
Technical Information: Sequence Test for Stocktaking by Sampling with Regular Stock Accounting (Eschborn, 1985)

Note: The recommendations are published in German only.

been permissible to determine the type, quantity and value of assets using recognized statistical sampling methods (HGB § 241 (1), first sentence), provided that:

1 The procedure is in accordance with GoB.
2 Recognized statistical methods are used.
3 The stated value of the inventory, determined according to the sample, agrees materially with that which would result from a full physical inventory.

To ensure the regularity of the sample-based inventory, the recommendations listed in Table 6.7 should be observed.

A distinction may be drawn between the valuation of the inventory and the valuation of the assets in the financial statements. For the inventory it is sufficient to value assets and liabilities at acquisition cost or production cost. There is no requirement that the lower market value should be taken into account.

The physical stocktaking and valuation can be further simplified by grouping certain assets together and valuing them using a weighted average (HGB § 240 (4)). The group value can also be used in the balance sheet. *Group valuation* is permitted for stocks and other movable assets, provided that they are of the same kind and of approximately similar value.

In addition it is permissible to value fixed assets and stocks that are regularly replaced, such as raw materials and supplies whose total value is not material, at a *fixed value* in both the inventory and the balance sheet (HGB § 240 (3)). The fixed value means that the stated quantity and value are kept constant for a certain period. As a general rule, a physical inventory need only be taken every three years.

7

The accounts of individual enterprises

1 THE OBLIGATION TO PREPARE ACCOUNTS

Sole proprietors and commercial partnerships are obliged to prepare financial statements, but these need consist only of a balance sheet (*Bilanz*) and a profit and loss account (*Gewinn- und Verlustrechnung*), even for large enterprises (see Table 7.1). Corporations, by comparison, must, in addition to a balance sheet and a profit and loss account,

Table 7.1 Components of financial statements, with time limits

Type of enterprise	*Criteria (two of the three)*	*Components of the financial report*	*Time limit after end of the financial year*
Large corporations	Balance sheet total over DM 15.5 million Annual turnover over DM 32.2 million No. of employees over 250	Balance sheet Profit and loss account Notes Management report	Three months
Medium-size corporations	Balance sheet total over DM 3.9 million Annual turnover over DM 8 million No. of employees over 50	Balance sheet Profit and loss account Notes Management report	Three months
Small corporations	Balance sheet total up to DM 3.9 million Annual turnover up to DM 8 million No. of employees up to 50	Balance sheet Profit and loss account Notes Management report	Six months
Sole proprietors and partnerships (large as defined in the *Publizitätsgesetz*)	Balance sheet total equal to or over DM 125 million Annual turnover equal to or over DM 250 million No. of employees equal to or over 5,000	Balance sheet Profit and loss account	Three months
Other		Balance sheet Profit and loss account	Within a regular period

prepare notes (*Anhang*) (see section 9 below) and also a management report (*Lagebericht*) (see Chapter 9, section 1).

For small unincorporated enterprises there is no statutory time limit on the preparation of the accounts. For large and medium-sized corporations, as defined in HGB § 267 (1) (exceeding two of the following figures on two successive balance sheet dates: balance sheet total DM 3.9 million, turnover DM 8 million, number of employees fifty), and for large enterprises, as defined in the PublG (exceeding two of the following three figures on three successive balance sheet dates: balance sheet total DM 125 million, turnover DM 250 million, number of employees 5,000) must prepare their accounts within three months (HGB § 264 (1), PublG § 5 (1)). Small corporations have six months (HGB § 264 (1)).

2 *GRUNDSÄTZE ORDNUNGSMÄßIGER BUCHFÜHRUNG* (GoB) AND THE 'TRUE AND FAIR VIEW'

The financial statements are to be prepared in accordance with *Grundsätze ordnungsmäßiger Buchfürung*, or GoB (principles of regular accounting; HGB § 243 (1)). Only for corporations is there the additional requirement that:

> the financial statements of the company must, in compliance with GoB, present a true and fair view of the net worth, financial position and results of the company. If special circumstances result in the financial statements not showing a true and fair view within the meaning of the first sentence, then additional disclosures are required in the notes.
>
> (HGB § 264 (2))

Before tackling the difficult subject of the relationship between GoB and a true and fair view, the GoB themselves and their relationship to the specific legal rules and to the purpose of the financial statements should first be explained.

When there are specific legal regulations on accounting matters they must normally be followed. Admittedly they are not, in themselves, GoB, but it is generally accepted that they are compatible with GoB. An example of a specific legal rule is the requirement in HGB § 249 (1) to set up a provision for guarantee expenses for which there is no contractual obligation. However, on many accounting questions there are no specific legal rules. Moreover, the existing legal rules are frequently ambiguous. For example, the rule on creating provisions does not specify the circumstances under which a provision is to be released. Such omissions and obscurities are to be dealt with in the light of GoB.

In earlier times GoB were interpreted inductively, that is, the accounting practice of reputable businessmen was drawn upon in order to remedy gaps and uncertainties. By contrast, one of the features of modern accounting law is that a good many of the principles are explicitly identified in the text. A survey of the codified GoB is given in Table 7.2. Part of the codified GoB – the substantive GoB – is particularly relevant to the financial statements. The more formal principles – for example, the principle of completeness – are significant both for book-keeping, in the narrow sense, and for the financial statements.

The GoB themselves need to be interpreted: for example, the codification of the prudence principle and the realization principle in HGB § 252 (1), fourth sentence, contains no statement on the extent of the prudence or realization criteria. Moreover, for certain accounting problems, different principles may offer different solutions. For example, in the translation of hedged foreign currency debtors and creditors, the requirement to write down current assets to market value (HGB § 253 (3)), the principle of item-by-item valuation (HGB § 252 (1), No. 3) and the prohibition on reporting unrealized profits (HGB § 252 (1), No. 4) would require the recognition of unrealized foreign currency losses. However, this solution would be incompatible with the customary interpretation of the prudence principle (HGB § 252 (1), No. 4). The prudence principle requires that such risks and losses should be accounted for only when they are in fact likely to occur. Such is not the case with hedged foreign currency positions. According to the current understanding of accounting law, when such contradictions occur, the principles (or their ranking) must be interpreted in the light of the purpose of the financial statements. The GoB are rules which the businessman has to follow in order to prepare a balance sheet that fulfils the legally defined purpose. The purpose of the financial statement is, as it were, the last authority for the interpretation of the content of the GoB.

In the case of hedged foreign currency positions, it would be argued that the prudence

Table 7.2 Codified *Grundsätze ordnungsmäßiger Buchführung* (GoB)

Formal codified GoB	*Bookkeeping (in the narrow sense)*	*Financial statements*
1 Completeness	HGB § 239 (2), 'The entries in the books and other necessary records must be made in a complete ...'	HGB § 246 (1), 'The financial statements must include all assets, liabilities, prepaid expenses, deferred income, revenues and expenses ...'
2 Correctness	HGB § 239 (2) (continued), '... correct ...'	–
3 Punctuality	HGB § 239 (2) (continued), '... timely ...'	HGB § 243 (3), 'The financial statements must be prepared within a period that conforms with orderly business conduct'
4 Order	HGB § 239 (2) (continued), '... and orderly fashion'	HGB § 243 (2), 'The financial statements must be well set out ...'
5 Clarity	–	HGB § 243 (2) (continued), '... and clear'
6 Auditability	HGB § 238 (1) sentences 2 and 3, 'The books must be kept in such a way that it is possible for an expert third party, within a reasonable period of time, to gain an insight into the transactions and position of the business. The business transactions must be traceable from their origin through to settlement'	–
7 Subsequent alterations	HGB § 239 (3), 'Upon alteration, the original contents must remain legible, whether or not the alteration is made originally or later'	–
8 Formal consistency	–	HGB § 252 (1) No. 1, 'The values of the opening balance sheet of one financial year must agree with those of the closing balance sheet of the previous financial year' HGB § 265 (1), 'The format, and, in particular the classification, must be maintained from one balance sheet to the next'

Substantive codified GoB	*Contents*
1 Historical cost	HGB § 253 (1), 'Assets are to be stated at no more than their acquisition cost or production cost, adjusted for depreciation'
2 Going concern	HGB § 252 (1) No. 2, 'The valuation should assume that the enterprise is a going concern, unless contradicted by the facts or the law'
3 Matching/Accruals	HGB § 252 (1) No. 5, 'Revenues and expenses are to be accounted for in the financial statements, regardless of the point in time of the related payments'
4 Item-by-item valuation	HGB § 252 (1) No. 3, 'The assets and liabilities are to be valued at the balance sheet date on an item-by-item basis'
5 Realization	HGB § 252 (4); 'Profits may be taken into account only if they are realized at the balance sheet date'
6 Imparity	HGB § 252 (1) No. 4, 'All foreseeable risks and losses are to be accounted for, even if unrealized' (in contrast to the position with profits)

7 Prudence	HGB § 252 (1) No. 4, 'Values must be determined prudently: namely, all foreseeable risks and losses which have arisen up to the balance sheet date must be taken into account, even if these only become known between the balance sheet date and the date of the preparation of the financial statements' (revealed value principle)
8 Substantive consistency (comparability)	HGB § 252 (1) No. 6, 'The valuation methods applied in the preceding financial statements should be retained'

Source: Ordelheide (1993: 260)

principle protects the creditors, but in this case their interests are not harmed. By contrast the interests of the shareholders would be prejudiced, because the distributable profit would be reduced by deductions for losses which could not occur. Consequently the principle of item-by-item valuation has been qualified in this case, following discussion in professional circles. This discussion found its expression in a proposed statement of the competent IdW committee, the HFA.

With the advent of the EC Fourth Directive, the German legislator was faced with the problem of reconciling this traditional system of the specific rules, the GoB and the purpose of the financial statements, on the one hand, with, the requirement to present a true and fair view on the other. An attempt was made in HGB § 264 (2), combined with the system of legal interpretation (see Chapter 6, section 2). It would seem doubtful whether the attempt has succeeded. There are those who argue that this article should be interpreted in accordance with the Fourth Directive in the sense that the true and fair view principle is valid also for the balance sheet and the profit and loss account unless there are specific legal rules that preclude doing so. Options, margins of error and legal uncertainties have to be interpreted with reference to the true and fair view. Other commentators advocate the so-called separation or disaggregation approach. On this interpretation the true and fair view basically has a bearing only on the notes, whereas the balance sheet and the profit and loss account have to be set up in accordance with the individual rules and the GoB. The separation argument is justified, in particular, by the observation that the financial statements consist of three integral parts – the notes, the balance sheet and the profit and loss account – and that, if due weight is given to the true and fair view in the notes, the financial statements as a whole will therefore present a true and fair view.

The practical consequences of these different approaches are admittedly somewhat limited. Since the substantive GoB are specifically named in the Fourth Directive and consequently, in German law, the overriding conclusion is that they, and with them the specific rules, are normally in agreement with the true and fair view. It may be possible to disregard specific rules or codified principles in order to present a true and fair view but only in highly unusual circumstances, if ever. Normally, according to German legal thinking, *lex specialis* overrides *lex generalis.*

Hence there can be an impact only in those cases when the specific rules and/or the codified principles still need to be interpreted in order to resolve an accounting problem. In the traditional view the decision would then be made with reference to the purpose of the financial statements, whereas, it is the intention of the Fourth Directive that the financial statements should be prepared so as to give a true and fair view.

Seen in the light of their role in the overall system of regulation, the functional interpretation of law and the application of the true and fair view seem very similar. Both are relatively imprecise and thus allow accepted interpretations of their meaning to become established, permitting the development and application of compromise solutions which reflect the interests of different parties. They also enable these solutions to be adapted over time as circumstances change.

Practical problems connected with the true and fair view requirement arise only when there are concrete differences between the true and fair view and the interpretation of GoB in the light of the purpose of the financial statements. As an example, German law generally forbids the reporting of unhedged foreign currency debtors and creditors at the current exchange rate in the accounts of the individual company when it would result in the debtors being valued above historical cost in Deutschmarks and the creditors being valued below historical cost. This follows from the German interpretation of the realization principle in article 31 of the Fourth Directive and in HGB § 252 (1), No. 4, and its specification within the historical cost principle (HGB § 253 (1)). The British understanding is that the true and fair view principle, and the realization principle based on it, seem to require valuation to be at the current exchange rate. If the British understanding of the realization principle were to prevail (for example, through a judgement of the European Court of Justice), the German interpretation of the Fourth Directive and of the HGB would be in conflict with it and hence would no longer be sustainable. At present the European interpretation of the true and fair view and of realized profit in articles 2.3 and 31.1.c.aa of the Fourth Directive is still a completely open matter. If the true and fair view requirement in the Fourth Directive were to be interpreted in the light of the particular situation, then both interpretations of the realization principles are defensible in law, since they are based on different capital market structures and other circumstantial factors.

3 FINANCIAL STATEMENT FORMATS

3.1 Balance sheet

The law prescribes the layout of the balance sheet (*Bilanz*) in varying degrees of detail, depending on the legal form of the organization, the industrial or commercial sector it operates in, and the size of the enterprise.

For sole proprietors and partnerships there is no prescribed format, provided they do not exceed the limits of the PublG (at least two of the following three criteria on three successive balance sheet dates: turnover DM 250 million; balance sheet total DM 125 million; employees 5,000). However, they must at least report the following items separately and break them down in sufficient detail: fixed assets, current assets, equity, liabilities, pre-paid and deferred items.

For sole proprietors and partnerships which are defined as large enterprises under PublG § 1 and for corporations, a specific format is laid down in HGB § 266. There are further references to format in other individual articles of the HGB and other laws. The legal format and the reference to other articles are presented in a consolidated form in Table 7.3. The positions preceded by a blob (•) are not in the legal format but derive from the individual articles.

Corporations must in addition prepare a 'schedule of fixed assets' (*Anlagespiegel*) covering the fixed assets and the capitalized business incorporation and expansion expenses (see Example 7.1). This presents the book value at the balance sheet date, with the accumulated historical cost and the additions, disposals, transfers, and write-ups of the financial year and the accumulated depreciation for all years (after setting off the previous years' write-ups).

The classifications in Table 7.3 are the legally prescribed minimum; they can be further subdivided. The legal requirement of a minimum level of classification does not mean that the published balance sheets of enterprises are always so detailed. More often than not, enterprises combine some items in their published balance sheets. In that case, however, the minimum detail as set out in Table 7.3 must be given in the notes.

3.2 Profit and loss account

3.2.1 Structure

Before the enactment of the Fourth Directive, German enterprises presented their profit and loss accounts (*Gewinn- und Verlustrechnungen*) in a form that Anglo-Saxons did not find easy to follow, known as the 'total costs' method (*Gesamtkostenverfahren* – format with classification of all expenses of the period by nature). Under the new law they now have the option, as an alternative, of using the 'cost of sales' method (*Umsatzkostenverfahren* – format with classification of expenses only related to sales of the period by function), which is similar to the US format. In Germany both types of profit and loss account are presented in vertical form, with revenue and expenses listed one after the other in a way that permits the calculation of informative subtotals. The alternative account form, used in other EC countries, is not legal in Germany.

A survey by Treuarbeit (1990: 97) revealed that up to 1988 twelve large corporations out of the 100 sampled had gone over to the 'cost of sales' method. A later survey showed that, of 150 medium-size corporations, only nine had done so (Ballwieser and Häger 1991: 119). Thus the 'total costs' method still predominates.

Table 7.4 presents the format according to the 'total costs' method and the 'cost of sales' method. The principle of completeness applies (HGB § 246): all revenue and expenses of the enterprise must be included. The profit for the year (item 20 or 19) comprises both the operating results and the financial results, also the capital gains and all extraordinary and prior year revenues and expenses.

In the format there is a division between operating results, financial results and extraordinary results. The operating results comprise items 1–8 in the total costs method (items 1–7 in the cost of sales method). The financial results comprise items 9–13 (8–12). Item 14 (13) is the sum of the operating results and the financial results, and presents the results of the ordinary business activity. The extraordinary results comprise items 15–17 (14–16).

The layout makes it clear that there is a difference in the calculation of operating results as between the two methods. The *cost of sales* method deducts from the sales only the costs which are attributable to them. The costs are classified according to cost centres (production, sales, administration). The *total costs* method, by contrast, presents all the costs of the period in the profit and loss account. They are classified by main cost

Table 7.3 Layout of the balance sheet

Assets

- Unpaid contributions on subscribed capital
  of which called (§ 272 (1))[1]
- Expenses for the start-up and expansion of the business

A Fixed assets
  I Intangible assets
    1 Concessions, trading and similar rights and values, and licences in such rights and values
    2 Goodwill
      of which 'fusion' surplus (AktG § 348 (2))
    3 Payments on account
  II Tangible assets
    1 Land, land rights and buildings, including buildings on third-party land
    2 Technical plant and machinery
    3 Other plant, factory and office equipment
    4 Payments on account and assets under construction
  III Financial assets
    1 Shares in affiliated enterprises
    2 Loans to affiliated enterprises
    3 Participations
    4 Loans to enterprises in which a participation is held
    • Loans to shareholders (GmbHG § 42 (3))
    5 Long-term investments
    6 Other loans
      of which to personally liable shareholders and their relatives (AktG § 286 (2))

B Current assets
  I Inventories
    1 Raw materials and supplies
    2 Work in progress
    3 Finished goods and merchandise
    4 Payments on account
  II Debtors and other assets
    1 Trade debtors[2]
    2 Amounts receivable from affiliated enterprises[2]
    3 Amounts receivable from enterprises in which a participation is held[2]
    • Amounts receivable from shareholders (GmbHG § 42 (3))[2]
    • Unpaid calls on subscribed capital (§ 272 (1))[2]
    • Unpaid supplementary calls (GmbHG § 42 (2))[2]
    • Payment obligations of personally liable shareholders (AktG § 286 (2))[2]
    4 Other assets[2]
      of which obligation of personally liable shareholders and their relatives (AktG § 286 (2))
  III Investments
    1 Shares in affiliated enterprises
    2 Own shares
    3 Other investments
  IV Cheques, cash, balances at the Bundesbank and Postgirobank, bank balances
  • Deferred taxes (prepaid) (§ 274 (2))

C Pre-paid expenses
  • Loan redemption premium (§ 268 (6))
  • Other pre-paid expenses
  • Deficit not covered by equity (§ 268 (3))
  • Share of losses of personally liable shareholders not covered by capital contribution (AktG § 286 (2))

Aktivselte

- Ausstehende Einlagen auf das gezeichnete Kapital, *davon* eingefordert (§ 272 Abs. 1)[1]
- Aufwendungen für die Ingangsetzung und Erweiterung des Geschäftsbetriebs (§ 269)

A Anlagevermögen

I Immaterielle Vermögensgegenstände

1 Konzessionen, gewerbliche Schutzrechte und ähnliche Rechte und Werte sowie Lizenzen an solchen Rechten und Werten
2 Geschäfts- oder Firmenwert, *davon* Verschmelzungsmehrwert (§ 348 Abs. 2 AktG)
3 Geleistete Anzahlungen

II Sachanlagen

1 Grundstücke, grundstücksgleiche Rechte und Bauten einschließlich der Bauten auf fremden Grundstücken
2 technische Anlagen und Maschinen
3 andere Anlagen, Betriebs- und Geschäftsausstattung
4 geleistete Anzahlungen und Anlagen im Bau

III Finanzanlagen

1 Anteile an verbundenen Unternehmen
2 Ausleihungen an verbundene Unternehmen
3 Beteiligungen
4 Ausleihungen an Unternehmen, mit denen ein Beteiligungsverhältnis besteht
• Ausleihungen an Gesellschafter (§ 42 Abs. 3 GmbHG)
5 Wertpapiere des Anlagevermögens
6 Sonstige Ausleihungen, *davon* an persönlich haftende Gesellschafter und deren Angehörige (§ 286 Abs. 2 AktG)

B Umlaufvermögen

I Vorräte

1 Roh-, Hilfs- und Betriebsstoffe
2 unfertige Erzeugnisse, unfertige Leistungen
3 fertige Erzeugnisse und Waren
4 geleistete Anzahlungen

II Forderungen und sonstige Vermögensgegenstände

1 Forderungen aus Lieferungen und Leistungen[2]
2 Forderungen gegen verbundene Unternehmen[2]
3 Forderungen gegenüber Unternehmen, mit denen ein Beteiligungsverhältnis besteht[2]
• Forderungen gegenüber Gesellschaftern (§ 42 Abs. 3 GmbHG)[2]
• eingeforderte Einlagen auf das gezeichnete Kapital (§ 272 Abs. 1)[2]
• eingeforderte Nachschüsse (§ 42 Abs. 2 GmbHG)[2]
• Einzahlungsverpflichtungen persönlich haftender Gesellschafter (§ 286 Abs. 2 AktG)[2]
4 Sonstige Vermögensgegenstände[2] *davon* an persönlich haftende Gesellschafter und deren Angehörige (§ 286 Abs. 2 AktG)

III Wertpapiere

1 Anteile an verbundenen Unternehmen
2 eigene Anteile
3 sonstige Wertpapiere

IV Schecks, Kassenbestand, Bundesbank- und Postgiroguthaben, Guthaben bei Kreditinstituten

• Aktivische latente Steuern (§ 274 Abs. 2)

C Rechnungsabgrenzungsposten

- Disagio (§ 268 Abs. 6)
- andere Rechnungsabgrenzungsposten
- Nicht durch Eigenkapital gedeckter Fehlbetrag (§ 268 Abs. 3)
- Nicht durch Vermögenseinlagen gedeckter Verlustanteil persönlich haftender Gesellschafter (§ 286 Abs. 2 AktG)

Table 7.3 Continued

Capital and obligations

A Equity
- I Subscribed capital or called capital (§ 272 (1))
- • Capital share of personally liable shareholders (AktG § 286 (2))
- II Capital reserve
  - *of which*: created during the financial year (AktG § 152 (2))
  - withdrawn during the financial year (AktG § 152 (2))
  - called supplementary contributions (GmbHG § 42 (2))
- III Profit reserves
  - 1 Legal reserve
  - 2 Reserve for own shares and for shares of a controlling enterprise or of an enterprise with a majority holding (§ 272 (4))
  - 3 Statutory reserves
  - 4 Other profit reserves, of which in conformity with AktG § 58 (2a) and GmbHG § 29 (4), 'are to be shown separately with the revenue reserves':
    - (a) 'the amounts that have been transferred by the general meeting from the *Bilanzgewinn* (balance sheet profit) of the previous year'
    - (b) 'the amounts that have been transferred from the profits of the current financial year'
    - (c) 'the amounts that have been withdrawn from reserves for the current financial year' (AktG § 152 (3))
- IV Profit (loss) brought forward
- V Profit (loss) for the current year
- Or IV and V together (§ 268 (1)):
  - *Bilanzgewinn/Bilanzverlust*
  - *of which* profit (loss) brought forward
- • Amount of higher valuation according to court decision (AktG § 261 (2))
- • Amount of higher valuation according to the results of the special audit (AktG § 261 (1))
- • Special item with a reserve component

B Provisions
- 1 Provisions for pensions and similar obligations
- 2 Tax provisions
- • Deferred taxation (§ 274 (1))
- 3 Other provisions

C Liabilities
- 1 Loans[3]
- 2 Liabilities to banks[3]
- 3 Payments received on account of orders[3] (if for inventory stocks, they may, as an alternative, be openly deducted from inventory stocks (§ 268 (5) sentence 2))
- 4 Trade creditors[3]
- 5 Liabilities on bills accepted and drawn[3]
- 6 Liabilities to affiliated enterprises[3]
- 7 Liabilities to enterprises in which a participating interest is held[3]
- • Liabilities to shareholders (GmbHG § 42 (3))[3]
- 8 Other liabilities
  - *of which* taxes
  - *of which* social security

D Deferred income

Passivseite

A Eigenkapital
- I Gezeichnetes Kapital oder Eingefordertes Kapital (§ 272 Abs. 1)
- • Kapitalanteil der persönlich haftenden Gesellschafter (§ 286 Abs. 2 AktG)
- II Kapitalrücklage
  davon: während des Geschäftsjahres eingestellt (§ 152 Abs. 2 AktG)
  für das Geschäftsjahr entnommen (§ 152 Abs. 2 AktG)
  Eingeforderte Nachschüsse (§ 42 Abs. 2 GmbHG)
- III Gewinnrücklagen
  1 gesetzliche Rücklage
  2 Rücklage für eigene Anteile und für Anteile eines herrschenden oder eines mit Mehrheit beteiligten Unternehmens (§ 272 Abs. 4)
  3 satzungsmäßige Rücklagen
  4 andere Gewinnrücklagen, davon gemäß § 58 Abs. 2a AktG bzw. § 29 Abs. 4 GmbHG, 'Zu den einzelnen Posten der Gewinnrücklagen sind ... jeweils gesondert anzugeben':
  (a) 'die Beträge, die die Hauptversammlung aus dem Bilanzgewinn des Vorjahrs eingestellt hat'
  (b) 'die Beträge, die aus dem Jahresüberschuß des Geschätsjahrs eingestellt werden'
  (c) 'die Beträge, die für das Geschäftsjahr entnommen werden' (§ 152 Abs. 3 AktG)
- IV Gewinnvortrag/Verlustvortrag
- V Jahresüberschuß/Jahresfehlbetrag

Oder IV und V zusammen (§ 268 Abs. 1):
  Bilanzgewinn/Bilanzverlust
  davon Gewinn-/Verlustvortrag
- • Ertrag aufgrund höherer Bewertung gemäß gerichtlicher Entscheidung (§ 261 Abs. 2 AktG)
- • Ertrag aufgrund höherer Bewertung gemäß dem Ergebnis der Sonderprüfung (§ 261 Abs. 1 AktG)
- • Sonderposten mit Rücklageanteil (§ 273)

B Rückstellungen
- 1 Rückstellungen für Pensionen und ähnliche Verpflichtungen
- 2 Steuerrückstellungen
- • Rückstellungen für latente Steuern (§ 274 Abs. 1)
- 3 Sonstige Rückstellungen

C Verbindlichkeiten
- 1 Anleihen[3]
- 2 Verbindlichkeiten gegenüber Kreditinstituten[3]
- 3 erhaltene Anzahlungen auf Bestellungen[3] (soweit auf Vorräte, alternativ auch offen von den Vorräten absetzbar, § 268 Abs. 5 S. 2)
- 4 Verbindlichkeiten aus Lieferungen und Leistungen[3]
- 5 Verbindlichkeiten aus der Annahme gezogener Wechsel[3]
- 6 Verbindlichkeiten gegenüber verbundenen Unternehmen[3]
- 7 Verbindlichkeiten gegenüber Unternehmen, mit denen ein Beteiligungsverhältnis besteht[3]
- • Verbindlichkeiten gegenüber Gesellschaftern (§ 42 Abs. 3 GmbHG)[3]
- 8 sonstige Verbindlichkeiten
  davon aus Steuern
  davon im Rahmen der sozialen Sicherheit

D Rechnungsabgrenzungsposten

Source: Schildbach (1992: 158–9).
Notes:
[1]The references are to the HGB unless otherwise specified.
[2]The amount receivable in more than one year's time is to be shown separately or disclosed in the notes.
[3]The following amounts are to be shown separately, under each heading:
- The amount due within one year (§ 268 (5)).
- The amount due after five years (§ 285 No. 1a).
- Liabilities which are secured by mortgages or similar claims (§ 285 No. 1b).

Example 7.1 **Statement of changes in intangibles, fixed assets and investments**

Intangible assets and property, plant and equipment

(in millions of DM)	9/30/91	Additions	Reclassifications	Retirements	9/30/92	Accumulated depreciation/ amortization	Net value as of 9/30/92	Net value as of 9/30/91	Depreciation/ amortization during the fiscal year
Intangible assets	971	411	–	450	932	497	435	275	248
Property, plant and equipment									
Land, equivalent rights to real property, and buildings, including buildings on land not owned	12,442	955	380	174	13,603	5,083	8,520	7,837	521
Technical equipment and machinery	11,985	1,081	421	802	12,685	9,436	3,249	2,961	1,083
Other equipment, plant and office equipment	14,836	2,357	259	1,570	15,882	12,382	3,500	3,325	2,248
Equipment leased to customers	2,961	649	(6)	647	2,957	2,047	910	896	501
Advances to suppliers and construction in progress	1,436	1,276	(1,054)	23	1,635	12	1,623	1,435	12
	43,660	6,318	–	3,216	46,762	28,960	17,802	16,454	4,365
	44,631	**6,729**	**–**	**3,666**	**47,694**	**29,457**	**18,237**	**16,729**	**4,613**

Additions to intangible assets and property, plant and equipment during the fiscal year amounted to DM 6,729 (1991: DM 8,651) million, which include the opening balance amounts of DM 1,072 million attributable to companies included in the consolidated financial statements for the first time.

Investments

(in millions of DM)	9/30/91	Additions	Reclassifications	Retirements	9/30/92	Accumulated write-downs	Accumulated equity-adjustment	Net value as of 9/30/92	Net value as of 9/30/91
Interests in subsidiaries	718	337	29	250	834	158	(95)	581	640
Interests in associated companies	2,876	81	(18)	201	2,738	–	(1,349)	1,389	1,494
Miscellaneous investments	805	315	(11)	78	1,031	344	–	687	526
	4,399	**733**	**–**	**529**	**4,603**	**502**	**(1,444)**	**2,657**	**2,660**

Source: Siemens AG, annual report, 1992.

Table 7.4 Layout of the profit and loss account

	Total cost method (HGB § 275 (2))		Gesamtkostenverfahren (§ 275 Abs. 2 HGB)
1	Turnover	1	Umsatzerlöse
2	Increase (decrease) in stocks of finished goods and work in progress	2	Erhöhung oder Verminderung des Bestands an fertigen und unfertigen Erzeugnissen
3	Other own work capitalized	3	Andere aktivierte Eigenleistungen
4	See below	4	Siehe unten
5	Cost of materials	5	Materialaufwand
	(a) Cost of raw materials, consumables and supplies, and of purchased merchandise		(a) Aufwendungen für Roh-, Hilfs- und Betriebsstoffe und bezogene Waren
	(b) Cost of bought-in services		(b) Aufwendungen für bezogene Leistungen
6	Employment costs	6	Personalaufwand
	(a) Wages and salaries		(a) Löhne und Gehälter
	(b) Social security and costs of pensions and other support		(b) Soziale Abgaben und Aufwendungen für Altersversorgung und für Unterstützung
7	Depreciation on	7	Abschreibungen auf
	(a) Intangible and tangible fixed assets and on capitalized business start-up and expansion expenditure		(a) Immaterielle Vermögensgegenstände des Anlagevermögens und Sachanlagen sowie auf aktivierte Aufwendungen für die Ingangsetzung und Erweiterung des Geschäftsbetriebs
	(b) Current assets, in so far as it exceeds the amount that is normal for the corporation		(b) Vermögensgegenstände des Umlaufvermögens, soweit diese in der Kapitalgesellschaft üblichen Abschreibungen überschreiten
4	Other operating income	4	Sonstige betriebliche Erträge
8	Other operating expenses	8	Sonstige betriebliche Aufwendungen
=	*Operating results (net sum of 1–8)*[1]	=	*Betriebliches Ergebnis (Summe 1–8)*[1]

	Cost of sales method (HGB § 275 (3))		Umsatzkostenverfahren (§ 275 Abs. 3 HGB)
1	Turnover	1	Umsatzerlöse
2	Production costs incurred to achieve the turnover	2	Herstellungskosten der zur Erzielung der Umsatzerlöse erbrachten Leistungen
3	Gross profit	3	Bruttoergebnis vom Umsatz
4	Selling expenses	4	Vertriebskosten
5	General administrative expenses	5	Allgemeine Verwaltungskosten
6	Other operating income	6	Sonstige betriebliche Erträge
7	Other operating expenses	7	Sonstige betriebliche Aufwendungen
=	*Operating results (net sum of 1–7)*[1]	=	*Betriebliches Ergebnis (Summe 1–7)*[1]
9 or 8	Income from participations	9 bzw. 8	Erträge aus Beteiligungen
10 or 9	Income from other investments and loans included in financial fixed assets[2]	10 bzw. 9	Erträge aus anderen Wertpapieren und Ausleihungen des Finanzanlagevermögens[2]
11 or 10	Other interest and similar income[2]	11 bzw. 10	Sonstige Zinsen und ähnliche Erträge[2]
12 or 11	Amortization of financial fixed assets and investments included in current assets	12 bzw. 11	Abschreibungen auf Finanzanlagen und Wertpapiere des Umlaufvermögens
13 or 12	Interest and similar expenses[2]	13 bzw. 12	Zinsen und ähnliche Aufwendungen[2]
	= Financial results (net sum of 9–13 or 8–12)[1]		= Finanzergebnis (Summe 9–13 bzw. 8–12)[1]
14 or 13	Result of ordinary business activity (net sum of 1–13 or 1–12)	14 bzw. 13	Ergebnis der gewöhnlichen Geschäftstätigkeit (Summe 1–13 bzw. 1–12)
15 or 14	Extraordinary income	15 bzw. 14	Außerordentliche Erträge
16 or 15	Extraordinary expenses	16 bzw. 15	Außerordentliche Aufwendungen

Table 7.4 Continued

17 or 16	Extraordinary results (net sum of 15 and 16 or 14 and 15)	17 bzw. 16	Außerordentliches Ergebnis (Summe 15 und 16 bzw. 14 und 15)
18 or 17	Taxes on profit	18 bzw. 17	Steuern vom Einkommen und vom Ertrag
19 or 18	Other taxes	19 bzw. 18	Sonstige Steuern
20 or 19	Profit/loss for year (net sum of 14 and 17–19 or 13 and 16–18)	20 bzw. 19	Jahresüberschuß/Jahresfehlbetrag (Summe 14 und 17–19 bzw. 13 und 16–18)

Source: Ordelheide (1993: 265).
Notes:
[1]The reporting of this item is not required by law.
[2] *Of which* from affiliated enterprises.

categories (materials, wages, depreciation). They are similarly deducted from turnover. However, when production is higher than sales, the increase in stocks is shown under item 2 as revenue. A similar procedure is followed for self-produced fixed assets (item 3). Where there is a reduction in stocks, item 2 shows a cost. Under both methods, the operating profit is the same, but there is a difference in the breakdown.

Example 7.2 **Total cost method and cost of sales method**

Item	*Year 1*	*Year 2*
Total cost method		
Turnover	–	+ 150
Change in stocks	+ 100	– 100
Cost of materials	– 40	–
Wages	– 50	– 15
Depreciation	– 20	– 5
All other expenses and revenues	–	–
Annual profit	– 10	+ 30
Cost of sales method		
Turnover	–	+ 150
Production costs incurred to achieve the turnover	–	– 100
Selling expenses	–	– 10
General administrative expenses	– 10	– 10
All other expenses and revenues	–	–
Annual profit	– 10	+ 30

With the total cost method, the total first year's expenditure of 40+50+20=110 is shown. It is assumed that, of this 110, only 100 is included in the balance sheet value of stocks. This increase in stocks is shown in the first year as revenue; the corresponding reduction in the second year, as a cost. It is assumed that the wages and depreciation of the second year cannot be included in the balance sheet value of stocks. The difference between the two methods is particularly clear with the cost of sales method in the first year. Here the only costs shown are the general administrative expenses, which may not be included in the value of stocks. In the second year the production costs incurred to achieve the sales are then shown as costs. In this example they are identical in amount to the reduction in stocks shown in the total cost method.

Source: Adler *et al.* (1989), § 275 Tz. 31. (Tz.: Textziffer – text number).

The total costs method has the advantage, from the viewpoint of small enterprises, that it is not necessary to maintain cost accounts. This argument carries little weight with larger corporations and large enterprises as defined by the PublG, for which the format rules were in fact conceived. Their accounting systems would normally be sophisticated enough to include a cost accounting system. Moreover, in assessing the position, it should be noted that in Germany the completed contract method must be used for calculating the profit on long-term production (see section 5.7.4). Under the total costs method the item 'Change in stocks' gives an indication of profit potential if there is some idea of the enterprise's profit margin. Admittedly the change in stocks can also be derived from the balance sheet. By contrast, companies that have gone over to the cost of sales method stress that, with it, the details of the profit calculation for external and internal reporting purposes are harmonized.

The disadvantage of the current rules is that, within the same industry, some enterprises choose the total costs method and others the cost of sales method. For example, Daimler-Benz, up to 1992 used total cost and Volkswagen uses cost of sales. Admittedly, comparability at the level of total costs may be established using supplementary information. The cost of materials and of wages needs to be given in the notes if the profit and loss account is to be made up according to the cost of sales method. Furthermore, depreciation is shown in the schedule of fixed assets or in the notes. There is still the snag that the cost of sales method is usual at the international level and those enterprises which choose the total costs method are not obliged to give the supplementary information which would make an international comparison possible.

3.2.2 Other operating revenues and expenses

The items 'Other operating revenues' (*sonstige betriebliche Erträge*) and 'Other operating expenses' (*sonstige betriebliche Aufwendungen*) have the character of general accounts. They include all operating revenues and expenses for which a separate heading is not provided. In the financial statements of many enterprises these items are highly significant. It is unsatisfactory that there is no legal obligation to give any further explanation in the notes. Some enterprises do admittedly provide a further breakdown in the notes on a voluntary basis.

Included in 'other revenue' are, for example:

1. Book profits on the disposal of fixed assets.
2. Write-ups of fixed assets and other write-ups.
3. Revenue from payments received in respect of debts written off.
4. Decreases in global and individual provision for doubtful debts.
5. Book profits from the sale or redemption of investments or other current assets, unless they are included in turnover.
6. Profits from foreign exchange transactions.
7. Revenue from the release of all types of provision other than tax provisions.
8. Remission of debts, unless included under other headings.
9. Reimbursements of costs.
10. A levy to cover administrative expenses (in the case of groups).

11 Revenue from activities outside the organization's normal business activities, such as renting or leasing.
12 Proceeds from insurance claims.
13 Claims for damage.
14 Canteen takings.
15 Amounts received in respect of payments in kind.

Included among the other operating expenses would be:

1 Losses resulting from the disposal of tangible fixed assets and financial fixed assets.
2 Losses from the disposal of current assets.
3 Amounts written off to debtors (to the extent that they do not exceed the normal level).
4 Transfers to the special item with a reserve component.
5 Donations.
6 Damage paid for.
7 Foreign exchange losses.
8 Additions to guarantees and other provisions which are not directly chargeable to other cost headings.
9 Expenditure on damages and other legal costs in lawsuits.
10 The costs of the supervisory board and the general meeting.
11 Subsidies paid to the parent enterprise.

3.2.3 Prior-year revenues and expenses

For prior-year items (*periodenfremde Erträge und Aufwendungen*) separate disclosure is not required and is hardly ever made. Frequently such items are to be found in the other operating expenses and revenues. However, if material, their amount and nature must be commented upon in the notes (HGB § 277 (4)). Frequently there are explanations in the management report.

3.2.4 Extraordinary revenues and expenses

The headings extraordinary revenues and expenses (*außerordentliche Erträge und Aufwendungen*) are for transactions that arise outside the ordinary run of the business (HGB § 277 (4)). Items are considered to be beyond the ordinary activities of the business only when they are, at one and the same time:

1 Of an unusual character.
2 Not regularly recurring.
3 Material.

According to the prevailing view, prior year revenues and expenses as such are not normally to be treated as extraordinary items. The detailed definition is a controversial topic in professional circles. Hence it is difficult to give an authoritative list of the items that should be included here.

Possible items are gains and losses on the sale or closure of a plant or department, gains and losses from the sale of participations, gains and losses from the sale of the business's land, provided it constitutes a significant part of the long term operating assets of the business and is not being held for resale, redundancy payments on the closure of a department (but not compensation in the context of rationalization), subsidies from partners, one-off payments in connection with the opening up of a market, changes in the company's production base and suchlike costs, remission of loans and reconstruction costs, gains and losses arising from mergers.

However, allowing for the size of the enterprise, the amounts – even when they may be considerable in absolute terms – are not material in total; thus even these items are shown with the other operating revenues and expenses. A glance at published financial statements reveals that often no extraordinary revenues or expenses are reported at all (for 80 per cent of large corporations and 85 per cent of medium-sized corporations).

There is a reason for this in that the HGB § 277 (4), requires the headings 'Extraordinary revenues' and 'Extraordinary expenses' to be commented on in the notes as regards their amount and nature in so far as the reported amounts are material to an understanding of the results. Enterprises avoid having to give this sort of commentary by defining the content of these headings in a restrictive manner. This is made possible by helpful interpretations in the legal commentaries on HGB § 277 (4).

3.3 Appropriation accounts

The principal function of the financial statements is to facilitate the regulation of distributions. In principle the reported profit for the year after the deduction of any losses brought forward and after mandatory transfers to reserves (see section 6 below and Chapter 6, section 1.1) is distributable. The part that it is planned to be distributed is termed the *Bilanzgewinn* (profit for distribution), that is, the profit after the partial or complete appropriations. In addition to a profit and loss account, AGs must prepare an appropriation account (*Ergebnisverwendungsrechnung*; AktG § 158 (1)). This account leads from the profit (or loss) for the year (see Table 7.4, item 20 or 19) to the *Bilanzgewinn* (see Table 7.5).

If the *Bilanzgewinn* is negative it is termed the *Bilanzverlust.* In that event the enterprise is not allowed to pay a dividend, as it has no disposable profits, and must carry the loss forward to the following year.

If the profit for the year exceeds the *Bilanzgewinn* the accounts present the other appropriations of the profit, in particular the making good of any loss brought forward and the various transfers to reserves. Where the profit is lower, the *Bilanzgewinn* shows the additional sources of the proposed dividend, notably the profits brought forward and transfers from profit reserves.

It is permissible to present the profits brought forward and the profit for the year in the balance sheet (see Table 7.3, headings A.IV and V). The capital section of the balance sheet, and notably the reserves, then shows the values before the appropriation of the profit for the year. However, this approach is rarely found in practice. As a rule, the balance sheet is drawn up after a partial appropriation of the year's profits has been made by the managing board and the supervisory board. Instead of the two headings 'Profit (Loss) for the year' and 'Profit (Loss) brought forward', there is a heading for

Table 7.5 Appropriation of profit

	Profit (loss) for the year		Jahresüberschuß/Jahresfehlbetrag
±	Profit (loss) brought forward	±	Gewinn-/Verlustvortrag
+	Transfers from the capital reserve	+	Entnahmen aus der Kapitalrücklage
+	Transfers from profit reserves:	+	Entnahmen aus Gewinnrücklagen
	From the legal reserve From the reserve for own shares From the statutory reserves From other profit reserves		aus der gesetzlichen Rücklage aus der Rücklage für eigene Aktien aus satzungsmäßigen Rücklagen aus anderen Gewinnrücklagen
−	Transfers to profit reserves:	−	Einstellungen in Gewinnrücklagen
	To the legal reserve To the reserve for own shares To the statutory reserves To other profit reserves		in die gesetzliche Rücklage in die Rücklage für eigene Aktien in satzungsmäßige Rücklagen in andere Gewinnrücklagen
=	*Bilanzgewinn/Bilanzverlust*	=	Bilanzgewinn/Bilanzverlust

Bilanzgewinn (*Bilanzverlust*), in which the profit (loss) brought forward is included (see Table 7.3). The capital section, particularly the reserves, then presents the position after the partial appropriation of the profit of the year, i.e. notably after the transfers to reserves made by the enterprise's management. For the final and complete appropriation of the year's profit, the resolutions of all the enterprises's official bodies (*Organe*) must be taken into account, i.e. including those of the annual meeting. This is rarely reported, since at the time when the financial statements are being prepared in order to be put before the annual meeting, its decision on the appropriation of the balance of profits is not yet known.

4 RECOGNITION OF ASSETS AND LIABILITIES

In German accounting law an explicit distinction is drawn between the rules that regulate the recognition of assets and liabilities (*Bilanzansatzvorschriften*; HGB §§ 246 ff.) and those that regulate their valuation (*Bewertungsvorschriften*; HGB §§ 252 ff.). The first-mentioned rules govern whether the inclusion of an economic advantage or economic burden in the balance sheet is mandatory, optional or prohibited. The latter rules govern the value to be placed on the item.

4.1 Assets

4.1.1 *Vermögensgegenstand/Wirtschaftsgut*

Table 7.6 presents all the rules governing what may be included on the assets side of the balance sheet. The most important principle is that all *Vermögensgegenstände* (property objects) must be included (HGB § 246 (1)). This is interpreted as meaning that, apart from explicit exceptions, *only Vermögensgegenstände* can be included. The exceptions are the mandatory pre-paid expenses and the prohibitions and options listed in Table 7.6. If these are disregarded, the necessary condition for the recognition of an asset is that the economic advantage represents a *Vermögensgegenstand. Vermögensgegenstände* comprise, in the first place, physical objects (see Table 7.3, headings A.II and B.I on the assets side) and certain rights (headings A.I,1, A.III, B.II–IV). But legislation has not restricted *Vermögensgegenstände* to physical objects and rights, as can be seen from the subheading for intangible assets set out in the HGB § 266 (2), A.I.1: in addition to concessions, industrial rights, similar rights and licences in such rights are listed 'similar *values* and licences in such *values*'.

The exact boundary between what may be counted as a *Vermögensgegenstand* and what may not is, in general, difficult to define, because the term *Vermögensgegenstand* is not defined by law. In professional circles different criteria for drawing the line have been developed.

1 One group demands that a *Vermögensgegenstand* should be marketable separately; this gives a narrow demarcation. Independent marketability would require that the *Vermögensgegenstand* should be obtainable separately from a third party (*Einzelbeschaffbarkeit*) and that it could also be disposed of separately to a third party (*Einzelveräußerbarkeit*). The ability to acquire the item separately should not be confused with acquisition for valuable consideration (*entgeltlicher Erwerb*), which will be considered later. The ability to acquire means the actual possibility of acquisition and thus also covers items that, in fact, are not acquired separately, such as joint products.
2 However, it is generally accepted that the rule about separate disposal can be safely ignored, since there exist *Vermögensgegenstände*, which, although they may be acquired separately, cannot be disposed of separately, but which must be included in the balance sheet when consideration is given to the purpose of the financial statements. This applies to trade marks, which can be individually 'acquired' by

Table 7.6 Capitalization of assets

Required	**Forbidden**	**Optional**
For all businesses:	*For all businesses*:	*For all businesses*:
• All *Vermögensgegenstände* (unless forbidden or optional): HGB § 246 (1) • All pre-paid expenses (transitory assets): HGB §§ 246 (1) and 250 (1) sentence 1	• Prohibition of offset: HGB § 246 (2) • Expenditure on the transformation of the enterprise and on the issue of equity: HGB § 248 (1) • Intangible fixed assets that have not been acquired for consideration: HGB § 248 (2)	• Goodwill: HGB § 255 (4) sentence 1 • Record expenditure on – Customs and consumption taxes on stocks – Turnover tax on payments on account: HGB § 250 (1) sentence 2 • Redemption premium on loans: HGB § 250 (3)
		Additional for corporations:
		• 'Fusion' surplus: AktG § 348 (2) • Expenses for the start-up and expansion of the business: HGB § 269 • Deferred taxes (pre-paid): HGB § 274 (2)

> registration but, in German law, may be sold only when the firm, or that part of the firm to which they belong, is sold at the same time. The rule about separate disposal is replaced by the criterion of theoretical ability to dispose of the asset. Other authors insist instead that a *Vermögensgegenstand* must be tangible. This test goes back to the jurisprudence of what used to be the highest fiscal court, the *Reichsfinanzhof* (RFH). In the view of that court a *Vermögensgegenstand* is 'a good that, on the disposal of the whole firm, is, as it were, palpable, i.e. it is a separate item of some consequence or is something that will provide a future benefit for the firm, but does not dissolve into the generality, i.e. does not show itself only as an increase in the goodwill of the whole enterprise'.

Despite this divergence of opinion over detail, there is a clear general trend. The ability to show economic benefits as assets is substantially restricted in commercial law by the criterion that an asset must be a *Vermögensgegenstand*, whatever detailed gloss is put upon the term.

Tax law does not use the term *Vermögensgegenstand*; it speaks instead of *Wirtschaftsgut* (income producing asset). However, the definition of assets for tax purposes complies with the GoB of commercial law, so that the interpretation of the term *Wirtschaftsgut* follows that of *Vermögensgegenstand*. Given that the interpretation of *Vermögensgegenstand* is contentious, differences may arise in practice. Even today the Federal Fiscal Court (BFH) tends towards a broader interpretation, whereas the Auditors' Institute prefers a more prudent interpretation, in order to reduce the risks its members incur when they accept assets that do not maintain their value. This can also be in the interests of the enterprise. If a cautious definition of an asset is accepted by the tax authority auditors, it means that taxation of income can be shifted to future periods. There can be an advantage even when the tax auditors object to the practice. As long as the tax audits are carried out only at lengthy intervals, it always pays to be prudent, given the interest gained by putting off payment of the tax, which in Germany is not penalized by an interest surcharge.

With this background, it is understandable that enterprises have not pushed for the incorporation into German law of options in the EC Fourth Directive concerning the recognition of assets that are not *Vermögensgegenstände* (e.g. development costs). The consequent weakening of the criteria of a *Vermögensgegenstand* would carry the hidden risk that such items must also be capitalized for tax purposes.

4.1.2 Prohibition on the capitalization of self-produced intangible fixed assets

With the exceptions listed in Table 7.6, the criterion that there must be a *Vermögensgegenstand* is a necessary but not a sufficient condition for the recognition of an asset. There is a prohibition on including self-produced intangible fixed assets in the balance sheet even when they are *Vermögensgegenstände* (HGB § 248 (2)). By contrast there is an obligation to recognize as assets self-produced intangible current assets, e.g. software produced by a software producer.

The prohibition of capitalization is based on the grounds that the value is particularly difficult to check, on account of the accumulation of various risks. When the asset is not acquired for consideration, there is, first, no confirmation of the asset's value by the market at the time of its acquisition; if there is no regular market, there is no way of checking its value later. Second, on account of its intangibility, it is difficult to check whether and to what extent the asset still exists. Third, since it concerns fixed assets, the impact of misjudged capitalization would be felt over a long time.

The effects of the prohibition can be avoided in part by creative accounting techniques. For example, when the intangible asset is provided as a contribution in kind on the formation of a company, it appears in the balance sheet of the promoting company, admittedly not as such, but in the guise of a participation in the newly formed company. If the latter then sells intangible fixed assets to the parent undertaking, they are treated as acquired assets. Of more practical importance is the 'asset deal' within a group, by which one domestic subsidiary sells all its assets and liabilities to another group company, as a rule another domestic subsidiary. In the sale contract the intangible assets are specified separately as extensively as possible, so that the other subsidiary can capitalize them as acquired assets. When there is an 'interlocking relationship' (fiscal unit, *Organschaft* – see Chapter 5, section 2.7) the profit made by the subsidiary that sold the assets is remitted to the parent undertaking. The latter sets off the profit received by writing down the value of its participation in the subsidiary, which is permissible in German law on account of the fall in value of the subsidiary following the remittance of the profits. Since this write-down is also recognized for corporation tax purposes, the whole 'asset deal' is, to that extent, tax-neutral. The newly capitalized intangible assets can now be depreciated over their useful life and thus reduce both the reported profit and the taxable profit.

However, the availability of this technique does not mean that the ban on capitalizing intangible fixed assets is systematically circumvented by most enterprises. In particular the effectiveness of this technique for tax purposes depends on the fulfilment of a number of conditions (not specified here) which is not always easy to achieve. Furthermore, the 'asset deal' may have external effects on the relationship between the legal structure and the management structure of the group, with disadvantages that can outweigh the taxation advantages.

4.1.3 Leasing

In German accounting law it is a basic principle that, in cases of dispute, it is the economic ownership and not the legal ownership that is conclusive for the balance sheet. However, given its imprecision, the principle is flexible, which has led to controversy, particularly in the case of leasing contracts. Depending on the form of the contract, leasing contracts range from those that are similar to purchase by instalments to those that are pure hiring. Financial leasing is particularly widespread: a lessor acquires capital goods and hands them over to the lessee to use for a fixed irrevocable term. The term is normally shorter than the expected business life of the asset but longer than fifty per cent of its life for tax purposes, given in the AfA tables (see section 5.3). The instalments paid over the period of the contract cover the lessor's acquisition cost, his interest and other costs, plus an addition for profit.

According to the IdW main technical committee's opinion of 1/1989, with such a contract the economic ownership of the goods passes to the lessee and thus the leased asset must be shown in the lessee's balance sheet. However, this view has not prevailed in practice. In financial statements it is much more common to use the tax accounting rules which are summarized in the following decrees of the Federal Ministry of Finance:

19 April 1971, *Leasing movable property*, BStBl I, 1971, pp. 264–6.
21 March 1972, *Leasing real property (full amortization contracts)*, BStBl I, 1972, pp. 188–9.
22 December 1975, *Partial amortization*, BB, 1976, pp. 72–3.
23 December 1991, *Leasing real property (partial amortization contracts)*, BStBl I, 1992, pp. 13–15.

Figure 7.1 gives a simplified overview, based on these decrees, of the interaction of the various criteria in determining whether the asset should be shown in the lessor's or the lessee's balance sheet. The criteria are not dissimilar to those of IAS 17, *Accounting for Leases*. However, the overall effect of the criteria is that, as a general rule, leased assets are shown in the lessor's balance sheet. But the lessee is obliged to furnish, in the notes to the accounts, information on commitments that do not appear in the balance sheet (HGB § 285, No. 3), which include commitments under leasing contracts.

4.1.4 Start-up expenses and goodwill

In the cases listed in Table 7.6 the law offers the option of capitalization, even though the items in question are not *Vermögensgegenstände*. The options relating to customs duties and consumption taxes and for turnover tax on payments on account are dealt with under pre-paid expenses (section 4.1.5 below); for deferred taxes (pre-paid) see section 7.

Expenditure on the start-up and expansion of the business (HGB § 269). Expenditure relating to the start-up and expansion of the business, but which may not be capitalized as *Vermögensgegenstände* (e.g. organization and planning costs), may be capitalized as a separate item. In the years following the investment they must be depreciated at a rate of at least 25 per cent per annum. The distribution of otherwise distributable reserves is blocked, to the amount of the capitalized asset, to ensure that the possibility of capitalization does not lead to an increase in creditors' risk. The capitalization in the financial statements has no effect on the tax computation, because otherwise the accounting convenience (*Bilanzierungshilfe*) introduced by this new rule would be partly lost. Nevertheless, this option is hardly ever used, because, according to some enterprises, the capitalization of such expenses would be interpreted as a signal of financial distress.

Goodwill (HGB § 255 (4)) and fusion surplus. Goodwill may be included in the balance sheet as the difference between the consideration paid on the acquisition of an enterprise and the value, at the date of acquisition, of the individual assets (*Vermögensgegenstände*) less the liabilities. That means that the equity which has to be set off is based on the current values of assets and liabilities. In addition, an 'acquisition' must have taken place. What is to be understood by 'acquisition' in this context can be derived only indirectly. The acquisition of shares in a corporation or a partnership is not considered an 'acquisition' for the purposes of the HGB § 255 (4), even when all the

Figure 7.1 Treatment of lease contracts in the financial statements

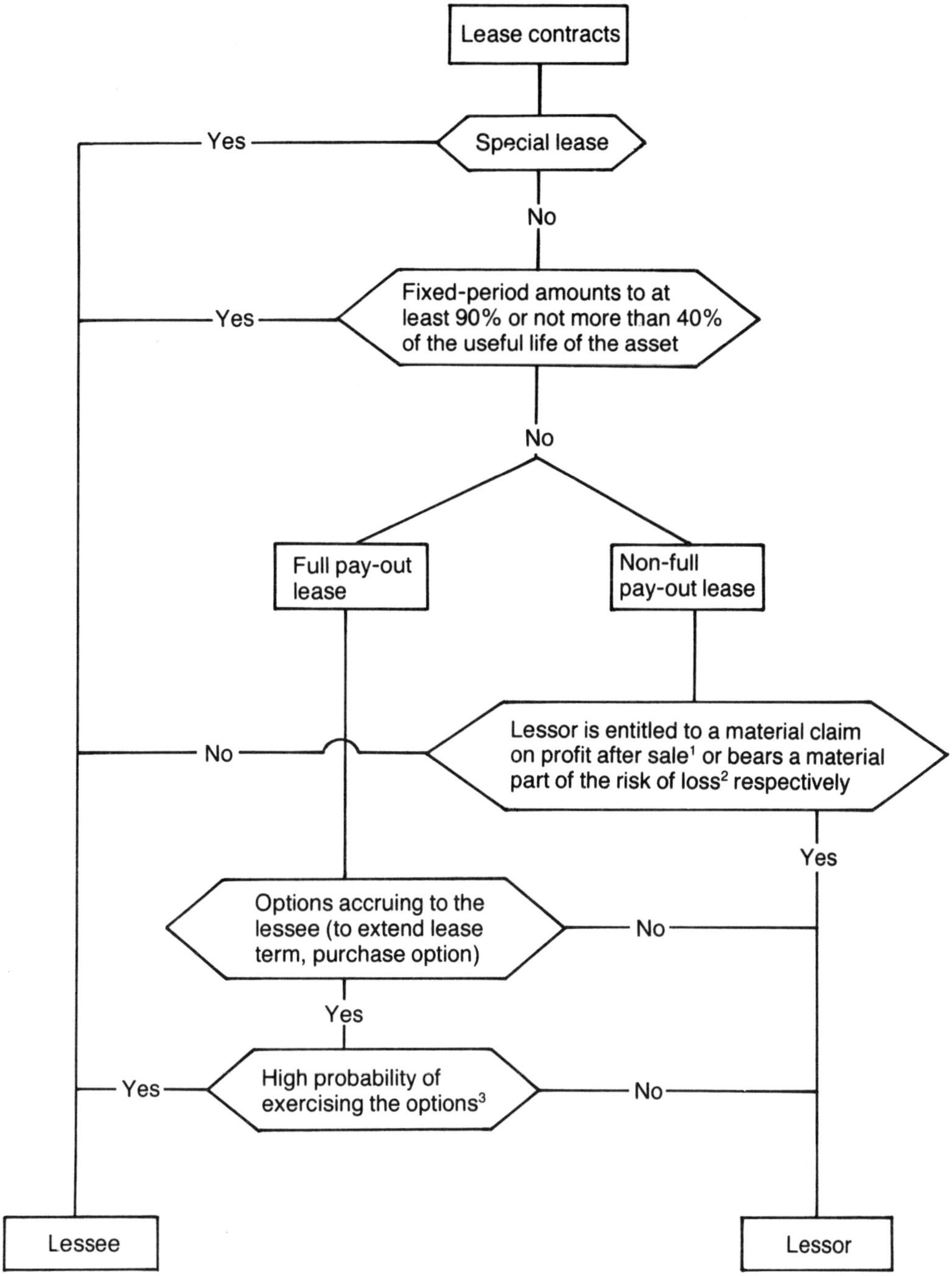

Source: Glasel (1991), slightly amended.

Notes:
[1] By virtue of tender rights or share of profit after sale.
[2] By virtue of options accruing to the lessee.
[3] i.e. The value of the option right is substantially lower than the market value.

shares are acquired. These shares are to be shown in the balance sheet of the acquiring company at acquisition cost and not at equity. Since the acquisition cost includes the value of goodwill, it is not permissible to show the latter separately. Also, for the same reason, there is no systematic depreciation of the goodwill. Furthermore, 'fusions' (legal mergers) of corporations, in which one or both corporations give up their legal identity, are not acquisitions for the purpose of the HGB § 255 (4). There are special rules for these, which are dealt with later. Finally, the capitalization of self-produced goodwill is ruled out (HGB § 248 (2); see section 4.1.2 above). Thus the reporting of goodwill in the balance sheet of the individual company under HGB § 255 (4) is limited to rare cases, such as:

1 The acquisition of a sole proprietorship, part of a business or a partnership, which is liquidated at the same time.
2 The acquisition of a corporation and the simultaneous liquidation of the corporation, in which less than 90 per cent of the consideration consists of newly issued shares of the acquiring company (see below).

Accordingly, only three out of 100 large corporations surveyed in 1988 (Treuarbeit 1990: 41) and five out of 150 medium-size companies (Ballwieser and Häger 1991: 72) reported a value for goodwill in their individual accounts.

When the acquired corporation 'fuses' with the acquiring corporation (legal merger), the acquired corporation loses its legal identity. The acquiring corporation includes in its balance sheet the individual assets and liabilities of the acquired corporation and the excess of the consideration over these values as 'fusion surplus'. There are special rules concerning the fusion surplus. When AGs and KGaAs fuse, the assets of the transferor are carried into the fused balance sheet of the transferee at their book value in the closing balance sheet of the transferor, so that the fusion surplus includes, in addition to the goodwill in the sense of HGB § 255 (4), the difference between the book values and the current values of the acquired assets and liabilities and, in appropriate cases, the full value of self-produced assets that were not included in the balance sheet (AktG § 348 (2)). A condition, among others, is that at least 90 per cent of the consideration consists of newly issued shares of the acquiring corporation. There are similar rules for the fusion of GmbHs (KapErhG § 27 (2)). The fusion surplus is reported in the balance sheet as goodwill and is treated as such.

When it is permissible to show goodwill as an asset, this is still only an option. If goodwill is not capitalized, its value is not shown as an acquisition in the schedule of fixed assets. Then this part of the enterprise's gross investment is not apparent. The full value of goodwill is charged against profits. This applies to all items capable of being reported as goodwill in the individual accounts and also to the fusion surplus. In the individual accounts, goodwill must not be charged directly against equity.

If the goodwill is capitalized it must be depreciated by at least a quarter in each of the years following the investment (method 1); but it is also possible to write goodwill off over the period during which the firm derives benefits (method 2), in which case there has to be a justification in the notes. This second possibility was made available to enterprises to facilitate compatibility with the tax rules. Under tax law the capitalization of goodwill in the sense of HGB § 255 (4) is mandatory and it must be written off on a straight-line basis over exactly fifteen years. Frequently this period is used in financial statements too. Where an exceptional fall in value can be proved, the tax rules require exceptional depreciation, called *Teilwertabschreibung.*

For group accounts the rules are different:

1 Goodwill that may not be capitalized in the balance sheet of the individual enterprise because it is part of the acquisition cost of the participation can be reported in the consolidated balance sheet when the participation is fully or proportionally consolidated or is valued using the equity method. This goodwill may be charged directly against the equity, or alternatively accounted for by the methods used in the individual accounts (see Chapter 8, sections 7 and 12).

2 For goodwill or a fusion surplus that already exists in the accounts of one of the individual enterprises either as an asset or as a direct charge against profits, the choice of capitalization or expensing can be made anew for the consolidated accounts. However, the rules that govern the accounts of the individual company must be followed; i.e. the direct charge against equity is not permissible in the consolidated accounts, either.

4.1.5 Pre-paid expenses and deferred income

Under this heading a distinction is drawn between transitory items and anticipated items. A transitory item arises when a cash transaction of the past year is to be treated as revenue or as an expense of a future period. In commercial law, *pre-paid expenses* may be included in the balance sheet only if they relate to a defined period after the balance sheet date – for example, rents paid in advance by enterprises for the first three months of the coming year (HGB § 250). Similarly, deferred income refers to receipts that represent revenue relating to a certain period after the balance sheet date (e.g. rents received in advance).

Anticipated items, the payment or receipts for which lie in the future but which are an expense or revenue of the past year, may not be reported under this heading but are shown as debtors or creditors, when they meet the conditions for recognition as such.

Under German law, liabilities are normally valued at the amount required to redeem them. If this exceeds the amount received on issue, the difference (the *redemption premium* or capitalized discount) may be shown as a deferred item. In the case of capitalization it should be written off over the term of the liability. If the redemption premium is not capitalized, it is charged in full against the first year's profit.

In addition, under the HGB § 250 (1) there is an option to capitalize as pre-paid expenses:

1 Customs duties and consumption taxes (e.g. the duty on beer; mineral oil taxes) to the extent that they relate to stocks on hand at the balance sheet date.

2 Turnover tax relating to payments on account at the balance sheet date either disclosed as liabilities or deducted from stocks.

These special rules can be explained by the relationship between the financial statements and the tax computation. Traditionally under tax law (EStG § 5 (4), second sentence, Nos 1–2) there has been an obligation to capitalize these payments as pre-paid expenses. Under HGB § 250 (1) they may now also be capitalized in the financial statements.

4.1.6 *Bilanzierungshilfe* (accounting convenience)

Bilanzierungshilfe is a concept which has become popular, especially since the introduction of the new accounting law. In its broad sense it embraces all legal options concerning the format, the recognition of assets and provisions, and the valuation. But normally it is used in a narrower sense for those options concerning the recognition of assets and the valuation which are not tax-relevant. This includes capitalization of start-up expenses, positive deferred taxes and interest payments which are made part of the capitalized production costs. A more flexible tax law would make the *Bilanzierungshilfe* a general concept, giving more asset-relevant information in companies' accounts. One way would be to allow the capitalization of self-produced intangible fixed assets as a *Bilanzierungshilfe*, which would not be taxed. The distribution of the additional profit would be prohibited by the obligation to create a special reserve. But such flexibility, despite being desirable, is not under discussion at present.

4.2 Liabilities and provisions

4.2.1 Basics

The law refers to obligations (*Schulden*), liabilities (*Verbindlichkeiten*) and provisions (*Rückstellungen*). In the HGB the term '*Schulden*' is used as a comprehensive term for liabilities and provisions. In accounting, liabilities are obligations, as a rule involving payment to third parties. Provisions, in so far as they have the character of liabilities, are distinguished from debts in that the legal existence and/or the amount of the liability is still uncertain. When the only uncertainty concerns the date at which the obligation has to be met, the commitment is generally reported as a liability.

According to the completeness principle of HGB § 246, all 'obligations' must be included in the accounts unless there is a contrary prohibition or option in the law. There are prohibitions and options relating to provisions, but none for liabilities.

The extent to which provisions may be included in the balance sheet has been a matter of controversy for decades. In this debate the 'static balance sheet' school (*statische Bilanzlehre*) are ranged against the 'dynamic balance sheet' school (*dynamische Bilanzlehre*). For the static school, the purpose of provisions is to ensure that all liabilities are reported, not excluding those where there is uncertainty concerning their existence and/or amount. According to the dynamic school, provisions refer additionally to deferred expenditure which has already arisen in the past period but the disbursement of which will occur only in a future period. Future outlays which have their economic origin in the past period should, in this way, be charged to the past period. Consequently the static school advocate only provisions which have the character of liabilities to third parties, whereas the dynamic school consider that, in addition, it is necessary to have provisions of an expense character (see section 4.2.3 below).

With each successive reform of the law there has been a stronger trend towards the dynamic view. Whilst the AktG of 1937 still stressed the liability character of provisions, the AktG of 1965 specifically permitted provisions for deferred maintenance and for land clearance. Under the latest Act these provisions have become mandatory (subject to certain qualifications) and options were created for further provisions for expenses.

Table 7.7 presents a summary of the types of provisions listed in the HGB § 249. The only other provision referred to in the law is provision for deferred taxation (HGB § 274). This is dealt with separately below (section 7). Where provisions are either mandatory or prohibited in the financial statements, the same rule is followed in the tax computation. However, if a provision is optional in commercial law, it is usually forbidden under tax law.

4.2.2 Provisions for uncertain liabilities and for anticipated losses on uncompleted transactions

Provisions for uncertain liabilities (*Rückstellungen für ungewisse Verbindlichkeiten*) and for losses on transactions not yet complete (*Rückstellungen für drohende Verluste aus schwebenden Geschäften*) are distinguished from provisions for expenses by the requirement that there has to be a liability towards a third party. With provisions for expenses the liability is more in the nature of an obligation of the enterprise towards itself. The obligation need not be actionable in the legal sense. It is sufficient for there to be a moral obligation or an obligation that a businessman would normally accept on considerations of profitability, for example the *Kulanzrückstellung* (the provision for liberal settlements of customers' complaints). Also included are obligations under public law, such as, for example, provisions based on the Environmental Protection Act.

A further condition for the creation of a provision is that, at the balance sheet date, the business event that gives rise to the obligation should already have occurred. Take, for example, the provision for liberal settlements of customers' complaints. It is sufficient that the goods have been delivered; it is not necessary for specific cases of damaged goods to have been notified. By contrast, a football club whose balance sheet date is 31 December cannot create a provision for the bonuses that would be payable to players if it won the championship, since a substantial part of the effort, and the event itself that gives

Table 7.7 Provisions according to HGB § 249

Provision	*Character*	*Financial statements*	*Tax computations*
Uncertain liabilities	Liability	Compulsory	Compulsory
Guarantees with no contractual commitment	Liability	Compulsory	Compulsory
Anticipated losses on uncompleted transactions	Liability	Compulsory	Compulsory
Deferred maintenance:			
Within next three months	Expense	Compulsory	Compulsory
Within next twelve months	Expense	Optional	Forbidden
Land clearance expenditure within next twelve months	Expense	Compulsory	Compulsory
Other expenses under § 249 (2)	Expense	Optional	Forbidden

rise to the obligation, still lie in the future. On the question of the business causation, there are endless legal wrangles in the tax courts, which are also of relevance to the financial statements, given the parallels between tax law and commercial law.

Finally, there is a requirement that there should be uncertainty concerning the existence and/or the amount of the liability. However, the liability must be sufficiently contingent for a reputable businessman to be likely to rate it as a commitment in assessing the net worth of his business. In principle the exposure on each individual commitment should be assessed separately. However, an assessment on the basis of average risk is permitted for mass transactions.

Provisions for losses on incomplete transactions can be seen as a special case of provisions for uncertain liabilities. They have to be set up for the excess, at the balance sheet date, of the commitment arising from an incomplete transaction over the value receivable.

Since provisions for liabilities are also deductible for tax purposes, enterprises and their advisers are particularly alert to opportunities for setting up such provisions. This is made clear by the major part that provisions represent of enterprises' finance (see Chapter 3, section 1). However, the influence of taxation is not the only reason for the high level of provisions. In Germany, by comparison with other countries, legislation on social and environmental protection is quite strict; this changes the enterprise's risk situation and necessitates the creation of provisions for uncertain liabilities higher than in countries with a more relaxed regime. Moreover the tax-deductibility of such provisions represents a hidden partial financing by the state (through lower tax receipts) of the environmental and social policy measures. The following paragraphs give a brief indication of the range of provisions to be found in Germany.

4.2.2.1 Provisions arising from employment relationships

Provisions for pensions (*Pensionsrückstellungen*) and similar commitments are based, above all, on a direct commitment by the enterprise to grant a benefit (pension) in the event of invalidity, death or old age. The risks (to the pensioner) are reduced by a form of insurance model of the business community, known as the *Pensionssicherungsverein* (Pension Guaranty Association), which takes over the pension commitment when the enterprise can no longer keep it up. In the case of such *commitments to direct support* entered into after 31 December 1986 a provision for pensions must be set up. There is an option allowing a provision to be set up in respect of commitments entered into before that date, or to expand an existing one. Pension provisions are calculated on an actuarial basis, with a choice of methods in calculating the present value of the liability. Transfers to these provisions are tax-deductible. However, the interest rate applied must not be under 6 per cent (EStG § 6a). Tax-deductibility and simultaneous retention for self-financing make the direct pension the most important form of contractual pension.

For *indirect arrangements, through a pension fund* (*Pensionskasse*), a provident fund or an insurance company there is no necessity to set up a provision straight away. The contributions the enterprise makes to the fund or company are treated as expenses in both the financial statements and the tax computation. However, if the pension fund or insurance company has insufficient assets to meet its commitments, then, in law, under certain circumstances the pensioner has a direct claim against the supporting enterprise. Where these obligations are imminent (e.g. following a sharp fall in the market value of the fund's investments) the parent undertaking is allowed to set up a provision under article 28 of the HGB Implementation Act. The reason why this provision is optional and not mandatory is essentially fiscal. The introduction under the new law of a mandatory provision for direct pension engagements led to a fall in tax revenue so great that the government did not want the additional budgetary burden that would have arisen from mandatory provision for indirect pension commitments. Given the authoritativeness principle, a mandatory provision would have had to be recognized for tax purposes. According to the invariable jurisprudence of the highest tax court (the BFH), a provision that is optional in the financial statements is to be disregarded for tax purposes.

Besides these, there are other provisions arising from an employment relationship that should be set up, for example for:

1 Benefits that the enterprise provides to compensate or ease the economic disadvantages suffered by its employees on the closure, relocation or merger of plants (*Sozialplanrückstellungen*, benefits from social plans).
2 Claims by employees for holidays outstanding at the balance sheet date.
3 Earnings protection when an employer, either under a collective agreement or under an individual contract, has an obligation to pay an employee at his previous salary level when he is moved to a lower-paid job (on age grounds, for example).
4 The proportional part of the Christmas bonus in enterprises with a year end other than 31 December.
5 Bonuses and gifts granted to employees on the occasion of a particular anniversary (e.g. a sixtieth birthday or thirty years' service (*Jubiläumsrückstellungen*)). The tax concessions in this field were greatly reduced in 1990.

4.2.2.2 Provisions relating to deliveries and services

Mandatory provisions can also arise in relation to deliveries and services, for example in respect of:

1 A claim for the compensation to which a sales representative is legally entitled after his departure if the enterprise subsequently derives substantial benefit from the business connections that the salesman has built up.
2 Liability for goods and services received before the balance sheet date which have yet to be invoiced.
3 Bonuses and rebates incurred in the past year which will be paid only in the coming year.
4 Commitments under warranties and guarantees, particularly in respect of product liability (*Produkthaftungsrückstellungen*).
5 Potential losses under forward contracts and options relating to foreign currency.
6 Risks arising from swap contracts, such as the obligation to make good the excess in a currency swap or the difference in an interest-rate swap.
7 The probable liability arising from the endorsement of a bill of exchange.

4.2.2.3 Provisions concerning continuous obligations

Provisions must be set up for impending costs under covenants, for example for:

1 Payments on reversionary commitments that exceed the depreciation on the property. A reversionary commitment is an obligation to transfer property to a third party, partly or wholly without compensation.
2 Renovation obligations under a lease.
3 Potential losses that would have to be borne by the lessor when an item is subsequently disposed of.
4 Potential losses under contracts entered into by the business.

4.2.2.4 Other reasons for provisions

There are numerous other occasions when provisions must be set up, for example for:

1 Demolition costs.
2 Debtor warrants.
3 Acceptance of guarantees.
4 Liability to third parties.
5 The cost of preparing the financial statements.
6 The infringement of patents or other rights.
7 The cost of lawsuits.
8 Land clearance commitments under public law.
9 Liability for mining subsidence.
10 Risks arising from the tax audit.
11 Fines (e.g. for infringement of the anti-trust or environmental regulations).

4.2.3 Provisions for expenses

The range of provisions has been further extended by HGB § 249 (2). The possibility of providing for expenses did not exist under the old law; it came about through the Fourth Directive. Under it, provisions can also be set up when goods are to be expended in a future period, exclusively and necessarily for internal business purposes, for a reason which goes back to a past period (*Aufwandsrückstellungen*). Instead of an obligation towards third parties there is, rather, an obligation of the business to itself. Such provisions are in principle optional. Hence they do not affect the tax computation.

There are two exceptions, when the provisions are mandatory:

1 For repairs and maintenance not undertaken in the past year but which are made good in the first three months of the following year.
2 For land clearance not undertaken in the past year but made good the following year.

These provisions, which are traditionally tax-deductible, remain mandatory. Had they been made optional in the financial statements they would no longer have been tax-deductible.

The preconditions to setting up the optional provisions for expenses are that:

1 The nature of the expenses is precisely defined.
2 The expenses are to be charged to the past year or to an earlier year.
3 At the balance sheet date it is as good as certain that the disbursement will be made.
4 There is uncertainty as to the amount or the date of the future disbursement.

Provisions for repairs and maintenance to be made good within three to twelve months of the balance sheet date may be set up regardless of these conditions (HGB § 249 (1), third sentence).

Examples of optional provisions for expenses are for:

1 The cost of major repairs to machines or buildings.
2 The cost of demolition or dismantling of buildings or production facilities.
3 The cost of security inspections and overhauls (e.g. of ships and aircraft).
4 The voluntary audit of the financial statements.

It is generally accepted that provisions may not be set up under HGB § 249 (2) for future selling and distribution expenses or for research and development activities. Nevertheless there is a danger that this regulation and the corresponding text of the Fourth Directive are so wide that there will be a blurring of the boundary between provisions and reserves, between charges against profit and appropriations of profit.

5 VALUATION RULES

5.1 Basic valuation principles

5.1.1 General

German accounting law, both for financial reporting and for tax purposes, is based on historical cost. Favourable experience with this system of valuation has discouraged the authorities from making use of the possibilities offered by article 33 of the Fourth Directive. Inflation accounting methods, which German researchers such as Mahlberg, Schmalenbach and Schmidt played such a major role in developing in the first decades of this century, may not be used in the financial statements. At best they would be permitted as voluntary additional calculations in the notes (see the corresponding recommendation of the IdW's main technical committee, HFA 2/1975). In practice, however, this is rare.

The regular valuation principles are brought together in HGB § 252 (1) (see also Table 7.2). The essential principle is the prudence principle (HGB § 252 (1), No. 4). It is made concrete through the acquisition cost principle, the principle of the lower of cost and market value and the realization principle, among others. In addition the following complementary and supporting principles should be noted:

1 The principle of balance sheet continuity (HGB § 252 (1), No. 1).
2 The 'going concern' principle (HGB § 252 (1), No. 2).
3 The principle of item-by-item valuation (HGB § 252 (1), No. 3).
4 The accrual principle (HGB § 252 (1), No. 5).
5 The consistency principle (HGB § 252 (1), No. 6).

Deviations from these principles are permitted only in justified exceptional circumstances. According to the usual understanding of the law, exceptions should be for specific cases in the accounts of individual enterprises and not for all enterprises nor for types of enterprises, such as corporations. It would not, therefore, be permissible to justify as an exception (and with reference to the 'true and fair view' principle; HGB § 264 (2)) the translation of foreign currency debtors and creditors at the current exchange rate, as some other countries propose (but see section 5.1.5 below on the consistency principle).

Given the clear distinction in the HGB between those regulations which concern the recognition of assets and liabilities and those relating to valuation, it is generally agreed that the principles outlined above do not apply to matters of content. Thus a change in recognition (e.g. by the capitalization of goodwill or the setting up of provisions for expenses) does not infringe the consistency principle.

5.1.2 The historical cost principle

The value to be placed on assets must on no account exceed the acquisition cost or the production cost – for depreciable fixed assets, the acquisition cost or production cost less systematic depreciation (known as the extrapolated acquisition cost or production cost): *Anschaffungskostenprinzip* – HGB § 253 (1), first sentence. This rule applies to tax as well. The acquisition cost or production cost forms the upper limit even when the value at the balance sheet date is manifestly higher and can be objectively and economically established with reference to the market price.

5.1.3 The principle of lower value

The acquisition cost or production cost, reduced as necessary by systematic depreciation, must or may be written down to the lower current value (*Niederstwertprinzip*). Such lower values are based partly on the GoB of the Commercial Code (see section 5.4 below) and partly on the values accepted for tax purposes, which are incorporated into the financial statements on the basis of the reverse authoritativeness principle (see section 5.5).

5.1.4 The realization principle

The realization principle (*Realisationsprinzip*) determines the events on which the realization of profit depends. Thus it marks the boundary between the historical cost principle and the principle of lower value. According to German understanding, the monetary claim that the enterprise has received in exchange for its endeavours must be basically free of risks relating to acquisition, production and sale. The remaining risks such as those concerning non-payment or warranties must be taken into account by writing down the value of the delinquent receivables or by setting up provisions. In concrete terms, for the realization of profit the following basic principles apply:

1 *Sale of the asset.* A profit is considered to have been realized, and hence can be

reported in the financial statements, when the asset has been delivered or constitutive possession has been agreed, the claim for payment has arisen and the price risk has been passed to the purchaser. Exceptions to these rules are permitted only when earlier recognition of profit does not lead to additional risks for the admission of the profit included in the monetary claim (see section 5.7.2 below on foreign currency translation and section 5.7.4 on long-term production).

2 *Sales on sale-or-return terms.* The point of realization is when the right to return the goods, or the time limit for returning them, has expired.
3 *Performance of contracts for the supply of services or work.* The relevant point of time is when the services or the work have been performed and the claim for recompense has arisen.
4 *Interest on fixed-interest securities and receivables.* Here there is a softening of the strict realization principle in that, independently of the due date, the proportional amount of revenue is treated as realized.
5 *Participation in the profits of enterprises.* When the investment is in a commercial partnership, the share of the profits is to be taken into account at the end of the accounting period (HFA/IdW statement 3/1976, p. 591). Dividends from corporations are normally considered to be realized at the time of the dividend resolution. Exceptionally, in the case of a parent undertaking, dividends can be treated as realized when the financial statements are adopted if a resolution for the distribution of the profits has been proposed, the parent undertaking, through its majority shareholding, can assure its adoption at the general meeting, and the parent undertaking's balance sheet date does not precede that of the subsidiary.

5.1.5 Other valuation principles

The principles that have been described above are supplemented and supported by further principles:

The principle of balance sheet continuity (Grundsatz der Bilanzkontinuität). The closing balance sheet of the previous period must be identical with the opening balance sheet of the following period.

The 'going concern' principle (Grundsatz der Unternehmensfortführung). The continuation of the enterprise is to be assumed unless refuted by law or by the actual circumstances. There is considerable debate about the circumstances in which this principle should not apply.

The principle of item-by-item valuation (Grundsatz der Einzelbewertung). The purpose of this principle is to prevent the offsetting of assets and liabilities, of expenses and revenues. First this assures more differentiated information. Second, and more important, in conjunction with the prudence principle, it prevents unrealized profits (which in principle should not be recognized) being offset against unrealized losses (which in principle should be recognized).

On grounds of simplification, partial exceptions to the principle of item-by-item valuation are permitted, for example:

1 Group or collective valuation.

2 Fixed valuation.
3 Average valuation or valuation by means of a usage monitoring function.
4 Limited netting in foreign currency translation.

The accrual principle (Verursachungsprinzip). Superficially this principle states the obvious, that the profit and loss account is a record not of receipts and payments but of revenues and expenses. However, in addition, there is an obligation to charge expenses as far as possible against the revenues that they occasion. This principle runs counter to the prudence principle. For example, development costs are occasioned by future production and accordingly should be capitalized and only later charged as expenses. In the other member states of the European Community the accruals principle is given greater weight relative to the prudence principle than is the case in Germany or some other countries such as Switzerland and Austria. In these countries it is subordinate to the prudence principle.

The consistency principle (Stetigkeitsgrundsatz). The valuation methods used in the previous year's financial statements should be retained. The old law did not require consistency in valuation methods. Nevertheless any changes and any significant effects on the results had to be reported in the notes. In the process of incorporating article 31.1.b of the Fourth Directive into German law an attempt was made to weaken this provision by a soft transformation (making it an enabling provision). But the formulation chosen for HGB § 252 (1), No. 6, 'the valuation methods ... should be retained', is generally interpreted as '... must be retained'.

Nevertheless in professional circles the consistency principle has been weakened by a helpful interpretation of the phrase 'valuation method'. A distinction is drawn between, for example, the valuation method for pension provisions and the mathematical parameters used in implementing the method (for example, the rate of interest). Consequently a change in the rate of interest is not a breach of the consistency requirement.

The consistency principle has been undermined further by the tendency to interpret far too liberally the permission to disregard the principle in exceptional circumstances. The following exceptions have been identified:

1 When the enterprise joins a group.
2 To achieve a valuation that is advantageous from a tax point of view.
3 Following a change in the interpretation of the law.
4 A change in the organization of the costing system.
5 A significant change in the utilization of capacity.
6 A significant change in the level of activity in the sector.

Particularly with the last two exceptions there is a danger of allowing what the consistency principle was intended to forbid. As long as accredited auditors go along with these exceptions – and such appears to be the case – it is difficult to prevent changes in valuation methods being used to manipulate asset values in line with the profitability or otherwise of the business.

5.2 Acquisition cost and production cost

According to the HGB § 255 (1), *acquisition costs* (*Anschaffungskosten*) are expenses incurred:

1 To acquire an asset (criterion of purpose).
2 To get it into a usable condition.
3 To the extent that they can be allocated directly to the specific asset (criterion of direct allocation).

They are made up of the following components:

Purchase price
\+ incidental costs of acquisition
\+ subsequent acquisition costs
− reductions in the acquisition costs (e.g. bonuses, rebates, discounts)
= acquisition costs.

There has been a wide-ranging and varied discussion on the detailed definition of the criteria (purpose, usable condition and direct allocation) and of the different components of acquisition costs. Conventions have been developed that ease the task of the enterprise's accountant in real situations. The conventions on the reporting of acquisition cost deals with the following practical situations:

1 The treatment of value-added tax.
2 What to do when the purchase price is excessive.
3 The purchase price when the asset is purchased from group enterprises or shareholders.
4 The purchase price in foreign currency (down-payments, purchases for cash, purchases on credit, purchases on credit with discounting the liability, purchases on credit with hedging).
5 The consideration of respites and payment by instalments.
6 Price under a purchase by means of annuity payments.
7 The consideration of escalator clauses (indexation clauses).
8 The consideration of the obligations given in consideration.
9 The inclusion of grants, subsidies and similar allowances (see section 5.7.3).
10 The purchase price of buy options.
11 The value when assets are exchanged.
12 The value when assets are acquired for no consideration.
13 The ascertainment of the individual purchase price by division of the total price.

The treatment of each individual case is governed by the principle that the acquisition must be profit-neutral (it neither increases nor decreases reported profits). This is achieved by valuing the acquired asset at acquisition cost. Profit neutrality means also neutrality at the level of the net assets. The acquisition of the asset occasions a fall in the value of the assets which is compensated by booking the acquired asset at a value that corresponds exactly to the reduction in the value of the other assets. For the calculation of profit, the acquisition must result in neither a profit nor a loss.

Self-produced assets are to be valued at *production cost* (*Herstellungskosten*). In

Table 7.8 Components of production cost according to the *Handelsgesetzbuch* (HGB) and *Einkommensteuerrichtlinien* (EStR)

HGB § 255 (2)	*Item*	*EStR section 33*
Compulsory	Direct material costs Direct manufacturing costs Direct special manufacturing costs Fictitious indirect material and manufacturing costs[1]	Compulsory
Optional	The appropriate portion, relating to the production period, of: • Necessary material overheads • Necessary manufacturing overheads • Depreciation of fixed assets, to the extent that it results from the production process	Compulsory
Optional	Costs of general administration Expenditure on social amenities, on voluntary staff benefits and on pensions Chargeable interest on loan capital relating to the period of production of an asset	Optional
Forbidden	Material and manufacturing overhead costs that: • Are inappropriate or • Are unnecessary or • Do not result from the production process Depreciation of fixed asset that: • Is not appropriate • Does not result from the production process Interest on loan capital that: • Is not chargeable • Does not relate to the period of production Selling expenses	Forbidden

Note: [1]Costs that are directly attributable but for which in fact no direct allocation is made, mainly for reasons of economy.

contrast to the position with acquisition cost, in the case of production cost enterprises have a choice between an upper and a lower limit (HGB § 255 (2)). The components of the upper and lower limits are shown in Table 7.8:

1 Certain administrative and staff costs may be capitalized. Selling expenses may not be included. This is generally held to apply also to direct selling costs.
2 The lower limit is set, in commercial law, by the expenses that can be allocated directly to the produced item, the direct costs. In practical terms this is the same as saying that, in law, the variable costs at least must be charged.

Because of the change in the commercial law rules introduced by the recent Act, there is a dispute over the lower limit of production cost for tax purposes. Table 7.8 gives the old rule, which is still being applied by the tax authorities. Certain overheads in respect of materials, and manufacturing overheads, whose capitalization is optional in commercial law, must be included for tax purposes.

In their financial statements enterprises as a rule use the lowest figure permitted for tax purposes. Given the authoritativeness principle, any higher figure would also have to be used in the tax computation, with unwelcome consequences. (Taxable profits would be brought forward in time.) On the other hand a further reduction to the even lower limit permitted by commercial law would be possible and would have no tax effects. But it is rarely done; on account of the consistency principle it is difficult to change the valuation methods when business conditions deteriorate. On account of the common difficulty of achieving a rapid reduction in fixed costs in these circumstances, there is a risk that the overhead costs would no longer be covered by the lower gross profit.

As with acquisition cost, so with production cost, there is a good deal of professional debate which is concentrated on the following detailed issues:

1 The demarcation of the boundary between what must be capitalized and what may be capitalized (the question of the lower limit).
2 The demarcation of the boundary between what may be capitalized and what must not be capitalized (the question of the upper limit).
3 Differences in the method of calculating the cost of materials used between production cost on the one hand and the profit and loss account on the other.
4 The treatment of wages and ancillary costs of employment.
5 Research and development costs as part of production cost.
6 The possibility of including taxes on consumption.
7 The treatment of overheads when producing at less than full capacity.
8 Transfers to provisions as part of production cost.
9 The dividing line between operating costs and non-operating costs.
10 The limitation of costs to the actual period of production.
11 The relationship between commercial law and tax law in the matter of the lower limit.
12 The definition of interest on debt which may be capitalized as part of the production costs.
13 The production cost in the case of long-term manufacturing operations.
14 The demarcation between selling costs, production costs and administrative costs.
15 The capitalization of subsequent production costs, for example expenditure on repairs and maintenance and on modernization.

5.3 Systematic depreciation

Depreciable fixed assets must be written down systematically (*planmäßige Abschreibung*). Depreciation must be maintained irrespective of the profit position of the enterprine and also when the current value of the object exceeds the (depreciated) acquisition costs. In *commercial law* any item may be depreciated using any of the recognized depreciation methods (straight-line, reducing balance, sum-of-the-years'-digits, progressive, stepped scale, production unit). As a rule, however, a depreciation method is in practice used in the financial statements only if it is also permitted for tax purposes. This avoids having to maintain two sets of asset schedules.

For tax, the equivalent of systematic depreciation in commercial law is the deduction for normal business wear and tear (*Absetzung für Abnutzung,* AfA in EStG § 7 (1)) or, in special cases, such as claypits, gravel pits and peat diggings, the deduction for depletion of a finite resource (*Absetzung für Substanzverringerung,* AfS in EStG § 7 (6)).

For the calculation of the AfA, normal wear and tear, the following methods are allowed:

1 Straight-line depreciation, for all depreciable items.
2 Reducing balance depreciation for all movable depreciable items, also for machines fixed to buildings. A fixed percentage rate is applied to the remaining balance. The percentage rate is limited by EStG § 7 (2), second sentence, for goods acquired after 29 July 1981 to:

   (a) Three times (two and a half times) the rate that would apply with straight-line depreciation.
   (b) With a maximum of 30 per cent (25 per cent).

   (The figures in brackets apply to goods acquired before 29 July 1981.) At any point in time, for any particular asset, one can switch from reducing balance to straight-line depreciation; but not vice versa. When the reducing balance method is used no further deduction for exceptional business wear and tear is permitted. (See section 5.5.1; EStG § 7 (2), second sentence.)
3 Stepped depreciation (with decreasing rates) for buildings that were constructed by the taxpayer or acquired in an unfinished state (EStG § 7 (5)). The current steps for buildings that form part of the business assets and are not used as dwellings and for which the application for the building permit was made after 31 March 1985 are: years 1–4: 10 per cent of the original cost each year; years 5–7: 5 per cent each year; years 8–25: 2½ per cent each year. The percentage rates and periods are changed from time to time for counter-cyclical policy reasons. In addition, there are numerous industrial planning rules that affect the depreciation of buildings.
4 The production unit method for movable fixed assets, where it is economically justified. The acquisition cost or production cost is allocated according to the demands made upon the asset (units produced, machine hours, kilometres driven).

Under commercial law, with all these methods of depreciation, the useful economic life of the asset must be estimated conservatively (HGB § 252 (1), No. 4). This principle also applies as regards tax. To simplify matters, the tax authorities, in conjunction with the industry associations, have drawn up depreciation tables (*Abschreibungs-Tabellen*) for all possible classes of depreciable assets other than buildings (*Bundesministerium für Finanzen* 1990). These set out the average asset life for items in each class. As a rule, these lives must form the basis of the tax computation. Any departure from them has to be justified. To avoid complications the same asset lives are often used in the financial statements. But it is always essential to check whether in each specific case the asset life is consistent with the prudence principle.

In addition, *geringwertige Wirtschaftsgüter des Anlagevermögens* (low-value fixed assets) may be regarded as a particular type of depreciation. Items with an acquisition or production cost not exceeding DM 800 may be written off immediately in the period of acquisition or production for both tax and financial reporting purposes. This little bonus from the taxman seldom comes amiss.

5.4 Exceptional depreciation in the financial statements

Table 7.9 outlines the rules on exceptional depreciation and value reductions in the financial statements (*außerplanmäßige Abschreibung*).

5.4.1 Fixed assets

There is an obligation to write fixed assets (*Anlagevermögen*) down to a 'lower attributable value' (*niedrigerer beizulegender Wert*) only when the fall in value is permanent. If it is not expected to be permanent, then exceptional depreciation is optional. In the case of corporations, taking account solely of commercial law (but see section 5.4.4), this option applies only to financial fixed assets. For all other fixed assets of corporations exceptional depreciation is forbidden when the fall in value is expected to be temporary. This rule is known as the weaker principle of lower value (*gemildertes Niederstwertprinzip*), on account of its optional character.

The term 'attributable value' is not defined by the law. Among accounting practitioners the following principles have gained acceptance:

1 *Non-depreciable assets.* As a rule, the basis is the replacement cost at the balance sheet date.
2 *Depreciable assets.* The appropriate value is the depreciated replacement cost

Table 7.9 Exceptional depreciation in the financial statements

Type of asset	*Type of depreciation*	*Corporations*	*Other enterprises*
Fixed	1 Exceptional depreciation with an anticipated permanent reduction in value: HGB § 253 (2) sentence 3	Compulsory	Compulsory
	2 Exceptional depreciation when the reduction in value is not expected to be permanent: HGB § 253 (2) sentence 3	Optional only for financial assets: HGB § 279 (1)[1]	Optional
Current	3 Write-down to the quoted or market value: HGB § 253 (3) sentence 1	Compulsory	Compulsory
	4 Write-down to the appropriate value: HGB § 253 (3) sentence 2	Compulsory if 3 not applied	Compulsory if 3 not applied
	5 Write-down to anticipate future necessary value corrections: HGB § 253 (3) sentence 3	Optional	Optional
Fixed and current	6 Depreciation on the basis of sound business judgement: HGB § 253 (4)	Forbidden	Optional
	7 Depreciation to a value justified only on tax grounds: HGB § 254	Optional with the reverse authoritativeness principle: HGB § 279 (2)	Optional

Note: [1]However, taking into account the reverse authoritativeness principle and HGB § 254, there is effectively an option for non-financial assets as well.

(replacement cost minus accumulated systematic depreciation). The accumulated systematic depreciation is calculated by applying, for the life of the asset to date, the depreciation method that was used for the historical cost, to the replacement cost.

3 *Participations.* The attributable value is calculated as the net present value of the future income stream. (Shares in other enterprises are to be treated as participations when there is a long-term connection with the other enterprise that is designed to serve the investing business. The indication of a participation is a holding of over 20 per cent of the nominal capital of the other enterprise (HGB § 271 (1), third sentence)).

4 *Securities that are part of fixed assets.* The 'attributable value' is the stock exchange or market price at the balance sheet date plus the (fictional) incidental costs of acquisition.

5 *Patents and similar rights.* The basis is the net present value of the future income stream (as with participations).

5.4.2 Current assets

In line with the HGB § 253 (3), first sentence, current assets (*Umlaufvermögen*) must be written down so that they are stated at the lower quoted price or market price at the balance sheet date. If no quoted or market price is available, they must be written down to the 'attributable value' (HGB § 253 (3), second sentence – see below). The obligation to write the current assets down is known as the 'strict lower value' principle (*strenges Niederstwertprinzip*).

In calculating the write-down, all the risks and losses that exist at the balance sheet date must be taken into account, even when they first become known between the balance sheet date and the date of the preparation of the financial statements (the 'revealed value principle', *Wertaufhellungsprinzip*).

The value to be derived from the quoted price or market price is the relevant price plus the incidental costs of acquisition. For the attributable value, the following conventions have become generally accepted:

1 Ascertainment of the value on the basis of data from the market regarding the supply of the goods for:

   (a) Raw materials and supplies.
   (b) Work in progress and finished goods, if it is possible to acquire these from a third party.

2 Ascertainment of the value on the basis of data from the selling market regarding:

   (a) Work in progress, finished goods and services performed.
   (b) Excess stocks of raw materials and supplies.
   (c) Securities.

3 Ascertainment of value on the basis of data from both markets, with the lower of the two values taken, for:

   (a) Merchandise.
   (b) Excess stocks of work in progress and finished goods.

In ascertaining value on the basis of data from the supply market, the so-called sunk replacement costs should be taken. These are to include the incidental costs of acquisition (as is also the case with the value derived from the quoted price). Deductions are required for obsolescence, damage, changes in fashion or changes in production processes – if necessary, right down to scrap value. Where the deductions are extensive, it is customary, and recognized for tax purposes, to make a global deduction based on the turnover rate, notwithstanding the principle of individual valuation. This is termed a write-off for non-marketability (*Gängigkeitsabschreibung*). There are conventions on how much may be deducted.

The current value of products on the basis of data from the selling market is calculated as follows:

forecast sales proceeds, calculated on a prudent basis
– sales deductions
– packaging and carriage outwards
– other selling expenses
– administrative costs that have yet to be incurred
– service of capital
– production costs that have still to be incurred (for unfinished products)
= attributable value at the balance sheet date

With current assets there is a further optional deduction for items whose value is expected to fall in the near future (after the balance sheet date) (HGB § 253 (3), third sentence). The fall in value must be expected within the next two years on the basis of criteria that can be subsequently verified. This deduction is relevant in the event, for example, of a slump in the prices of raw materials and supplies, difficulties in sales, a fall in the stock exchange prices of securities or fluctuations in credit rating.

5.4.3 Depreciation on the basis of sound business judgement

For non-corporations a further optional write-off is available. They are permitted, under the HGB § 253 (4), to effect write-offs in excess of those allowed under the rules described above if that is what a sound businessman would do. In practice this rule gives them a free hand to create hidden reserves by means of wide-ranging write-downs. This possibility is open even to large enterprises subject to the PublG.

For corporations, however, the lower attributable value is a firm value. This means principally that no further write-off below this value is permitted. The rule was brought in with the AktG of 1965 in order to limit management's scope for reducing the potential for dividends. For sole proprietors and partnerships the protection of distributions is left to the contract between the parties. Hence they were allowed scope for additional write-offs.

5.4.4 Depreciation based exclusively on tax-driven values

The relationship between the financial statements and the tax computation has already been outlined in general terms in Chapter 6, section 1.3. The consequence in commercial law is regulations that permit the inclusion in the financial statements of value reductions that are justified only on tax grounds. For non-corporations this is permitted by the HGB § 254. Thus it is possible for these predominantly smaller enterprises to prepare only one set of accounts for both financial reporting and tax purposes.

However, corporations can use tax-driven value reductions in their financial statements only if, under tax law, they are a condition of the recognition of depreciation in the calculation of taxable profit (the reverse authoritativeness principle). Under the old law this was often not the case. However, the Tax Amendment Act of 1990 (§ 5 (1), second sentence) states that, in general, tax options may be exercised only in agreement with the financial statements. In this way the traditional tax-driven German system of financial reporting, which might have been impaired by the Fourth Directive, has been preserved, in a roundabout way, by tax law. Take as an example the prohibition on exceptional depreciation of non-financial assets where the decrease in value is not permanent, laid down in the HGB § 279 (1), which is made an option because of a corresponding option provided for in the tax laws (see section 5.5.2 below) that is accepted for commercial accounts owing to the authoritativeness principle (see HGB § 279 (2)).

This is seen by many, even in Germany, as a defect in the financial statements. But it should be noted that the defect is mitigated by the following regulations:

1 The distortion in the presentation of assets (but not of profits) can be avoided by reporting the tax-driven part of the depreciation as a separate liability: the *Sonderposten mit Rücklageanteil* (special item with a reserve component; HGB § 281 (1)). This option is open to all enterprises, including non-corporations. In addition, information must be given about the specific tax regulations on which the tax-driven depreciation is based. Transfers to the special item are to be reported in the profit and loss account under 'Other operating expenses'. The item has to be written back to the respective expense items:

    (a) According to the tax rules, e.g. in the event of abolition of the tax allowance.
    (b) In the event of disposal of the asset.
    (c) In the event of the replacement of tax depreciation by depreciation according to commercial law.

2 Corporations must disclose in the notes the amount of depreciation charged in the year solely on the basis of tax regulations, separately for fixed and for current assets.

With this information it is possible to arrive at a separate calculation of the profit that would have been reported had tax depreciation not been used in the financial statements. But while profit may be recalculated, the information in the notes does not suffice for calculating the cumulative effect on the balance sheet.

5.5 Special write-offs in the tax computation

The equivalents of the forms of exceptional depreciation listed in rows 1–6 of Table 7.9 for tax purposes are:

1 The deduction for exceptional wear and tear (EStG § 7 (1), fifth sentence).

2 The *Teilwertabschreibung* ('part of the whole value' depreciation).

Furthermore there are also special depreciation allowances for tax purposes.

5.5.1 Deduction for exceptional wear and tear

The trigger for the deduction for exceptional wear and tear is damage on unusual technical grounds, such as, fire, flood, insect infestation or dry rot, or a fall in value for economic reasons, such as a fall in demand, a considerable increase in the price of raw materials or a new invention.

Formally the deduction for exceptional wear and tear is optional. However, since, as a rule, the same circumstances must lead to an exceptional depreciation charge being taken into the financial statements on account of the permanent fall in value, the deduction is also mandatory for tax purposes, given the authoritativeness principle.

5.5.2 *Teilwertabschreibung* ('part of the whole value' depreciation)

The *Teilwert* is a value exclusively for tax purposes. The EStG defines *Teilwert* as the amount that the purchaser of the whole enterprise would pay for the individual item out of the global price; at the same time there is no question but that the purchaser will keep the item in the business.

The writing down of an asset's value for tax purposes to a lower *Teilwert* is relevant to all assets. Admittedly it is formally only an option (EStG § 6 (2), second sentence). However, it becomes mandatory on account of the authoritativeness principle when there is an obligation to record exceptional depreciation in the financial statements for the same event.

1 For fixed assets the tax deduction corresponds in content to the exceptional depreciation prescribed by the HGB § 253 (2), third sentence. If the fall in value is permanent, the exceptional depreciation is obligatory. If the fall in value is temporary, there is still a tax option, which, in contrast to the position with the financial statements of corporations, is not limited solely to financial fixed assets.
2 For current assets, the strict principle of lower value applied in the financial statements leads to an obligation to take exceptional depreciation in the tax computation as well.

The option in commercial law of effecting anticipated write-offs in respect of future falls in value does not apply with tax. However, a decision of the highest tax court (BFH) has accepted that account may be taken of price movements in a period of up to four to six weeks after the balance sheet date in the case of goods with strongly fluctuating prices.

The underlying idea of the *Teilwert* is that the market value of the enterprise is equal to the sum of all *Teilwerte.* If one disregards ideal economies of the Arrow–Debreu type, there are obvious problems with such a value concept. There is an insufficiently objective basis on which to set a fictional purchase price for the enterprise, for example as the net present value of expected profits. For quoted enterprises the market value of the shares is certainly a basis for an approximation. But, even if a satisfactory purchase price were to be achieved, it might not be possible to apportion it among the individual assets because the profits are generated by the assets in combination (joint production).

For these reasons jurisprudence has developed the 'supposed *Teilwert*', based on the prices or costs of the goods in question or of comparable goods. This is not so much a system as a complicated piece of casuistry which can be only briefly outlined here:

1 For current assets the *Teilwert* is, as a rule, the replacement cost.
2 For non-depreciable fixed assets the *Teilwert* is the original acquisition or production cost, even in subsequent years.
3 For depreciable fixed assets the *Teilwert* is equal to the acquisition or production cost, reduced by the AfA depreciation charge.

The taxpaying company can reject these suppositions and set a lower *Teilwert*. The most relevant grounds would be that:

1 The replacement cost has fallen since the *Teilwert* was originally set.
2 The selling price of the product has fallen since the *Teilwert* was originally set, so that the forecast proceeds no longer cover the full costs plus an average profit (*Einkommensteuerrichtlinien*, EStR, Income Tax Regulations, section 36).
3 It is now recognized that the acquisition or construction was a mistake.

In particular the first two grounds lead to the tax depreciation charge becoming close to the exceptional depreciation charged in the financial statements (to the lower attributable value). The essential difference is that, on account of the '*Teilwert* suppositions' in the tax laws, the burden of proof regarding the lower value lies with the taxpayer.

5.5.3 Special depreciation allowances for taxation

The purpose of special depreciation allowances, increased depreciation or additional value abatements (hereafter referred to collectively as 'special depreciation allowances') is the granting of a special tax concession through manipulation of the profit figure. Ideally these special allowances should not appear as expenses in the financial statements. The root cause and the reasons why they nevertheless appear in the financial statements of German enterprises were outlined in Chapter 6, section 1.3. In practice there are (were) important special depreciation allowances for:

1 Investment in the former German Democratic Republic.
2 Depreciable fixed assets situated in Berlin (BerlFG § 14). These are being phased out.
3 Environmental protection facilities (EStG § 7d).
4 Warehouses, factories and agricultural buildings of German people expelled or persecuted during and after the Second World War (EStG § 7e).
5 Movable fixed assets and certain buildings in agriculture (*Einkommensteuer-Durchführungsverordnung* (EStDV), Ordinance Regulating the Income Tax Law, §§ 76–8).
6 Certain depreciable fixed assets in coal mining and ore mining (EStDV § 81).

5.6 Writing back

The principle of lower value is qualified by the rules relating to *writing back* (*Wertaufholung*). If, after the value of an asset has been written down by exceptional depreciation, its value subsequently rises, there is, for non-corporations, the option of writing up the value of the asset to this higher value (HGB § 253 (5)). The upper limit of the writing up is the historical cost less systematic depreciation if the current value exceeds this adjusted historical cost. Otherwise the current value is the upper limit.

For corporations, there is an obligation to write up the value (HGB § 280 (1)) when exceptional depreciation has been taken under the HGB § 253 (2), third sentence, HGB § 253 (3) or HGB § 254, first sentence. However, in practice this obligation is rendered largely ineffective by an exemption. There is no obligation to write back:

1 When it is permissible to retain the lower value for tax purposes.
2 When the lower value may be used for tax purposes only when it is also retained in the financial statements.

Without this exemption the application of the authoritativeness principle would act to the taxpayer's disadvantage if the write-back was made in the financial statements. This reverse authoritativeness principle antedates the Fourth Directive. But with the enactment of the provisions of the Fourth Directive it has been strengthened, in particular through the amendment of EStG § 5 (see section 5.4.4 above). The practical effect has been to seriously undermine the Fourth Directive's ideas on writing-back.

5.7 Particular valuation rules

5.7.1 LIFO and other simplified valuation methods

According to the HGB § 256, the average cost method and also LIFO or FIFO may be chosen to calculate the acquisition and production cost of items of stock. Note that the homogeneity of the items is a prerequisite. However, this choice, in respect of the commercial accounts, is not much used in practice. Enterprises do not want to keep two inventory records. They choose a method allowed for tax purposes which is then used in the commercial accounts as well.

1 Up to 31 December 1989 only the average cost method was applicable for tax purposes. The LIFO and FIFO methods could be chosen only if the actual sequence of utilization was equivalent to the one assumed under the respective methods. A separate issue is the availability of LIFO for certain kinds of precious metals.
2 Since 1 January 1990 LIFO has been generally accepted for tax purposes as well (EStG § 6 (1), No. 2a). The same prerequisites apply as with commercial accounts. The changes in the LIFO method in times of rising prices is, by general consensus, an admissible breach of the consistency principle.

Currently there is lively debate as to which of the different methods (quantity LIFO; permanent or period LIFO; double extension, chainlink or retail LIFO) is permissible under the GoB.

5.7.2 Foreign currency translation

German law does not regulate the translation of foreign currency items in the accounts of the individual company, debtors and creditors in particular, except in the case of banks. For banks there is a legal rule (HGB § 340h) based on article 39 of the European Community's Bank Accounts Directive. For other enterprises the principles of foreign currency translation have emerged from the professional debate. Under them, translation differences, like all valuation differences, must pass through the profit and loss account. Direct transfer to reserves, common in some other countries, is unknown in Germany. The following points of detail should be noted:

1 Negative translation differences (write-downs of assets and write-ups of liabilities) following a translation at the current rate are a charge against profit, in line with the general valuation principles:

   (a) Obligatory for current assets, and also for fixed assets, when the fall in value is expected to be permanent.
   (b) Optional for expected temporary falls in the value of fixed assets.

2 Positive translation differences which remain after netting are not taken into account (it would be an infringement of the realization principle), i.e. the asset (liability) continues to be reported at the lower (higher) historical value in the home currency.
3 Positive translation differences that offset negative differences are taken into account under certain circumstances. There is controversy over the extent to which the principle of item-by-item valuation may be departed from.

Under the *Revised Proposals for a Declaration on Foreign Currency Translation in the Annual Accounts of Enterprises and Groups* of the IdW's main technical committee (1986), netting is allowed, as are hedging transactions and 'closed positions'. Debts and liabilities relating to deliveries and services can be covered, including the rights and obligations arising from incomplete transactions. Fixed assets may not be covered, because, in their case, there is no certainty at any given time that the foreign currency gains and losses will be offset by monetary transactions. There is no requirement for the due dates to be identical, provided that the timing differences can be bridged by borrowing, lending and forward contracts. This pronouncement represented a weakening of the principle of item-by-item valuation but left many points open. Hence the continuing controversy in the professional literature.

5.7.3 Government grants

Government grants are payments by public authorities made to enterprises for no consideration which are neither loans nor equity contributions. There is general agreement that such grants should ultimately be credited to the profit and loss account; they may not be credited directly to reserves. However, there is no agreement over when they should be credited to profit or how they should be presented in the balance sheet and the profit and loss account. Usually a distinction is drawn between taxable grants (*Zuschüsse*, subsidies) and non-taxable grants (*Zulagen*, allowances). A further distinction depends on whether they are granted in respect of investment expenditure ('investment subsidies or allowances') or in respect of recurring or non-recurring expenditure ('expenditure subsidies').

Since there are no rules under commercial law, in practice the tax rules are frequently applied in the commercial account as well:

1 The full amount of an investment allowance is normally credited as revenue in the year of the investment or when the allowance is received.
2 Investment subsidies can be either offset against the acquisition cost of the asset or credited immediately for the full amount as revenue (EStR, section 34).

In 1984 the main technical committee (HFA) of the IdW issued a recommendation on the commercial accounting treatment of grants, with a view to standardizing divergent practices. The following procedures are proposed in respect of non-repayable grants:

1 *Crediting to profit.* Investment subsidies and allowances should be credited to profit as revenue over the economic life of the asset in respect of which they were granted. Expenditure subsidies and allowances should be accounted for in the same way as the expenditure which the grant serves to cover. The immediate credit of the full amount to profit is recommended only in exceptional cases, e.g. when the later costs relating to the subsidized assets are anticipated by exceptional depreciation or when losses are compensated, as in a reconstruction.
2 *Timing considerations.* If the right to the grant is acquired before the money is received, then, when all the conditions for the receipt of the grant have been fulfilled, a debtor is to be set up, with a credit to the profit and loss account. When, on the other hand, the grant is received before all the conditions have been fulfilled, then it should be recorded as a liability and credited to the profit and loss account only when all the conditions have been fulfilled.
3 *Reporting of investment subsidies and allowances.* The gross method (reporting an item on the liabilities side of the balance sheet which is gradually written off against profits) is preferred to the net method (set-off against acquisition cost). However, the net method is still regarded as acceptable. With the gross method, the credit to the profit and loss account should be shown as a separate item or included with other operating revenue or set off against depreciation.
4 *Reporting of expenditure subsidies.* Expenditure subsidies may be set off against corresponding expenditure in the profit and loss account only when both items relate to the same period. In other cases they should be reported as other operating revenue.

Frequently grants are made subject to reimbursement requirements under which there is an obligation to repay the grant under certain conditions ('conditionally repayable grants'). The accounting treatment depends on the nature of the conditions. If the grant has to be repaid when the enterprise earns a profit (as with a grant for the reconstruction of an enterprise), then, in the year when a profit is made, a creditor must be set up through a charge against profits for the amount of the refund due. If initially there is an obligation to repay which is cancelled when, for example, the underlying purpose of the financial support has been achieved, the grant should first be treated as a liability and the profit and loss account credited only when the conditions have been fulfilled.

5.7.4 Long-term made-to-order production

There are no particular rules on how to account for long-term production (*langfristige Auftragsfertigung*). The realization of profit is determined according to general valuation principles, by which the upper limit of the asset's value is set by the acquisition cost/ production cost. Interim profits may not be included in the asset's value. Thus accounting for an uncompleted contract by the 'percentage of completion' method is not permissible. This does not mean that it is completely impossible to report realized interim profits. If it is agreed that the contracted goods are to be produced and delivered in separate, completed parts, the goods will be accepted as such by the customer and account rendered as such by the supplier, before the final account is settled, then the profit element in the partial delivery can be reported as realized. In such a case, receivables (less any pre-payments) and turnover, including the profit element, would be accounted for and the unfinished contract transferred to expenses. If there are still risks to be taken into account (e.g. for guarantees) the appropriate provisions should be set up. There is controversy over the specific details of the conditions for the realization of interim profits. For some, there is an obstacle when, even though an account has been rendered for part of the contract, there is still considerable risk attaching to the whole contract, e.g. technical risks. Since this is not uncommon, the completed contract method is usually applied, particularly as the method is acceptable for tax purposes. Consequently enterprises with long-term production contracts often possess a substantial invisible cushion of profits relating to contracts not yet fully completed.

Marketing expenses may not be included in the value of the asset under HGB § 255 (6), which follows article 39.2 of the Fourth Directive. This prohibition also applies, in the accepted view, to special direct selling costs in long-term production contracts. There is some argument about the extent to which the costs of obtaining and preparing the contract are marketing costs and the extent to which they are production costs. The majority view tends towards a rather restrictive interpretation.

Interest on debt capital may be included in the cost of the asset when it can be attributed to the financing of the contract. This is often the case with long-term production, or it can be achieved by appropriate drafting of the credit contract.

6 EQUITY

6.1 The regulation of equity as part of the law on capital maintenance

The effort to reduce the risks of creditors through the maintenance of equity capital corresponds with the high level of debt financing of German enterprises. Legal rules are the predominant means of ensuring that corporations do not allow their capital base to shrink, particularly AGs (see Chapter 6, section 1.1). By contrast, with unincorporated enterprises, for example partnerships, the matter is settled largely by private contract.

The capital maintenance rules for corporations apply to the various separate accounts relating to capital. The relevant items on both the assets and the capital side of the balance sheet are shown in Table 7.10. They are examined here in detail, because equity capital is particularly important for financial analysis.

6.2 Subscribed capital

6.2.1 Amount, types and presentation

The subscribed capital is termed *Grundkapital* in the balance sheet of an AG and a KGaA, and *Stammkapital* in the balance sheet of a GmbH. The minimum amount of *Grundkapital* (for an AG) is DM 100,000; of *Stammkapital* (for a GmbH), DM 50,000.

The subscribed capital of an AG is divided into shares (*Aktien*) with a minimum denomination of DM 50. Where the capital is divided into different classes of shares (ordinary shares, *Stammaktien*; various types of preference shares, *Vorzugsaktien*) the total amount for each class must be disclosed separately in the balance sheet (AktG § 152 (1), second sentence). In Germany bearer shares are the norm. With this type of share, the holder of the certificate can enforce the rights attached to it. Transfer of the shares takes place without formalities by agreement and delivery on the part of the owner. Registered shares, where the shareholder's name is recorded in the corporation's share register and which can be transferred only by endorsement and inscription in the share register, are common only in certain sectors, notably insurance. This is because, in that sector, the nominal value is often not fully paid up. The minimum paid-up contribution is 25 per cent of the nominal value plus the difference between the issue price and the nominal value (share premium). Registered shares are also used to thwart take-over

Table 7.10 Statement of equity according to the Commercial Code

Assets side		*Capital side*	
A	Unpaid contributions to the subscribed capital *of which* called (HGB § 272 (1) sentence 2)	A	Equity
	–	I	Subscribed capital (HGB § 272 (1); see also AktG § 152 (1); GmbHG § 42 (1))
	–	II	Capital reserve (HGB § 272 (2); see also AktG § 152 (2))
	–		1 Called supplementary contributions (for GmbH) (GmbHG § 42 (2) sentence 3)
C	Current assets	III	Profit reserves (HGB § 272 (3))
II	Receivables and other assets		1 Legal reserve (AktG § 150)
	4 Called, unpaid contributions to the subscribed capital (HGB § 272 (1) sentence 3 *or* called supplementary contributions from the shareholders of a GmbH (GmbHG § 42 (2))		2 Reserve for own shares (HGB § 272 (4))
			3 Statutory reserves
			4 Other reserves
		IV	Profit/loss carried forward (HGB § 266 (3))
		V	Profit/loss for the year (HGB § 266 (3))
III	Securities	VI	Balance sheet profit/loss – *of which* carried forward (according to HGB § 268 (1)) (as an alternative to IV and V above)
	2 Own shares		
	–		
	–		
	–	B	Special item with a reserve component in accordance with HGB § 273 in conjunction with HGB § 247 (3)
E	Loss not covered by equity capital (HGB § 268 (3))		
		C	–

Source: Coenenberg (1992: 166).

bids, in that the transfer of ownership is made conditional on the approval of the corporation's executive board (registered shares not freely transferable). In 1992 the Aachener und Münchener Lebensversicherung AG tried to avoid being taken over by the French insurance group, Assurances Générales de France, in this way.

Take-overs are also hindered by shares with several votes, known as multiple-voting shares (*Mehrstimmrechtsaktien*). They may no longer be issued (AktG § 12 (2), second sentence). However, multiple-voting shares already in existence when the AktG came into force in 1965 retain their voting rights.

The shares in a GmbH – called *Stammeinlagen* – must have a nominal value of at least DM 500; the nominal value must be divisible by 100. A condition for the effective legal formation of a GmbH is a minimum paid-in share capital of DM 25,000.

Where the subscribed capital is not fully paid up, the unpaid contributions may be presented in the balance sheet in different ways (HGB § 272 (1), second and third sentences). They can be shown on the assets side as a separate item above the fixed assets (see Table 7.10). The called contributions should in that case be shown separately. However, it is also permissible, on the face of the balance sheet, to deduct the uncalled unpaid contributions from subscribed capital. In that case the called contributions are to be disclosed under the current assets as receivables (see also Table 7.10).

6.2.2 Increase in subscribed capital

The increase in the subscribed capital of an AG (KGaA) requires:

1 A resolution of the general meeting to that effect with a three-quarters majority. (The articles can require a different majority.)
2 The implementation of the increase in capital.
3 A notice in the commercial register.

The capital of an AG (KGaA) can be increased in one of four ways.

1 *Capital increase for consideration* (*Kapitalerhöhung gegen Einlagen*). With this, the regular capital increase, the AG receives new resources in the form of cash or contributions in kind.
2 *Conditional capital increase* (*bedingte Kapitalerhöhung*). Contributions are received in this case as well, depending on whether new shares are issued following a conversion or on the exercise of subscription rights. The nominal value of the conditional capital may not exceed half the subscribed capital. This form of increase of capital is normally used:

   (a) For the redemption of convertible debt.
   (b) In connection with the 'fusion' of several enterprises.
   (c) For the granting to the corporation's employees of the right to subscribe to new shares in consideration of monetary claims relating to the employees' share of profits.

3 *Authorized capital* (*genehmigtes Kapital*). In this case the general meeting delegates to the management its right to increase capital – for a maximum of five years. The

executive board is empowered to issue new stock for a consideration up to the limit of the authorized capital.

4 *Capital increase out of company funds* (*Kapitalerhöhung aus Gesellschaftsmitteln*). In contrast to the other forms, in this case the capital is increased not through contributions but through the conversion of the corporation's reserves.

With a GmbH there are only two possibilities: the capital increase for consideration or that out of company funds. There are the same preconditions as for an AG (three-quarters majority, implementation, inscription in the commercial register).

6.2.3 Reduction of subscribed capital

When the reduction in capital serves to offset accumulated losses it is known as a nominal reduction. Where it leads to their contributed capital being returned to the owners it is known as an effective reduction. There are particular rules for the protection of creditors which are set out in Table 7.11 for the different forms of capital reduction.

6.3 Capital reserve

In accordance with HGB § 272 (2), the following amounts are to be credited to capital reserve (*Kapitalrücklage*):

1 The amount received; on the issue of shares (including rights), in excess of the nominal value.
2 The amount received on the issue of bonds in consideration for stock conversion rights and option rights.
3 The amount contributed by shareholders in consideration for preferential rights on their shares.
4 The amount of other capital contributions from stockholders.

For a GmbH no particular conditions are attached to the retransfer of the capital reserve. For an AG or KGaA the matter is regulated by rules which cover both the conditions and the purpose.

6.4 Profit reserves

The part of the year's profit that is not distributed is transferred to the profit reserves (*Gewinnrücklagen*). The following profit reserves must be disclosed separately:

1 Legal reserve.
2 Reserve for own shares.
3 Statutory reserve.
4 Other profit reserves.

6.4.1 Legal reserve

The legal reserve (*gesetzliche Rücklage*), which only an AG has to set up (not a GmbH), serves to limit the distribution of profit, as does the capital reserve. Each year 5 per cent of the profit must be transferred to the legal reserve until the balance of the reserve plus the share premiums included in the capital reserve equals 10 per cent of the subscribed capital or such higher percentage as may be set in the AGs articles. Any loss carried forward from previous years must first be deducted from the year's profit. The use of the legal reserve is governed by the same rules as the capital reserve.

Table 7.11 Types of capital reduction

Regular capital reduction	*Simplified capital reduction*	*Capital reduction through retirement of stock*
Legal rule		
AktG §§ 222–8	AktG §§ 229–36	AktG §§ 237–9
Purpose of the capital reduction		
Set-off of losses or repayment of capital	Set-off of value reductions, covering of other losses or transfer to the legal reserve (AktG § 229 (1))	Set-off of losses or reimbursement of capital
Point at which the capital reduction becomes effective		
When the capital reduction resolution is inscribed in the commercial register (AktG § 224)	Can already be taken into account in the annual accounts for the year before the capital reduction resolution (AktG § 234 (1)); otherwise with the entry of the capital reduction resolution in the commercial register (AktG § 229 (3) in conjunction with § 224)	For shares that have already been acquired, with the entry of the capital reduction resolution in the commercial register; for shares that have to be acquired, with its cancellation; for shares which are compulsorily cancelled under a provision in the articles, with the compulsory cancellation (AktG § 238)
Implementation of the capital reduction		
By reduction in the nominal value of the shares (cancellation) (AktG § 222 (4))	By reduction of the nominal value of shares (cancellation) or by consolidation of shares (AktG § 229 (3) in conjunction with § 222 (4))	By the compulsory cancellation of shares or the repurchase of shares (AktG § 237 (1))
Protection of creditors		
By provision of security for all creditors who come forward within six months of the publication of the capital reduction resolution and who cannot demand payment (AktG § 225 (1)). Payments to shareholders may be made only after the end of a six-month waiting period (AktG § 225 (2))	Through a prohibition on distributions whilst the legal reserve is less than 10% of the subscribed capital (AktG § 233); through the prohibition of distributions higher than 4% in the two years following the reduction in capital (AktG § 233 (2))	By provision of security for all creditors who come forward within six months of the publication of the capital reduction resolution and who cannot demand payment, by a prohibition on payments to shareholders for six months after the publication of the entry (AktG § 237 (2) in conjunction with § 225 (2))

Source: Coenenberg (1992: 176).

6.4.2 Reserve for own shares

When an AG or a GmbH acquires its own shares, it must set up a 'reserve for own shares' (*Rücklage für eigene Aktien*) to an amount corresponding to the value of the own shares shown on the other side of the balance sheet (HGB § 272 (4)). Own shares include not only those held in the corporation itself but also those held in a parent company which itself holds a majority of the respective company's shares or which controls it (HGB § 272 (4), fourth sentence). The transfer to this reserve must be made from the year's profit or from available disposable reserves. Thus it serves the purpose of maintaining the capital of the company by restricting future distributions (see Chapter 6, section 1.1).

The reserve may be released only when the shares are issued, sold or redeemed, or to the extent of any value reductions effected in respect of the corresponding asset on the other side of the balance sheet.

6.4.3 Statutory reserves

Statutory reserves (*satzungsmäßige Rücklagen*) are those that are set up in accordance with provisions in the corporation's memorandum or articles of association. They may be set up in connection with a purpose laid down therein, for example the maintenance of capital, rationalization and suchlike matters. Their release is subject to conditions laid down in the articles which are binding for the supervisory board and executive board in the same way as legal regulations.

6.4.4 Other profit reserves

The remainder of the year's profit, after setting off profit/loss carried forward, which is not transferred to any of the above mentioned reserves (sections 6.4.1–3 above) and which is not distributed is included in 'Other profit reserves'.

Whilst for the shareholders of a GmbH there are no legal restrictions on transfers to and from other profit reserves, for an AG or KGaA there are certain legal rules that must be observed (see, for details, Chapter 6, section 1.1).

6.5 Special item with a reserve component

This item (labelled *Sonderposten mit Rücklageanteil*) in the balance sheet includes that part of depreciation taken for tax purposes that is not directly deducted from the asset value (see section 5.4.4 for details). In addition this item is used to report those tax allowances that are granted in the form of a tax-free reserve. In this case it is more a question of the tax payment being postponed, for, when the special item is released, tax must be paid on the corresponding amount. When it comes to the calculation of equity as part of the financial analysis of the balance sheet, the special item commonly is reduced by the amount of the future tax payable before being included with the equity. Some examples of such tax-free reserves are:

1 Reserves for profits on the disposal of certain fixed assets (so-called 6b reserve, from

the EStG § 6b). Under this regulation, enterprises are permitted either to deduct the profit on the disposal of certain assets from the acquisition cost or production cost of a similar asset acquired in the same or an earlier period, or alternatively to transfer the profit to a tax-free reserve.

2 Reserve for replacement (EStR, section 35). When the taxpayer is deprived of an asset against his will, e.g. by fire, theft or expropriation, he can transfer to this reserve the difference between the compensation received and the book value of the asset at the time of the loss.
3 Reserve for government grants (EStR, section 34 (3)).
4 Reserve under the Promotion of Urban Construction Act, § 32, in conjunction with EStG § 6b.
5 Reserve under the law on tax measures relating to the closure of coal mines.
6 Conversion reserve under section 8 of the Conversion Tax Act.
7 Reconstruction reserve under EStG § 6b.
8 Reserve under section 6 of the Development Areas Act.

7 DEFERRED TAXATION

Deferred taxation (*Steuerabgrenzung*) was unknown in German financial reporting before the implementation of the Fourth and Seventh Directives. This was connected with the fact that deferred taxation was less significant in Germany compared with say the English-speaking countries on account of the close relationship between the balance sheet and the tax computation. For individual accounts deferred taxation is regulated by the HGB § 274. HGB § 274 is formulated in such a way that it is possible for enterprises largely to avoid having to calculate and report deferred taxation, apart from provisions for taxes which were already required by the old law. The regulation distinguishes between deferred tax as a liability (HGB § 274 (1)) and deferred tax as a pre-payment (HGB § 274 (2)). If the tax expense relating to the current or earlier years is too low, because the taxable profit is lower than the reported profit, and if this lower tax expense will probably be made up in later years, then a provision must be set up for the amount of the probable tax charge in subsequent years in accordance with HGB § 249 (1), first sentence. It should be disclosed separately in the balance sheet or in the notes. The provision is to be released as soon as the higher tax charge occurs or is no longer likely to arise. In the opposite case, the reporting of deferred taxes as a pre-payment is optional. There is an additional requirement that, in that case, the amount of the profit reserves available for distribution after payment of dividends (increased by any profits brought forward or reduced by any losses brought forward) should be at least equal to the amount of the pre-paid taxes. The pre-payment has to be transferred to the profit and loss account as soon as the tax saving occurs or ceases to be likely.

These regulations have been the subject of exhaustive professional discussion. Most commentators have interpreted them in accordance with the principles of the 'dynamic balance sheet' school: all timing differences, both debit and credit, should be brought together and the net balance reported as deferred tax. The legal rules in HGB § 274 would then apply only to the net balance of deferred tax. However, some commentators interpret HGB § 274 in accordance with the 'static balance sheet' school; the purpose of deferred taxation is to assure due disclosure of assets and liabilities. The legal formulation of HGB § 274 favours such an interpretation, as it draws a clear distinction between deferred taxes as an asset and deferred taxes as a liability and lays down for each a particular treatment in the balance sheet – accounting convenience and provision. Moreover it may be argued that, since provisions may not be set off against other items in the balance sheet, then, for that part of the timing difference which leads to a liability, there is an obligation to set up a provision for deferred taxation, whereas for that part which leads to an asset there is no such obligation; it is optional. Since, in any case, with the reference to HGB § 249 (1), first sentence, the law assumes that deferred taxation provisions relate only to uncertain liabilities, only those differences are taken into account that result in future payments. With such an interpretation there is no great difference between the treatment of deferred tax as outlined and the old regulation under which provisions had to be set up for tax. On these grounds many enterprises have declined to modify their traditional practice.

8 HIDDEN RESERVES

The balance sheets of German enterprises contain hidden reserves (*stille Rücklagen*) – the more successful the enterprise, the more hidden reserves it is likely to have. The scale of these hidden reserves occasionally becomes evident. For example, the debt crises of recent years (Latin America, Eastern Europe) have had little impact on the balance sheets of German banks. Nowadays the criticism of hidden reserves is a good deal less fierce than it was a few decades ago. At the time of the reform of the AktG in 1937 there was a lively, detailed and acrimonious debate on all aspects of hidden reserves. This was understandable, for in effect the 1937 AktG set no lower limit on the value of assets. The fundamental valuation provision (§ 133) of the 1937 law was interpreted as banning overvaluation completely but as not prohibiting undervaluation.

For the better appreciation of subsequent developments, and of the current situation, it is helpful to define and categorize the various types of hidden reserve. Hidden reserves are the amount by which the book value of an asset is less than some other value. Depending on the value selected for comparison, a distinction is drawn between hidden historical cost reserves and hidden current value reserves.

1 Hidden historical cost reserves arise when, for example, in the annual accounts assets with an individual cost of less than DM 800 (*geringwertige Wirtschaftsgüter*) are fully written off in the year of acquisition. The write-off is allowable for tax purposes (EStG § 6 (2)) and it is customary to show it in the financial accounts because otherwise, on account of the authoritativeness principle, the tax deduction would not be accepted.
2 Hidden current value reserves necessarily arise under German law when the current value exceeds the historical cost, but also when write-downs, permitted for tax purposes, make the book value less than the current value.

For ease of understanding it is also helpful to differentiate hidden reserves according to the reason for their creation:

1 *Arbitrary reserves.* These arise through the application of accounting and valuation measures that can no longer be credibly justified by current events or the expectation of future events and which therefore result in values that no longer lie within the limits set by GoB, e.g. values that are less than the minimum permissible under the GoB, the omission of assets, the inclusion of fictitious liabilities and provisions.
2 *Discretionary reserves.* These may arise from a particularly prudent appraisal of future events, e.g. taking a short view of the economic life of depreciable assets, or taking into account factors that justify setting up a provision and in the valuation of the provision.
3 *Mandatory reserves.* The legal prohibition on the capitalization of self-produced fixed intangible assets necessitates the creation of a hidden reserve when a valuable asset has been created. The authoritativeness principle used in tax computations is often the source of economic pressure, as demonstrated above in the case of the hidden reserve relating to fixed assets with an individual cost of less than DM 800.

Arbitrary reserves are not allowed under German law. Evasion of this prohibition is discouraged by the threat in the Act of penalties such as special audits, the accounts being declared void, fines and imprisonment. However, the dividing line between an arbitrary reserve and a discretionary reserve is often rather blurred and hard to pin down.

Discretionary reserves are set up following a decision of the enterprise's management. The reform of the AktG in 1965 considerably reduced the opportunities for AGs and KGaAs, as the ceiling set by § 133 of the 1937 law was replaced by the 'fixed value' principle. In writing down assets or writing up liabilities a specific value must be stated which is determined officially in line with the definition given in the law. The Accounting Directives Act of 1985 extended this rule to GmbHs, which in fact had tended to follow the practice of AGs even before then. For commercial partnerships the provision in HGB § 253 (4) permitting further write-offs, if they seem necessary to a reasonable businessman, in practice affords opportunities of creating very substantial discretionary reserves, if not arbitrary reserves.

Accounting options in the law also permit enterprises to effect write-offs even when the resulting values seem relatively improbable. The relevant legal options are set out in Table 7.12, which indicates those that are not available to corporations and outlines the tax treatment. When the creation of a hidden reserve is not accepted for tax purposes the corresponding charge has to be borne wholly by the profit after tax. The impact of these measures is therefore considerable by comparison with those that are accepted for tax purposes. Often the result is that the former measures are not applied. An illustration of the effect is given by the provisions for expenses that are permitted by HGB § 249 (2). In practice, it would seem that less use is made of this opportunity than would be expected on legal grounds. Table 7.12 also indicates the extent to which corporations must disclose the amount of discretionary reserves. Thus certain discretionary reserves can be detected by financial analysts, who can correct for them in appraising the annual accounts. This is true only when the reserves are created: as a rule, transfers from such reserves remains hidden.

Discretionary reserves can arise even where the accounting rules offer no choice. They are based on a particularly prudent judgement in relation to future events, e.g. the

Table 7.12 Main options for capitalization and valuation

		Financial statement		*Tax account*	
	Item	*Sole proprietor; commercial partnership*	*Corporation*	*Sole proprietor; commercial partnership*	*Corporation*
1	Start-up and business expansion expenses; capitalization and depreciation method		•		
2	Goodwill; capitalization and depreciation method	•	•		
3	Disagio; capitalization	•	•		
4	Provisions for expenses; capitalization	•	•		
5	Acquisition costs; public grants			•	•
6	Production costs; direct or full costs	•	•	•	•
7	Production costs; inclusion of interest on debt	•	•	•	•
8	LIFO; average	•	•	•	•
9	Fixed value	•	•	•	•
10	Provisions for anticipated losses; direct or full costs	•	•	•	•
11	Systematic depreciation methods	•	•	•	•
12	Depreciation accord to sound business judgement	•			
13	Exceptional depreciation/Part-of-the-whole-value depreciation: temporary fall in value of financial fixed assets	•	•	•	•
14	Exceptional depreciation/Part-of-the-whole-value depreciation: temporary fall in value of non-financial fixed assets	•	•	•	•
15	Special depreciation allowances for taxation	•	•	•	•
16	Writing back exceptional depreciation; depreciable fixed assets	•	•	•	•
17	Writing back exceptional depreciation: non-depreciable fixed assets and current assets	•	•	•	•
18	Writing back special depreciation allowances for taxation	•	•	•	•

Note:
Disclosure of changes of items 1 and 2 in the schedule of fixed assets; disclosure in the notes of:
- The hidden current value reserves of item 8.
- The depreciation of items 13–15.
- The write-back for other than tax reasons (item 16).

economic life of an asset or the anticipation of events that would justify the setting up of a provision. It is difficult to control such hidden reserves by accounting rules, because the enterprise's management necessarily has access to privileged information which it uses in its own interests. It does not help to require the enterprise to provide information on amounts shown. Hence such reserves remain hidden as regards both their creation and their disposal.

Whereas management has the discretion to create reserves, it does not always have the same discretion over their availability. For example, where a hidden reserve is built up through a very cautious estimate of an asset's economic life, it is automatically run down in the period following the estimated economic life, during which no depreciation is charged. It is not easy to change the estimate of the economic life, as that would be a breach of the consistency principle. Similarly, hidden reserves arising from the valuation of stocks at direct cost are continuously being released automatically. Again the application of the consistency principle generally requires this valuation method to be retained, substantially limiting the availability of the reserve. Admittedly enterprises are permitted to change their valuation methods, but only for convincing reasons and not constantly. Moreover the change must be disclosed, and often the effect of the change is stated in the management report, particularly in the case of quoted corporations, such as Daimler-Benz in 1989. Nor can provisions simply be written back. Under HGB § 249 (2), third sentence, they may be released only when the reason for setting them up has disappeared. In general, there is much less flexibility in the release of hidden reserves than in creating them. However, this does not mean that the potential of release is insignificant.

The obligation to account for deferred taxation also tends to limit the effect of discretionary reserves. But this is relevant only when the charge is not recognized for tax purposes and the tax paid is accounted for as a pre-payment (see section 7 above).

Mandatory reserves. When German enterprises are reproached about hidden reserves it should be borne in mind also that many hidden reserves are imposed by accounting and valuation rules based on the prudence principle and by the link between the accounts and taxation which is favoured by the state. The first point is in complete agreement with the valuation principles of article 31 of the Fourth Directive, but the reverse authoritativeness principle is allowed but arguably in conflict with the objectives of the Fourth Directive. Therefore the current efforts of the IASC, FEE and ASB to shift accountancy in continental Europe closer to the Anglo-American model start logically with the Fourth Directive. In this connection there is, perhaps, insufficient recognition of the close interrelationship in Germany and elsewhere between the prudence principle (associated with the interconnection of accounts and taxation) and the capital and labour markets. With respect to mandatory hidden reserves there is a clash of interests that involves more than mere accounting rules. Here there is said to be a confrontation between different conceptions of the enterprise. In Germany and other countries of continental Europe it is seen not just as an economic but as a social entity, in itself worth maintaining over the long term (the stakeholder perspective). In the United States, by contrast, it is regarded purely as an investment object (the shareholder perspective).

In any assessment of the role of hidden reserves there is yet another reason to differentiate Germany from other countries. In all other European countries it is permissible to revalue assets above historical cost, albeit in some cases such as France on pain of tax penalties. When the increase in value is credited directly to reserve and the cost (i.e. depreciation) is later calculated on the basis of the higher asset value, then profits are reduced by amounts that may not be charged in Germany. It is sometimes argued that this bar to (for example) tackling the problem of inflation is compensated for by greater opportunities of creating hidden reserves. Revaluation seems to be rare outside the Netherlands and the United Kingdom. It is expressly excluded by the United States rules.

The non-availability of revaluation means that the reduction of profits by virtue of the creation of hidden reserves necessarily results in a corresponding increase in profits in succeeding periods, the latest being when the asset is disposed of or when the provision is released. In any single accounting period the reduction in profits will be more or less compensated for by the release of hidden reserves built up in earlier periods. In the case of groups with many individual valuation items there will be comparatively little change in the overall balance of the hidden reserves and thus the effect of the creation of hidden reserves on the profits will be small. This may well explain, at least partially, why comparative analysis of German and American accounts comes to rather similar conclusions on the question of the interrelation between profits and share prices (see Harris and Lang 1992).

Hidden reserves have a stronger influence on the equity of German enterprises. They go some way to explaining why the equity ratio is comparatively low by international standards. They distort other indicators that use equity – for example, the return on equity or horizontal balance sheet ratios.

9 THE NOTES ON THE ACCOUNTS

In addition to the balance sheet and the profit and loss account, the notes on the accounts (*Anhang*) are an essential, mandatory part of the financial statements of corporations. The three elements constitute a composite whole. The German view is that the three elements together must present a true and fair view, not each element separately. Table 7.13 lists the items of information that must be disclosed, either in the notes alone or, at the discretion of the enterprise, in the balance sheet/profit and loss account, together with the legal reference. The following items are of particular interest:

Accounting and valuation methods (items 6–9). In relation to matters where more than one method of accounting is permitted, or where no particular method is prescribed, information must be provided on the method actually used. In particular, the method of foreign currency translation must be explained. When there has been a change of method, the fact must be disclosed, together with the effect – but not the amount – on the net worth, financial position and the results.

Effect of accounting methods applied solely for tax reasons (items 12, 13, 17, 18). The amounts should be disclosed of depreciation of fixed and current assets solely for tax reasons and of write-backs of assets omitted for tax reasons. In respect of these matters, disclosure is necessary of the extent to which the annual results have been influenced and to which future charges are affected. The use of the word 'extent' implies that a quantitative assessment of the effect on the reported profit is not required.

Extraordinary depreciation (items 15, 16). The amount must be disclosed of extraordinary depreciation of fixed assets and of any precautionary write-downs of current assets.

Information on receivables and liabilities (items 33–5, 48; see HGB § 266 (2) and (3)).

Table 7.13 Checklist for the notes

No.	*Information to be disclosed*	*Section*
	I General information on the annual accounts	*HGB*
1	General rule	264 (2) sentence 2
2	Breach of the principle of consistent presentation	265 (2) sentence 2
3	Lack of comparability of previous year's figures	265 (2) sentence 2
4	Adaptation of previous year's figures	165 (2) sentence 3
5	Several industrial sectors	265 (4) sentence 2
	II Basic principles of accounting and valuation	
6	Accounting and valuation methods	284 (2) No. 1
7	Basis of foreign currency translation	284 (2) No. 2
8	Deviations from accounting and valuation methods	284 (2) No. 3
9	Effect of these deviations on net worth, financial position and results	284 (2) No. 3
10	Difference in valuation with FIFO, LIFO or average cost	284 (2) No. 4
11	Interest on loan capital included in production cost	284 (2) No. 5
12	Effect on profits of taxed-based depreciation	285 No. 5
13	Future charges arising from (12)	284 No. 5
14	Systematic depreciation of goodwill	284 No. 13
15	Extraordinary depreciation of fixed assets	277 (3) sentence 1
16	Write-downs of current assets.	277 (3) sentence 1
17	Write-ups not due to tax grounds	280 (3)
18	Write-downs of fixed and current assets made for tax reasons	280 (2) No. 1
	III Explanations concerning the balance sheet and the profit and loss account	
	1 Balance sheet	
	(a) *To be disclosed by all types of corporation*	
19	Inclusion under several balance sheet headings	265 (3) sentence 1
20	Breakdown of combined balance sheet headings	265 (7) No. 2
21	Profit/loss carried forward after appropriations	268 (1) sentence 2
22	Schedule of fixed assets	268 (2) sentence 1
23	Book value as assumed acquisition cost or production cost in the schedule of fixed assets	Art. 24 (6) sentence 3 EGHGB
24	Depreciation of the current year	268 (2) sentence 3
25	Anticipated assets	268 (4) sentence 2
26	Anticipated liabilities	268 (5) sentence 3
27	Premium on redemption of a debt (*disagio*)	268 (6)
28	Contingent liabilities	268 (7)
29	Start-up costs	269 sentence 1
30	Special item with a reserve component	273 sentence 2 and 280 (1) sentence 2
31	Provision for deferred taxes	274 (1) sentence 1
32	Pre-paid deferred taxes	274 (2) sentence 2
33	Liabilities with a remaining term of more than five years	285 No. 1a
34	Security for liabilities	285 No. 1b
35	Analysis of (33) and (34)	285 No. 2
36	Disclosure of holdings	285 No. 11
37	Explanation of other provisions	285 No. 12
38	Deficit on pension provision	Art. 28 (2) EGHGB
	(b) *To be disclosed by AGs and KGaAs*	*AktG*
39	Transfer to profit reserves	58 (2a) sentence 2

No.	*Information to be disclosed*	*Section*
40	Movements on capital reserve	152 (2)
41	Movements on profit reserves	152 (3)
42	Types of share capital	160 (1) No. 3
43	Subscribed shares on an increase in capital	160 (1) No. 3
44	Authorized capital	160 (1) No. 4
45	Convertible bonds, etc.	160 (1) No. 5
46	Profit participation rights, etc.	160 (1) No. 6
	(c) *To be disclosed by GmbHs*	*GmbHG*
47	Transfer to profit reserves	29 (4) sentence 2
48	Receivables and payables in respect of members	42 (3)
	2 Profit and loss account	
	(a) *To be disclosed by all types of corporation*	*HGB*
49	Breakdown of combined headings	265 (7) No. 2
50	Extraordinary income and expense	277 (4) sentence 2
51	Income and expense unrelated to accounting period	277 (4) sentence 3
52	Transfers from special item with a reserve component	281 (2) sentence 2
53	Transfers to special item with a reserve component	281 (2) sentence 2
54	Analysis of turnover	285 No. 4
55	Tax on ordinary and extraordinary profits	285 No. 6
56	Cost of materials and labour with the cost of sales method	285 No. 8
	(b) *To be disclosed by AGs and KGaAs*	*AktG*
57	Development from annual profit to balance sheet profit	158 (1) sentence 2
	IV Other information	*HGB*
	(a) *To be disclosed by all types of corporation*	
58	Other financial commitments	285 No. 3
59	Other financial commitments to affiliated enterprises	285 No. 3
60	Number of employees	285 No. 7
61	Total remuneration of members of the executive and supervisory boards	285 No. 9a
62	Total remuneration of former board members	285 No. 9b
63	Provision for pensions (including unaccrued amounts) for former board members	285 No. 9b sentence 3
64	Advances to board members	285 No. 9c
65	Commitments in favour of board members	285 No. 9c
66	Names of members of the supervisory board and of heads of the executive board	285 No. 10
67	Non-disclosure of holdings	286 (3) sentence 3
68	Separate listing of holdings	287 sentence 3
69	Group accounts exempting from obligation to prepare consolidated accounts	291 (2) No. 3
70	Name of holding company	285 No. 14
	(b) *To be disclosed by AGs and KGaAs*	*AktG*
71	Reserved shares	160 (1) No. 1
72	Own shares	160 (1) No. 2
73	Reciprocal holdings	160 (1) No. 7
74	Holdings of a size that has to be disclosed	160 (1) No. 8
75	Application of reductions in capital	240 sentence 3
76	Special audit on account of inadmissible undervaluation	261 (1)

Source: Schülen (1992), B410.

Receivables and payables are to be analysed according to due date: receivables in two classes (up to one year; over one year); payables in three classes (up to one year; up to five years; over five years). In addition separate disclosure must be made of receivables and payables with regard to affiliated undertakings and undertakings in which a participating interest is held. The total amount of payables that are secured by mortgages or similar rights, and the type and form of security, must be disclosed. This information must be shown separately for each item in the balance sheet. The total amount must be disclosed of financial commitments that are not included in the balance sheet (for example, long-term rental or leasing contracts, investment plans in progress, future major repairs, environmental measures, long-term purchase obligations or forward foreign exchange contracts); the amount in respect of affiliated undertakings must be shown separately.

Information on the development of equity in the statement of appropriation of profit (item 57; see Table 7.5). The additional information on the development of equity, stated under items 39–48, must be provided.

Information on employees (item 60). The average number of persons employed during the year should be given, broken down by group.

Remuneration and benefits of board members (items 61–5). Although there are strict data security laws, and a large number of people refused to reply to the question on personal income on the recent census form, enterprises are nevertheless required to furnish information relating to the management, consisting of the separate totals, for the supervisory board and the executive board, of:

1 The remuneration of board members.
2 The remuneration of former board members and their dependants.
3 The pension provision and unaccrued liability in respect of former members.
4 Advances to members.
5 Commitments in favour of members.

The requirement to provide this information is an indication of the powerful position of the trade unions in society.

Information on shareholdings (items 36, 67, 68, 73, 74). Corporations must disclose the name and registered address of other enterprises in which they, or persons acting on their behalf, own a fifth or more of the shares, together with the percentage share of equity and last year's results. Many enterprises do not include this list in their accounts. There are two reasons for the omission. First, the list need not be included in the notes if it is deposited in the commercial register. Second, it may be omitted when it is not significant for the presentation of a true and fair view, or when, on the basis of sound business judgement, its publication is thought likely to cause material harm to the interests of the company or the other enterprise. Many enterprises avail themselves of these options.

8
Group accounts

---

1 INTRODUCTION

1.1 Historical development of the rules on group accounts

The first proposals concerning the publication of group accounts (*Konzernabschluß*) in Germany are to be found in the AktG amendment of 19 September 1931. This amendment, prompted by the collapse of several important groups of companies, in addition to enacting some rules on the disclosure of group links in the individual accounts of enterprises, authorized the government to issue regulations on group accounts. But group accounts were not in fact regulated by law. The position remained unaltered with the reform of the AktG in 1937. After the Second World War the allied occupation authorities in West Germany issued regulations on the drawing up of group accounts. Following the American model, groups in the coal, iron and steel industries had to supplement the *Geschäftsbericht* (annual report) of the holding company by a consolidated balance sheet and a consolidated profit and loss account. The group accounts had to be audited and confirmed by the holding company's auditors. The publication of these group accounts induced important groups in other industries, in subsequent years, to publish their own group accounts voluntarily.

The rules relating to group accounts were first codified comprehensively in the AktG of 1965. Joint stock corporations were obliged to draw up group accounts (whole-group consolidations and sub-group consolidations). The enterprises to be included in the consolidation were defined. The rules were set out relating to the consolidation of capital and debt, the elimination of intra-group profit, the drawing up of the consolidated profit and loss account and of the consolidated annual report, and, finally, the audit, filing and disclosure of the group accounts. In addition, in 1969 the PublG was enacted, which required the holding companies of groups above a certain size, irrespective of their legal form, to draw up group accounts on the basis of the regulations relating to joint stock corporations and to publish at least a consolidated balance sheet.

The rules of the AktG and the PublG relating to group accounts remained unchanged for some time thereafter. Only since the implementation of the Fourth, Seventh and Eighth EC Directives in law by the *Bilanzrichtliniengesetz* of 19 December 1985 (BiRiLiG, Accounting Directives Act) have there been important changes, in which Anglo-American consolidation procedures have been assimilated.

1.2 The function of group accounts

In contrast to the accounts of the individual enterprise, the group accounts do not form the basis either of the calculation of the dividend payable to the shareholders of the holding company or of the tax calculation. In this respect group accounts in Germany have no immediate effects, in contrast to the position in, say, Spain or the United States. In fact the situation is undoubtedly more complex.

1 The taxable profit is established, as before, solely on the basis of the accounts of the individual enterprises in the group. Nevertheless the first signs are evident of the recognition in tax law of the group as an economic entity, in the tax treatment of transactions between group enterprises on the 'arm's length' principle and the equalization of profits and losses between group enterprises (the *Organschaft*) which is possible under certain conditions (see Chapter 5, section 2.7).
2 In practice, the group accounts frequently play a role in the calculation of the amount to be reported as distributable profit (*Bilanzgewinn*) by the holding company. The reason would seem to be that, if the holding enterprise's results were substantially lower, the shareholders would demand either an explanation or a higher dividend. To eliminate this source of inconsistencies, many German groups even endeavour to report the *same* distributable profit for the holding enterprise as for the group.

However, the main role of the group accounts is to provide information. According to the general rule set out in HGB § 297 (2), second sentence, group accounts must, in compliance with the *Grundsätze ordnungsmäßiger Buchführung* (GoB), present a true and fair view of the assets, liabilities, financial position and profit and loss of the group. Moreover the net worth, financial position and results are to be disclosed as if the consolidated enterprises constitute a single business entity (see HGB § 297 (3), first sentence). Hence the group accounts give a view of the group as an economic entity in the same way as the accounts of an individual enterprise that is a separate economic and legal entity (*Fiktion der rechtlichen Einheit* or *Einheitsgrundsatz,* the legal entity fiction or entity principle).

The basis of the legal entity fiction is the so-called 'entity theory', according to which the shareholders of all consolidated enterprises are regarded as shareholders of the entity to which the group accounts relate. This concept is also followed extensively in the legal provisions of the HGB. Questions of legal interpretation too are normally argued on the basis of the entity theory because of the general principle in HGB § 297 (3), first sentence.

Despite this creation of a new reporting entity (the group), and despite functions other than those of the individual accounts, legislation has refrained from separating the group accounts from the individual accounts completely. Rather the basis of the group accounts is the accounting and valuation rules prescribed for the individual accounts of the parent enterprise. German groups may not draw up their group accounts according to different foreign or international rules (e.g. those of the FASB, IASC or other international organizations). Thus the position is rather different from that in certain other countries, e.g. France. Moreover the group accounts do not replace the individual accounts, as is sometimes the case in other countries. Group accounts and individual accounts are independent reporting instruments which supplement each other in their information function. But some groups, for example Siemens, have gone over to referring solely to the group accounts in the *Geschäftsbericht* (annual report).

2 THE LEGAL REGULATION OF GROUP ACCOUNTS

As indicated in Chapter 6, section 2, the German financial reporting system has a legalistic character. The legal provisions concerning group accounts are set out in detail in the HGB §§ 290–315 and the PublG §§ 11–15. Whereas the regulations in the HGB apply to all holding enterprises which have the legal form of a corporation (AG, KGaA, GmbH), the regulations of the PublG apply to enterprises of other legal forms (particularly commercial partnerships, sole proprietors and co-operatives), subject to certain size criteria (see section 3.1 below for details).

Moreover all the above regulations apply only to groups that are headed by a single holding enterprise (*Unterordnungskonzern*, group of subordinated affiliates). Since the law does not regulate the financial reporting of groups in which private persons or a family or several enterprises share control (*Gleichordnungskonzern*, equal ranking group), it is possible to circumvent the legal obligation to prepare group accounts by setting up the group as an equal ranking group. Nor do the regulations apply to legal mergers (*Fusionen* or *Verschmelzungen*) in which one enterprise gives up its separate legal personality and its assets and liabilities are taken over by another enterprise. For such legal mergers there are special regulations, which are not dealt with here.

Figure 8.1 shows the relevant provisions of the HGB and the PublG relating to the preparation of group accounts. The provisions of the HGB take up most of the table. For large enterprises that are not corporations there are special rules, which do not originate from the Seventh Directive, concerning the obligation to prepare group accounts and the scope of consolidation. However, such enterprises are subject to the HGB rules relating to the other consolidation steps (standardization of the content of the underlying individual accounts, capital and debt consolidation, elimination of intra-group profit, consolidation of revenues and expenses, and, finally, deferred taxation). On foreign currency translation there are no provisions either in the HGB or in the PublG; instead there are recommendations of the auditors' institute, the *Institut der Wirtschaftsprüfer* and of the working group on external company accounting of the *Schmalenbach-Gesellschaft/Deutsche Gesellschaft für Betriebswirtschaft*, which are not legally binding.

3 THE OBLIGATION TO PREPARE GROUP ACCOUNTS

3.1 Consolidation of the whole group

The group accounts and the group management report must be prepared by the domestic holding enterprise of a group (*obligation to prepare*). A corporation incurs this obligation when the group exceeds two of the following three limits on two consecutive balance sheet dates: balance sheet total DM 39 million (DM 46.8 million), turnover DM 80 million (DM 96 million), number of employees 500 (HGB § 293 (1)). The amounts have to be calculated on the basis of the group accounts (the unbracketed figures) or on

Figure 8.1 The system of legal regulation of group accounts

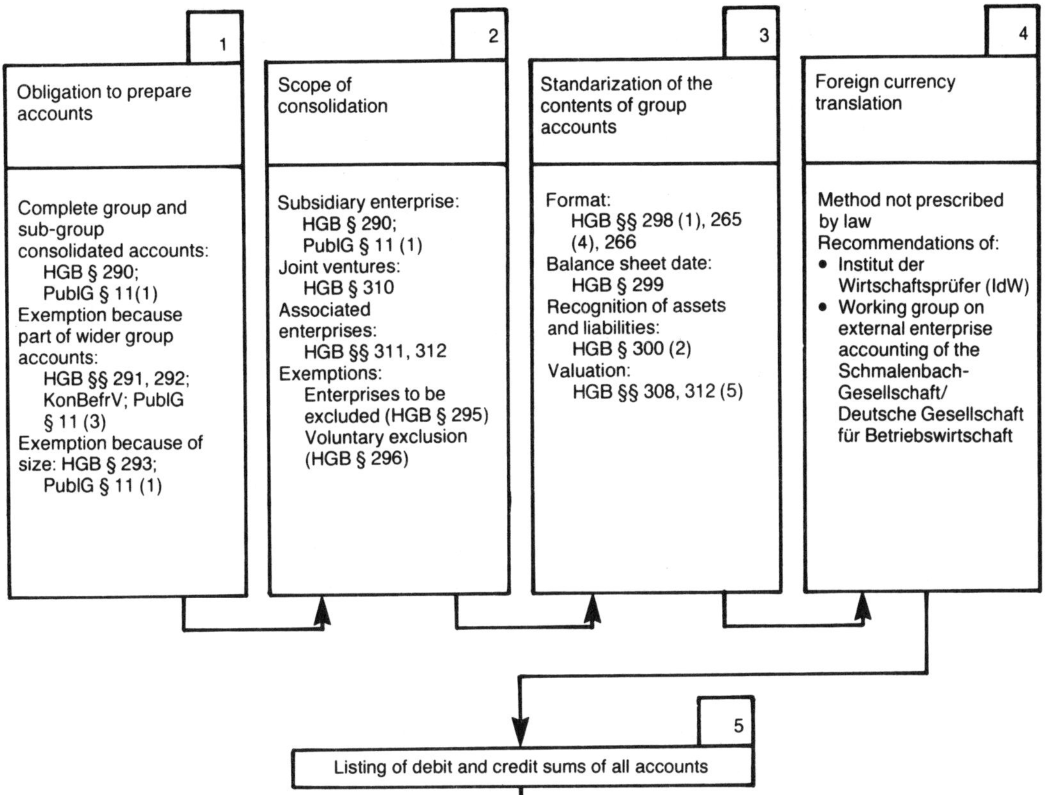

6

	Subsidiary enterprises Full consolidation	*Joint ventures* Proportional consolidation	*Associated enterprises* Equity method
Capital consolidation	HGB §§ 301, 302, 307, 309	HGB § 310 (2)	HGB § 312 (1)–(3)
Debt consolidation	HGB §§ 303, 305	HGB § 310 (2)	Not prescribed by law
Elimination of intra-group profits	HGB §§ 304, 305	HGB § 310 (2)	HGB § 312 (5)
Consolidation of revenues and expenses	HGB § 305	HGB § 310 (2)	–
Deferred taxation	HGB § 306	HGB § 310 (2)	Not prescribed by law

the gross sum of the accounts of all the enterprises in the group (the figures in brackets).

Parent undertakings that are not corporations are obliged under the PublG § 11 (1) to prepare group accounts if they head a large group. The limits set in the PublG are higher than those in the HGB. On three consecutive balance sheet dates two of the following three limits need to have been exceeded: DM 125 million consolidated balance sheet total; DM 250 million turnover with enterprises that are not part of the group (i.e. with third parties); 5,000 employees in domestic group enterprises. As an exception to this rule, parent undertakings in the form of sole proprietorships and general partnerships composed entirely of natural persons need not prepare group accounts if their activity is limited to portfolio management and does not include the management of the group (PublG § 11 (5), second sentence).

As the law stood before the implementation of the Seventh Directive, the enterprises in a group were differentiated from other enterprises solely on the criterion of unified management (*einheitliche Leitung*). This term is virtually equivalent in meaning to 'integrated business planning'. This latter economic approach has also been taken into the new law:

1 An enterprise is a parent undertaking under the PublG when it manages another enterprise (the subsidiary enterprise) on a unified basis (PublG § 11 (1)).
2 For a corporation to be a parent enterprise under the HGB there is an additional condition, that it should own a participating interest in the subsidiary enterprise as defined in HGB § 271 (1) (HGB § 290 (1)).

The unified management must actually be practised in reality if there is to be a legal obligation to prepare group accounts. It is not sufficient that the parent undertaking has the option of practising unified management; it must also avail itself of the opportunity. The law sets out certain indicators of unified management. First it is assumed that unified management exists when the parent undertaking owns the majority of the capital (AktG § 18 (1), third sentence, and § 17 (2)). The parent undertaking may refute this assumption. Second a control contract leads to an irrefutable assumption of unified management.

The criterion of unified management embodies in law the economic concept of the firm as applied to the group. Under this concept the boundary of the group is where the entity's management ends and where co-ordination through market forces begins. Ideally, in principle, the concept of unified management includes those cases of economic entities, where an obligation to prepare group accounts is desirable. Certainly the disadvantage of the concept is that it is insufficiently formalized in terms of objective criteria (substance over form). Rules in the HGB are not only the embodiment of certain economic ideas but also, at the same time, rules for organization and co-ordination in a world of conflicting interests. The management of a group has an incentive to exclude from the consolidation enterprises which, although members of the group from an economic point of view, would not improve its financial picture if included. The criterion of unified management does not altogether prevent such 'cheating', since it may be extremely difficult to verify from outside whether or not an enterprise is in fact managed by another. So there have undoubtedly been cases of bogus contracts being given the nod by which the parent undertaking apparently relinquishes control in order to avoid including a subsidiary enterprise (in fact but not in law) in the consolidation.

The criteria developed in Anglo-American accounting take greater cognizance of these organizational aspects. Here the test is not the exercise of unified management but comprises objective indicators in the form of certain rights of control (the control concept): form over substance. In line with the Seventh Directive, this criterion has been included in the new accounting law (HGB § 290 (2)) as regards holding undertakings that are corporations. Hence corporations are obliged to prepare group accounts if in fact management is unified and/or if they are entitled to the following rights of control over another enterprise:

1 A majority of votes.
2 The right to appoint the majority of the members of its administrative, executive or supervisory bodies.
3 The contractual right of control.

Considered as rights of the parent undertaking for this purpose are the rights belonging to other subsidiaries (HGB § 290 (3)), since the parent undertaking can use such rights for itself on its own behalf, given its influence over its subsidiaries.

The two criteria – unified management and the existence of certain rights of control – are independent of each other. This means that, if only one of the criteria applies to a corporation, there is an obligation to prepare group accounts. Hence the range of corporations that are obliged to prepare group accounts is defined relatively broadly in Germany by comparison with other countries.

The right to exercise a dominant influence over another enterprise can be provided for in a contract or in the enterprise's articles. The latter is a particularly important locus for limited liability companies, whose articles or memorandum can include such a provision. The criterion of the right to appoint members of another enterprise's boards applies only when the parent undertaking is also a shareholder.

3.2 Consolidation of sub-groups

In a group with several layers, those subsidiary enterprises that also control subsidiaries are, at the same time, parent undertakings according to the definition in section 3.1. As such, in principle, they are obliged to prepare group accounts on the 'Christmas tree principle', that is, they must prepare group accounts for the sub-group. Such enterprises are exempted from the obligation, however, if:

1 They do not exceed two of the size limits set by HGB § 293 (for corporations) or PublG § 11 (for other enterprises), or
2 A higher-level parent undertaking prepares group accounts and if it fulfils the conditions set out in HGB § 291 or in the *Konzernabschlußbefreiungsverordnung* (KonBefrV, Group Accounts Exemption Order) of 2 October 1991 issued under HGB § 292. HGB § 291 concerns parent undertakings resident in the European Community; KonBefrV, by contrast, refers to parent undertakings resident outside the Community.

Figure 8.2 presents a review of the detailed provisions. Of particular interest are the

Figure 8.2 Exemption from sub-group consolidation

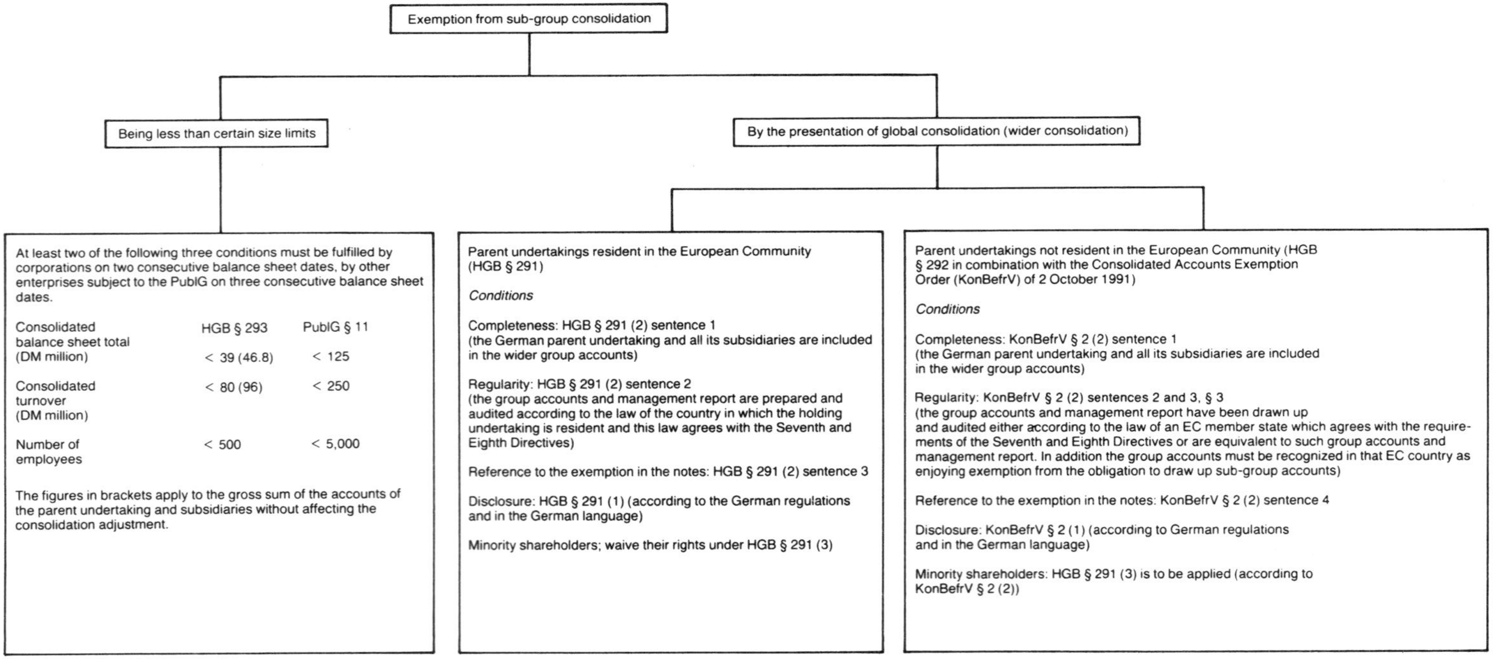

requirements regarding the acceptability/regularity of the group accounts of parent undertakings which are not resident in the European Community. The criterion of acceptability is met, according to the KonBefrV, if the group accounts and group management report have been drawn up and audited according to the requirements of the law of an EC member state which is harmonized with the requirements of the Seventh and Eighth Directives, or they are equivalent to such accounts. It is not necessary for the group accounts to be drawn up in line with German consolidation rules. The foreign group accounts must, however, also be recognized in the foreign country as affording exemption from the obligation to draw up sub-group accounts. The order (KonBefrV) does not specify in detail what is meant by 'equivalent'. So far there has been no public pronouncement on the subject. The European Commission has laid down the basic principles of the equivalence of third-country financial statements in its document XV/109/90 rev. 2. Occasional consideration seems to have been given to how to apply the basic principle to the interpretation of the 'equivalence' required by the order (KonBefrV). It seems that 'equivalence' is achieved when the minimum requirements of the Fourth and Seventh EC Directives are met.

4 THE SCOPE OF CONSOLIDATION

As the law stood before the implementation of the Seventh Directive the demarcation between the group and the market was clear and straightforward, like the dividing line between the firm and the market in the ideal model of micro-economic theory. The new law attempts to take account of the fact that the transition from unified management to (complete) independence is a grey area by means of a graduated concept of the group. Depending on the intensity of the influence, the enterprises are (1) consolidated fully (*Vollkonsolidierung*), (2) consolidated proportionately (*Quotenkonsolidierung*) or (3) consolidated by the equity method (*Equitykonsolidierung*).

4.1 The full consolidation set

The nucleus of the group consists of the set of the parent undertaking and the subsidiary enterprises. All must be fully consolidated (*Vollständigkeitsgrundsatz*, the principle of completeness). This includes foreign subsidiaries. The test of a parent–subsidiary relationship is the existence of unified management or the legal relationships that define a group (see section 3.1 above).

The exceptions to the principle of completeness are to be found in HGB §§ 295–6. They are set out in Figure 8.4.

The inclusion of a subsidiary is illegal only if its activities are so different from those of the other enterprises that its inclusion in the group accounts would be incompatible with the obligation to give a true and fair view of the assets, liabilities, financial position and profit or loss (HGB § 295 (1)). It is not sufficient that the enterprise belongs to a different sector of industry (HGB § 295 (2)). The assessment of what constitutes the activities of a group is to be interpreted much more widely. For example, a marketing finance enterprise that is part of a motor car group serves the group's activities (motor car manufacture) and must therefore be included. Possible obstacles to inclusion would

Figure 8.3 The graduated concept of the group

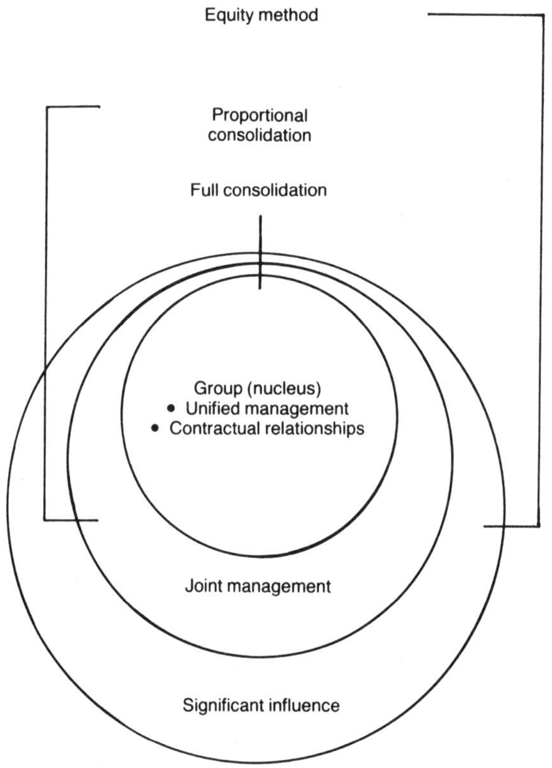

be, for example, that the enterprise's assets were subject to significantly different legal regulations, for example those of the Charities Act (*Gemeinnützigkeitsrecht*) or the Supervision of Insurance Companies Act (*Versicherungsaufsichtsgesetz*). Prevailing opinion is that the inclusion of independent charitable funds (provident funds) would not be permissible because it would give an unduly favourable impression of the group's financial position. The assets of the provident funds would belong not to the group but to the fund's beneficiaries.

The parent undertaking has an option to exclude a subsidiary if:

1 Severe long-term restrictions substantially hinder the parent undertaking in the exercise of its rights over the assets and management of the subsidiary (for example, following the installation of state management after a *coup d'état*).
2 The information necessary for the preparation of the group accounts cannot be obtained without disproportionate expense or undue delay (for example, on the first balance sheet date immediately following the acquisition of a subsidiary).
3 The shares of the subsidiary are held solely with a view to their subsequent resale.
4 The subsidiary is not material in respect of the obligation to give a true and fair view.

Figure 8.4 Criteria for the definition of businesses to be consolidated fully

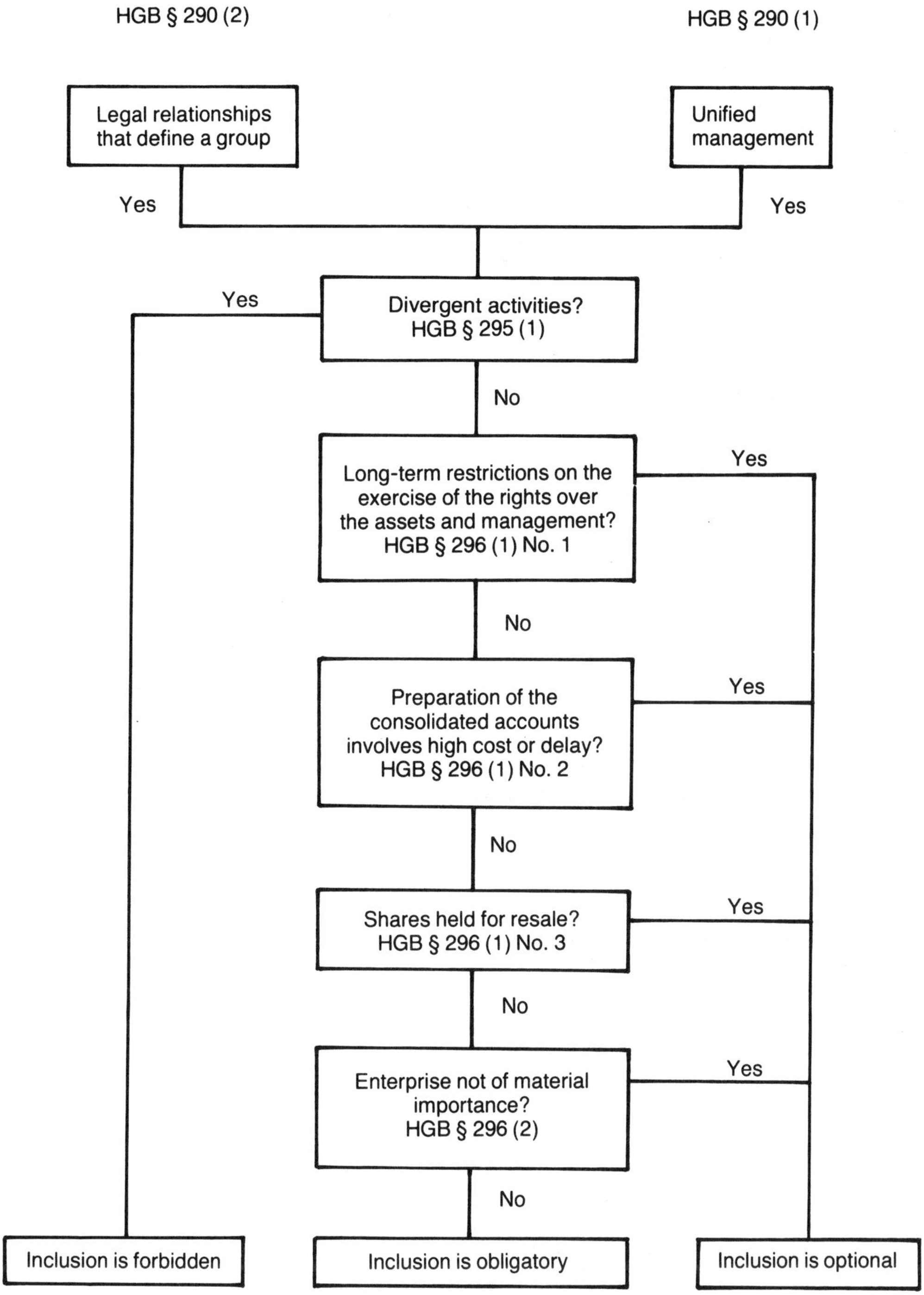

There are no other grounds for excluding a subsidiary. If a subsidiary is excluded from the full consolidation it should be checked as to whether it fulfils the conditions for inclusion as an associated enterprise as set out in HGB § 311 (see section 4.3).

Treuarbeit (1990) analysed this matter in a study of the 1989 group accounts of 100 large groups. Only ten cases were noted referring to HGB § 295 or to the circumstances mentioned in that section. By contrast, seventy-six groups made use of the exclusion option available under HGB § 296. The reasons given were:

1 Not material: seventy-four cases.
2 Limitations of the parent undertaking's rights: twenty-five cases.
3 Problems in obtaining the necessary information: four cases.
4 Intention of resale: four cases.

(More than one reason could be given.)

4.2 The proportional consolidation set

The full consolidation set is complemented by the proportional consolidation set (*Quotenkonsolidierungskreis*). It is made up of enterprises that a parent undertaking can only control jointly with one or more other economically independent enterprises (HGB § 310). The joint character of the control normally finds its expression in that the controlling enterprises have equal shares in the capital of the joint venture and possess equal powers of control. Certainly equal shares of capital are not a compulsory requirement. The assets and profits of a joint venture are attributed to the participating parent undertaking on a proportional basis (see section 12 below). However, it is also possible (an option) to consolidate participation in joint ventures according to the equity method rather than proportionally.

4.3 The equity method consolidation set

The set of enterprises consolidated using the equity methods comprises, in addition to joint ventures that are not proportionately consolidated, the associated enterprises (*assoziierte Unternehmen*). These are enterprises in respect of which the parent undertaking holds a participating interest, either directly or indirectly, and exercises a significant influence (*maßgeblicher Einfluß*) over operational and financial policy (HGB § 311); according to the law there is a presumption of a participating interest (*Beteiligung*) when the share of capital is more than 20 per cent (HGB § 271 (1)), and there is a refutable presumption of significant influence with 20 per cent or more of the votes (HGB § 311). Qualitative indications of the exercise of a significant influence are not specified in the law. The criteria that are given in IAS 28 (5):

1 Representation on the executive or supervisory board.
2 Participation in business policy-making.
3 Considerable business relationships.
4 Interchange of management personnel.
5 The provision of technological information.

These are compatible with the HGB rules and are suitable for contributing to the assessment of significant influence under the HGB.

Finally, included in the set of enterprises that are consolidated using the equity method are those subsidiary enterprises that are not fully consolidated owing to exemption under HGB § 295 (compulsory exclusion) and HGB § 296 (optional consolidation). Since unified management or the existence of certain control rights covers significance influence, these enterprises have to be consolidated by the equity method. In each case, however, it is necessary to check whether, in fact, the conditions for the application of the equity method apply.

According to HGB § 311 (2) the equity method need not be applied when the participating interest is not material in arriving at a true and fair view.

5 STANDARDIZATION OF THE ACCOUNTS OF INDIVIDUAL ENTERPRISES

Enterprises operating in different industries and different countries mostly use different charts of accounts and, in consequence, different account classifications, with the accounts themselves all differing in content. In addition the balance sheet dates are not always the same. In Germany, to ensure comparison of like with like, the individual accounts of the consolidated enterprises must, following the legal fiction of the group as an entity, be drawn up according to uniform legal rules of classification, valuation and accounting, and on the same balance sheet date. Any departure from this standard has to be resolved before the individual financial statement can be consolidated, otherwise, an interim financial statement must be prepared.

5.1 Format

According to HGB § 298 (1), the group accounts are to use the classifications set out in the regulations covering the individual accounts of large corporations. (For the detailed regulations see Chapter 7, section 3.) Normally, this leads to the reclassification of the individual accounts of small and medium-sized corporations as well as those of foreign enterprises (*Handelsbilanz I*, balance sheet I). Moreover reclassification may be necessary because, when considered from the point of view of the group as an entity, individual items in the accounts may have to be presented quite differently. For example, what is extraordinary expenditure for the individual enterprise may be an ordinary business expense for the group. Where this is a choice, group management must decide on a single method of classification. The basic principles of economy and materiality set bounds to the practical achievement of uniform accounts, particularly in respect of foreign subsidiaries. In these marginal cases the extra expense of reclassification has to be weighed against the impairment of the information content of the group accounts.

5.2 Content

Occasionally, foreign financial statements will make use of accounting and valuation rules that diverge from German law. Even within Germany it is possible for, say, a subsidiary which takes the form of a commercial partnership to use different accounting rules from those employed by a corporation as parent undertaking. Before consolidation the individual accounts of such enterprises must be modified, using the accounting rules that apply to the parent undertaking. (For capitalization rules see HGB § 300 (2); for valuation see HGB § 308.)

Where the law allows a choice of accounting treatment (see Chapter 7) a different method may be adopted for group accounts, so that even the parent undertaking may have a different accounting policy in the group accounts from that followed in the individual accounts. Thus, where the parent undertaking is a corporation, standardization of the accounting and valuation rules for the assets and debts of all consolidated enterprises is achieved on the basis of the strict rules that apply to corporations. The conflict between the integrity of the individual accounts and the aim of uniform accounting and valuation is resolved by relinquishing the authoritative character of the individual accounts. If the parent undertaking is a partnership (*Personengesellschaft*) under the PublG, the group accounts may follow the valuation rules that apply to partnerships, with all the opportunities for creating and releasing hidden reserves. These rules can be applied to the assets and liabilities of the corporations that are included in the group accounts of a sole proprietor, even though the assets and liabilities are valued in the individual accounts according to the strict rules that apply to corporations. The parent undertaking must then accept that such consolidated accounts do not exempt the subsidiary corporations from the obligation, in appropriate circumstances, to prepare group accounts for a sub-group (PublG § 13 (3), third sentence).

Departures from the basic principle of uniform valuation (*Grundsatz einheitlicher Bewertung*) are permitted only:

1 On the inclusion of items in the accounts of banks and insurance businesses which are valued according to the special rules applicable in this financial sector (HGB § 308 (2), second sentence).
2 If the effect of modifying the valuation is not material to the presentation of a true and fair view (HGB § 308 (2), third sentence).
3 In 'exceptional cases' which have to be justified (HGB § 308 (2), fourth sentence), e.g. acquisition of an important subsidiary shortly before the group balance sheet date.
4 Where valuations permitted under tax law are maintained in the group accounts (HGB § 308 (3)).

This last provision can have the effect that valuations for tax purposes also influence the group accounts and reduce their information content. (On the influence of valuations according to tax law on the individual accounts see Chapter 6, section 1.3.) Certainly the use of valuations undertaken for tax purposes is an option which, in practice, few enterprises take up. Parent undertakings whose subsidiaries have made large special write-offs for tax purposes reverse these in the group accounts, in order to increase the equity. The procedure has no retrospective effect on the tax computation, as the group accounts are not authoritative for tax purposes.

5.3 Common balance sheet date

'The group accounts are to be prepared at the balance sheet date of the accounts of the parent undertaking or at the different balance sheet date of the most important or of a majority of the consolidated enterprises' (HGB § 299 (1)). The balance sheet date for the group accounts can, to this extent, be chosen freely from the indicated alternatives.

Should the financial year of a consolidated enterprise differ from that of the group, then for consolidation purposes interim accounts (*Zwischenabschluß*) should be prepared which take the same period as the group accounts (HGB § 299 (2)). Only in a case where the balance sheet date of the subsidiary is less than three months prior to that of the group is there no requirement to prepare interim accounts. It would still be necessary to take account of or to disclose important events concerning the assets and liabilities, the financial position or the profit or loss of a consolidated undertaking which have occurred between that undertaking's balance sheet date and the consolidated balance sheet date.

6 FOREIGN CURRENCY TRANSLATION

The BiRiLiG of 1985 left largely open the question of foreign currency translation (*Währungsumrechnung*), among other things, on account of the continuing technical controversy. In contrast to the position with the individual accounts, there is as yet no accepted convention concerning group accounts. The prevailing view is that, for the time being, foreign currency translation should remain unregulated, pending further experience of the application of the methods. It is up to the enterprise to decide on the translation method and whether translation differences should be treated as an element of profit or transferred direct to reserves. The only requirement of the Commercial Code (HGB § 313 (1) No. 2) is that information should be given on the translation methods. As a result of this lack of regulation there are almost as many variations in foreign currency translation as there are reporting enterprises. Since different methods can have substantially different impacts, the effect is to reduce considerably the comparability of the accounts of German enterprises with significant foreign interests. At present discussion is centred on four methods; the other methods can all be derived by combining elements of these four:

1 The pure closing rate method (*reine Stichtagskursmethode*).
2 The modified closing rate method (*modifizierte Stichtagskursmethode*).
3 The pure temporal or 'equivalence' method (*reine Zeitbezugsmethode*).
4 The modified temporal or 'equivalence' method (*modifizierte Zeitbezugsmethode*).

6.1 Closing rate method

6.1.1 Pure closing rate method

All assets and liabilities, revenues and expenses (including the profit) are translated at the exchange rate ruling at the balance sheet date (closing rate). Negative and positive translation differences are transferred direct to equity, bypassing the profit and loss account. The equity, after addition or deduction of the translation difference, is finally also translated at the closing rate.

6.1.2 Modified closing rate method

Balance sheet items are translated at the closing rate; profit and loss items are translated at the average exchange rate for the period. The profit figure is either recalculated as the difference between the translated revenues and expenses (in effect it is translated at the average rate), or it is translated at the closing rate. In the second case the difference arising from translating the profit and loss items at average rate and the net profit at closing rate is reported as other revenues or expenses. All other translation differences are transferred, as with the pure closing rate method, direct to equity.

6.2 Temporal method

6.2.1 Pure temporal method

Balance sheet

1 Translation of the separate assets and liabilities with reference to the timing of the values: historical values in foreign currency with reference to the historical rate, current values with reference to the closing rate.
2 Ascertainment of the corresponding current value in Deutschmarks (= current value in the foreign currency at the closing rate) or the historical cost in Deutschmarks (= historical cost in the foreign currency at the historical rate).
3 Comparison of the historical cost in Deutschmarks with the current value in Deutschmarks for each item and choice of the value to be used for the Deutschmark balance sheet through analogous application of the rules for the individual balance sheet (extended historical cost principle, extended principle of lower value, extended realization principle).
4 Frequently, simplified methods are used. The comparison of the historical cost in Deutschmarks with the current value in Deutschmarks is not always made systematically for every item, but only when a lower current value in Deutschmarks is evident. Furthermore inventories are usually translated at the closing rate.

Profit and loss account

1 Translation of revenues and expenses that are not value adjustments of balance sheet items (e.g. wages, taxes) at the exchange rate ruling at the time of the transaction.
2 Translation of other items (e.g. depreciation) at the exchange rate appropriate to the corresponding asset or liability.
3 The profit is calculated as the difference between the translated revenues and expenses.

6.2.2 Modified temporal method

1 Translation of the individual items in the balance sheet and the profit and loss account in principle as with the pure temporal method, except for debtors and creditors. To the extent that receivables and payables have similar payment dates, on the revaluation (devaluation) of the home currency, the payables (receivables) are also translated at the closing rate. In that case the imparity principle which requires unrealized losses to be accrued but prohibits recognition of unrealized profits (see Table 7.4) is applied only to the net balance of receivables and payables.

2 As opposed to the pure temporal method, the profit is translated at the closing rate and is not calculated as the difference between translated revenues and translated expenses. In order to make the profit and loss account add up, the difference that is thereby created is shown as 'other revenues' or 'other expenses'. Translation differences in the balance sheet are either shown as a separate item or charged to equity.

The effects of the temporal method (both the pure and the modified versions) and of the pure closing rate method are demonstrated in Example 8.1.

6.3 Which method?

As indicated at the beginning of this section, it is not always possible to classify the methods used in practice by reference to the theoretical methods that have been presented here. Therefore the classification in empirical surveys has to be relatively crude. According to a survey of 100 large German groups by Treuarbeit (1990), of the sixty-seven groups that gave information on foreign currency translation, twenty-one groups chose the pure closing rate method and twenty-six the modified closing rate method. In all other cases different rates were used, which gives grounds for supposing that most could be consistent with variations of the temporal method (see also Zillessen 1982 and Busse von Colbe *et al.* 1989: 204–10, which produced results different from those of Treuarbeit 1990). It is impossible to be more precise, owing to lack of sufficient information in the accounts. However, the pure temporal method would seem to be seldom used.

There are recommendations on foreign currency translation from both the *Institut der Wirtschaftsprüfer* and the working party of the *Schmalenbach-Gesellschaft/Deutsche Gesellschaft für Betriebswirtschaft eV*. The Institut der Wirtschaftsprüfer recommended that either the closing rate or the temporal method could be used, so long as the method chosen was used as consistently as possible over time for all the accounts in the group. With the temporal method there was an option concerning the treatment of the translation difference: it could be regarded either as an element of profit (the pure form of the temporal method) or transferred to reserves (modified form). The working group on external company accounting of the *Schmalenbach-Gesellschaft/Deutsche Gesellschaft für Betriebswirtschaft eV* (Busse von Colbe 1989: 51–63) also allowed for this option, but, in contrast to the IdW, the working group expressed a clear preference for the temporal method. All these statements have the status of recommendations only and are not legally binding on enterprises.

Example 8.1 **Foreign currrency translation of the statements of subsidiaries**

The holding enterprise (P) owns 100 per cent of the shares of the foreign subsidiary (F). F's balance sheet and profit and loss account are presented in a simplified form in Tables 8.1.1–2. The following assumptions are made concerning the individual items and the exchange rate.

- *Foreign exchange rate.* Revaluation of the home currency (DM) during the financial year. Exchange rate: before the revaluation, 1 FC (Foreign Currency) = 1 DM; after the revaluation, 2 FC = 1 DM.
- *Tangible fixed assets.* Book value at the beginning of the financial year, FC 46 million. Depreciation on these assets for the financial year, FC 2 million. Current value of these assets at the end of the financial year, FC 100 million. Additional tangible fixed assets acquired after the revaluation: acquisition cost FC 16 million.
- *Raw materials.* Book value at beginning of year, FC 24 million; market value at end of year, FC 50 million; no change in stocks during the year.
- *Finished goods.* Book value at beginning of year, FC 20 million; market value at end of year, FC 32 million; no change in stocks during the year.
- *Debtors and liabilities.* Denominated in FC and have similar due dates. No change in balances during the year.
- *Equity.* No change during the year.
- *Profit and loss account.* All revenues and expenses relating to transactions occurred after the revaluation.
- The profit for the year in the balance sheet is equal to the balance sheet profit (*Bilanzgewinn*).

Table 8.1.1 Balance sheets at 31 December 19X1

	F's balance sheet (FC million)		*Closing rate method*			*Pure temporal method*			*Modified temporal method*		
			Exchange rate (DM per FC)	F's balance sheet (DM million)		Exchange rate (DM per FC or explanation)	F's balance sheet (DM million)		Exchange rate (DM per FC)	F's balance sheet (DM million)	
	1		2	3		4	5		6	7	
	Debit	Credit		Debit	Credit		Debit	Credit		Debit	Credit
Assets											
1 Fixed assets	60		0.5	30		44×1+16×0.5	52		44×1+16×0.5	52	
2 Stocks: raw materials	24		0.5	12		1	24		1	24	
3 Stocks: finished goods	20		0.5	10		See text	16		See text	16	
4 Debtors	16		0.5	8		0.5	8		0.5	8	
5 Cash	4		0.5	2		0.5	2		0.5	2	
6 Translation difference				35						7	
Liabilities and equity											
7 Subscribed capital		40	1		40	1		40	1		40
8 Profit reserves		30	1		30	See text		15	1		30
9 Provisions		10	0.5		5	1		10	1		10
10 Liabilities		30	0.5		15	1		30	14×1+16×0.5		22
11 *Bilanzgewinn*		14	0.5		7			7	0.5		7
Total	124	124		97	97		102	102		109	109

Table 8.1.2 Profit and loss accounts for 19X1

		Closing rate method		Pure temporal method		Modified temporal method	
	Profit and loss (FC million)	*Exchange rate (DM per FC)*	*Profit and loss (FC million)*	*Exchange rate (DM per FC)*	*Profit and loss (FC million)*	*Exchange rate (DM per FC)*	*Profit and loss (FC million)*
	1	*2*	*3*	*4*	*5*	*6*	*7*
1 Turnover	240	0.5	120	0.5	120	0.5	120
2 Change in stocks	–		–		–		–
3 Other operating revenues	8	0.5	4	0.5	4	0.5	4
4 Cost of materials	122	0.5	61	0.5	61	0.5	61
5 Wages	100	0.5	50	0.5	50	0.5	50
6 Depreciation	2	0.5	1	1	2	1	2
7 Other operating expenses	8	0.5	4	0.5	4	0.5	4
8 Interests and similar expenses	2	0.5	1	0.5	1	0.5	1
9 Operating results	14	0.5	7	Balance	6	Balance	6
10 Losses from currency translation					14		
11 Translation difference (other revenues)							1
12 Profit of the year	14	0.5	7	Balance	−8	0.5	7
13 Withdrawals from profit reserves	–		–	Balance	15		–
14 *Bilanzgewinn*	14	0.5	7	0.5	7	0.5	7

Tables 8.1.1–2 present the impact of the different foreign currency translation methods on the balance sheet and profit and loss account.

Closing rate method (*Stichtagskursmethode*)

Since the opening equity is translated at historical cost, a translation difference of DM 35 million (debit) arises following the devaluation of the FC. This difference represents the unrealized losses on the various assets and the unrealized gains on the various liabilities. Under the pure closing rate method this difference is set off against equity; for exposition purposes it is shown separately in Table 8.1.1. In the group accounts it is set off against the profit reserves. In the profit and loss account there is, in this example, no translation difference, since all items (including the net profit) are translated at the same rate.

Example 8.1 Continued

Pure temporal method (*reine Zeitbezugsmethode*)

Under this method the historical cost in DM and the current value in DM are compared for each item and one of these values is chosen for the DM balance sheet on the basis of the accounting rules used in the holding enterprise's individual accounts. As regards the tangible fixed assets, this leads to the valuation of the existing fixed assets on the basis of their historical cost less depreciation translated at the historical exchange rate (FC 44 million × 1 DM/1 FC = DM 44 million), since an evaluation on the basis of current value translated at the current exchange rate (FC 100 million × 0.5 DM/1 FC = DM 50 million) would lead to a breach of the extended historical cost principle and to the reporting of unrealized gains. With the newly acquired assets there is no problem (FC 16 million × 0.5 DM/1 FC = DM 8 million), since the historical rate and the current rate are identical. For the stocks the comparison of the historical cost in DM and the current value in DM is made as follows:

Raw materials

Book value in FC × historical rate = FC 24 million × 1 DM/1 FC = DM 24 million
Current value in FC × current rate = FC 50 million × 0.5 DM/1 FC = DM 25 million

Finished goods

Book value in FC × historical rate = FC 20 million × 1 DM/1 FC = DM 20 million
Current value in FC × current rate = FC 32 million × 0.5 DM/1 FC = DM 16 million

Since the strict principle of lower value applies to stocks in the accounts of the individual enterprise, the raw materials are reported at DM 24 million and the finished goods at DM 16 million. Similar principles are applied to the monetary items. Receivables and cash are translated at the current rate, because of the devaluation of the foreign currency; by contrast, liabilities and provisions are translated at the historical rate (because for liabilities the principle of highest value is applied). In total there is an unrealized translation loss of DM 14 million, which is made up of losses in respect of finished goods (DM 4 million), receivables (DM 8 million) and cash (DM 2 million). In the profit and loss account, the profit for the year is the operating result (the difference between the translated revenues and the translated expenses) less the translation difference of DM 14 million. The difference between the translated operating results with the closing rate method (DM 7 million) and with the pure temporal method (DM 6 million) is caused by the different treatment of depreciation. With the temporal method (in contrast to the closing rate method) depreciation is translated at the exchange rate applied to the original assets, i.e. the historical cost. After the translation loss of DM 14 million has been deducted from the operating result there is a loss for the year of DM 8 million. When, as in the example, the same dividend is to be paid as with the closing rate method, this is possible only if DM 15 million is taken from the profit reserves.

Modified temporal method (*modifizierte Zeitbezugsmethode*)

In this example there are two differences by comparison with the pure temporal method. First, only the excess of liabilities over debtors (DM 14 million) is translated at the historical rate, so that there is an unrealized gain on liabilities of DM 8 million. Second, the profit of the year is translated at the closing rate (and not found by difference). The difference that thereby arises between the translated profit of the year and the net balance of translated revenues and expenses is included with 'other revenues'. In the balance sheet the result of these procedures is a translation difference of DM 7 million (debit). If this is set off against equity, the profit reserves become DM 23 million. This amount differs from the one reported under the pure temporal method by just the amount of unrealized profits of DM 8 million on liabilities.

7 CONSOLIDATION OF CAPITAL

There are basically two methods of consolidating capital:

1 Accounting for the subsidiaries at market value. The market value at the time of acquisition is equal to the acquisition cost of the shares in the subsidiary. This method of consolidation of capital is known as the purchase method (*Erwerbsmethode*).
2 Accounting for the subsidiary's assets and liabilities at their book value in the subsidiary's own accounts (pooling of interests method, *Interessenzusammenführungsmethode*). However, the choice of this method is subject to certain conditions (see section 7.2 below for details).

7.1 Purchase method

7.1.1 First consolidation

According to HGB § 301, when using the purchase method a group has a choice between two variants: the book value method (*Buchwertmethode*; HGB § 301 (1), second sentence, No. 1) or the revaluation method (*Neubewertungsmethode*; HGB § 301 (1), second sentence, No. 2). The same method should be used for all subsidiaries in order to ensure that the group accounts are comprehensible. However, this is not a legal requirement. In the following paragraphs the operation of the two variants is described in detail; initially it is assumed that there are no minority shareholders.

7.1.1.1 Without minority shareholders

In the case of the consolidation of the capital of a subsidiary whose shares are 100 per cent owned by consolidated enterprises, there is no material difference (in the end result) between the book value method and the revaluation method. With the book value method (*Buchwertmethode*) the first step is to replace, in balance sheet II (*Handelsbilanz II*) of the parent undertaking, the shares in the subsidiary with the assets and liabilities taken from the subsidiary's balance sheet II (HGB § 300 (1)). Balance sheet II is the balance sheet after effecting the adjustments resulting from the standardization of the balance sheet contents (see section 5 above) and, in appropriate cases for subsidiaries, the translation from a foreign currency (see section 6 above). The second step is to take account of the consolidation difference, since the value of the shares in the subsidiary will not, as a rule, be equal to the net assets, except in the case where the parent undertaking formed the subsidiary.

If the value of the shares is greater than the value of the net assets (a positive consolidation difference, *aktivischer Unterschiedsbetrag*), in German law the values of the assets and liabilities of balance sheet II must be adjusted so that they reflect their current value (HGB § 301 (1), third sentence). For example, if land is acquired whose book value is less than its current value, the book value must be adjusted to ensure that, in the group accounts, the land is shown at its current value. The difference between the book value of assets and their current value is often referred to as 'hidden current value reserves' (*stille Tageswertrücklagen*), or 'hidden reserves' for short. If the subsidiary owns intangible assets which it has developed itself and which it may not capitalize in its individual financial statements (see Chapter 7, section 4.1.2), these will normally have been paid for by the parent undertaking in the purchase price of the shares and, accordingly, are to be shown in the consolidated financial statements. The total of these value adjustments usually accounts for only part of the consolidation difference. The remainder, if any, of the consolidation difference has to be shown in the consolidated financial statements as goodwill (*Geschäftswert*). With the revaluation method (*Neubewertungsmethode*) the equity of the subsidiary is revalued before being set against the value of the subsidiary's shares in the parent undertaking's balance sheet (HGB § 301 (1), second sentence, No. 2). As the subsidiary's asset values have already been adjusted, the whole of the consolidated difference is goodwill. For 100 per cent-owned subsidiaries the results of the two methods are identical.

In theory the application of the revaluation method could lead to a total value of net assets higher than the book value of the subsidiary's shares in the parent undertaking's balance sheet. However, the possibility is excluded by law, since revaluations are permissible only to the extent that the subsidiary's net assets do not exceed the acquisition cost to the parent undertaking of the shares in the subsidiary (HGB § 301 (1), fourth sentence). The same applies when the book value method is chosen. Value adjustments may be made only to the extent of the consolidation difference (*Unterschiedsbetrag*). Which asset values may be adjusted (the imputation problem) is not prescribed by law; there is a choice of method. The law's aim is to ensure that the asset value adjustments made as part of the capital consolidation are based on payments (acquisition cost), that is, the sum of the value adjustments is limited to the difference between a subsidiary's net assets and the acquisition cost to the parent undertaking of the subsidiary's shares. This procedure is compatible with German accounting regulations for the financial statements of the individual enterprise and also makes sense in economic terms. With the purchase method, the acquisition of a subsidiary is treated like any other investment. The acquisition cost of the acquired enterprise is recorded in the balance sheet. The special feature is that the acquisition cost is broken down as between the separate assets and liabilities of the subsidiary. Example 8.2 shows how the valuation adjustments are limited to the acquisition cost of the participation.

If, from the beginning, the subsidiary's net assets are greater than the acquisition cost of the parent's investment, then the negative consolidation difference (*passivischer Unterschiedsbetrag*) must be shown in the consolidated balance sheet, according to HGB § 301 (3), first sentence, after correcting for any overstatement of net assets (i.e. when, in the subsidiary's balance sheet, the book value of assets is greater than their true value or the book value of liabilities is less than their true value). The assets and liabilities of the subsidiary less the consolidation difference again equal in total the acquisition cost of the investment. The cause of a negative consolidation difference is frequently that the purchase price has taken account of certain expected future losses of the subsidiary, the full effect of which are not yet recorded in its balance sheet. In such a case, as the losses occur, they are charged against the negative consolidation difference, so that the losses are compensated. They were already taken into account in the calculation of the purchase price of the investment.

The law does not specify where, on the liabilities side of the balance sheet, a negative

Example 8.2 **First consolidation without minority shareholders**

Acquisition cost of shares in a 100 per cent owned subsidiary: DM 32 million
Equity in subsidiary's balance sheet II: DM 22 million
Subsidiary's assets (DM million):

	Book value in balance sheet II	*Difference between current value and book value*
Building plot	3	+10
Land and building	10	+7
Self developed patent	0	+7
Plant and machinery	8	−8
Total	21	16

The consolidation difference of DM 10 million occurring under the book value method (DM 32 million less DM 22 million) is used to adjust the assets as follows. First the plant and machinery are written off completely (DM 8 million). The sum of possible positive value adjustments (building plot, land and buildings, and the patent) is DM 24 million (10 + 7 + 7). However, by law the total of the value adjustments is limited to DM 18 million (the consolidation difference of 10 and the negative value adjustment of 8 that has already been made). How this figure of DM 18 million should be divided among the different assets is not prescribed by law. In the literature the pros and cons of various methods are argued, but it is not possible to go into them here. In what follows, only the calculation for the proportional imputation method is outlined. The correction factor is 75 per cent (18 : 24).

Value adjustments	DM million
Building plot, 75 per cent of 10	7.50
Land and buildings, 75 per cent of 7	5.25
Patent, 75 per cent of 7	5.25
Total	18.00

If the write-down of the plant and machinery (DM 8 million) is deducted from the total of the value adjustments (DM 18 million), we arrive at the amount of the consolidation difference (DM 10 million). This is the case with both the book value method and the revaluation method.

consolidation difference is to be presented. In the literature it is considered permissible to show it as a separate item between reserves and provisions, but also as a separate item within either the reserves or the provisions, depending on the nature of the item. (See also the comments in the section on subsequent consolidation (*Folgekonsolidierung*).) According to the survey by Treuarbeit (1990), of thirty-one groups which reported a negative consolidation difference, twenty-eight showed it as part of the equity, one showed it between reserves and provisions and two included it with provisions.

Example 8.3 **Presentation of a negative consolidation difference: extracts from the accounts of three groups**

	DM
BILFINGER & BERGER AG GROUP ACCOUNTS, 31 DECEMBER 1989	
Reserves	
I Capital reserve	172,448,000
II Profit reserves (four separate items)	115,859,000
III Consolidation difference	34,086,000
Total	332,393,000
RUHRKOHLE AG GROUP ACCOUNTS, 31 DECEMBER 1989	
Other provisions	4,604,650,000
Among them provisions for:	
• Sales area	865,709,000
• Filling in of shafts, recultivation and environmental protection	558,909,000
• Social benefits	1,186,656,000
• Anniversary expenses	337,260,000
• Taxes	318,530,000
of which deferred	(29,343,000)
• Capitalized pension obligations	235,300,000
• Difference from the consolidation with the character of a provision	187,505,000

SÜDZUCKER AG

'In the consolidated balance sheet, the capital reserve includes a consolidation difference of DM 17.7 million.'

7.1.1.2 With minority shareholders

If the shares of the subsidiary are not 100 per cent-owned by the consolidated enterprises, because some shares are owned either by outsiders or by non-consolidated subsidiaries, then there is a material difference between:

1 The book value method.
2 The revaluation method.

With the book value method (*Buchwertmethode*), the procedure is the same at first as was shown for the 100 per cent-owned subsidiary except that the consolidation difference is calculated on the basis of the share of the subsidiary's equity that is owned by the parent. In addition, the question arises as to how this consolidation difference may be used in value adjustments for individual assets: whether these can be made only in proportion to the parent's share (the 'share method', *Anteilsmethode*) or whether the whole consolidation difference may be used so that some assets can be put in the consolidated balance sheet at the full acquisition cost at the time of first consolidation (the 'allocation' method, *Zuteilungsmethode*). Both methods can be combined (the 'shared allocation' method, *anteilige Zuteilungsmethode*). The law does not state categorically which method should be used. As long as it is certain that the values used comply with the unitary entity principle (see section 1.2 above), and that the value adjustments do not exceed the consolidation difference, then, according to some commentators, all three methods are compatible with the law (option).

For the other shareholders' part of the subsidiary's net assets, a separate item must be disclosed within the equity section of the consolidated balance sheet, representing the minority interest of other shareholders, with an appropriate description. In the case of the book value method, it is equal to the appropriate share of net assets (or equity) as given in the subsidiary's balance sheet II.

With the revaluation method (*Neubewertungsmethode*) the value adjustments relating to the other shareholders' part of the net assets are affected and the minority interest is corrected accordingly. If there is no imputation problem, the assets are shown at their full

Example 8.4 **First consolidation with minority shareholders**

This example uses the same data as Example 8.2, except that the subsidiary is only 60 per cent owned. According to the book value method, the consolidation difference is DM 18.8 million (32 million less 60 per cent of 22 million). Of this amount, DM 16 million is used up in the revaluation of assets.

Value adjustments (DM million):

	Book value	*Adjustment*	*Calculated acquisition cost at the time of first consolidation*
Building plot	3	+10	13
Land and buildings	10	+7	17
Self-developed patent	0	+7	7
Plant and machinery	8	−8	0
Total	21	+16	37

The remainder of the consolidation difference, that is, DM 2.8 million (18.8 million less 16 million), is shown as goodwill. Under the book value method the minority interest (*Minderheitenanteil*) is calculated at DM 8.8 million (40 per cent of 22 million).

Under the revaluation method the equity of the subsidiary after the value adjustments is DM 38 milion (22 million + 16 million). The value adjustments of DM 16 million can be made in their entirety and, in contrast to Example 8.2, there is no imputation problem. In this case the minority interest comes to DM 15.2 million (40 per cent of 38 million). The parent's share of the subsidiary's equity comes to DM 22.8 million (60 per cent of 38 million). The consolidation difference is DM 9.2 million (32 million less 22.8 million), which, in accordance with HGB § 301, is shown in the balance sheet as goodwill.

(DM million)	*Book value method*	*Revaluation method*
Building plot	13	13
Land and buildings	17	17
Self-developed patent	7	7
Plant and machinery	0	0
Goodwill (*Geschäftswert*)	2.8	9.2
Minority interest (*Minderheitenanteile*)	8.8	15.2

In comparing the two methods it is clear that, in both cases, the full value adjustments of DM 16 million are applied to the assets. However, with the book value method, the value adjustments are credited entirely (i.e. at 100 per cent, which is more than the 60 per cent share) to the parent's share of the subsidiary's equity, which has the effect of reducing goodwill. With the revaluation method, the minority interest is credited with its share of the value adjustments, which results in it being shown at a higher amount (by DM 6.4 million, being 40 per cent of 16 million).

actual value at the time of the first consolidation. In addition the full amount of the goodwill that relates to the parent is shown in the consolidated balance sheet. However, an increase in the minority interest through the addition of its imputed share of the goodwill would be illegal (HGB § 307 (1), second sentence). Goodwill is shown in the consolidated balance sheet only to the extent that it relates to the parent undertaking.

Example 8.4 highlights the differences between the book value method and the revaluation method.

7.1.2 Subsequent consolidation

In subsequent consolidations (*Folgekonsolidierungen*) the question is how to treat the value adjustments, the goodwill, or, in appropriate cases, the negative consolidation difference. In effect the value adjustments remain tied to the assets and liabilities to which they belong.

1 If the book value of a *depreciable fixed asset* that is taken into the consolidated balance sheet is increased, then, from the viewpoint of the group, the book value, increased by the amount of the value adjustment, represents the acquisition cost. This increased acquisition cost is to be written off in accordance with the legally permitted methods. Frequently the elements of the (subsidiary's) existing depreciation plan are adopted and the value adjustments are depreciated in the same way as the original book value in the subsidiary's accounts. For this a complementary calculation or complementary consolidated book-keeping is necessary. However, it is also possible to set up a new depreciation plan just for the group accounts.
2 If value adjustments have been made in respect of *land* or of *finished products*, then, when these assets are subsequently disposed of, their cost, for the purposes of reporting the profit on disposal, is not the book value in the subsidiary's accounts but rather the value shown in the group accounts, that is, the book value in the subsidiary's accounts plus the value adjustments.
3 *Provisions* that have been set up in the group accounts can be used or released only in the group accounts.

Concerning the subsequent accounting treatment of the goodwill arising from the first consolidation, there are, according to HGB § 309, three possibilities. It may be:

1 Written off to the profit and loss account within the four years following the year of acquisition.
2 Written off to the profit and loss account systematically over the expected life. There is no legal limit on how long this may be.
3 Set off directly against the reserves in the consolidated balance sheet, thus not affecting profit.

Under HGB § 301 (3), third sentence, there is also the possibility of setting off goodwill against a negative consolidation difference arising from the consolidation of another subsidiary.

Charging goodwill against the consolidated reserves is a rule that found its way into German law from British practice via the Seventh Directive. It is contrary to certain basic principles that in Germany have for years applied to the individual accounts. In the individual accounts, acquired goodwill must be amortized via the profit and loss account (HGB § 255 (4); see also Chapter 7, section 4.1.4). This breach of established principle was accepted into legislation only to avoid German enterprises being at a disadvantage in reporting profits.

In the case of a negative consolidation difference (*passivischer Unterschiedsbetrag*) the law (HGB § 301 (3), third sentence, and § 309 (2)) provides for the following accounting treatments in subsequent consolidations:

1 Release to the profit and loss account.
2 Retention in the consolidated balance sheet.
3 Offsetting against goodwill.

According to HGB § 309 (2), a negative consolidation difference may be released to the profit and loss account only if:

1 An unfavourable development in the profitability of the enterprise that was foreseen at the time of acquiring the shares, or at first consolidation, has occurred, or if expenditure that was anticipated at the time has to be charged, or
2 It is established at the balance sheet date that it relates to a realized profit.

In the first case, the consolidation difference is of the nature of negative goodwill. In the second, there are two possibilities. On the one hand, the difference arises when it is no longer considered that the losses which were anticipated at the time of acquisition will occur. On the other hand, there can be the special case where the shares in the subsidiary were acquired through the disposal/exchange of a real asset (for example, real property or another shareholding) and that thereby a profit on disposal of this asset was realized.

When positive and negative consolidation differences are set off against each other, this is allowed only as regards the book value of goodwill after (for example) depreciation. The amounts in question must be shown in the notes, to the extent that they have been set off (HGB § 301 (3), third sentence).

7.1.3 The sale of a subsidiary enterprise

When an enterprise, which until now has been fully consolidated, is sold or otherwise disposed of (e.g. by liquidation), there is an impact on the presentation of the net worth, financial position and results. According to the legal entity fiction (*Fiktion der rechtlichen Einheit*, HGB § 297 (3), first sentence) the event must be presented in the group accounts as it would be in the accounts of a single entity, where disposal of assets, etc., are accounted for separately. If the aim is to account for the disposal following this fiction of separate disposals, then the proceeds from the sale of the shares must be divided among the separate departing assets, etc., in the same way as, on the first consolidation, the acquisition cost of the shares was divided among the incoming assets, etc. The current disposal proceeds must then be set off against the book value of the assets in the consolidated balance sheet immediately prior to the disposal of the subsidiary. The separate gains and losses on disposal must then be shown in the profit and loss account as they would be shown in the individual accounts of a separate legal entity.

As a rule, however, the reporting of separate gains and losses on the disposal of a subsidiary is too expensive. The following procedure is simpler and permitted by law:

1 In the *balance sheet* the retired fixed assets are shown as a separate column in the fixed assets schedule, entitled 'Retirements arising from changes in the scope of the group accounts', or are included together with the other disposals (originating from the accounts of the parent undertaking and other subsidiaries).
2 In the *profit and loss account* the assets of the subsidiary being sold are combined under a separate heading, 'Costs relating to the disposal of subsidiary companies', or is included in other business expenses. Correspondingly the debts of the subsidiary being sold and the disposal proceeds are shown as revenue from the sale of shares in subsidiaries or as other business income. Netting one item off against the other would violate the general prohibition of offsetting income and expenses, which, under HGB § 298 (1), also applies to the group accounts.

In order to ensure that the consolidated results are shown in accordance with the principle of the legal entity fiction, when a subsidiary leaves the group the disposal proceeds and the book value of the subsidiary from the viewpoint of the group must be disclosed separately. Hence, for a 100 per cent-owned subsidiary an appropriate presentation is:

  proceeds of the sale of shares
− book value of the subsidiary in the consolidated balance sheet (thus including any differences between the book value of assets and their current value still remaining from the first consolidation)
+ debts of the subsidiary according to the consolidated balance sheet (thus including any differences between the book value of debts and their current value still remaining from the first consolidation)
− goodwill arising from the first consolidation that has not yet been written off
+ any remaining negative consolidation difference from the first consolidation
= gain/loss on disposal of the subsidiary from the viewpoint of the group

Where there still remains a positive consolidation difference (*aktivischer Unterschiedsbetrag*) from the first consolidation, it must be included in the value of the subsidiary sold, after including hidden reserves and debts as required by the HGB § 301 (1), third sentence. Otherwise only part of the subsidiary's assets and debts that were employed during the time that it belonged to the group would be reckoned as cost. Outlays for assets cannot simply be ignored in the group accounts. On the other side, any remaining negative consolidation difference (*passivischer Unterschiedsbetrag*) must be transferred to the profit and loss account, since otherwise the net assets of the subsidiary, which on the disposal are shown as expenses, will be reported at a higher amount than the group paid. The pagatoric principle (*pagatorisches Prinzip*), one of the fundamental principles underlying German accounting law, would be violated. The pagatoric principle means that the profit must be calculated in such a way that the sum of profit over the lifetime of an enterprise equals the total cash flow.

This explanation on the disposal of a subsidiary is consistent with the legal entity fiction and the pagatoric principle. Since the rules relating to the disposal of a subsidiary are not expressly specified in the law, it can happen that some groups fail to include remaining consolidation differences in the value of the assets sold and thus distort the results.

An analogous situation arises when there is a fundamental change in how a subsidiary is accounted for in the group accounts, particularly when a subsidiary that has been fully consolidated in the past must be excluded from the consolidation and shown as an investment at historical cost. Most of the rules explained above, concerning the elimination of consolidation differences, etc., apply, *mutatis mutandis*, to this situation. However, when the only change in the accounting treatment of a subsidiary is from full consolidation to proportional consolidation or the equity method, there is no gain or loss on disposal to be reported.

7.2 Pooling of interests method

With the BiRiLiG of 19 December 1985 a second Anglo-American method of capital consolidation, besides the purchase method, was introduced into German law: the pooling of interests method (*Interessenzusammenführungsmethode*), set out in HGB § 302. This method differs from the purchase method in that:

1 The offsetting of the carrying value of the shares owned by the parent undertaking in a subsidiary is limited to the subsidiary's nominal capital. (Reserves and any carried forward profits are not taken into account.)
2 The resultant consolidation difference is not included with the assets and liabilities in the consolidated balance sheet but is included with the reserves.

However, the fact that the book value of the parent undertaking's investment is set solely against its share of the subsidiary's subscribed capital is less significant than it might appear at first sight. When, for example, a positive consolidation difference (*aktivischer Unterschiedsbetrag*) is deducted from the reserves, the effect is the same as when, with the purchase method, the book value of the investment is set off against the parent undertaking's share of the subsidiary's total equity (share capital plus reserves). Moreover, when it is noted that, with the purchase method in Germany, goodwill may be written off direct to reserves, thus not affecting the profit, the difference arising from the different procedure of the pooling of interests method is limited to the reporting of a possible acquired share of annual profits at the time of first consolidation and the prohibiting of the revaluation of assets of the acquired enterprise.

In contrast to the purchase method, the pooling of interests method has scarcely been mentioned in German literature and is seldom found in practice. In its survey Treuarbeit (1990) did not come across a single instance of the method being applied among respondent groups. One can only speculate on the reasons:

1 The restricted range of conditions under which the method may be applied militate against it becoming more significant. It may be used only for subsidiaries that are wholly consolidated in the consolidated balance sheet (i.e. not for proportionally consolidated subsidiaries or associated enterprises). Furthermore, under the terms of HGB § 302 (1), the pooling of interests method can be used only when:

(a) Ninety per cent of the subsidiary's subscribed capital belongs to the parent undertaking.
(b) The shareholders of the acquired enterprise in the main received as consideration for their shares not cash but instead shares in one of the consolidated undertakings (exchange of shares).
(c) Any agreed cash payment (e.g. for fractions of shares) did not exceed 10 per cent of the nominal value of the shares.

All three conditions must be met.

If these conditions are compared with those required in the United States, where the method originated, it is clear that there the conditions are even more rigorous than in Germany. APB Opinion 16 specifies twelve preconditions for the application of the pooling of interests method. Nevertheless the method is used much more frequently in the United States than in Germany. This suggests that there are further grounds for its infrequent use.

2 Whereas, in the United States, the pooling of interests method is compulsory when the twelve preconditions of APB Opinion 16 are met, in Germany the purchase method is always permitted for fully consolidated subsidiaries. When the conditions of HGB § 302 (1) are met, there is a choice between the purchase method and the pooling of interests method. There is no obligation to use the pooling of interests method. Perhaps the advantages of the pooling of interests method are not great enough to make it worth while employing, in parallel, two different consolidation methods in the group accounts. As has been demonstrated above, the essential differences of the pooling of interests method from the purchase method are limited, first to being able to report, as part of the consolidated profit, the parent undertaking's share of the subsidiary's annual profit at the time of first consolidation and, second, to maintaining the subsidiary's assets at their own original book value (not restating them at current value). By contrast, in the United States, the differences are greater because writing goodwill off directly against reserves, and so bypassing the profit and loss account, is not permitted.

3 A further explanation for the slight importance of the pooling of interests method could lie in the low propensity of German enterprises to use share exchanges as a method of acquiring subsidiaries. Frequently, to effect a share exchange, an enterprise would have to increase its share capital, which, fundamentally, requires the approval of a qualified majority of the shareholders. In the resolution proposing the increase in capital it would moreover be necessary to exclude the pre-emptive rights of the existing shareholders (wholly or partially), or at least to get some shareholders to waive their pre-emptive rights.

8 CONSOLIDATION OF INTRA-GROUP BALANCES

Intra-group debts appear in the individual balance sheets of the consolidated enterprises as corresponding receivables and payables. These amounts, unless they are immaterial, have to be eliminated from the gross sum of the balance sheet (*Schuldenkonsolidierung*, HGB § 303).

Example 8.5 **Consolidation of intra-group balances**

On 2 January 1988 one group enterprise, L (Lender), advances a loan to another group enterprise, B (Borrower). The loan is for a nominal amount of DM 30,000 at a discount of 20 per cent and is repayable by B on 31 December 1993. Thus B receives DM 24,000 on 2 January 1988 and has to repay DM 30,000 on 31 December 1993.

Initially, in L's balance sheet, the loan is shown as an asset at its acquisition cost of DM 24,000 and, in B's balance sheet, as a net liability of DM 24,000 (loan of DM 30,000 less capitalized discount (*Disagio*) of DM 6,000). B writes off the discount as an expense against profits in six equal instalments over the years 1988–93. L respects the prudence principle and reports the discount only in 1993, when the whole of the amount of DM 6,000 is taken to income and, simultaneously, added to the value of the loan. (The above treatment of the loan in the balance sheets of L and B is only one of several possibilities.)

Table 8.5.1 shows in rows 1–4 the impact of these operations on the gross sum of the balance sheets and on the yearly profit, calculated as the sum of the individual profits. The interest payments of B and the interest receipts of L are assumed to be equal and are ignored.

Table 8.5.1 Impact of the inter-enterprise loan: Increase (+) or reduction (−) in items in the gross sum of the balance sheets and in the gross sum of the annual profits, together with the difference arising from consolidation of inter-enterprise balances (DM 000, calculated at the end of each year)

	Item	*1988*	*1989*	*1990*	*1991*	*1992*	*1993*
1	Loan from L to B	+24	+24	+24	+24	+24	
2	Owed by B to L	+30	+30	+30	+30	+30	
3	Capitalized discount in B's balance sheet	+5	+4	+3	+2	+1	
4	Gross sum of the annual profit	−1	−1	−1	−1	−1	+5
5	Difference arising from the consolidation of inter-enterprise balances (1+3−2)	−1	−2	−3	−4	−5	
6	Change in the difference compared with the previous year	−1	−1	−1	−1	−1	+5
7	Annual consolidated profit	0	0	0	0	0	0

Row 1 shows the loan from L to B of DM 24,000 and row 2 the amount of DM 30,000 owed from B to L as they appear in the individual balance sheets of L and B; they are included at these amounts in the gross sum of the balance sheets. The capitalized discount (row 3) is reduced annually by the amount of the amortization. Each year, from 1988 to 1993, this amortization reduces the profits of B by DM 1,000. In 1993 the profit of L is increased by the credit of DM 6,000, and thus, for that year, the gross sum of the annual profits is DM 5,000 (row 4). Row 5 shows the excess of the credits (amount owed by B to L) over the debits (loan and capitalized discount). The change in this difference compared with the previous year is given in row 6. It is clear that the change in the difference arising from the consolidation of inter-enterprise balances (row 6) and the effect of the inter-enterprise financial operations on the sum of the annual profits inevitably move in parallel. Thus the change in the consolidation difference as compared with the previous year is to be deducted from the sum of the annual profits; the brought forward balance of the consolidation difference is to be set off against the consolidated reserves or disclosed as a separate item of equity. (The brought forward balance of the consolidation difference has already influenced the consolidated profits of the previous year(s).) The consequence of this procedure is that financial operations within the group have no effect on the consolidated profit (row 7).

If the amounts of the intra-group receivables and payables tally, there is no problem in offsetting and it has no effect on profit. Otherwise there will be a difference, arising from the fact that the receivable in one subsidiary's balance sheet is not valued at the same figure as the corresponding payable in the balance sheet of another subsidiary (or the parent). This difference is often referred to as the difference arising from the consolidation of intra-group balances (*Unterschiedsbetrag aus der Schuldenkonsolidierung*); the difference can be either positive (a net asset, *aktivischer Unterschiedsbetrag*) or negative (a net liability, *passivischer Unterschiedsbetrag*).

The dominance of the prudence principle (*Vorsichtsprinzip*) in German financial reporting means that the consolidation difference is usually a credit. Such a difference arises, for example, from the setting up of provisions for uncertain liabilities, for imminent losses on unsettled business or for guarantees given to consolidated undertakings, because the corresponding assets are not shown in the balance sheet of the other enterprise. It can also arise in respect of the charge to the profit and loss account concerning the reduction in the value of a receivable on account of its low (or zero) rate of interest or the write-off of an intra-group receivable. In all these cases, intra-group expenditure and revenue arise which affect the profits in the accounts of the individual enterprises and hence the gross sum of the balance sheet. The setting up of the provision or the write-off of the receivable lowers the profit in the accounts of the individual enterprise and increases the consolidation difference. Since such intra-group debts and provisions could not occur within a single legal entity, the intra-group expenses and revenue they induce and the resultant changes in the profit have to be reversed in the group accounts. For a year when the consolidation difference relating to intra-group debts is increased (reduced), the annual profit in the gross sum of accounts should be increased (reduced) accordingly. Example 8.5 makes the relationships clearer.

9 ELIMINATION OF INTRA-GROUP PROFITS

German law does not lay down explicit rules for the elimination of the profit on deliveries of goods or services between group enterprises (*Zwischengewinnelimininierung*). The obligation arises in an indirect fashion from the terms of HGB § 304, under which assets that result wholly or partially from deliveries of goods or services between enterprises included in the consolidation are to be included in the consolidated balance sheet at an amount at which they could be included if all the consolidated enterprises formed a single legal entity. The amount is the acquisition cost to the group, in the case of assets that have been acquired from outside the group, or the group's production cost otherwise. To put it another way, the valuation rules that apply to the individual accounts are to be applied, by analogy, to the group accounts.

In the individual accounts, there is a degree of latitude in valuing assets between the costs that must be capitalized and the costs that may be capitalized (see Chapter 7, section 5.2, for details). Thus, for the purposes of the elimination of intra-group profits, a value for the group's production cost can be chosen that lies between the lower and upper limits of acceptable cost. It should be noted that there can be a difference between production cost from the viewpoint of the supplying enterprise and production cost from the viewpoint of the group. Thus it is possible that certain costs which may not be capitalized in the accounts of the individual enterprise may, or even must, be capitalized in the group accounts. For example, the cost of transporting goods from the supplying to the receiving enterprise are distribution costs from the viewpoint of the supplying enterprise but internal transport costs and therefore production costs from the viewpoint

Example 8.6 **Elimination of intra-group profits**

L sells finished goods to A at a price of DM 15 per unit. The selling price is made up of:

	DM per unit
L's direct production cost (which must be capitalized in L's balance sheet)	6.00
Share of L's operating and administrative overheads	3.00
Share of advertising cost	2.50
Directly attributable transport costs	1.50
L's profit	2.00
	15.00

Since the market price was DM 16, and since there was no reason to reduce the value (e.g. on account of damage to the goods), A, in its balance sheet, valued the goods at the acquisition cost of DM 15.00 per unit, plus DM 1.50 per unit for additional supplementary acquisition costs which it had incurred (e.g. for unloading the goods). By comparison, the lower and upper limits of the group's production cost are calculated as follows:

	DM per unit
L's direct production cost	6.00
+ A's supplementary acquisition costs	1.50
+ Directly attributable transport costs	1.50
= Total of the group's costs that must be capitalized	9.00
= Lower limit of the group's production cost	
+ Operating and administrative overheads	3.00
= Total of the group's costs that may be capitalized	
= Upper limit of the group's production cost	12.00

A's supplementary acquisition costs must be capitalized by the group when they are charged by an enterprise external to the group. If these supplementary costs arose from the employment of a group enterprise, it should be taken into consideration that only that part of the acquisition cost which is properly so classifiable must be capitalized and/or that not all the supplementary costs (e.g. advertising costs, profit mark-up) may be capitalized from the viewpoint of the group.

The amount of intra-group profit to be eliminated depends on the value to be placed on the finished goods. Given the latitude in assessing production cost from the group's viewpoint, conceivable values are between the lower limit of group production of DM 9.00 per unit and the upper limit of DM 12.00 per unit. If the finished goods are valued at DM 9.00 per unit, the amount of intra-group profit to be eliminated is DM 7.50 (DM 16.50 less DM 9.00); if the goods are valued at DM 12.00 per unit, the profit to be eliminated is only DM 4.50.

If the example is changed to make the intra-group transfer price only DM 7.00, instead of DM 15.00, then there is an intra-group loss calculated on the basis of the group production cost of between DM 0.50 and DM 3.50. This loss must be eliminated by increasing the value of the inventory of finished goods.

The situation is different again if it is assumed that the market price is DM 10.00 per unit (with the intra-group transfer price at its original level of DM 15.00 per unit). On account of the strict application of the principle of lower value to current assets (for details see Chapter 7, section 5.1.3), in the individual accounts the goods must be valued at the lower market value of DM 10.00 plus the supplementary acquisition cost of DM 1.50. Since the value of the goods in the individual balance sheet (DM 11.50) lies between the upper and lower limit of the group's production cost, this amount is a permissible value under the terms of HGB § 304 and is used in the consolidation accounts. There is no intra-group profit to be eliminated.

of the group. Furthermore, by a strict application of the entity principle, operating and administrative costs of the receiving enterprise, which cannot be included in the acquisition cost of its inventory, may be included in the group's production cost of the inventory. This even applies to the administrative costs of the parent undertaking, even when it was not party to the intra-group delivery. However, it is not permissible to capitalize any profit mark-up of the delivering enterprise or distribution costs that are such from the point of view of the group.

There is a basic obligation to eliminate intra-group results. Intra-group profits and intra-group losses must both be eliminated. The law allows two exemptions. The first arises when the goods or services are delivered at normal market rates and the calculation of the intra-group profit or loss would require unreasonably high costs (HGB § 304 (2)). Normally, by using appropriate estimates, the costs can be reduced to such a low level that, in reality, the exemption will remain an exception. Much more use is made of the second rule; the elimination of intra-group profit or loss need not be affected when it is not material for the presentation of a true and fair view of the net worth, financial position and results of the group.

According to the survey by Treuarbeit in 1990, eighty-two of the 100 groups in the sample provided information on the elimination of intra-group results in the general exposition on methods of consolidation. In most cases (sixty-four) the explanation was limited to a general comment on the application of the respective rule. Seventeen groups refrained (partially or wholly) from the elimination of intra-group results. Thirteen justified this on the grounds of immateriality, the remaining four by reference to normal market rates in conjunction with unreasonably high costs.

10 CONSOLIDATION OF REVENUES AND EXPENSES

The treatment of intra-group deliveries of goods and services in the consolidated profit and loss account is dealt with in HGB § 305 (*Aufwands- und Ertragskonsolidierung*). Internal sales and other revenue from deliveries of goods and the provision of services between consolidated enterprises are to be offset against the corresponding expenses, in so far as they do not relate to increases in stocks of finished goods or work in progress or to own work that has been capitalized. If, after the setting-off of internal expenses and revenues, there remains a positive balance (intra-group profit), then the consolidated profit must be reduced. If the balance is negative (intra-group loss) the consolidated profit must be increased.

The offsetting of revenues and expenses may be omitted, if the amounts to be eliminated are immaterial for the presentation of a true and fair view (HGB § 305 (2)).

11 DEFERRED TAXATION

As regards deferred taxation (*latente Steuern*), the same basic considerations apply to the group accounts as to the individual accounts (see Chapter 7, section 7). However, the particular characteristic in the group accounts is that deferred taxation is made up of two components:

1 Those amounts which are taken from the individual accounts of the consolidated undertakings.
2 The additional deferred taxation that arises from standardization of the accounts, the translation of foreign currency items and other consolidation measures.

For the first component the rule in HGB § 274 applies; for the latter that in HGB § 306. The significant difference between the two rules is that, in the group accounts, there is an obligation to report deferred taxation in the balance sheet even when it is to be shown on the assets side. Accordingly, this new instrument of deferred taxation is much more relevant to the group accounts than it is to the individual accounts. Certainly the importance of deferred taxation is basically limited, in that foreign currency translation and capital consolidation regularly lead to differences, the reversal of which, at the time of their creation, is not foreseeable or lies so far in the future that they should be understood less as timing differences than as being of a quasi-permanent nature. Hence they are not taken into account in the computation of deferred taxation. Furthermore, if the differences are considered as a whole, then too there is no deferred taxation to account for, even if there are individual differences which reverse themselves over time, provided that the total amount of deferred taxation remains unchanged from period to period on account of equal disposals and additions. This consideration is important in Germany, because often an existing basic amount of deferred taxation is classified as permanent and, for that reason, is not reported (*Bodensatztheorie*, theory of permanent average balances). The basic amount can be fixed as a global sum for all differences or only for individual classes, depending on the cause of the deferred taxation, e.g. consolidation of intra-group balances, elimination of intra-group profit or intra-group dividends. Given that the transmission of the profits of subsidiaries, intra-group sales with intra-group profit and intra-group loans are normally not a unique occurrence but are repeated year by year, it is clear that in Germany the amount of unreported deferred taxation can take on considerable dimensions.

A further question unresolved by the law concerns the tax rate to be used in the calculation of deferred taxation. In principle, there are the following alternatives:

1 The tax rate of the enterprise that originated the entry which affected the profit.
2 The effective marginal tax rate of the business transaction.
3 The top tax rate of the holding undertaking.
4 The average tax burden of the consolidated profits of the enterprises involved over the effective life of the business transaction in question.
5 An average tax rate for the group.

Prevailing opinion in the literature favours the use of a uniform rate for the whole group. In practice a fixed rate of 50 per cent is common (Treuarbeit 1990: Tz (text number) 435).

For the calculation of the amount of deferred taxation when the tax rate changes, two methods are discussed in the literature: the liability method and the deferral method. The consensus is that either method is legally permissible.

12 PROPORTIONAL CONSOLIDATION AND THE EQUITY METHOD

12.1 Proportional consolidation

For the proportional consolidation (*Quotenkonsolidierung*) of a joint venture, the same consolidation steps should be followed as for the full consolidation of a subsidiary undertaking. The rules relating to format, recognition and valuation of assets and liabilities must be adapted to those of the parent undertaking, the capital, debts, income and expenditure must be consolidated, the intra-group profit must be eliminated and the deferred taxes must be calculated (HGB § 310 (2)). The difference is that all this is done only in respect of the parent undertaking's share. The assets, debts, etc., contained in the individual accounts of the joint venture are only taken into the group accounts *pro rata* (HGB § 310 (1)). Accordingly debts of the joint venture to its owners and profits on transactions between the joint venture and its owners are only partially offset and eliminated. Consequently, as regards its assets and profits, the joint venture is split in two. One part belongs to the group, the other part to the other owners. In some groups (for example, VIAG) joint ventures form a considerable proportion of the total number of undertakings in the group. In these cases, proportional consolidation presents a more accurate picture of the size of the group (in particular as represented by its turnover), and the return on sales, than would the equity method.

12.2 Equity valuation

In contrast to its prohibition in the individual accounts, equity valuation is obligatory for associated enterprises in the group accounts (HGB § 311). There are two reasons for this. First, the group accounts have no formal role in determining distributions, only an information disclosure role. Second, equity valuation is supported by relatively objective indicators. At the moment of the acquisition of the participating interest, the equity method value coincides with the acquisition cost. Subsequently lower or higher values are derived from the changes in the capital and reserves of the associated undertaking (HGB § 312 (4)). The profits of the associated undertaking are added to the book value of the participating interest via the profit and loss account, and dividends are deducted, with the effect that the book value of the participating interest increases in line with the retained profits.

Apart from basing changes in value on capital and reserves, the equity method is also subject to consolidation rules (for details see HGB § 312). In principle it would have been possible to prescribe all corrections that apply in a proportional consolidation and which have an effect on the equity. However, the standardization of asset capitalization and valuation rules is optional and the elimination of intra-group profits is necessary only when the information required for the calculation is available. There is no obligation on the associated enterprise to give the information. Moreover the two exemptions from the obligation to eliminate intra-group profits that are granted to subsidiaries also apply, by analogy, to associated enterprises. There are, first, sales at normal market rates coupled with unreasonably high cost of eliminating the profit, and, second, immaterial amounts. For these reasons the elimination of intra-group profits on transactions with associated enterprises is rare.

According to Treuarbeit (1990), of 100 selected groups, only eighteen gave information on the elimination of intra-group profits; fifteen of them reported that they had (partially) refrained from the elimination of intra-group profits. In all fifteen cases the reason given was that the amount was immaterial; in three cases it was additionally stated that the required information was not available.

In addition the law does not require a correction of equity for a difference on consolidation of intra-group receivables and liabilities. Thus, in practice, the consolidation is confined largely to capital. The writing off of the value adjustments arising from the capital consolidation and of goodwill (see section 7.2.2 above) reduces the value of the participating interest.

In general the equity value is calculated as follows:

	acquisition cost
+(−)	share of the annual profit (loss)
−	dividends received
−	write-off of the value adjustments arising from the capital consolidation
−	write-off of goodwill arising from the capital consolidation
+	credits in respect of releasing a negative consolidation difference to the profit and loss account
+(−)	effect of (possible) standardization of accounting rules
−(+)	effect of elimination of intra-group profit (loss)
−(+)	any exceptional write-off (write-back) of the book value of the participating interest
+(−)	increase (reduction) in capital
=	equity value (value of participating interest)

The value of the participating interest may be shown either:

1 Inclusive of the share of goodwill (the book value method – *Buchwertmethode* – according to HGB § 312 (1) No. 1), or
2 With goodwill shown separately (known as the capital share method – *Kapitalanteilsmethode* – according to HGB § 312 (1) No. 2).

When the book value is applied for the first time, the difference arising from the capital consolidation, that is, the share of goodwill and of hidden reserves (*stille Tageswertrücklagen*), has to be given in the consolidated balance sheet or in the notes.

13 THE NOTES ON THE GROUP ACCOUNTS

The group accounts are comprised of three equal-ranking components: the balance sheet, the profit and loss account and the notes (*Anhang*). The notes (the legal provisions are in HGB § 313) serve to interpret, correct, alleviate and complement the two other components, with which they are closely correlated.

The interpretation role of the notes is to explain the accounting, valuation and consolidation methods used in the balance sheet and the profit and loss account, both in general terms (e.g. information on the consolidation methods used) and in relation to specific items in the balance sheet and profit and loss account (e.g. explanation of the deferred taxes in the balance sheets of consolidated undertakings). Furthermore information should be given on deviations from the methods that were used previously and on other variations as compared with the previous accounts, to the extent that they are significant, together with justification for the changes.

The correction function of the notes is particularly evident when comprehensive quantitative information is given on changes as compared with the previous year. In the alleviation function, the equal ranking of the notes becomes evident. In certain specific cases defined by law it is possible to present information in the notes which should otherwise be shown in the balance sheet or profit and loss account (e.g. presentation of changes in fixed assets (fixed asset movement schedule) and formation expenses). The notes, by appropriate use of options, can make the accounts much more comprehensible. Conversely there is a danger that too much information will be shunted into the notes from the balance sheet and the profit and loss account so that the latter become an empty shell.

Finally, in fulfilling the complementary function, the notes make available supplementary information which under the prevailing rules does not appear in the consolidated balance sheet or the profit and loss account. An example of the supplementary information provided in the notes is the total of other financial obligations that do not appear in the consolidated balance sheet but which are significant for the evaluation of the financial position of the group (HGB § 314 (1) No. 2) or the analysis of turnover by areas of activity and by geographically defined markets (HGB § 314 (1) No. 3). Other complementary information, some of which may be provided voluntarily, concerns holdings of shares (name, registered office and proportion of capital owned relating to consolidated subsidiaries, associated enterprises and proportionately consolidated joint ventures and other participating interests). Similarly information is given on the labour force and on expenditure and loans in connection with the group's supervisory and executive bodies (e.g. the total emoluments of current and former members of those bodies: supervisory board, executive board or similar bodies of the parent (and subsidiary) undertakings, in each case separate totals for current and former members). It is precisely this supplementary information that is of particular interest to the trade unions.

The above-mentioned items of information are only examples. Which information, explanations and justifications must be shown separately in the notes on the group accounts is set out in detail in HGB §§ 313 f. In some cases, and under certain conditions, the presentation of the information is optional.

9 Supplementary reports

1 THE MANAGEMENT REPORT

In accordance with HGB § 264 (1), corporations are obliged to prepare an annual management report (*Lagebericht*), which in the case of large and medium-size corporations has to be audited and published. The preparation of a management report is also required of enterprises, other than corporations, that exceed the limits of the PublG (see Chapter 7, section 1), and which are neither partnerships (*Personengesellschaften*) nor sole proprietors (PublG § 5 (2)).

The management report is an independent instrument of management reporting which complements the accounts by providing information on the enterprise's business situation and development. Only in the management report can the management take a view of the enterprise's position, taking account of the business, technical, legal, social and economic aspects of its activities.

The contents of the management report are defined in HGB § 289, which sets out the minimum requirements. These also apply, analogously, to undertakings that are required to prepare annual accounts under the PublG.

The management report must at least set out the development of the business and the position of the corporation so as to provide a true and fair view (HGB § 289 (1)). What is meant by 'development of the business and the position' is not defined in the law. It is generally accepted, however, that users should, in particular, be provided with the following information:

1 *A report on conditions in general* in the relevant sector of the economy (the economic state of the industry/ies in which the enterprise is active) and in the economy as a whole, and their effects on the company.
2 *A report on the enterprise's performance* (purchasing, production, sales); for example, information on the production or sales programmes, major rationalization, the state of the order book, the competitive situation, and changes in turnover in important branches of the firm's activities.
3 *A report on the financial situation,* in so far as it is not clear from the annual accounts (in particular information on liquidity).
4 *A report on matters affecting employees* and employment relations (for example, information on fundamental changes in the labour force, the effects of collective agreements or plant-level settlements concerning wages, hours of work or pensions, the basic impact on the enterprise of legal provisions in the social field).
5 *A report on structural changes in the enterprise* (organization, legal relationships, partners); for example, information on the signing of 'enterprise agreements' (*Unternehmensverträge*), membership of business associations and employers' organizations.

In addition to the current information required under HGB § 289 (1), the following future oriented matters should be dealt with separately (HGB § 289 (2)):

1 *Post-balance sheet events* of particular importance: for example, information on fundamental changes in the circumstances of the enterprise, any reduction in capacity, plant closures, important new investment programmes, industrial disputes, significant measures relating to equity or debt capital.
2 *The immediate prospects of the company:* for example, information on the expected short-term economic outlook in the industries in which the enterprise operates, expected price trends in its main purchasing and selling markets, expectations concerning orders in the current year.
3 *Research and development:* owing to the danger of revealing sensitive information to competitors if too much detail, particularly output-oriented data, were to be provided (for example, information on the results of individual research projects or on patents applied for), most enterprises limit their comments to a general statement on the resources employed in this field.

These are the essential elements of the management report. However, given the lack of specificity in the law, very considerable latitude is left to the management.

Parent undertakings, which under the terms of the HGB or PublG are obliged to prepare group accounts, must, in addition to their own management report, prepare a group management report (*Konzernlagebericht*) (HGB § 290 (1), and PublG § 13 (1)). The contents of the group management report, and the minimum requirements, are set out in HGB § 315, which by analogy applies also to groups that are obliged to prepare group accounts under the PublG. The wording of the article is practically identical to that concerning the management report of the individual corporation. Thus the points made above can be applied equally to the group management report. However, the latter is not simply the sum of the management reports of all the consolidated enterprises. Rather it should deal with the group as an economic entity.

Since all the documents concerning the annual accounts and reports of both the parent undertaking and the group are commonly presented in a single publication, the management report of the parent undertaking and the management report of the group are frequently combined in a single integrated report. This avoids repetition and the need for cross-referencing and is not against the law.

2 THE INTERIM REPORT

2.1 The obligation to report and the purpose of the report

Under § 44b of the *Börsengesetz* (BörsG, Stock Exchange Act), the issuers of listed securities are obliged to publish regularly at least one interim report (*Zwischenbericht*) during the financial year which, on the basis of figures and explanations, conveys a true and fair view of the financial position and of the general course of business of the issuer during the period covered by the report. The interim report has to appear in one of the official periodicals (e.g. the federal official gazette, the *Bundesanzeiger*) no later than two months after the end of the reporting period. If the issuer is subject to legal obligation to publish group accounts, the interim report can cover either the group or the individual enterprise (the parent undertaking), an option which must invite criticism, since any quoted corporation should be able to present interim group accounts. The purpose of the interim report is to inform the stockholders promptly of the position and the prospects of the enterprise and thus provide them with a basis for their investment decisions. Early information is particularly useful because the individual and group accounts have to undergo a lengthy process of preparation, audit and certification before they are published and are often not available until up to six months after the balance sheet date. Many German enterprises go beyond the minimum legal requirements and publish quarterly reports (*Quartalsberichte*), letters to shareholders (*Aktionärsbriefe*) and similar statements. This alone indicates that there is a demand for such information supplementary to the annual accounts. There is, however, no danger that the interim reports will displace the annual accounts, for the following reasons:

1 The interim report fulfils a purely information function, with the stockholder envisaged as the principal recipient. Creditors, generally, obtain their information from other sources (see Chapter 3 and Chapter 6, section 1.2). Apart from the penalties for not meeting the requirements as to preparation and publication, the interim report has no legal consequences and can have no effect on claims on profit. In contrast to the position with the annual accounts, there is no obligation to audit the interim report.
2 It is not necessary to include in the interim report a figure for profit based on the principle of single-assets valuation. The core of the report is rather a general verbal run-down (partly complemented by figures) on the development of sales and orders, the state of the order book, the use of capacity and the position concerning finance and profits. In this respect the interim report is not dissimilar to the enterprise's management report.
3 On account of its content, the interim report, in contrast with the annual accounts, is construed very much as an assessment of the enterprise from the short-term point of view.

2.2 Compulsory content

The contents of the interim report and, in particular the figures and explanations to be given and the date and form of publication, are specified in the *Börsenzulassungs-Verordnung* of 15 April 1987 (BörsZulV, Stock Exchange Listing Requirements Order). In principle, the interim report must permit an assessment of the issuer's activity during the period of the report (BörsZulV § 53). It must contain figures and commentary relating to the operations and results of the issuer. At a minimum the following figures and information are required (BörZulV § 54):

1 The figure for turnover and the comparable figure for the previous year (BörZulV § 54 (1)).
2 The profit either before or after tax according to the accounting principles laid down by the HGB, and the corresponding figure for the previous year (BörZulV § 54 (1)). It should be noted that the profit stated in the interim report, in contrast to that announced in the annual financial statements, is based very substantially on estimates and projections. Moreover, the stock exchange control authorities permit corporations that are quoted solely on a German stock exchange to report, subject to certain conditions, the interim profit purely on an estimated basis.
3 When an interim dividend is paid (which is rare), the results after tax and the amount of the dividend (BörZulV § 54 (2)). As German corporations are not permitted to pay interim dividends, this rule applies only to foreign companies.
4 When the figures have been audited, the audit certificate, including any additional remarks, reserves or withholding of opinion.

In the commentary, the issuer is also obliged (BörsZulV § 55) to give further information on:

1 The analysis of turnover (as a rule, by industrial sector and geographical markets).
2 The state of the order book.
3 The development of costs and prices.
4 The number of employees.
5 Capital investments.
6 Events of particular importance that could affect the profitability of operations.

3 ADJUSTED EARNINGS (DVFA/SG)

Apart from the accounts of the individual enterprise, the group accounts and the interim report, there is a further item of information that is worthy of mention: the results according to DVFA/SG, which listed companies frequently present on a voluntary basis. This result is calculated using a procedure that has been developed by the *Deutsche Vereinigung für Finanzanalyse und Anlageberatung* (DVFA, German Association of Financial Analysts and Investment Consultants) in conjunction with the *Schmalenbach-Gesellschaft/Deutsche Gesellschaft für Betriebswirtschaft* (SG, the Schmalenbach Society/German Association for Business Economics). The starting point of the calculation is the published consolidated profit or loss. Unconsolidated subsidiaries and associated companies are taken into account in an approximate fashion, if they are

Table 9.1 Worksheet for the ascertainment of the DVFA/SG profit

A *Ser. no. of item*		*B* *Description of item according to the annual accounts or other sources*	*C* *DM million gross*	*D* *DM 000s net*
1		**Net profit/loss for the year** as disclosed in the profit and loss account or profit transferred/loss assumed		
2	−	**Start-up expenses** which have been capitalized [in the following years the depreciation on these expenses must then be eliminated]		
3		**Fixed asset items to be adjusted**		
3.1		Intangible assets and goodwill		
3.1.1	+	Amortization on goodwill		
3.1.2	+	Amortization of hidden reserves, which have been released in capital consolidation		
3.2		Tangible assets		
3.2.1	+	Special tax-deductible depreciation		
3.2.2	−	Write-ups		
3.2.3	±	Profit/loss from disposals, if they result from exceptional, very rare transactions		
3.2.4		Valuation of own-manufactured assets [should be adjusted if not valued at direct cost plus an appropriate portion of material overheads and labour overheads (including depreciation)]		
3.2.5	+	Investment grants and allowances		
3.3		Financial assets		
3.3.1	+	Amortization (as a result of a temporary impairment)		
3.3.2	−	Write-ups		
3.3.3	±	Profit/loss from disposals, if they result from exceptional, very rare transactions		
3.3.4	±	Items to be adjusted in the equity accounted valuations		
3.4		3.1 to 3.3, subtotal		
4		**Current asset items to be adjusted**		
4.1		Inventories and work in progress		
4.1.1	+	Transfers to valuation reserves		
4.1.2	−	Transfers from valuation reserves		
4.1.3	+	Depreciation on current assets exceeding the usual level		
4.1.4	+	Net changes of imported goods write-down		
4.2		Receivables and debt discount		
4.2.1		Receivables:		
		+ Transfers to valuation reserves		
		− Transfers from valuation reserves		
4.2.2		Debt discount (should not be adjusted if it is spread over the term of the loan)		
4.3		4.1 to 4.2, subtotal		
5		**Liability items to be adjusted**		
5.1		Special items with reserve element		
5.1.1	+	Transfers to special items		
5.1.2	−	Transfers from special items		
5.2		Accruals		
5.2.1		Accruals for pensions (correction for exceptional or discretionary transfers or contributions):		
	±	Changes to the method of computation		
	+	Correction of previous under-accruals		
	−	Shortfall in charge for year		
	−	Income from release		
5.2.2		Other accruals:		
		Net changes of taxed accruals		
	±	Other accruals to be adjusted		
	−	Income from release		

Table 9.1 Continued

A *Ser. no. of item*		*B* *Description of item according to the annual accounts or other sources*	*C* *DM million gross*	*D* *DM 000s net*
5.3		5.1 to 5.2, subtotal		
6		**Foreign currency and other influences**		
6.1		Foreign currency influences		
6.1.1	±	Change of translation differences, balance sheet, if it affected the profit (cannot be applied automatically to differences in respect of countries with extremely high inflation rates)		
6.1.2	±	Translation differences, profit and loss account (if the profit for the year is computed by netting income and expenses translated at different rates against each other there should be discussion with the enterprise whether or not a translation profit or loss should be taken into account)		
6.2		Other influences		
6.2.1	±	Changes in accounting policies, if significant in amount and rare in occurrence		
6.2.2	±	Measures taken by shareholders, if significant in amount and rare in occurrence		
6.3		6.1 to 6.2, subtotal		
7		**Adjustments, total** (No. 2 + 3.4 + 4.3 + 5.3 + 6.3)		
8		**Earnings according to the DVFA/SG method** (group) (No. 1 + No. 7)		
9		**Determination of the earnings per share according to the DVFA/SG method**		
		Earnings according to the DVFA/SG method (group) (No. 8)		
9.1		Minority interest in result for period		
9.2		Earnings according to the DVFA/SG method without minority interest		
9.3		Average number of shares entitled to dividends in the current financial year		
9.4		Earnings per share according to the DVFA/SG method (before adjustments; before dilution) (No. 9.2):(No. 9.3)		
10		**Adjustment factor** (adjustment of earnings per share calculation on the occasion of increase in capital)		
11		**Adjusted earnings per share according to the DVFA/SG method**		
12		**Earnings per share according to the DVFA/SG method 'fully diluted'** (only in cases where there are conditionally outstanding shares [relating to issued convertible or option bonds] which could join the share capital already issued with a claim to a share of the profit)		

Source: Busse von Colbe *et al.* (1991: appendix 1).

Key

A Serial number of item.

B Description of item according to the annual accounts or other sources or as proposed by DVFA/SG.

C The relevant income or expenditure item is entered gross here, i.e. before tax. If an income source is not taxable, even taking deferred taxes into consideration, the gross amount is the same as the net amount and should thus be entered directly into column D. Similarly, any item of expenditure which is not tax-deductible should also be entered directly into column D.

D The net amounts derived by applying the appropriate tax rates to the gross amounts are to be entered here.

material. Corrections are made for special factors such as extraordinary or unusual items and for disposal matters. This last factor refers to the latitude permitted in matters of valuation (e.g. options for capitalizing expenses, tax concessions, stock valuation and the creation of provisions) both over time within the individual enterprise and between enterprises. However, not all corrections are updated in subsequent periods (no clean surplus concept). Not all the factors mentioned can be derived from the published accounts, so that the announcement of its results according to DVFA/SG is an additional and voluntary measure of disclosure by the enterprise. Revealing hidden reserves is not part of the correction of the results (see Table 9.1, which contains the worksheet for ascertaining the DVFA profit). The aim is rather, on the best comparable basis, and in the context of conservative German accounting principles, to:

1 Show the trend of results over time.
2 Present a reliable basis for the forecasting of future results.
3 Permit comparisons between different enterprises of their business success (Busse von Colbe *et al.* 1991: 5).

On account of differences between national accounting principles, inter-firm comparability is largely restricted to German enterprises.

10

Audit and disclosure

1 THE AUDITING PROFESSION AND THE AUDIT OF THE FINANCIAL STATEMENTS

1.1 The *Wirtschaftsprüfer*

The annual accounts and the management reports, including the bookkeeping, of corporations that are not 'small' as defined in HGB § 267 (1) and of large enterprises as defined in PublG § 1, must be examined by an independent auditor to check that they satisfy the requirements of the law and of the enterprise's articles ('Audit requirement', HGB § 316 (1), PublG § 6). There is also a requirement that the group accounts and the group management report of corporations must be audited (HGB § 316 (2)), as must those of large enterprises of other legal forms (PublG § 14).

The auditor of the annual accounts is appointed by the shareholders; in the case of the group accounts, it is the shareholders of the parent undertaking who are responsible (HGB § 318 (1)). With limited liability companies, the articles of association may provide otherwise. Who may be appointed as auditor and what requirements he must fulfil are specified in detail by law. According to HGB § 319 (1) only *Wirtschaftsprüfer* and *Wirtschaftsprüfer* firms may act as auditors. For the audit of the annual accounts of medium-size limited liability companies a second category of auditor is approved: the sworn-in auditor (*vereidigter Buchprüfer*) and firms of sworn-in auditors. The difference between the *Wirtschaftsprüfer* and the sworn-in auditor lies in the training, which is stricter for the former. In principle, candidates for the profession of *Wirtschaftsprüfer* must have a university degree and at least five years' practical experience. There is an extensive final examination. Moreover, efforts are made deliberately to keep the examination difficult so as to ensure that only really suitable candidates are admitted to the profession. The aim is to ensure that the level of technical competence in the profession remains high. It is also claimed that this policy regulates access to the market.

The *Wirtschaftsprüfer* and the sworn-in auditor alike must be impartial and independent. According to the guidelines that govern the professional conduct of both categories, the auditor must 'in his findings, judgements and decisions be free of all influences, commitments and considerations'. In HGB § 319 (2) and (3) certain specific cases of non-independent relationships between the *Wirtschaftsprüfer*/sworn-in auditor and the client are set out, which bar their appointment as auditors:

(2) No *Wirtschaftsprüfer* or sworn-in auditor may be appointed as auditor if he or any person involved in the conduct of his business:

1 Owns shares in the corporation to be audited.
2 Is a legal representative or member of the supervisory board or an employee of the corporation to be audited, or was such in the last three years prior to his appointment.
3 Is a legal representative or member of the supervisory board of a legal entity, shareholder of a partnership or owner of an enterprise to the extent that the legal entity, partnership or sole proprietor is related to the company or owns more than 20 per cent of the shares of the company.
4 Is an employee of an enterprise that is related to the corporation to be audited or owns more than 20 per cent of the shares in that corporation, or is the employee of a natural person who owns more than 20 per cent of the shares of the corporation to be audited.
5 Has participated in the keeping of the accounting records or in the preparation of the financial statements of the corporation to be audited beyond the level of auditing.
6 Is a legal representative, employee, member of the supervisory board or shareholder of a legal entity or natural person or of a partnership or owner of a sole proprietorship to the extent that the legal entity or natural person, the partnership or one of its shareholders or the sole proprietorship may not be an auditor of the corporation to be examined pursuant to No. 5 above.
7 Employs a person on the audit who may not be an auditor in accordance with Nos. 1–6 above.
8 Has in each of the last five years drawn more than half the total revenue from his professional activities from examination and advisory services for the corporation to be audited or from enterprises in which the company to be audited owns more than 20 per cent of the shares and where the same situation is also expected to apply in the current year. The *Wirtschaftsprüferkammer* (chamber of *Wirtschaftsprüfer*) may agree to temporary exceptions in cases that might otherwise involve hardship.

(3) A *Wirtschaftsprüfer* firm or a firm of sworn-in auditors may not be appointed as auditor if:

1 It holds shares in the corporation to be audited or is related to the latter or if its related company holds more than 20 per cent of the shares of the company to be audited or is related to the latter.
2 In its capacity as shareholder of a legal entity or partnership pursuant to paragraph (2), No. 6, or pursuant to paragraph (2), Nos. 5, 7 or 8, it may not be the auditor.
3 In the case of a *Wirtschaftsprüfer* firm or firm of sworn auditors which is a legal entity, a legal representative or shareholder who owns more than 50 per cent of the voting rights of the shareholders or, in the case of another *Wirtschaftsprüfer* firm or firm of sworn auditors, a shareholder may not be an auditor in accordance with paragraph (2), Nos. 1–4.
4 One of its legal representatives or one of its shareholders may not be an auditor in accordance with paragraph (2), No. 5 or 6, or
5 One of its supervisory board members may not be an auditor in accordance with paragraph (2), No. 2 or 5.

The legal position of the *Wirtschaftsprüfer* and the sworn-in auditor is set out, for the whole of Germany, in the Regulation governing the Profession of *Wirtschaftsprüfer* (*Wirtschaftsprüferordnung*). This order provides that the profession is to be self-governing; this function is assured by the *Wirtschaftsprüferkammer* (chamber of *Wirtschaftsprüfer*). The chamber is a public law body under the official supervision of the Federal Minister of Economics. All *Wirtschaftsprüfer* (numbering 6,906 at 1 July 1991), *Wirtschaftsprüfer* firms (1,328 at 1 July 1991) and sworn-in auditors (5,690 at 1 July 1991) are required to be members of the chamber.

By contrast membership of the *Institut der Wirtschaftsprüfer in Deutschland eV* is voluntary. The institute was formed in 1932 through the reorganization of the *Institut für das Revisions- und Treuhandwesen*, which had been founded two years earlier. Shortly afterwards, the institute was assigned the role of regulating the profession of *Wirtschaftsprüfer* with its associated public functions on a self-governing basis. Today self-government of the profession is the responsibility of the chamber. It still figures as one of the tasks of the institute, however, under the terms of its constitution, along with the promotion of the next generation of *Wirtschaftsprüfer* through professional education and safeguarding the interests of the profession as a whole. A further task is to contribute to the implementation and interpretation of accounting rules through recommendations, opinions and other declarations. The recommendations and opinions of the institute are admittedly not accounting standards, but they carry considerable weight, since every *Wirtschaftsprüfer* is obliged to take notice of them both for professional and for legal liability reasons. The *Wirtschaftsprüfer* may not depart from them without good reason.

1.2 Audit of the individual accounts and the group accounts

The scope of the audit of the accounts and of the group accounts must be sufficient to determine whether the legal requirements (primarily HGB §§ 238–314) and the additional provisions of the company's statutes have been observed. Furthermore, the management report (group management report) should be examined to check whether it agrees with the individual accounts (group accounts), and whether the other information contained in the management report (group management report) does not give a false impression of the position of the enterprise (group) (HGB § 317 (1)). The audit of the financial statements includes an audit of the books of accounts.

In addition, when the group accounts incorporate the accounts of individual enterprises that have not been audited, the auditor of the group accounts must check whether the individual accounts comply with the principles of regular accountancy and whether the rules for including them in the group accounts have been observed. This is not a requirement of the Seventh EC Directive.

The auditor must make out a written report on the results of his audit. Under the terms of HGB § 321 (1), this audit report (*Prüfungsbericht*) must state specifically whether the books of account, the financial statements and the management report comply with the legal requirements and whether the legal representatives have provided the information and explanations requested of them. In addition, the essential items in the annual accounts must be analysed and explained. Negative variances by comparison with the previous year in net worth, in the financial position or in the results should be included in the report, with adequate explanation. This also applies to losses that have had a significant influence on the results. If the auditor has discovered facts which endanger the enterprise or serious violations by the legal representatives, he must report on them (HGB § 321 (2)).

In principle, in a joint stock corporation, only the management board and the supervisory board have a right to receive the full audit report – the shareholders' meeting and the individual stockholder have no such right. They, like others, such as creditors, are informed of the outcome of the audit through the audit opinion (*Bestätigungsvermerk*) on the financial statements. The precise text of the audit opinion is set out in the law (HGB § 322 (1); see an example of the text in Appendix A); it should be extended when additional comments appear necessary.

1.3 Audit of the interim report

There is no legal requirement for the interim report to be audited. When an audit is carried out the audit opinion, together with additional remarks or restrictions or even a disclaimer of opinion, has to be disclosed completely (BörsZulV § 54 (3)). The scope of the audit and of the audit report depend on the audit agreement. In its opinion No. 2 of 1988 the IdW stated its position concerning the minimum scope of a non-statutory audit.

2 DISCLOSURE

2.1 Corporations

Corporations must lodge the following documents with the commercial register (*Handelsregister*) where the corporation is located (see Table 10.1):

1 The adopted annual accounts of the individual enterprise (*Einzelabschluß*).

Table 10.1 Disclosure

Large corporations	*Medium-size corporations*	*Small corporations*	*Large enterprises under the PublG*
Disclosure in the federal gazette and filing with the commercial register	Filing with the commercial register (notification in the federal gazette of the commercial register and the number where they are filed)	Filing with the commercial register (notification in the federal gazette of the commercial register and the number where they are filed)	Disclosure in the federal gazette and filing with the commercial register
Documents to be published: • Balance sheet • Profit and loss account • Notes (list of participating accounts[4]) • Management report • Audit opinion • Report of the supervisory board • Proposal and resolution concerning the appropriation of profit (if not apparent from the annual accounts) • Record of the stockholders' meeting (for joint stock corporations)[4] • List of shareholders (for limited liability companies)[4]	Documents to be published: • Balance sheet (special form) • Profit and loss account • Notes (shortened form) • Management report • Audit opinion • Report of the supervisory board • Proposal and resolution concerning the appropriation of profit (if not apparent from the annual accounts) • Record of the stockholders' meeting (for joint stock corporations) • List of shareholders (for limited liability companies)	Documents to be published: • Balance sheet • Notes, with no items relating to the profit and loss account • Proposal and resolution concerning the appropriation of profit (if not apparent from the annual accounts) • Record of the stockholders' meeting (for joint stock corporations) • List of shareholders (for limited liability companies)	Documents to be published: • Balance sheet (equity shown as one figure[1]) • Profit and loss account[2] • Notes[3] • Management report[3] • Audit opinion • Report of the supervisory board where there is a supervisory board • Resolution concerning the appropriation of profit[2] (indication of the year's profits), if not apparent from the balance sheet
Time limit: nine months after the balance sheet date	Time limit: nine months after the balance sheet date	Time limit: twelve months after the balance sheet date	Time limit: as for large corporations

Notes

1 Applies only to commercial partnerships.

2 Instead of the profit and loss account and the resolution concerning the appropriation of profit, sole proprietors and commercial partnerships are permitted to disclose an annex to the balance sheet containing the information set out in PublG § 5 (5), third sentence.

3 Does not apply to sole proprietors and commercial partnerships.

4 These items need not be published in the federal gazette.

2 The audit opinion (*Bestätigungsvermerk*).
3 The management report (*Lagebericht*).
4 The control report of the supervisory board (*Bericht des Aufsichtsrats*).
5 The resolution (proposed or adopted) for the appropriation of the year's profits (*Vorschlag für und Beschluß über die Verwendung des Ergebnisses*) (the duty of disclosure, HGB § 325 (1)).

The commercial register is administered by the competent local first-instance court. Anyone may inspect the register (HGB § 9 (1)). There is no central commercial register. In relation to the filing of the above documents with the commercial register there are graduated disclosure requirements, depending on the size of the corporation (for the size categories see Chapter 7, section 1).

1 *Large corporations* must first publish these documents in the *Bundesanzeiger* (federal official gazette), which is the official medium of the Federal Ministry of Justice for official announcements.
2 *Medium-size corporations* need only file a simplified balance sheet and may omit certain items from the notes, as specified in detail in HGB § 327.
3 *Small corporations* need, moreover, not disclose their profit and loss account or the items in the notes that relate to the profit and loss account (HGB § 326). In addition the time limit for filing is twelve months, instead of nine months. As with medium-size corporations, it is not necessary to publish in the federal gazette in full; it is sufficient merely to indicate at which commercial register and under what number the documents have been lodged.

The legal representatives of a corporation which has to prepare group accounts have the same disclosure obligations, in principle, as the legal representatives of large corporations (HGB § 325 (3)). The publication of the group accounts does not release management from the obligation to disclose the accounts of the individual enterprise. Since each set of financial statements has a different function, so each is subject to the disclosure requirements, as long as the other conditions are fulfilled. Within nine months of the balance sheet date the group accounts, together with the group management report and audit opinion, has to be published in the federal gazette (*Bundesanzeiger*). Quoted joint stock corporations often voluntarily disclose their accounts earlier. The notification of publication and the relevant documents are to be lodged with the competent commercial register. Quoted joint stock corporations must publish their interim report, within two months of the end of the period covered by the report, by reproducing it in at least one journal authorized to print mandatory stock exchange announcements, or in the federal gazette, or as a separate publication. If the interim report does not appear in the federal gazette, then information must be inserted in the gazette on where the interim report is being published and how the public may obtain a copy.

Whether these disclosure rules are respected is another matter. Such evidence as exists is sobering. A survey of the *Land* of Lower Saxony was undertaken by Ballwieser and Häger (1991): they found an average filing rate of 11.9 per cent for the 1988 financial statements of corporations. (Admittedly this was a sample survey: it was based on the replies of twenty-one of the seventy-three commercial registration courts in Lower

Saxony.) As regards disclosure by GmbHs, in January 1989 the journal *Impulse* sent a questionnaire to about half the commercial registration courts in Germany: the finding was that only about 7 per cent of GmbHs respect the disclosure obligation (*Impulse*, April 1989, pp. 166–9). The main reasons behind this reluctance to disclose are:

1 Concern about suffering a competitive disadvantage, in that outsiders, competitors in particular, would learn too much.
2 The excessive additional cost.
3 The lightness and the low risk of penalties for failure to observe the disclosure rules.

2.2 Other legal entities

It is understandable that corporations which raise finance on the capital market, those classed as public corporations (*Publikumsgesellschaften*), should be obliged to disclose their position as to net worth, finance and results. German law, however, compels corporations that are not public (for example 100 per cent-owned subsidiaries) and large enterprises of other legal forms to publish their annual accounts. In such cases the disclosure is intended to benefit creditors, employees and their organizations. It enables them to gain a better understanding of the economic position of the enterprise. However, it may also be useful to other parties concerned. Without disclosure, external parties might perceive their risks as higher, and, under the condition of a functioning market, they would demand an additional risk premium on the price or allow for the element of risk in some other way.

For large enterprises as defined in PublG § 1, the disclosure regulations for large corporations apply correspondingly (for details see Table 10.1). Where the enterprise is in the legal form of a sole proprietor or a partnership, it need only file the balance sheet and an annex to the balance sheet in accordance with PublG § 5. This annex contains information on turnover, investment income, personnel costs, valuation and depreciation methods, and the number of employees, but not the year's profit. According to the PublG concerning group accounts, parent undertakings of other legal forms are subject to the same obligations concerning disclosure as parent undertakings in the form of a corporation (PublG § 15).

Part III
Appendices

A Illustrative financial statements
B Comparison with IAS
C EC Directives and German legislation
D Useful information

Appendix A
Illustrative financial statements

1 INTRODUCTION

The consolidated financial statements reproduced on the following pages are from Siemen's English-language Annual Report and German-language *Geschäftsbericht.* The consolidated group includes Siemens AG and other companies in Germany and elsewhere in which Siemens AG directly or indirectly has a majority of the voting rights. A separate report (*Jahresabschluß der Siemens AG*) is published relating to the operations of the controlling company, Siemens AG.

Siemens AG is a well known multinational company with about 60 per cent of its revenue arising in Germany, 20 per cent elsewhere in Europe and 20 per cent in other parts of the world. Its activities cover a number of areas relating to the electrical and electronics sectors, including power generation and transmission, communication networks and information systems. In 1992, fourteen companies in the new German federal states (*Länder*) were included in the consolidated financial statements for the first time.

SIEMENS AG
Report for the fiscal year
ended September 30, 1992

Contents

Siemens at a glance

Siemens*	1991	1992	Change
New orders	82,166	85,409	+ 4%
Sales	73,008	78,509	+ 8%
Employees	402,000	413,000	+ 3%
Capital expenditures and investments	5,595	8,574	+ 53%
Research and development	7,892	8,385	+ 6%
Net income	1,792	1,955	+ 9%
as a percent of sales	2.5	2.5	
as a percent of shareholders' equity	9.9	10.0	
Total dividend of Siemens AG	686	727	+ 6%
Dividend per share in DM	13.00	13.00	

Amounts in millions of German marks (DM) unless stated otherwise

*Siemens includes Siemens AG and companies in Germany and other countries in which Siemens AG directly or indirectly has a majority of the voting rights and which are included in the consolidated financial statements.

The Annual Report contains the consolidated financial statements of Siemens AG, the Managing Board's combined general review of Siemens AG and Siemens worldwide consolidated for the 1992 fiscal year, as well as additional information not required by law.

The annual financial statements of Siemens AG have received an unqualified audit opinion from KPMG Deutsche Treuhand-Gesellschaft AG Wirtschaftsprüfungsgesellschaft, and will be published in the German Federal Gazette and filed with the Commercial Registries of the Berlin-Charlottenburg and Munich District Courts. These financial statements can be obtained in German free of charge from Siemens AG, Infoservice ZI/Z004, P.O. Box 23 48, D-8510 Fürth 2, Germany.

Consolidated financial statements
Siemens worldwide consolidated balance sheet

as of September 30
(in millions of DM)

Assets	Note	1992	1991
Intangibles, fixed assets and investments			
Intangible assets	(5)	435	275
Property, plant and equipment	(5)		
At cost		46,762	43,660
Less accumulated depreciation		(28,960)	(27,206)
		17,802	16,454
Investments	(6)	2,657	2,660
		20,894	19,389
Current assets			
Inventories	(7)	26,275	24,774
Less advances received from customers		(19,993)	(16,535)
		6,282	8,239
Receivables and miscellaneous assets	(8)		
Accounts receivable – trade		14,459	14,387
Other receivables and miscellaneous assets		10,445	8,818
		24,904	23,205
Marketable securities and notes	(9)	16,600	15,088
Other liquid assets		3,077	3,478
		50,863	50,010
Prepaid expenses		43	69
Total assets		71,800	69,468

Shareholders' equity and liabilities	Note	1992	1991
Shareholders' equity			
Capital stock of Siemens AG	(10)		
Common stock (total number of votes 55,025,662)		2,752	2,593
Preferred stock (total number of votes 923,634)		46	46
		2,798	2,639
Additional paid-in capital	(10)	8,590	6,244
Retained earnings	(11)	6,991	7,735
Unappropriated consolidated net income		727	686
Minority interests	(12)	1,235	1,345
		20,341	18,649
Accrued liabilities	(13)		
Pension plans and similar commitments		14,761	13,957
Other accrued liabilities		20,220	20,137
		34,981	34,094
Debt	(14)	4,531	4,575
Other liabilities	(14)		
Accounts payable – trade		4,854	4,912
Additional liabilities		6,675	6,851
		11,529	11,763
Deferred income		418	387
Total shareholders' equity and liabilities		71,800	69,468

Konzernabschluß
Bilanz Siemens Welt

zum 30. September 1992
in Millionen DM

Aktiva	Anhang	30.9.1992	30.9.1991
Anlagevermögen			
Immaterielle Vermögensgegenstände	(5)	435	275
Sachanlagen	(5)		
Anschaffungs- und Herstellungskosten		46762	43660
Kumulierte Abschreibungen		-28960	-27206
		17802	16454
Finanzanlagen	(6)	2657	2660
		20894	19389
Umlaufvermögen			
Vorräte	(7)	26275	24774
Erhaltene Anzahlungen		-19993	-16535
		6282	8239
Forderungen und Sonstige Vermögensgegenstände	(8)		
Forderungen aus Lieferungen und Leistungen		14459	14387
Übrige Forderungen und Sonstige Vermögensgegenstände		10445	8818
		24904	23205
Wertpapiere und Schuldscheine	(9)	16600	15088
Flüssige Mittel		3077	3478
		50863	50010
Rechnungsabgrenzungsposten		43	69
Summe Aktiva		71800	69468

Passiva	Anhang	30.9.1992	30.9.1991
Eigenkapital			
Gezeichnetes Kapital	(10)		
Stammaktien (Gesamtstimmenzahl 55025662)		2752	2593
Vorzugsaktien (Gesamtstimmenzahl 923634)		46	46
		2798	2639
Kapitalrücklage	(10)	8590	6244
Gewinnrücklagen	(11)	6991	7735
Konzerngewinn		727	686
Anteile in Fremdbesitz	(12)	1235	1345
		20341	18649
Rückstellungen	(13)		
Pensionen und ähnliche Verpflichtungen		14761	13957
Übrige Rückstellungen		20220	20137
		34981	34094
Finanzschulden	(14)	4531	4575
Andere Verbindlichkeiten	(14)		
Verbindlichkeiten aus Lieferungen und Leistungen		4854	4912
Übrige Verbindlichkeiten		6675	6851
		11529	11763
Rechnungsabgrenzungsposten		418	387
Summe Passiva		71800	69468

Consolidated financial statements
Siemens worldwide consolidated statement of income

for the fiscal years ended September 30
(in millions of DM)

	Note	1992	1991
Net sales	(15)	78,509	73,008
Change in inventories and additions to self-produced plant and equipment	(16)	3,204	3,300
Total operating performance		81,713	76,308
Other operating income	(17)	5,326	5,089
Cost of materials	(18)	(35,450)	(32,360)
Personnel costs	(19)	(33,873)	(31,817)
Depreciation and amortization		(4,613)	(4,400)
Other operating expenses	(20)	(11,826)	(11,107)
Net income from investment in other companies	(21)	56	(153)
Net interest income	(22)	1,864	1,859
Income before income taxes		3,197	3,419
Income taxes	(23)	(1,242)	(1,627)
Net income		1,955	1,792

Appropriation of net income	1992	1991
Net income	1,955	1,792
Minority interests in net income of consolidated subsidiaries	(203)	(155)
Minority interests in net loss of consolidated subsidiaries	43	211
Balance brought forward from prior year	6	–
Transfers to retained earnings	(1,074)	(1,162)
Unappropriated consolidated net income (dividend of Siemens AG)	727	686

Konzernabschluß
Gewinn- und Verlustrechnung Siemens Welt

1. Oktober 1991 bis 30. September 1992
in Millionen DM

	Anhang	1991/92	1990/91
Umsatzerlöse	(15)	78509	73008
Bestandsveränderung und andere aktivierte Eigenleistungen	(16)	3204	3300
Gesamtleistung		81713	76308
Sonstige betriebliche Erträge	(17)	5326	5089
Materialaufwand	(18)	-35450	-32360
Personalaufwand	(19)	-33873	-31817
Abschreibungen auf Immaterielle Vermögensgegenstände und Sachanlagen		- 4613	- 4400
Sonstige betriebliche Aufwendungen	(20)	-11826	-11107
Beteiligungsergebnis	(21)	56	- 153
Zinsergebnis	(22)	1864	1859
Ergebnis der gewöhnlichen Geschäftstätigkeit		3197	3419
Ertragsteuern	(23)	- 1242	- 1627
Jahresüberschuß		1955	1792

Verwendung des Jahresüberschusses	1991/92	1990/91
Jahresüberschuß	1955	1792
Konzernfremden Gesellschaftern zustehender Gewinn	- 203	- 155
Auf konzernfremde Gesellschafter entfallender Verlust	43	211
Gewinnvortrag aus dem Vorjahr	6	-
Einstellungen in Gewinnrücklagen	- 1074	- 1162
Konzerngewinn (Dividende der Siemens AG)	727	686

Consolidated financial statements
Siemens worldwide consolidated statement of changes in financial position

for the fiscal years ended September 30
(in millions of DM)

	1992	1991
Cash flow		
Net income	1,955	1,792
Depreciation, amortization and write-downs	4,735	4,440
Increase in medium- and long-term accrued liabilities	189	565
	6,879	6,797
Funds invested in operating assets		
Capital expenditures for property, plant and equipment	(5,560)	(5,003)
Expenditures for acquisition of investments	(3,014)	(592)
Increase in inventories	(910)	(2,042)
Increase in receivables	(2,121)	(2,648)
Change in miscellaneous balance sheet items	134	816
	(11,471)	(9,469)
Financing from operations		
Increase in advances received from customers	3,247	1,808
Increase in other liabilities	109	325
	3,356	2,133
Other financing activities		
Increase in paid-in capital	2,505	351
Reduction of debt	(158)	(593)
	2,347	(242)
Change in liquid assets	1,111	(781)
included therein: Marketable securities and notes	1,512	(598)
Other liquid assets	(401)	(183)
Liquid assets at September 30	19,677	18,566

Konzernabschluß
Kapitalflußrechnung Siemens Welt

1. Oktober 1991 bis 30. September 1992
in Millionen DM

	1991/92	1990/91
Cash flow		
Jahresüberschuß	+ 1955	+ 1792
Abschreibungen auf Anlagevermögen	+ 4735	+ 4440
Erhöhung mittel- und langfristiger Rückstellungen	+ 189	+ 565
	+ 6879	+ 6797
Mittelbindung		
Investitionen in Sachanlagen	– 5560	– 5003
Investitionen für den Erwerb von Beteiligungen	– 3014	– 592
Erhöhung der Vorräte	– 910	– 2042
Erhöhung der Forderungen	– 2121	– 2648
Veränderung sonstiger Bilanzpositionen	+ 134	+ 816
	– 11471	– 9469
Finanzierung aus dem Geschäft		
Erhöhung der Erhaltenen Anzahlungen	+ 3247	+ 1808
Erhöhung der Anderen Verbindlichkeiten	+ 109	+ 325
	+ 3356	+ 2133
Sonstige Finanzierungsvorgänge		
Erhöhung des eingezahlten Eigenkapitals	+ 2505	+ 351
Verminderung der Finanzschulden	– 158	– 593
	+ 2347	– 242
Veränderung der Liquidität	+ 1111	– 781
davon Wertpapiere und Schuldscheine	+ 1512	– 598
Flüssige Mittel	– 401	– 183
Liquidität, Stand 30.9.	19677	18566

Auditors' report

The consolidated financial statements, which we have audited in accordance with professional standards, comply with the German legal provisions. With due regard to the generally accepted accounting principles, the consolidated financial statements present a true and fair view of the Siemens group's assets, liabilities, financial position and earnings. The general review of the Managing Board is consistent with the consolidated financial statements.

KPMG Deutsche Treuhand-Gesellschaft
Aktiengesellschaft
Wirtschaftsprüfungsgesellschaft

Berlin and Frankfurt on Main
Munich, January 5, 1993

Schnicke	Dr. Schulz
Wirtschaftsprüfer	Wirtschaftsprüfer

(independent auditors)

Bestätigungsvermerck

Der Konzernabschluß entspricht nach unserer pflichtgemäßen Prüfung den gesetzlichen Vorschriften. Der Konzernabschluß vermittelt unter Beachtung der Grundsätze ordnungsmäßiger Buchführung ein den tatsächlichen Verhältnissen entsprechendes Bild der Vermögens-, Finanz- und Ertragslage des Konzerns. Der Konzernlagebericht steht im Einklang mit dem Konzernabschluß.

KPMG Deutsche Treuhand-Gesellschaft
Aktiengesellschaft
Wirtschaftsprüfungsgesellschaft

Berlin und Frankfurt a.M.
München, den 5. Januar 1993

Schnicke	Dr. Schulz
Wirtschaftsprüfer	Wirtschaftsprüfer

Consolidated financial statements
Notes

(1) Principles of consolidation
The worldwide consolidated financial statements include virtually all the domestic (German) and foreign subsidiaries. In addition to Siemens AG, 67 (1991: 57) subsidiaries in Germany and 224 (1991: 231) subsidiaries in foreign countries have been consolidated. 320 (1991: 306) companies that are either inactive or have a low business volume are not included in the consolidated financial statements, because they have little or no significance for the presentation of Siemens' overall position. Their sales account for less than three percent of consolidated sales. In addition, we have omitted retirement benefit corporations, whose assets are assigned for a specific purpose, as well as those companies whose shares were acquired exclusively for investment purposes.

Investments in 36 (1991: 50) associated companies and in two subsidiaries which we had already recorded at our proportionate interest in their net worth in fiscal 1991, have been accounted for using the equity method. An additional 137 (1991: 131) other associated companies were not accounted for in this manner because of their relative immateriality.

The principal subsidiaries and associated companies are listed on pages 46 and 47, including their sales, shareholders' equity and earnings. A complete list of our holdings is being filed with the Commercial Registries of the Berlin-Charlottenburg and Munich District Courts.

In consolidating our investment in subsidiaries, we offset the purchase price against the value of Siemens' interests in the shareholders' equity of the consolidated subsidiaries at the time of their acquisition or initial consolidation. Any resulting goodwill is offset against retained earnings. The same principles are applied in consolidating companies under the equity method. Our share in the net income of the companies accounted for under this method is shown in the statement of income under net income from investment in other companies.

In the consolidated financial statements, we eliminate intercompany profits as well as sales, expenses and income within the Siemens organization and all receivables and liabilities between consolidated companies. Since the intercompany profits of the companies accounted for under the equity method are insignificant, they are not eliminated. Interim statements are used for consolidated subsidiaries whose fiscal year differs from that of Siemens AG.

(2) Foreign currency translation
In the individual financial statements, we translate receivables and liabilities in foreign currency at the rate existing at the transaction date or the rate at the balance sheet date, whichever is lower. When foreign currency receivables and liabilities of our subsidiaries outside Germany have been hedged by forward exchange transactions, they are valued at the corresponding hedging rate.

Accruals are established to cover impending losses from hedging operations.

In the consolidated financial statements, intangible assets, property, plant and equipment, and investment in subsidiaries and other companies of our foreign subsidiaries are translated at historical exchange rates. Their other assets and liabilities are translated at the year-end current rate (the average of the buying and selling rates).

Revenues and expenses included in the statement of income are translated at average rates for the year, except for depreciation, amortization and write-downs on intangibles, fixed assets and investments, which are translated at historical rates.

When our subsidiaries' financial statements are translated into German marks, the resulting balance is recorded in one of two ways in accordance with the convention of conservatism. A net translation loss is charged against earnings, while a net translation gain is offset by an accrual for exchange risks, which is used to cover translation losses in subsequent years.

(3) Principles of accounting and valuation
The financial statements of Siemens AG and its domestic and foreign subsidiaries are prepared according to uniform principles of accounting and valuation. To ensure uniformity of valuation within the worldwide Siemens consolidated financial statements, the tax-deductible valuation adjustments and special reserves included in the individual financial statements of the domestic companies have been reversed in the consolidated financial statements. In accordance with §17 of the German DM Opening Balance Sheet Act (DMBilG), the special reserves in the individual financial statements of the companies in the new German federal states have been offset against the special loss accounts and allocated to the retained earnings of the worldwide consolidated financial statements. Valuations in the statements of companies accounted for under the equity method that deviate from these uniform principles have not been adjusted on the basis of immateriality.

Insofar as intangible assets have been acquired for consideration, they are carried at acquisition cost and are amortized up to a maximum of five years. Any goodwill resulting from consolidation is offset against retained earnings.

Property, plant and equipment is recorded at acquisition or production cost, less scheduled depreciation. Depreciation is taken on residential, office and factory buildings for a maximum of 50 years, on technical equipment and machinery for a maximum of 10 years, and on other equipment and plant and office equipment, in general, over five years. Equipment leased to customers is depreciated according to the useful lives of the product groups. In the Federal Republic of Germany, we use the declining balance method for the depreciation of property, plant and equipment to the extent possible under the tax laws, at the

Consolidated financial statements
Notes

maximum allowable rates, switching to the straight-line method as soon as the latter results in higher depreciation. Additional depreciation is taken where a write-down in book value is deemed necessary. Minor fixed assets are fully expensed in the year of acquisition.

Significant investments in associated companies are accounted for using the equity method, thereby reflecting our proportionate interest in their net worth. Interests in nonconsolidated subsidiaries and other associated and related companies are valued at the lower of cost or market. Loans made as investments and bearing nominal or no interest are stated at their discounted cash value.

Materials, supplies, merchandise for resale, and advances to suppliers are carried in inventories at the lower of cost or market. Work in process and finished products are stated at production cost. Production cost includes materials, direct labor and production overhead which must be capitalized in accordance with the provisions of the German tax laws. The cost of unbilled contracts is valued according to the same principles. We use the LIFO method for certain metals. Purchases from consolidated companies are stated in inventory according to the uniform capitalization policy required by the German Commercial Code. A reasonable and sufficient allowance is made for declines in value due to slow-moving items, technical obsolescence and reductions in fair value.

Receivables and miscellaneous assets are carried at the lower of cost or market. Accounts receivable due after one year which bear nominal or no interest have been discounted.

Marketable securities and notes are stated at the lower of cost or market. In Germany, lower valuations are retained to the extent permissible under the tax laws.

Accrued liabilities include reasonable and sufficient allowance for all perceivable risks. In Germany, the accruals for pension plans are set up according to actuarial principles, using the method of computation provided for in the German Income Tax Act. Foreign subsidiaries establish accruals for pension plans, as required, according to comparable principles.

Deferred taxes are recorded following the liability method. These taxes are provided for the temporary differences between the financial reporting basis and the tax basis of the consolidated assets and liabilities. Deferred assets and liabilities are netted, with any resulting credit balance being recorded as an accrual for deferred taxes. A net deferred tax receivable balance will be recorded only if it is derived from consolidation entries.

Intangibles, fixed assets and investments of our subsidiaries in the highly inflationary economies of Argentina and Brazil are recorded at acquisition or production cost and translated at historical exchange rates. Other assets and liabilities are stated at their current value or replacement cost and translated at the year-end current rate (the average of the buying and selling rates). The difference between this amount and the lower acquisition or production cost is, as a rule, largely neutralized by translation at the prevailing year-end current rate.

For improved clarity of the consolidated financial statements, the inflationary components contained within interest income (expense) and within foreign exchange gains (losses) have been eliminated from the financial statements of our subsidiaries in countries with highly inflationary economies and reclassified to other operating expenses.

Certain items on the consolidated balance sheet and in the consolidated statement of income have been combined to provide greater clarity. These items are shown separately in the Notes to consolidated financial statements (Notes).

The consolidated financial statements are denominated in millions of German marks (DM).

(4) Acquisition of subsidiaries and associated companies
During the 1992 fiscal year, Siemens AG increased its interest in the shareholders' equity of Siemens Nixdorf Informationssysteme AG (SNI), Paderborn, to 100%.

By September 30, 1991, Siemens AG had acquired 78% of the shareholders' equity of SNI. Following the purchase of additional shares of SNI under a tender offer for publicly held outstanding shares and on the basis of previously made agreements with the Nixdorf family and family-related trusts, Siemens AG held more than 95% of the capital stock of SNI at the beginning of 1992. The Annual Shareholders' Meeting of SNI on March 5, 1992 resolved that the Company be integrated into Siemens AG under §320, par. 1 of the German Stock Corporation Act. This resolution was approved by the Annual Shareholders' Meeting of Siemens AG on March 12, 1992. The integration was recorded in the Commercial Registry of the Paderborn District Court on April 15, 1992 and, thereby, became legally effective.

Pursuant to §320, par. 4 of the German Stock Corporation Act, all shares not yet held by Siemens AG passed to Siemens AG with the recording in the register. Pursuant to §320, par. 5 of the German Stock Corporation Act, Siemens AG has undertaken to offer SNI shareholders who did not tender their shares a settlement of one share of common stock of Siemens AG with a par value of DM50 in exchange for six shares of (common or preferred) stock of SNI, each with a par value of DM50; holdings of less than six shares will receive cash in the amount of DM156.50 per share of SNI. The exchange ratio is based on an appraisal by certified public accountants dated March 5, 1992.

In fiscal 1992, ROLM Company, Norwalk, Connecticut, which had been held on a 50/50 basis by Siemens and International Business Machines Corporation, Armonk, New York, became wholly-owned by us. The company, which had been accounted for on the basis of our proportionate interest in its net worth in prior years, has been fully included as a subsidiary in the consolidated financial statements as of July 1, 1992.

Fourteen companies that were newly formed or acquired in the new German federal states in fiscal 1991 were included in the consolidated financial statements for the first time in fiscal 1992.

A total of 15 subsidiaries in Germany and 16 subsidiaries in other countries were consolidated for the first time, while five German companies and 23 companies outside Germany are no longer included in the consolidated financial statements.

Goodwill in the amount of DM1,934 million, which resulted from the initial consolidation of equity interests in subsidiaries and associated companies, was offset against retained earnings.

The changes in the number of consolidated companies did not have a material effect on Siemens' overall position.

(5) Intangible assets and property, plant and equipment

(in millions of DM)	9/30/91	Additions	Reclassifications	Retirements	9/30/92	Accumulated depreciation/amortization	Net value as of 9/30/92	Net value as of 9/30/91	Depreciation/amortization during the fiscal year
Intangible assets	971	411	–	450	932	497	435	275	248
Property, plant and equipment									
Land, equivalent rights to real property, and buildings, including buildings on land not owned	12,442	955	380	174	13,603	5,083	8,520	7,837	521
Technical equipment and machinery	11,985	1,081	421	802	12,685	9,436	3,249	2,961	1,083
Other equipment, plant and office equipment	14,836	2,357	259	1,570	15,882	12,382	3,500	3,325	2,248
Equipment leased to customers	2,961	649	(6)	647	2,957	2,047	910	896	501
Advances to suppliers and construction in progress	1,436	1,276	(1,054)	23	1,635	12	1,623	1,435	12
	43,660	6,318	–	3,216	46,762	28,960	17,802	16,454	4,365
	44,631	6,729	–	3,666	47,694	29,457	18,237	16,729	4,613

Additions to intangible assets and property, plant and equipment during the fiscal year amounted to DM6,729 (1991: DM8,651) million, which include the opening balance amounts of DM1,072 million attributable to companies included in the consolidated financial statements for the first time.

Consolidated financial statements
Notes

(6) Investments

(in millions of DM)	9/30/91	Additions	Reclassi-fications	Retire-ments	9/30/92	Accumulat-ed write-downs	Accumulat-ed equity-adjustment	Net value as of 9/30/92	Net value as of 9/30/91
Interests in subsidiaries	718	337	29	250	834	158	(95)	581	640
Interests in associated companies	2,876	81	(18)	201	2,738	–	(1,349)	1,389	1,494
Miscellaneous investments	805	315	(11)	78	1,031	344	–	687	526
	4,399	733	–	529	4,603	502	(1,444)	2,657	2,660

The additions to interests in subsidiaries and associated companies relate predominantly to the acquisition of equity interests.

Retirements in interests in subsidiaries resulted primarily from their initial consolidation. Retirements in interests in associated companies mainly include the sale of the equity interest in Fides Industrie-Beteiligungsgesellschaft mbH, Munich.

Our share in the net income of subsidiaries and associated companies accounted for under the equity method amounted to DM36 (1991: DM92) million during the fiscal year.

Miscellaneous investments include interests in other companies, as well as loans, primarily residential construction loans.

Write-downs of DM89 million on interests in subsidiaries and of DM33 million on miscellaneous investments were made during the fiscal year.

(7) Inventories

(in millions of DM)	9/30/92	9/30/91
Materials and supplies	2,448	2,512
Work in process	4,489	4,798
Finished products and merchandise	5,140	5,478
Cost of unbilled contracts	12,598	11,055
Advances to suppliers	1,600	931
	26,275	24,774

(8) Receivables and miscellaneous assets

(in millions of DM)	9/30/92	Due after one year	9/30/91	Due after one year
Accounts receivable – trade	14,459	981	14,387	1,657
Other receivables and miscellaneous assets				
Receivables from nonconsolidated subsidiaries	2,249	32	1,259	46
Receivables from associated and related companies	2,753	1,499	2,202	992
Miscellaneous assets	5,443	713	5,357	947
	10,445	2,244	8,818	1,985
	24,904	3,225	23,205	3,642

Miscellaneous assets include our interests in subsidiaries in the amount of DM1,308 (1991: DM1,473) million, which were acquired exclusively as financial investments. This item also includes a large amount of accrued interest income.

(9) Marketable securities and notes

(in millions of DM)	9/30/92	9/30/91
Treasury stock	57	13
Stock certificates	1,850	1,733
Fixed-income securities	13,264	11,580
Notes	1,429	1,762
	16,600	15,088

In fiscal 1992, Siemens AG purchased 608,369 shares of common stock, with a total par value of DM30 million, or 1.2% of the capital stock, at an average price of DM639.80 per share, in order to offer them to employees for purchase. Including the 32,505 shares of treasury stock held at the beginning of the fiscal year, 476,364 shares, with a total par value of DM24 million, or 0.9% of the capital stock, were sold to employees at a preferential price of DM391 per share. At the close of the fiscal year, 164,510 shares of common stock, having a total par value of DM8 million, or 0.3% of the capital stock, remained in treasury. They are valued at DM347 per share.

The fixed-income securities include shares of investment funds in the amount of DM3,965 (1991: DM3,604) million.

Our security holdings include debentures and bonds issued by Siemens companies.

For tax reasons, write-downs of DM108 million made in prior years were not reversed in fiscal 1992, although the market price of such securities increased during the year. This reduced net income in fiscal 1992 by DM45 million.

(10) Capital stock and additional paid-in capital
The capital stock of Siemens AG amounts to DM2,798 million and is divided into 55,025,662 common shares and 923,634 preferred shares, each with a par value of DM50. Each share is entitled to one vote. Under conditions set forth in §23 of the Articles of Association, preferred stock is entitled to six votes per share in a second vote that may be demanded by the holders of preferred stock.

During the fiscal year, capital stock increased by a total of DM159 million through the issuance of 2,993,583 common shares from the other authorized capital as a result of the exercise of option rights under the warrants attached to the 1986/2001 U.S. dollar zero coupon bonds issued by Siemens Western Finance N.V. as well as through the issuance of 188,410 common shares from the other authorized capital as a result of the settlement offered to former shareholders of SNI.

The premium of DM1,707 million paid on the option rights that were exercised, and of DM120 million paid for the settlement offered to SNI shareholders was recorded as additional paid-in capital.

The authorized capital of Siemens AG remained unchanged at DM800 million. On March 28, 1991, the Annual Shareholders' Meeting authorized the Managing Board to issue DM500 million in new shares with subscription rights for shareholders as well as for holders of stock warrants (authorized capital I) and DM300 million in new shares for which the subscription right of shareholders is excluded (authorized capital II). These authorizations will expire on March 1, 1996. A law suit contesting these resolutions was brought by a shareholder. In its verdict rendered on April 2, 1992, the Munich Regional Court dismissed the complaint with respect to the authorized capital I and upheld the complaint with respect to the authorized capital II. The verdict, however, is not final, since both parties have appealed.

The other authorized capital amounts to DM164 (1991: DM300) million. Of this amount, DM150 million is reserved to secure the rights to purchase common shares of Siemens AG under the warrants attached to the 8% U.S. dollar bonds of 1992/2002 issued by Siemens Capital Corporation. The stock warrants grant option rights for a total of 3,000,000 common shares, which may be exercised until June 2, 1998. The option period is automatically extended for periods of one year terms – but not more than two years – if the market price of the Siemens share falls below the option price within one reference period. The option price is DM693. The premium of DM519 million paid on the stock warrants was recorded as additional paid-in capital.

The other authorized capital of DM5 million provides for the settlement offered to SNI shareholders who have not tendered their shares by September 30, 1992.

The remaining other authorized capital of DM9 million secures the rights to purchase common shares of Siemens AG that were granted to the holders of the 6¼% 1987/94 DM bonds with warrants issued by Siemens Nixdorf International Finance B.V. and to the holders of the Nixdorf 1989/97 convertible loans following the integration of SNI AG into Siemens AG.

Option rights under the 1986/2001 U.S. dollar zero coupon bond issue for 2,993,583 shares were exercised during the fiscal year, at a share price of DM620. Warrants for only 6,405 shares were not exercised when the option period expired in June 1992.

(11) Retained earnings
Retained earnings include a reserve for treasury stock in the amount of DM57 (1991: DM13) million. The reserve was increased by DM44 million through transfers from other retained earnings.

Consolidated financial statements
Notes

After deducting the treasury stock reserve, other retained earnings amounted to DM6,934 (1991: DM7,722) million. We transferred DM1,074 (1991: DM1,162) million to other retained earnings from the consolidated net income of DM1,955 (1991: DM1,792) million. Goodwill of DM1,934 million resulting from the initial consolidation of interests in subsidiaries and associated companies was offset against other retained earnings.

Due to the consolidation of our companies in the new German federal states, other retained earnings include a small amount of special reserves pursuant to the German DM Opening Balance Sheet Act (DMBilG) which remained after offsetting such reserves against special loss accounts.

(12) Minority interests
Minority interests represent the minority shareholders' proportionate share of the equity of consolidated subsidiaries, primarily our companies in Austria and Switzerland, as well as Siemens Stromberg-Carlson, Boca Raton, Florida, and, in fiscal 1991, the minority interests in SNI.

(13) Accrued liabilities
The accruals for pension plans at Siemens AG and its domestic subsidiaries provide for the contractual retirement benefits of employees and retirees not subject to collective bargaining agreements. In addition, the accruals provide for 80% of the retirement benefits of employees covered by such collective bargaining agreements as well as their claims for transitional payments. Retirement benefit corporations in Germany provide for the remainder of Siemens AG's pension obligations to employees subject to collective bargaining agreements and to their surviving dependents. In addition, accruals are established for the retirement benefits of the employees and retirees of our foreign subsidiaries, unless the obligations are covered by pension funds. Moreover, the obligations of our U.S. subsidiaries to provide postretirement benefits other than pension for active and retired employees are shown here.

The pension commitments of Siemens AG and its subsidiaries are fully covered by accruals for pension plans and the funds of the retirement benefit corporations.

Other accrued liabilities include DM2,131 (1991: DM2,106) million in provisions for taxes. In addition, this item consists primarily of accruals for personnel costs, warranty obligations, anticipated losses on contracts, penalties for contract performance delays, and expenses for contracts already billed.

(14) Debt and other liabilities

(in millions of DM)	9/30/92	Due within one year	9/30/91	Due within one year
Debt				
Bonds and debentures	2,225	3	1,213	3
Loans from banks . .	1,920	1,498	2,344	1,775
Notes and other loans	386	99	1,018	761
	4,531	1,600	4,575	2,539
Other liabilities				
Accounts payable – trade.	4,854	4,640	4,912	4,652
Additional liabilities				
Liabilities to nonconsolidated subsidiaries	239	165	524	479
Liabilities to associated and related companies	310	272	444	302
Miscellaneous liabilities	6,126	5,494	5,883	5,205
	6,675	5,931	6,851	5,986
	11,529	10,571	11,763	10,638

Debt increased as a result of the 8% U.S. dollar bonds with warrants issued by Siemens Capital Corporation.

Tax liabilities totaling DM961 (1991: DM989) million are included in miscellaneous liabilities. This item also contains liabilities amounting to DM995 (1991: DM988) million mandated by the social security program, which consist of outstanding statutory social welfare contributions and statutory retirement benefit obligations in foreign countries.

Siemens AG has made commitments to lenders of public funds that it will not encumber its real estate.

We have furnished security for debt and other liabilities totaling DM351 (1991: DM691) million. Debt in the amount of DM181 (1991: DM167) million is secured by mortgages. In Germany, debt in the amount of DM23 million is secured by claims under a Hermes export credit guaranty. In addition, we assigned receivables from export orders in accordance with the guidelines of AKA Ausfuhrkredit-Gesellschaft mbH, receiving loans from AKA in the amount of DM16 million in the form of notes payable. In some countries, we have executed promissory notes and pledged securities, in conformity with local practice, to secure our debt.

Debt and other liabilities with a remaining term of more than five years totaled DM2,269 (1991: DM1,327) million.

Bonds and debentures (in millions)currency	Foreign DM		
Siemens Beteiligungen AG, Zurich 4¾% 1983/93 Swiss franc debentures	Sfr	100	114
Siemens Capital Corporation, Wilmington, Delaware 8% 1992/2002 U.S. dollar bonds with warrants	U.S.$	1,000	1,410
Siemens Ltd., Bombay			
15% 1971/92 Indian rupee bonds	IRs	20	1
15% 1981/92 Indian rupee bonds	IRs	50	2
Siemens Nixdorf International Finance B.V., Vianen, Netherlands 6¼% 1987/94 DM bonds with warrants			500
Siemens Western Finance N. V., Willemstad, Curação 1986/2001 U.S. dollar zero coupon bonds with warrants	U.S.$	144	198
			2,225

(15) Net Sales
Net sales include our income from leasing and license agreements. A breakdown of net sales by business segment and region is given on page 45.

(16) Change in inventories and additions to self-produced plant and equipment
Change in inventories and additions to self-produced plant and equipment totaled DM3,204 (1991: DM3,300) million, of which DM1,124 (1991: DM1,700) million relates to the increase in inventories of finished products and work in process and in the cost of unbilled contracts. DM2,080 (1991: DM1,600) million in additions to self-produced plant and equipment was capitalized.

(17) Other operating income
Other operating income includes, in particular, foreign exchange and securities gains, income from various services, subsidies for research and development, Berlin sales tax benefits and capital investment grants, income from the reversal of accruals, and gains on the sale of investments.

(18) Cost of materials
The cost of materials amounted to DM35,450 (1991: DM32,360) million. This included DM26,775 (1991: DM24,110) million for materials, supplies, and merchandise purchased for resale, and DM8,675 (1991: DM8,250) million for purchased services from third parties.

(19) Personnel costs
Personnel costs consist of wages and salaries totaling DM27,043 (1991: DM25,373) million, statutory social welfare contributions and expenses related to employee benefits of DM4,396 (1991: DM4,103) million, and expense for pension plans of DM2,434 (1991: DM2,341) million.

The average number of employees during the fiscal year was 417,800 (1991: 406,000); they were engaged in the following activities:

	1992	1991
Manufacturing	172,000	172,700
Sales	145,000	135,500
Research and development	48,000	46,800
Administration and general services	52,800	51,000
	417,800	406,000

(20) Other operating expenses
Other operating expenses include the expenses for write-downs on investments, marketable securities and notes totaling DM465 (1991: DM110) million and miscellaneous taxes in the amount of DM477 (1991: DM553) million.

The translation of financial statements into German marks resulted in a loss of DM138 (1991: DM255) million in fiscal 1992.

Furthermore, other operating expenses consist mainly of administrative, marketing and selling expenses such as rentals, travel expenses, sales commissions, insurance and other overhead; additions to accruals; securities and foreign exchange losses; and bad debt expenses.

(21) Net income from investment in other companies

(in millions of DM)	1992	1991
Income from investment in other companies	77	48
Income under profit-and-loss transfer agreements	24	25
Share in earnings resulting from equity consolidation	36	92
Losses absorbed under profit-and-loss transfer agreements	(81)	(318)
	56	(153)

Consolidated financial statements
Notes

Net income from investment in other companies includes DM48 (1991: DM22) million in income from subsidiaries.

The income from subsidiaries and associated companies consolidated under the equity method consists primarily of our share in the earnings of Bosch-Siemens Hausgeräte GmbH, Munich; GPT Holdings Ltd., London; and companies in the United States.

Losses absorbed under profit-and-loss transfer agreements relate primarily to our companies in the new German federal states.

(22) Net interest income
Interest and similar income of DM2,706 (1991: DM2,885) million exceeded interest and similar expenses of DM842 (1991: DM1,026) million by DM1,864 (1991: DM1,859) million. Interest and similar income includes DM216 (1991: DM135) million attributable to subsidiaries. The interest expense attributable to subsidiaries is not significant.

(23) Income taxes
Income taxes include German corporate income and local income taxes, as well as the comparable foreign taxes relating to income. Such taxes are determined in accordance with the tax laws applicable to the individual companies. In addition, income taxes include the deferred taxes resulting from temporary differences. Income tax expense was reduced by DM40 (1991: DM98) million in tax credits that relate to income from investments in domestic companies. Taxes not based on income, at DM477 (1991: DM553) million, are included in other operating expenses.

(24) Remuneration of the Supervisory Board and the Managing Board, and loans granted
Provided that shareholders approve the proposed dividend at their Annual Shareholders' Meeting on March 11, 1993, the amount authorized to be paid for the fiscal year will be DM1.1 (1991: DM1.1) million for the Supervisory Board; DM21.0 (1991: DM22.9) million for the Managing Board; and DM16.0 (1991: DM17.2) million for former members of the Managing Board and their surviving dependents. Pension commitments to former members of the Managing Board and their surviving dependents are covered by an accrual of DM136.7 (1991: DM126.7) million.

Loans to members of the Managing Board totaled DM0.9 (1991: DM1.8) million (repaid in 1992: DM0.9 million). These loans bear interest of up to six percent and have contractual terms of up to 10 years.

The members of the Supervisory and Managing Boards of Siemens AG are listed on pages 3 and 50, respectively.

(25) Guarantees and other commitments

(in millions of DM)	9/30/92	9/30/91
Contingent liabilities on notes	340	440
Guarantees	57	127
Warranties	1,672	1,480
Collateral for third party liabilities	2	5

(26) Other financial obligations
At September 30, 1992, we had leased from leasing companies 74 properties, 14 of which were located outside Germany. In fiscal 1992, the rental expense under these leases was DM127 (1991: DM129) million. The discounted value of our payment obligations under these leasing agreements amounts to DM879 (1991: DM928) million. Under the terms of the leases, the agreements do not convey the ownership rights to the leased properties; therefore, they are not capitalized in the consolidated financial statements.

We also have payment obligations with a discounted value of DM1,088 (1991: DM1,008) million under long-term lease agreements for movable assets and real property. The rental expense in fiscal 1992 amounted to DM176 (1991: DM160) million.

We are committed to making capital contributions of DM34 (1991: DM45) million to other companies, including DM10 (1991: DM37) million to subsidiaries. We have made commitments in the amount of DM579 (1991: DM439) million, including DM577 (1991: DM437) million to nonconsolidated subsidiaries, as limited partners pursuant to §171 of the German Commercial Code. In addition, commitments exist in the amount of DM16 (1991: DM26) million, including DM10 million in fiscal 1991 to nonconsolidated subsidiaries, pursuant to §24 of the German Limited Liability Companies Act (GmbH Act).

We are jointly and severally liable and have capital contribution obligations as a partner in companies formed under the German Civil Code, through which we have concluded profit-and-loss transfer agreements with other companies, as a partner in a general partnership, and as a participant in various joint activities.

(27) Segment information
Siemens is a supplier of electronic and electrical products, systems and equipment. Activities in other lines of business are not significant.

Sales and capital expenditures of the domestic and foreign subsidiaries are assigned to the Group that has the worldwide responsibility for that business activity. Net sales in the table below include intersegment shipments.

By business segment	Net sales		Capital expenditures	
(in millions of DM)	1992	1991	1992	1991
Power Generation (KWU)	6,570	4,955	523	394
Power Transmission and Distribution	5,568	5,307	219	221
Industrial and Building Systems	8,717	8,774	272	214
Drives and Standard Products	6,686	6,522	316	420
Automation	5,811	5,680	216	237
Private Communication Systems	5,383	5,105	516	431
Public Communication Networks	13,165	11,260	472	434
Defense Electronics	1,460	1,679	52	76
Automotive Systems	2,540	2,127	241	219
Transportation Systems	2,718	2,141	132	79
Medical Engineering	7,887	7,429	347	375
Semiconductors	1,881	2,029	470	345
Passive Components and Electron Tubes	1,488	1,591	116	139
Electromechanical Components	855	832	87	68
Audio and Video Systems	261	249	16	14
SNI	13,010	12,125	712	708
Osram	3,119	2,971	310	328
Other	1,251	1,446	543	301
Less intersegment shipments	(9,861)	(9,214)	–	–
	78,509	73,008	5,560	5,003

Siemens does an extensive international business. Fifty-four percent of total sales are made to customers outside Germany. The geographic breakdown of sales by customer location is shown on page 26.

Our 202 operating companies outside Germany earned net income of DM562 million in fiscal 1992, compared with DM652 million in 1991. A regional breakdown of the net sales and capital expenditures of Siemens AG and its domestic and foreign subsidiaries is shown in the table below.

By region	Net sales		Capital expenditures	
(in millions of DM)	1992	1991	1992	1991
Germany	56,339	51,245	3,568	3,105
Attributable to exports	[19,864]	[17,982]		
Europe excluding Germany	23,485	23,338	1,160	1,061
Included therein: European Community	[15,183]	[14,761]	[782]	[680]
North America	8,716	8,517	515	502
Latin America	1,417	1,563	92	115
Asia	2,582	2,715	184	183
Other regions	1,178	1,100	41	37
Less intersegment shipments	(15,208)	(15,470)	–	–
	78,509	73,008	5,560	5,003

Berlin and Munich, December 14, 1992

Siemens Aktiengesellschaft

The Managing Board

Principal subsidiaries and associated companies

	Sales * (DM million)	Shareholders' equity * (DM million)	Earnings* (DM million)	Siemens' share (%)
I. Subsidiaries				
1. Germany				
Siemens Nixdorf Informationssysteme AG, Paderborn	10,233.8	1,509.6	(515.8)	100
Osram GmbH, Berlin and Munich	1,910.4	647.6	87.0	100
Siemens Anlagentechnik und Energieverteilung Leipzig GmbH, Leipzig	497.3	158.9	(18.7)	100
Vacuumschmelze GmbH, Hanau	382.0	98.8	0.8	100
Siemens Private Kommunikationssysteme Vertriebs-GmbH, Berlin	423.7	70.1	0.5	100
Siemens Audiologische Technik GmbH, Erlangen	97.9	55.0	1.6	100
Siemens Kabelwerk Schwerin GmbH, Schwerin	169.4	51.6	(24.7)	100
Siemens Übertragungssysteme GmbH, Greifswald	132.4	43.4	2.6	100
WSSB Verkehrstechnik GmbH, Berlin	182.8	38.5	(0.6)	100
Rofin-Sinar Laser GmbH, Hamburg	79.0	32.7	(12.5)	100
NRG Nuklearrohr-Gesellschaft mbH, Duisburg	63.9	31.5	1.7	100
Siemens Finanzierungsgesellschaft für Informationstechnik mbH, Munich	104.6	1,921.1	149.7	100
Siemens Miet- und Portfolio-GmbH & Co. OHG, Berlin	328.2	561.7	109.6	100
Siemensstadt-Grundstücksverwaltung GmbH & Co. OHG, Berlin	236.6	189.8	108.2	100
Sietec Systemtechnik GmbH & Co. OHG, Berlin	323.4	169.2	165.9	100
Duewag AG, Krefeld-Uerdingen	506.5	12.0	(10.1)	96
Siemens Solar GmbH, Munich	34.4	60.0	(93.9)	51
Siemens Matsushita Components GmbH & Co. KG, Munich	594.2	66.6	(34.7)	50***
2. International				
A. Europe				
Siemens Beteiligungen AG, Zurich	–	1,554.8	130.5	100
Siemens S.A., Saint-Gilles (Brussels)	1,433.3	410.3	64.3	100
ATEA N.V., Herentals/Belgium	399.0	53.7	17.8	100
Siemens A/S, Ballerup (Copenhagen)	487.8	77.6	23.5	100
Siemens Osakeyhtiö, Espoo (Helsinki)	296.8	44.3	(19.7)	100
Siemens S.A., Saint-Denis (Paris)**	773.3	70.5	(18.0)	100
Siemens Automotive S.A., Toulouse	361.5	89.5	16.7	100
Siemens A.E., Elektrotechnische Projekte und Erzeugnisse, Athens**	183.6	43.6	6.4	100
Siemens plc, Sunbury-on-Thames (London)**	1,256.7	423.7	32.8	100
Siemens Plessey Electronic Systems Ltd., Chessington, Surrey**	622.1	48.5	(32.0)	100
Siemens Ltd., Dublin	113.5	8.2	3.6	100
Siemens Telecomunicazioni S.p.A., Cologno Monzese (Milan)	1,008.6	234.3	28.7	100
Siemens S.p.A., Milan	1,676.6	175.8	(15.4)	100
Siemens Nederland N.V., The Hague	902.3	239.7	22.5	100
Siemens A/S, Oslo**	727.4	135.6	13.5	100
Siemens AG Österreich, Vienna**	3,184.9	406.2	53.6	74
Siemens S.A., Lisbon**	578.9	150.3	6.9	100
Siemens-Elema AB, Solna (Stockholm)	624.7	165.9	34.3	100
Siemens AB, Stockholm	293.2	14.3	4.5	100
Siemens-Albis AG, Zurich	1,209.0	303.3	30.7	78
Siemens S.A., Madrid	1,043.2	200.9	(8.2)	100
Simko Ticaret ve Sanayi A.Ş., Istanbul	393.3	30.1	5.4	51
Türk Siemens Kablo ve Elektrik Sanayii A.Ş., Mudanya	214.3	48.4	21.2	55
Osram S.A., Molsheim/France	262.9	52.7	2.7	100
Osram Ltd., Wembley (London)	186.7	52.6	0.4	100
Osram Società Riunite Osram Edison-Clerici S.p.A., Milan	424.0	78.3	6.8	100
Osram S.A., Madrid	91.4	20.5	(1.6)	90
Siemens Nixdorf Information Systems S.A./N.V., Brussels	433.8	159.3	14.7	100
Siemens Nixdorf Information Systems S.A., Cergy (Paris)	488.1	17.2	(77.1)	100
Siemens Nixdorf Information Systems Ltd., Bracknell (London)	357.9	31.1	(5.5)	100
Siemens Data S.p.A., Milan	662.4	78.5	3.7	51
Siemens Nixdorf Informatiesystemen B.V., Vianen/Netherlands	224.1	49.6	8.4	100
Siemens Nixdorf Informationssysteme Ges.m.b.H., Vienna	384.6	87.9	10.3	100
Siemens Nixdorf Informationssysteme AG, Kloten (Zurich)	307.5	57.5	0.3	100
Siemens Nixdorf Sistemas de Información S.A., Tres Cantos (Madrid)	395.7	0.5	(120.8)	100

at September 30, 1992

	Sales * (DM million)	Shareholders' equity * (DM million)	Earnings * (DM million)	Siemens' share (%)
B. North America				
Siemens Corporation, New York, NY (consolidated financial statements)	7,561.1	1,324.9	(427.6)	100
including: ROLM Company, Norwalk, CT				
ROLM Systems, Santa Clara, CA				
Siemens Automotive L.P., Auburn Hills, MI				
Siemens Communication Systems, Inc., Boca Raton, FL				
Siemens Components, Inc., Iselin, NJ				
Siemens Energy & Automation, Inc., Atlanta, GA				
Siemens KWU, Inc., New York, NY				
Siemens Medical Corporation, Iselin, NJ				
Siemens Private Communication Systems, Inc., Boca Raton, FL				
Siemens Nixdorf Information Systems, Inc., Burlington, MA	160.0	15.2	(98.8)	100
Siemens Automotive Ltd., Chatham, Ontario	457.2	94.0	18.8	100
Siemens Electric Ltd., Pointe Claire (Montreal)	370.0	55.0	(14.1)	100
C. Latin America				
Siemens S.A., Buenos Aires	396.2	19.1	(56.3)	100
Siemens S.A., São Paulo **	360.7	181.7	(3.4)	87
Siemens S.A., Bogotá	66.5	38.2	8.1	94
Siemens S.A. de C.V., Mexico City **	228.1	116.9	15.1	100
Siemens S.A., Caracas	78.5	3.5	0.9	100
Osram Argentina S.A.C.I., Buenos Aires	65.6	35.7	(4.6)	66
Osram do Brasil-Companhia de Lâmpadas Elétricas S.A., Osasco	113.8	24.8	(14.5)	100
Osram S.A. de C.V., Naucalpan (Mexico)	53.7	24.2	0.3	100
Siemens Western Finance N.V., Willemstad, Curaçao	–	49.7	(1.3)	100
D. Asia				
Siemens Ltd., Bombay	227.5	53.0	8.2	51
Siemens K. K., Tokyo	179.3	35.2	4.3	83
Siemens Components (Advanced Technology) Sdn. Bhd., Malacca (Malaysia)	167.6	30.4	6.4	100
Siemens Pakistan Engineering Co. Ltd., Karachi	104.9	14.1	4.7	64
Siemens Components (Pte) Ltd., Singapore	510.8	88.2	33.6	100
Taicom Systems Ltd., Taipei	415.1	159.6	54.8	55
Osram-Melco Ltd., Yokohama	171.3	72.7	0.5	51
E. Africa				
Siemens Ltd., Johannesburg **	888.6	122.2	20.3	52
F. Australia				
Siemens Ltd., Richmond (Melbourne)	251.8	56.7	7.3	100
II. Associated companies				
1. Germany				
Bosch-Siemens Hausgeräte GmbH, Munich	5,817.7	691.0	172.4	50
Linotype-Hell AG, Eschborn	756.7	409.4	12.2	33
Mannesmann Tally GmbH, Elchingen	435.6	46.0	(71.2)	49
Tela Versicherung Aktiengesellschaft, Berlin and Munich	285.7	285.4	6.1	50
2. International				
GPT Holdings Ltd., London **	3,150.9	1,201.3	239.1	40
Siecor Corporation, Hickory, NC **	539.9	177.1	33.7	50

* These figures comply with the financial statements prepared in accordance with the specific generally accepted accounting principles in each country and do not reflect the amounts included in the consolidated financial statements. Shareholders' equity and earnings are translated at the year-end current rate, and sales are translated at average rates for the year.

** Sales, shareholders' equity and earnings according to the consolidated financial statements

*** Subsidiary pursuant to §290, par. 2(1) of the German Commercial Code

Commentary and analysis

Consolidated financial statements

Net income
as a percent of

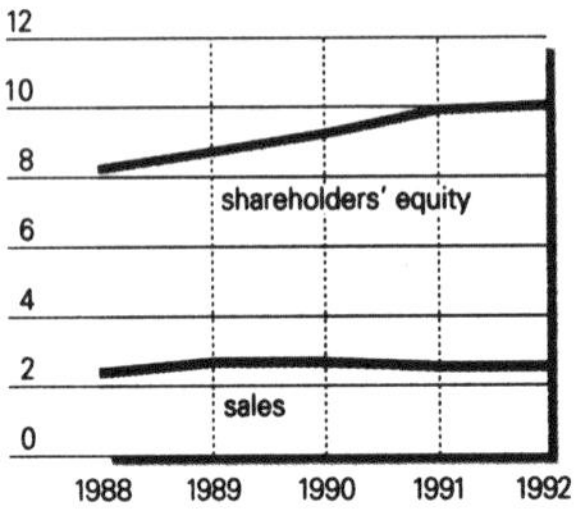

Shareholders' equity and debt
(in billions of DM)

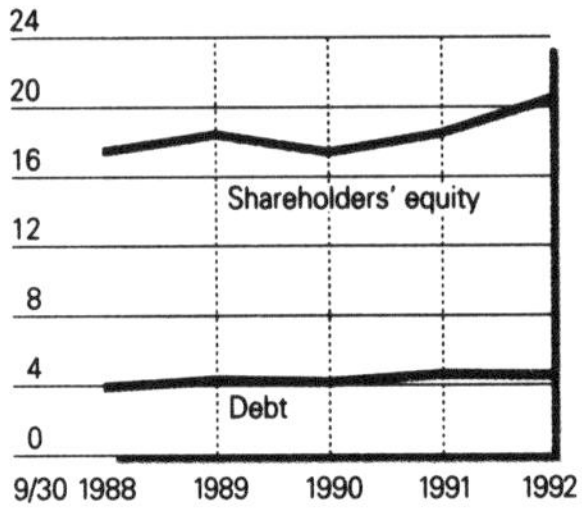

Capital spending and cash flow
(in billions of DM)

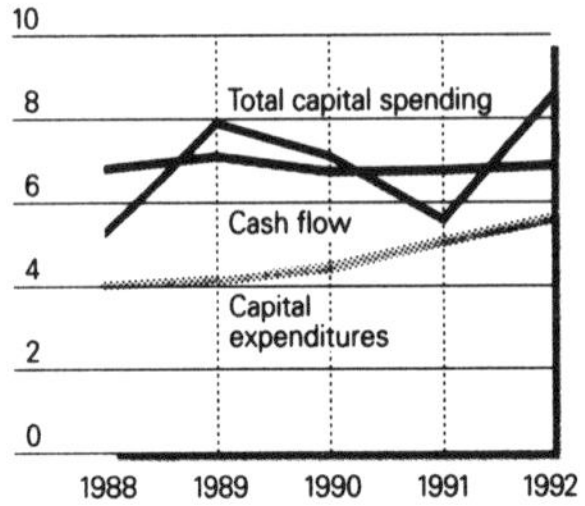

Fourteen companies in the new German federal states were included in the consolidated financial statements for the first time in fiscal 1992. ROLM Company, Norwalk, Connecticut, which had previously been accounted for under the equity method, has been fully included in the consolidated financial statements as of July 1, 1992, after it became wholly-owned by Siemens. Moreover, the remaining outstanding shares of Siemens Nixdorf Informationssysteme AG (SNI), Paderborn, were acquired during fiscal 1992; this company had already been included in last year's consolidated financial statements. Goodwill in the aggregate amount of DM1.9 billion, which resulted from the initial consolidation of equity interests in subsidiaries and associated companies, was offset against retained earnings.

The changes in the number of consolidated companies did not have a material effect on Siemens' overall position.

Increase in net income
Net sales increased DM5.5 billion, or eight percent, to DM78.5 billion in fiscal 1992. Total operating performance, i.e., the sum of net sales, increase in inventories, and additions to self-produced plant and equipment, rose seven percent to DM81.7 billion, lagging slightly behind the growth in sales resulting from a smaller increase in inventories compared to fiscal 1991.

The cost structure remained virtually unchanged. As in fiscal 1991, the two largest cost categories, materials and personnel, accounted for 84% of total operating performance. Depreciation and amortization totaled DM4.6 (1991: DM4.4) billion. In contrast to the prior year, a net income from investment in other companies was recorded for fiscal 1992. In fiscal 1991, net income from investment in other companies had been adversely affected by higher losses absorbed from east German companies.

Interest income continued to be considerably higher than interest expense. Totaling DM1.9 billion, net interest income remained at last year's level. Overall, interest income declined due to the significant reduction in long-term interest-bearing customer receivables, in spite of higher income from the larger securities portfolio. At the same time, replacement of higher-interest debt reduced interest expense.

Income before income taxes amounted to DM3.2 (1991: DM3.4) billion. Income tax expense declined as a result of lower taxable income in Germany and at subsidiaries abroad. The lower income tax rate was also brought about by reduced losses of several subsidiaries, notably SNI. After income taxes of DM1.2 billion, net income totaled DM1,955 million, nine percent more than a year earlier. While the return on sales remained unchanged at 2.5%, return on shareholders' equity improved moderately to 10.0%.

Cash flow remains high
Cash flow, i.e., the sum of net income plus depreciation, amortization, write-downs and the increase in medium- and long-term accrued liabilities, reached DM6.9 (1991: DM6.8) billion, representing 8.8% (1991: 9.3%) of net sales.

Due to the sharp rise in the acquisition of investments, capital spending, at DM8.6 billion, was considerably higher than in fiscal 1991. At DM5.6 (1991: DM5.0) billion, expenditures for property, plant and equipment significantly exceeded depreciation and amortization. They were fully funded by cash flow, i.e., by internally generated funds.

Together with cash flow, the strong DM3.4 billion cash inflows provided by operations, which relate almost exclusively to advances received from customers, financed all capital spending, as well as most of the current asset requirements.

The proceeds from the exercise of stock warrants attached to the 1986/2001 zero coupon bonds and the issuance of the new 8% U.S. dollar bonds of 1992/2002 with warrants in June 1992 produced a cash surplus at the close of the fiscal year. Liquid assets increased by DM1.1 billion.

Well-balanced assets and capital structure
The Company's total assets grew to DM71.8 billion, a DM2.3 billion increase over the prior year. This growth was essentially produced by the expanded volume of business.

Total intangibles, fixed assets and investments rose to DM20.9 billion and now account for 29% (1991: 28%) of the balance sheet total; 97% of these assets is covered by shareholders' equity. The increase in inventories to DM26.3 billion relates predominantly to the systems business. At 76% (1991: 67%), a considerably higher percentage of inventories was financed by advances received from customers (DM20.0 billion). As a result, net inventories after deduction of advances declined by DM2.0 billion. Reflecting the expanded volume of business, receivables increased to DM24.9 billion. Investments in marketable securities and other liquid assets rose to DM19.7 billion.

Liquid assets are invested primarily in fixed-income securities and notes of top-grade issuers; most of them (over 60%) are denominated in German marks. Of the total portfolio, DM1.9 billion will mature during fiscal 1993 and DM1.8 billion in the following year. Eleven percent of the investments in marketable securities consists of stock certificates.

Capital stock and additional paid-in capital rose by DM2.5 billion due to the exercise of options rights under the warrants attached to the 1986/2001 zero coupon bonds, the issuance of new shares of stock as a result of the settlement offered to former shareholders of SNI, and the inclusion of the value of the warrants attached to the 1992/2002 bond issue. Goodwill in the amount of DM1.9 billion, which resulted from the initial consolidation of equity interests in other companies, was offset against retained earnings.

Balance sheet structure (in billions of DM)

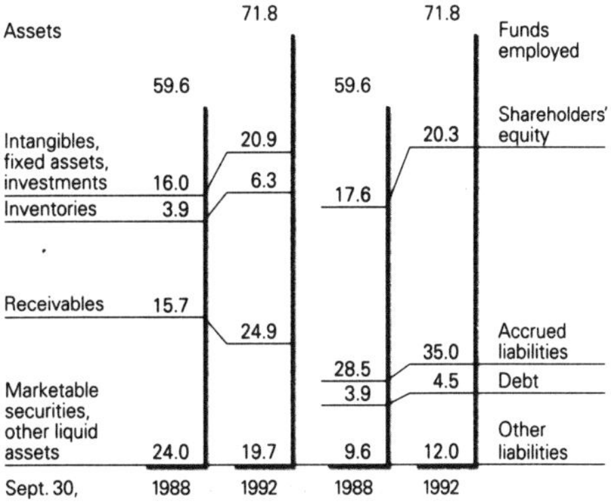

Shareholders' equity was increased by DM1.7 billion to a total of DM20.3 billion and now finances 28% (1991: 27%) of consolidated assets.

As in fiscal 1991, accrued liabilities, at DM35.0 billion, again accounted for 49% of total shareholders' equity and liabilities.

Debt remained at the prior year's level of DM4.5 billion, because the cash provided by the 8% U.S. dollar bond issue was used to replace some of the higher-interest borrowings. Just under one-half of total debt, most of which is incurred outside Germany as a hedge against foreign exchange risks, is denominated in U.S. dollars. Two-thirds of total debt are due after one year. At September 30, 1992, debt represented only 22% (1991: 25%) of shareholders' equity.

This low debt level and the high proportion of liquid assets demonstrate the financial strength of the Company. In spite of the significant growth in consolidated assets in recent years, our balance sheet has a solid structure, by both German and international standards.

Share performance

Changes in Siemens dividend
in DM

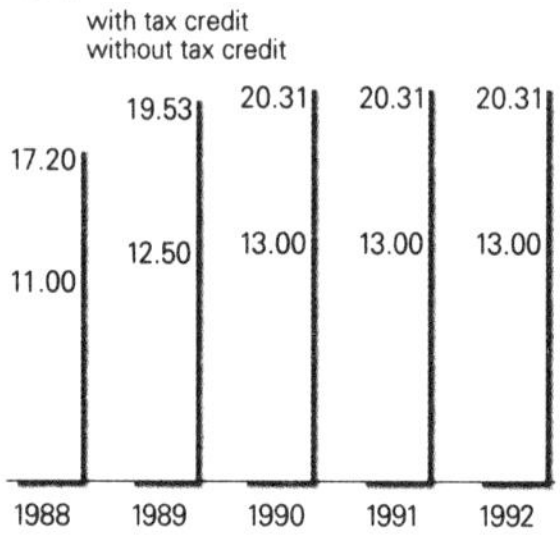

Per-share data
in DM

	1991	1992
Net income without minority interests	35.00	32.10
Dividend	13.00	13.00
Dividend with tax credit	20.31	20.31
Cash flow	130.00	120.10
Shareholders' equity (Sept. 30)	328.10	341.50
Market price (Sept. 30)	637.10	570.70
Shares issued (Sept. 30, in millions)	52.7	55.9

Share price trend
Around the turn of the year, positive growth expectations for the western economies sparked a significant advance of the German equity market. During the spring of 1992, the Siemens share price rallied to a high of DM703.90 for the year on May 25, 1992.

In early June, though, economic expectations, some of them overly enthusiastic, were reappraised. This reevaluation was also prompted by the weakening U.S. dollar, which has adverse effects on exports for German industry. Consequently, analysts revised their corporate earnings expectations downward. The Siemens share price was also affected by this general trend. At the close of fiscal 1992, it was quoted at DM570.70, down from DM637.10 a year earlier.

Earnings/dividend
For the fifth year in a row, Siemens posted increased earnings. Net income for the year was DM1.955 billion, up from DM1.792 billion in fiscal 1991. At the Annual Shareholders' Meeting, the Supervisory and Managing Boards of Siemens AG will again recommend a dividend of DM13.00 per share. Due to the higher number of shares outstanding, the total dividend payout for 1992 will increase to DM727 million, compared with DM686 million for 1991.

Warrants expired
The warrants attached to the U.S. dollar zero coupon bonds issued in 1986 entitled the holders of these warrants to purchase shares of Siemens common stock at a price of DM620 until June 19, 1992. A total of 99.79% of these warrants were exercised, increasing the number of shares of Siemens common stock by 2,993,583. These shares are entitled to the full dividend for the 1992 fiscal year.

In addition to the original warrant premium of DM601 million, which was collected at the time of issue in 1986, exercise of the option rights during fiscal 1992 increased shareholders' equity by an additional DM1.86 billion.

New debt with equity warrants
On June 2, 1992, Siemens Capital Corporation, a U.S.-based subsidiary, issued U.S.$1 billion in bonds with warrants attached. These

Stock market trend (fiscal 1988–1992)
(Index of adjusted quarterly closing prices: year-end 1958=100)

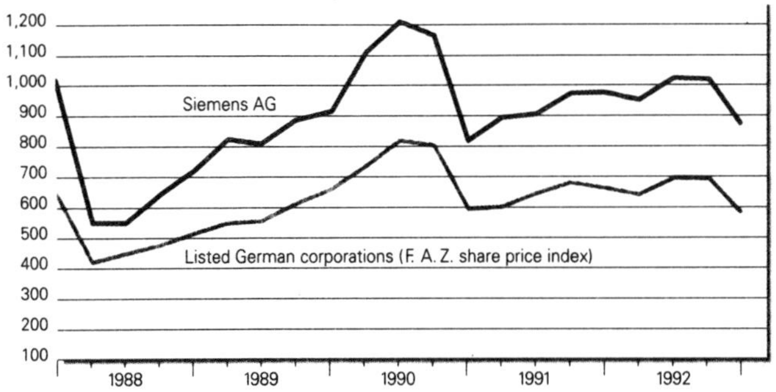

Fiscal 1992 highs and lows of the Siemens share (in DM)

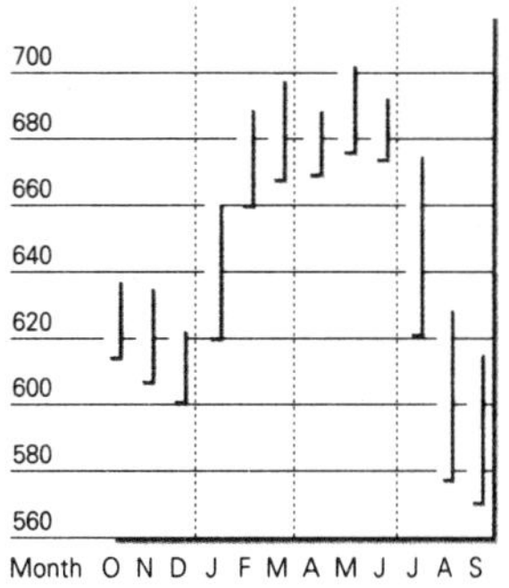

warrants entitle the holders to purchase Siemens common stock at a price of DM693 at any time between August 4, 1992, and June 2, 1998. This exercise period will be extended for a maximum of two years, should the price of Siemens common stock be lower than the exercise price within ten working days prior to May 2, 1998, or May 2, 1999.

The total of U.S.$1.32 billion raised by this issue was employed for partial repayment of higher-cost borrowings and for financing our growing business in the U.S. on a hedged basis.

SNI integration
A voluntary tender offer made in the autumn of 1991, as well as the acquisition of the remaining shares of SNI still in the hands of its former majority shareholder, enabled Siemens AG to increase its holdings in SNI from approximately 78% to 95.2%. In March 1992, the annual shareholders' meetings of both companies passed resolutions integrating SNI into Siemens AG pursuant to §320 et.seq. of the German Stock Corporation Act. The integration became effective on April 15, 1992 upon being recorded in the commercial register. Under the applicable provisions of the German Stock Corporation Act, the remaining shares of SNI devolved on Siemens AG. As indemnification, the SNI shareholders have been offered one common share of Siemens AG in exchange for six shares of SNI stock; holdings of less than six shares will receive cash in the amount of DM156.50 per share of SNI. By September 30, 1992, 188,410 new Siemens shares entitled to the fiscal 1992 dividend were issued for this purpose.

Employee stock
Under our annual employee stock offering, approximately 69% of all eligible employees purchased around 553,000 shares of common stock of Siemens AG in the spring of 1992. Since the purchase price was significantly higher this time than in the prior year, the acceptance rate was slightly lower than the long-standing average of roughly 70%. The shares required for this offering were purchased on the open market.

Quarterly figures

(in billions of DM)	10/1/91 – 12/31/91	1/1/92 – 3/31/92	4/1/92 – 6/30/92	7/1/92 – 9/30/92
New orders	20.1	22.5	20.5	22.3
Sales	16.2	19.6	19.2	23.5
Capital spending	2.2	2.5	1.5	2.4
Net income after taxes	0.4	0.5	0.5	0.6

Five-year summary

Assets/funds employed Sept. 30,	1988	1989	1990	1991	1992
Siemens worldwide					
Property, plant and equipment	13,623	14,379	14,870	16,729	18,237
Investments	2,341	2,646	3,698	2,660	2,657
Intangible assets, fixed assets and investments	15,964	17,025	18,568	19,389	20,894
as a percent of balance sheet total	27%	26%	29%	28%	29%
Inventories	3,917	6,888	7,314	8,239	6,282
Receivables and miscellaneous assets	15,768	19,244	19,221	23,274	24,947
Securities and other liquid assets	23,968	21,239	19,347	18,566	19,677
Total assets	59,617	64,396	64,450	69,468	71,800
Capital stock and additional paid-in capital	7,263	7,690	8,532	8,883	11,388
Retained earnings and minority interests	10,371	10,864	9,025	9,766	8,953
Shareholders' equity	17,634	18,554	17,557	18,649	20,341
as a percent of balance sheet total	30%	29%	27%	27%	28%
Accruals for pension plans	10,665	11,990	12,735	13,957	14,761
Other accrued liabilities	17,854	18,820	19,101	20,137	20,220
Total accrued liabilities	28,519	30,810	31,836	34,094	34,981
as a percent of balance sheet total	48%	48%	49%	49%	49%
Debt	3,904	4,227	4,058	4,575	4,531
as a percent of shareholders' equity	22%	23%	23%	25%	22%
Other liabilities	9,560	10,805	10,999	12,150	11,947
Total funds employed	59,617	64,396	64,450	69,468	71,800

Earnings/dividend	1988	1989	1990	1991	1992
Siemens worldwide					
Income before taxes	2,475	2,788	2,823	3,419	3,197
Income taxes	1,084	1,211	1,155	1,627	1,242
Net income	1,391	1,577	1,668	1,792	1,955
as a percent of sales	2.3%	2.6%	2.6%	2.5%	2.5%
as a percent of shareholders' equity	8.2%	8.7%	9.2%	9.9%	10.0%
Total dividend of Siemens AG	538	622	678	686	727
Dividend per share (in DM)	11	12.50	13	13	13

Employees* (in thousands) Sept. 30,	1988	1989	1990	1991	1992
German operations	223	227	230	243	253
International operations	130	138	143	159	160
Siemens	353	365	373	402	413
Personnel costs	1988	1989	1990	1991	1992
Siemens	23,847	25,904	26,988	31,817	33,873

Research and development	1988	1989	1990	1991	1992
Siemens	6,480	6,875	6,980	7,892	8,385
as a percent of sales	10.9%	11.2%	11.0%	10.8%	10.7%

*Without temporary student workers and trainees

Amounts in millions of DM

New orders	1988	1989	1990	1991	1992
German business	24,294	27,531	28,432	36,746	40,174
International business	30,447	35,338	39,312	45,420	45,235
Siemens	54,741	62,869	67,744	82,166	85,409
Change over prior year	+9%	+15%	+8%	+21%	+4%

Sales	1988	1989	1990	1991	1992
German business	30,755	28,449	28,352	33,263	36,475
International business	28,619	32,679	34,833	39,745	42,034
Siemens	59,374	61,128	63,185	73,008	78,509
Change over prior year	+15%	+3%	+3%	+16%	+8%

Capital spending	1988	1989	1990	1991	1992
in Germany	2,846	2,697	3,882	3,332	5,861
International	2,364	5,175	3,184	2,263	2,713
Siemens	5,210	7,872	7,066	5,595	8,574
Acquisition of investments	1,121	3,746	2,675	592	3,014
Capital expenditures	4,089	4,126	4,391	5,003	5,560
Depreciation of property, plant and equipment	3,715	4,057	3,975	4,400	4,613
as a percent of capital expenditures	91%	98%	91%	88%	83%

Cash flow	1988	1989	1990	1991	1992
Siemens	6,812	7,072	6,765	6,797	6,879
as a percent of sales	11.5%	11.6%	10.7%	9.3%	8.8%

Siemens AG
Balance sheet
and statement of income
in billions of DM (condensed version)

for the fiscal years ended September 30,	1991	1992
Net sales	39.3	43.3
Total operating performance	40.9	44.8
Cost of materials	(19.1)	(21.6)
Personnel costs	(16.5)	(17.4)
Other expenses/income	(3.3)	(3.7)
Income before income taxes	2.0	2.1
Income taxes	(0.7)	(0.9)
Net income	1.3	1.2

as of September 30,	1991	1992
Property, plant and equipment	5.8	6.3
Investments	15.8	18.2
Fixed assets and investments	21.6	24.5
Inventories	1.8	1.8
Receivables	17.1	20.1
Marketable securities, other liquid assets	9.7	9.0
Total assets	50.2	55.4
Shareholders' equity	16.5	19.6
Accrued liabilities and special reserves	25.7	26.5
Debt	0.5	0.6
Other liabilities	7.5	8.7
Total shareholders' equity and liabilities	50.2	55.4

Appendix B
Comparison with IAS

The intention here is to draw a brief comparison between German accounting regulations and the accounting principles embodied in the standards of the International Accounting Standards Committee. The explanation of the German position is necessarily abridged, and the reader should refer to the appropriate chapter earlier in the book for a detailed review. The IAS rules are assumed to be known and are not explained in detail. In general the comparison is based on the regulations for corporations. The approach adopted is to follow the numerical sequence of the thirty-one International Accounting Standards (IAS) published in *IAS 1991/1992* (as of 1 January 1991).

IAS 1 *Disclosure of accounting policies*

In Germany, corporations are required to state in both the notes on the individual accounts and in the notes on the group accounts the accounting policies followed in the preparation of the financial statements. Among other things the following must be disclosed (see Chapter 7, section 9):

1 The accounting and valuation methods applied to the items in the balance sheet and the profit and loss account.
2 The bases for translation into Deutschmarks where the financial statements contain headings which include amounts in foreign currency or which originated in foreign currency.
3 Justified deviations from these accounting and valuation methods; their effect on net worth, the financial position and the results must be disclosed separately.

Generally speaking, German rules are in line with IAS 1.

IAS 2 *Valuation and presentation of inventories in the context of the historical cost system*

Inventories are valued at the lower of cost or market value (see Chapter 5, section 5.1.3). It should be noted that in Germany (in contrast to IAS 2) it is possible to effect further write-downs so long as they are based on sound business judgement and necessary in order to avoid a valuation change in the near future as a result of value fluctuations.

For the valuation of homogeneous items of stock, LIFO, FIFO and other methods of determining the sequence of utilization are explicitly permitted by commercial law so long as they are consistent with GoB. However, since for tax purposes only the average cost method and LIFO are permitted (but only since 1990 and only under certain conditions) in the annual accounts the average cost method is frequently applied.

IAS 4 *Depreciation*

There are no significant differences between the regulations of this standard and practice in Germany.

IAS 5 *Information to be disclosed in financial statements*

German financial statements would for the most part meet IAS 5 requirements. The main exceptions are:

1 German enterprises are not obliged to disclose the current market value of marketable securities.
2 Under IAS 5 only the accumulated depreciation of property, plant and equipment has to be disclosed. By contrast, in Germany, full information on all classes of fixed assets must be disclosed. The schedule of fixed assets reports the original acquisition cost or production cost and the accumulated depreciation since acquisition, together with additions, disposals, transfers and write-ups of the reporting period, to give the carried forward book value.
3 In Germany more information is given on the due dates of receivables and payables than is required under IAS 5. Receivables are classified into two groups (time to maturity under one year; one year or over) and payables in three groups (time to maturity under one year; one to five years; over five years). (See Chapter 7, section 9.)

IAS 7 *Statement of changes in the financial position*

No such statement is required either of individual or of group accounts, even if in practice most of the large corporations provide some sort of funds flow or cash flow analysis.

IAS 8 *Unusual and prior-period items and changes in accounting policies*

In contrast to IAS 8, in Germany, prior-period items and the amount of the adjustments, if any, resulting from changes in accounting policies *must* affect the profit of the year. Prior-period items are not disclosed separately, unless they are at the same time extraordinary. (See Chapter 7, section 3.2.4.)

In order to calculate the DVFA/SG profit (see Chapter 9) the disclosed net profit (or loss) for the year is adjusted by income and expense items which are in a broader sense extraordinary, or exceptional, or which are the result of the application of different accounting options.

IAS 9 *Accounting for research and development activities*

In Germany research and development costs which are not incurred under a contract may not be capitalized separately. (See Chapter 7, section 4.1.2.) Since the basic research and the general development of the product clearly precede production, the associated costs may not be capitalized as part of production costs. (See Chapter 7, section 5.2.)

IAS 10 *Contingencies and events occurring after the balance sheet date*

German enterprises have to provide for contingent losses, but must not recognize any contingent gains. (See Chapter 7, sections 4.2.2 and 5.1.)

A contingent liability that has not been accrued (e.g. contingent liabilities relating to guarantees, security granted for third-party liabilities) must be disclosed on the face of the balance sheet or in the notes. In contrast to IAS 10, profit is charged with any impending losses arising from such commitments.

The regulations of IAS 10 concerning events occurring after the balance sheet date do coincide closely with the German revealed value principle. (See Chapter 7, section 5.4.2.)

IAS 11 *Accounting for construction contracts*

In contrast to IAS 11, only the completed contract method is allowed in Germany. (See Chapter 7, section 5.7.3.) The realization principle requires a sales event and a completed transfer to the customer of the object to be produced and delivered. However, if impending losses become apparent during production, then a provision for impending losses on uncompleted contracts must be set up following the imparity principle.

IAS 12 *Accounting for taxes on income*

The IAS 12 rules and the German rules are similar only in the case of the consolidated accounts (Chapter 8, section 11). In the accounts of the individual enterprise, given that reporting tax as a prepayment is optional and given that the formulation of HGB § 274 is vague, the full reporting of deferred taxation and its complete omission are both equally possible. (See Chapter 7, section 7.)

IAS 13 *Presentation of current assets and current liabilities*

There are no significant differences between this standard and the corresponding regulations in the HGB.

IAS 14 *Reporting financial information by segment*

In Germany, segment information is required only for sales and only to the extent that the areas of activity and geographically defined markets differ significantly from each other, taking into account the sales organization for the goods and services typical of the enterprise's ordinary business. In contrast to IAS 14 no further details are required. The disclosures need not be made in so far as the analysis is likely significantly to harm the corporation or an enterprise in which the corporation holds at least a fifth of the shares. (See Chapter 7, section 9.) These regulations apply both as regards individual accounts and as regards group accounts.

IAS 15 *Information reflecting the effects of changing prices*

There is no such requirement in Germany. The only exception is the obligation to disclose in the notes undervaluations resulting from the application of simplified valuation methods such as LIFO. (See Chapter 7, section 8.)

IAS 16 *Accounting for property, plant and equipment*

The general terms of IAS 16 concerning assets carried at historical cost are in conformity with German GoB. In both individual accounts and group accounts, revaluing upwards is forbidden (with the exception of write-ups that reverse previous write-downs which are no longer justified; under no circumstances should the asset's book value exceed the original historical cost).

IAS 17 *Accounting for leases*

In Germany the accounting treatment of a finance lease usually follows its treatment for income tax purposes. The criteria in determining whether the asset should be shown in the lessor's or the lessee's balance sheet are not dissimilar to those of IAS 17. (See Chapter 7, section 4.1.3.) However, the overall effect of the criteria is that, in Germany, as a rule, leased assets are shown in the lessor's balance sheet. But the lessee is obliged to furnish, in the notes on the accounts, information on commitments under leasing contracts.

For operating leases there are no material differences between the accounting treatment in Germany and the IAS 17: the rental payments are expensed by the lessee and recorded as income by the lessor in the periods to which they relate.

IAS 18 *Revenue recognition*

The interpretation of the realization principle is broadly in line with IAS 18. Differences are:

1. Where goods are sold on extended credit there is no partial recognition of either the sale or the implicit interest. It is recognized in full at the realization date, depending upon when the ownership risk passes. (See Chapter 7, section 5.1.4.)
2. The selling price of a product is not generally broken down in order to ascribe different parts of the price to different elements of the contract such as credit, warranty, etc.

IAS 19 *Accounting for retirement benefits in the financial statements of employers*

In contrast to IAS 19, in Germany there is a difference in accounting for a direct commitment by the enterprise to grant a benefit (pension) and indirect arrangements (the funding of pension obligations). For commitments to direct support given after 31 December 1986 a provision for pensions must be set up. They are calculated on an actuarial basis. For indirect arrangements, through a pension fund, a provident fund or an insurance company, there is usually no necessity to set up a provision. The contributions that the enterprise makes to the fund or company are treated as expenses in the financial statements. But see also Chapter 7, section 4.2.2.1.

IAS 20 *Accounting for government grants and disclosure of government assistance*

In Germany accounting for grants and subsidies is a disputed matter. The main technical committee of the IdW recommends with respect to non-repayable grants that investment subsidies and allowances should be credited to profit as revenue over the economic life of the asset in respect of which they were granted. Expenditure subsidies and allowances should be accounted for in the same way as the expenditure which the grant serves to cover. (See Chapter 7, section 5.7.2.) This approach is in line with IAS 20. However, the alternative approach is also encountered in practice, namely the reporting of the gross purchase price and the immediate crediting of the whole grant to income.

IAS 21 *Accounting for the effects of changes in foreign exchange rates*

In Germany, in contrast to IAS 21, there are no regulations for the translation of the statements of subsidiaries for inclusion in group accounts, so that in principle all methods are applicable. The IdW, however, recommends that either the closing rate or the temporal method should be used. The working group on external enterprise accounting of the Schmalenbach-Gesellschaft also allows this option but expresses a clear preference for the temporal method. (See Chapter 8, section 6.)

As regards foreign currency transactions, the main differences are that (see Chapter 7, section 5.7.1):

1 The direct transfer of translation differences to reserves is unknown in Germany.
2 Positive translation differences which remain after netting are not taken into account.
3 Positive translation differences that offset negative differences are taken into account only under certain circumstances.

IAS 22 *Accounting for business combinations*

1 With the purchase method in IAS 22 there is no guarantee that the value of assets is limited to the resources expended to acquire them, i.e. the revaluation of the subsidiary's assets is not limited to the acquisition cost to the parent undertaking of the subsidiary. Thus it is possible that a figure for positive goodwill before the revaluation of the subsidiary's assets may be converted into negative goodwill after revaluation (which is not consistent with HGB).
2 Under IAS 22, paragraph 19, the goodwill arising on the acquisition of a subsidiary can either be amortized to income on a systematic basis over its useful life or set off immediately against equity. Depreciation within the four years following the year of acquisition is not prescribed. If it relates to negative goodwill, a negative consolidation difference can be treated as potential revenue (see paragraph 25) which is to be recognized in the periods in which the expected lower profits occur. (This is consistent with the HGB rules for the release of negative goodwill to the profit and loss account.) However, if the negative goodwill arises from a 'lucky buy' it should be allocated to the non-monetary assets in proportion to their fair values. (See IAS 22, paragraph 25.) This is not permitted in the HGB.
3 Under IAS 22, paragraphs 26–8, the minority interest can be recorded either on the basis of the pre-acquisition values of the subsidiary's net assets (this corresponds to the HGB's book value method) or on the basis of the post-acquisition restated fair values (this corresponds to the HGB's revaluation method, when there is no imputation problem). By contrast to the HGB rule, under IAS 27, paragraph 33, the minority interest should not be presented as part of the equity in the balance sheet.

(For details see Chapter 8, section 7.)

IAS 23 *Capitalization of borrowing costs*

German regulation is very similar to IAS 23 – borrowing costs incurred during the production of an asset may be capitalized in the carrying value of the asset, but this is optional and in fact rarely done by German corporations. (See Chapter 7, section 5.2.)

IAS 24 *Related-party disclosures*

There is no general prescription as such which calls for disclosure of related-party transactions in general. However, disclosures are made in specific areas:

1 Corporations have an obligation to provide information on the existence of relationships between enterprises in the notes on the financial statements and the obligation to record enterprise contracts in the commercial register. (See Chapter 2, section 3.)
2 Subsidiary AGs must prepare a dependence report that deals with the measures the AG has taken at the instigation or in the interests of the controlling enterprise or of an enterprise that is closely related (see Chapter 2, section 3.)
3 For certain items, e.g. receivables and payables, there must be an indication in the balance sheet and in the profit and loss account of the extent to which they relate to subsidiaries or participating interests.

IAS 25 *Accounting for investments*

Investments classified as current assets are valued at the lower of cost or market (quoted) value. In contrast to IAS 25 there is also an optional deduction for items for which, in the near future (after the balance sheet date) a fall in value is anticipated. Each asset must be valued individually and not on a portfolio basis, and no disclosure of market values is required. (See Chapter 7, section 5.4.2.)

Fixed assets are carried at the lower of cost or 'attributable value' and must always be considered individually. For participations the attributable value is usually calculated as the net present value of the future income stream. There is an obligation to write down to a lower 'attributable' value only when the fall in value is permanent. If it is not expected to be permanent, then exceptional depreciation is optional. (See Chapter 7, section 5.4.1.)

Investments must not be revalued upwards; the acquisition cost forms the upper limit even when the value at the balance sheet date is manifestly higher and can be objectively and economically established with reference to the market price. (See Chapter 7, section 5.1.2.)

IAS 26 *Accounting and reporting by retirement benefit plans*

See comments on IAS 19.

IAS 27 *Consolidated financial statements and accounting for investments in subsidiaries*

1 Differences in the obligation to prepare group accounts (see Chapter 8, section 3):

(a) In IAS 27, paragraph 10, the group is defined in terms of the control concept. Control is assumed to exist when the parent undertaking can exercise more than 50 per cent of the votes, either directly or indirectly. If the parent undertaking can prove that, notwithstanding the majority of votes, no control is in fact exercised, then there is no need to prepare consolidated accounts. In Germany, by contrast, a majority of votes creates an obligation to prepare consolidated accounts, subject to the exclusion rules of the HGB §§ 295–6.

(b) For the IASC, control may be established even when there is no majority of votes if certain other rights or agreements exist, as set out in IAS 27, paragraph 10 (a)–(d). In Germany, too, the existence of these rights creates an obligation to prepare consolidated accounts, whether or not there is a majority of votes. Furthermore there is an obligation to prepare consolidated accounts, independently of the existence of certain legal relationships, if the parent undertaking in fact exercises unified management (the economic concept of group).

2 Differences in the scope of consolidation (see Chapter 8, section 4). In IAS 27 there are fewer exceptions to the basic obligation to include all domestic and foreign subsidiaries, as compared with the HGB. According to IAS 27 even subsidiaries with a substantially different activity are to be included. In the case of shares held for sale or of considerable limitations on the rights over the assets or management, the subsidiaries *should* be excluded, according to IAS 27. (In the HGB it is an option.) The optional exclusion on grounds of disproportionate expense or delay in obtaining information, as well as when the subsidiary is immaterial, that are part of the HGB's provisions, are not explicitly referred to in IAS 27 but would seem also to agree with IASC rules because of the materiality principle which applies generally to all IAS statements.

3 Differences in the standardization of the accounts of the individual enterprises (see Chapter 8, section 5):

(a) According to both IAS 27, paragraph 32, and the HGB, uniform accounting policies are to be used in the consolidated accounts. In Germany, in contrast to the IAS, the subsidiaries' accounts must be adapted to the accounting principles applicable to the parent undertaking. IAS 27 requires only 'uniform accounting policies'.

(b) According to IAS 27 the proportion of the non-uniform items should be disclosed; this information is not required by the HGB.

4 Differences in the elimination of intra-group profits (see Chapter 8, section 9). In Germany, elimination of intra-group profits need not be effected if:

(a) The deliveries or services are provided at normal market rates and the calculation of the intra-group profit or loss would involve unreasonably high costs, or

(b) It is not material for the presentation of a true and fair view of the net worth, financial position and results of the group.

Neither exemption is found in IAS 27. However, since the materiality principle applies to all IAS standards, there should be no significant difference between paragraph 30 of IAS 27 and the HGB.

IAS 28 *Accounting for investments in associates*

In Germany the equity method is used in group accounts for the investments of associates, joint ventures that are not proportionately consolidated and those subsidiary enterprises that are not fully consolidated because of compulsory exclusion and optional exclusion. In the HGB there is no provision that the equity method should not be applied when there are long-term restrictions on the transfer of funds to the investors. (See Chapter 8, section 4.3.)

Furthermore there are the following essential differences between IAS 28 and the HGB:

1 According to IAS 28 the equity value can be accounted for only according to the book value method; in Germany enterprises have a choice between the book value method and the capital share method. (For details see Chapter 8, section 12.)
2 In contrast to the HGB there is no obligation to eliminate inter-company profits, even when the necessary information is known or available. (See Chapter 8, section 12.)

The equity method is prohibited in the individual accounts; there, the acquisition cost forms the upper limit.

IAS 29 *Financial reporting in hyperinflationary economies*

Germany would not be considered a hyperinflationary economy within the terms of this standard. There are no accounting regulations dealing with such conditions.

IAS 30 *Disclosures in the financial statements of banks and similar financial institutions*

There are special legal standards for banks and insurance companies which are not explicitly dealt with in this book. The relevant laws and rules will be found in Figure 6.2(c).

IAS 31 *Financial reporting of interests in joint ventures*

Germany has special legal forms (e.g. the civil law partnership) which can be used to encapsulate different forms of joint venture. There are no special treatments in the financial statements.

Where there is a jointly controlled entity, proportional consolidation can be applied. But it is also possible to consolidate participation in joint ventures according to the equity method. (See Chapter 8, section 4.)

Appendix C
EC Directives and German legislation

The European Fourth Company Law Directive (78/660/EEC) and the Seventh Directive (83/349/EEC) were adopted in Germany through the *Bilanzrichtliniengesetz* (BiRiLiG) of 19 December 1985.

The regulations of the directives were mainly incorporated into the *Handelsgesetzbuch* (HGB). A number of individual laws were also affected, however. The influence of the Fourth and Seventh Directives can be found in the *Aktiengesetz* (AktG), the *Gesetz betreffend die Gesellschaften mit beschränkter Haftung* (GmbHG), the *Publizitätsgesetz* (PublG), the *Wirtschaftsprüferordnung* (WPO), the *Gesetz über das Kreditwesen* (KWG), the *Versicherungsaufsichtsgesetz* (VAG), the *Gesetz über die Auflösung und Löschung von Gesellschaften und Genossenschaften* (LöschG) and other laws, which were affected to a lesser extent. The *Einführungsgesetz zum HGB* (EGHGB) consists mainly of the transitional provisions to the *Bilanzrichtliniengesetz* (BiRiLiG).

The purpose of the following tables is to review the text of the Fourth and the Seventh Directives article by article alongside the respective German statutes. The descriptions are confined to the adaptations in the HGB, which form the largest group of implementations. The third column indicates the contents of the relevant article of the directive. In the case of national options the adaptation chosen in Germany is briefly described as well. For the exact adaptation of certain articles in the German HGB, please refer to the original text or one of the commentaries listed in the bibliography.

THE FOURTH DIRECTIVE

Fourth Directive	*HGB (unless otherwise stated)*	*Content*
Art. 1	Second section of the third book-definition in the heading	Definition of companies which come within the purview of the adopted regulations.
Art. 2 (1)	§§ 242, 264 (1) sentence 1	Components of the financial statement (balance sheet, profit and loss account, notes).
Art. 2 (2)	§ 243 (2)	The financial statements must be clear and well set out.

Fourth Directive	*HGB (unless otherwise stated)*	*Content*
Art. 2 (3)	§ 264 (2) sentence 1	True and fair view.
Art. 2 (4)	§ 264 (2) sentence 2	Additional information required if the true and fair view cannot be achieved.
Art. 2 (5) national option	Not adopted expressly	Deviation from national accounting principles to achieve the true and fair view.
Art. 3	§ 265 (1)	Deviations from the format concerning the balance sheet and the profit and loss account/principle of continuity.
Art. 4 (1) sentence 1	§ 266 (1), § 275 (1)	Format of the balance sheet and the profit and loss account.
Art. 4 (1) sentences 2–3 national option	§ 265 (5)	Further subdivision of items of the balance sheet and the profit and loss account or addition of new items – adopted.
Art. 4 (2)	§ 265 (6)	Deviations from the prescribed headings in the balance sheet and the profit and loss account.
Art. 4 (3) national option	§ 265 (7)	Integration of items for the purpose of clarity or in the event of materiality – adopted.
Art. 4 (4) national option	§ 265 (2)	In case of non-comparability of preceding year figures, these figures may either be adapted or reported upon in the balance sheet notes; in Germany, adaptation of the preceding year figures is not admitted, but further comments in the notes are required in the event of non-comparability.
Art. 4 (5)	§ 265 (8)	Items for which no amount is shown can be dropped.
Art. 5 national option	Not adopted	Special format for the accounts of investment companies.
Art. 6 national option	§ 268 (1)	Adaptation of the balance sheet and profit and loss account formats to show the appropriation of the year's result; in Germany the balance sheet may be prepared before appropriation of the annual profit or after partial or full appropriation of profit.
Art. 7	§ 246 (2)	Prohibition of offsetting.
Arts 8, 9, 10 national option	§ 266	National option for the choice of the balance sheet format; Germany has authorized only the horizontal presentation of the balance sheet (art. 9).
Art. 9 (assets A and liabilities A) national option	§ 266	Presentation of the share capital – adopted.
Art. 9 (assets B) national option	§ 269	Formation expenses to be included under intangible assets; in Germany this item to be disclosed in the balance sheet above fixed assets under the heading 'Start-up and business expansion expenses'.
Art. 9 (assets C.I.2 (b)) national option	§ 266	Concessions, patents, licences and trade marks: Germany does not permit the inclusion of such items in the balance sheet if they have been produced by the enterprise itself.
Art. 9 (assets C.I.1) national option	Not adopted	Cost of research and development: European states had to determine the capitalization, depreciation and restriction on profit distribution concerning the expenses for basic and applied research and development. In Germany none of the options is permitted. The expenses are charged immediately to the profit and loss account when incurred.

Fourth Directive	*HGB (unless otherwise stated)*	*Content*
Art. 11 national option	§ 266 (1) sentence 3, § 267 (1), § 268 (4) sentence 1, § 268 (5) sentence 1	Definition of size classes – adopted.
Art. 12	§ 267 (1) and (4) sentence 1	The consequences of the prescribed criteria apply only if they are exceeded or fallen short of in two successive financial years.
Art. 12 (2)	§ 267 (1) Nos. 1 and 2	Translation of the size criteria in national currencies.
Art. 12 (3)	§ 267 (1) No. 1	Definition of the balance sheet total.
Art. 13	§ 265 (3) sentence 1	Asset or liability included under several headings.
Art. 13 (2)	§ 265 (3) sentence 2	Own shares held may be shown only under the special heading provided for the purpose.
Art. 14	§ 251, § 268 (7)	Contingent liabilities which do not appear on the balance sheet: in Germany, contingent liabilities have to be shown separately as a below-the-line item in the balance sheet or in the notes.
Art. 15 (1)	§ 247 (2)	Assignment of items to fixed assets or current assets according to the purpose which the item is to serve.
Art. 15 (2)	§ 247 (2)	Fixed assets to include only those items that are required for long-term use.
Art. 15 (3) (a)	§ 268 (2)	Fixed asset movement schedule.
Art. 15 (3) (b)	EGHGB Art. 24 (6) sentences 1 and 3	Simplifications in the schedule when the adopted regulations are applied for the first time.
Art. 15 (3) (c)	Not adopted	Fixed asset movement schedule in the event of revaluation.
Art. 15 (4)	§ 268 (2), EGHGB art. 24 (6)	Application of art. 15 to 'start-up and business expansion expenses' also.
Art. 16	§ 266 (2) A II 1	Definition of land, land rights and buildings according to national law.
Art. 17 national option	§ 271 (1) sentences 1 and 2	Presumption of participating interests: in Germany it is assumed that holdings in an enterprise whose nominal value exceeds in total 20% of the nominal capital are participating interests.
Art. 18 sentence 1	§ 250 (1)	Pre-paid expenses and deferred income.
Art. 18 sentence 2 national option	§ 268 (4) sentence 2	Option to show items in the receivables account; in Germany this must be explained in the notes.
Art. 19	§ 253 (2) and (3)	Definition of value adjustments.
Art. 20	§ 249 (1)	Provisions.
Art. 20 (2) national option	§ 249 (2)	Provisions of precisely determined expenses which are probable or certain at the balance sheet date – adopted.
Art. 20 (3)	§ 249 (3) sentence 1	Provisions may not be set up for offsetting asset diminution, i.e. for value adjustment purposes.
Art. 21 sentence 1	§ 250 (2)	Pre-paid expenses and deferred income.
Art. 21 sentence 2 national option	§ 268 (5) sentence 3	Set-up of pre-paid expenses in the liability accounts; in Germany this option is adopted under provision of further explanations in the notes.

Fourth Directive	*HGB (unless otherwise stated)*	*Content*
Art. 22 national option	§ 275 (1)–(3)	Presentation of the profit and loss account; national option between the classifications of arts. 23–6 of the Fourth Directive: in Germany arts 23 and 25 are adopted (see below).
Art. 23	§ 275 (2)	Classification adopted in German law (provision of company option between the classification of arts 23 and 25).
Art. 24	Not adopted	See art. 22.
Art. 25	§ 275 (3)	See art. 23.
Art. 26	Not adopted	See art. 22.
Art. 27	§ 267 (1) and (2), § 276	Simplifications of the profit and loss account, dependent upon size.
Art. 28	§ 277 (1)	Definition of sales.
Art. 29	§ 277 (4)	Definition of extraordinary revenues and extraordinary expenses.
Art. 30 sentences 1–2 national option	§ 275 (2) No. 19 and (3) No. 18	Option of one-line entry for taxation in the profit and loss account – adopted.
Art. 30 sentence 3	§ 285 No. 6	In the event of adoption of the option of sentences 1–2, the extent to which taxes on income and profits affect the results from ordinary activities and the extraordinary results is to be shown in the notes.
Art. 31 (1) (a)	§ 252 (1) No. 2	General valuation principles: Going concern.
Art. 31 (1) (b)	§ 252 (1) No. 6	Valuation methods once applied should be retained (consistency principle).
Art. 31 (1) (c)	§ 252 (1) No. 4	Prudence principle.
Art. 31 (1) (c) (aa)	§ 252 (1) No. 4	Realization principle.
Art. 31 (1) (c) (bb)	§ 252 (1) No. 4	Anticipation of future risks.
Art. 31 (1) (c) (cc)	Not adopted expressly	Diminution in value.
Art. 31 (1) (d)	§ 252 (1) No. 5	Matching/accrual principle.
Art. 31 (1) (e)	§ 252 (1) No. 3	Valuation on an item-by-item basis.
Art. 31 (1) (f)	§ 252 (1) No. 1	Formal consistency.
Art. 31 (2)	§ 284 (2) No. 3, § 252 (2)	Deviations from the principles must be explained in the notes.
Art. 33 national option	Not adopted	Revaluation of assets and set-up of revaluation accrual.
Art. 34	§ 269	Start-up and business expansion expenses: depreciation and non-distributable reserve.
Art. 35 (1) (a)	§ 253 (1) sentence 1	Valuation at acquisition cost or production cost.
Art. 35 (1) (b)	§ 253 (2) sentences 1 and 2	Systematic depreciation.
Art. 35 (1) (c) (aa)	§ 253 (2) sentence 3, § 279 (1) sentence 2	Value adjustments to financial fixed assets.
Art. 35 (1) (c) (bb)	§ 253 (2) sentence 3, § 279 (1) sentence 2	Value adjustments to fixed assets for permanent impairment of value.

Fourth Directive	*HGB (unless otherwise stated)*	*Content*
Art. 35 (1) (c) (cc)	§ 277 (3) sentence 1	Disclosure of information in the notes concerning the value adjustments mentioned in (aa) and (bb).
Art. 35 (1) (c) (dd)	§ 280 (1)	Requirement to reinstate original values (writing back). Writing back may be dispensed with if the lower valuation can be maintained for the purposes of determining taxable income and if it is a prerequisite of such retention that the lower value is also retained in the financial statements.
Art. 35 (1) (d)	§ 247 (3), §§ 254, 273, 279 (2), § 280 (2) and (3), § 281	Exceptional value adjustments for tax purposes.
Art. 35 (2)	§ 255 (1)	Acquisition costs comprise incidental costs.
Art. 35 (3) (a)	§ 255 (2) sentences 1–5	Production costs comprise costs that are directly attributable.
Art. 35 (3) (b)	§ 255 (2) sentence 3	Production costs also include part of the indirect costs.
Art. 35 (4)	§ 255 (3), § 284 (2) No. 5	Capitalization of interest costs on the construction of fixed assets; disclosure in the notes.
Art. 36 national option	Not adopted	Depreciation regulation for investment companies.
Art. 37 (1) national option	Not adopted	Recognition of research and development costs.
Art. 37 (2) national option	§ 255 (4) sentences 1–3, § 285 No. 13	Depreciation of goodwill: member states may allow goodwill to be amortized over a period of more than five years – adopted.
Art. 38	§ 256	Simplified valuation methods.
Art. 39 (1) (a)	§ 253 (1) sentence 1	Valuation of current assets at acquisition cost or production cost.
Art. 39 (1) (b)	§ 253 (3) sentences 1 and 2	Value adjustments to current assets.
Art. 39 (1) (c) national option	§ 253 (3) sentence 3, § 277 (3) sentence 1	Exceptional value adjustments for anticipated fluctuations in value – adopted; disclosure in the notes.
Art. 39 (1) (d)	§ 280 (1)	Requirement to reinstate original value (writing back).
Art. 39 (1) (e)	§ 247 (3), §§ 254, 273, 279 (2), §§ 280 (2) and (3), § 281	Exceptional value adjustments for tax purposes.
Art. 39 (2) national option	§ 255 (1)–(3), § 284 (2) No. 5	Selling expenses not part of production cost. Option of including interests in stocks: in Germany, interest on loan capital used to finance the production of the asset may be included to the extent that it was incurred during the period of production.
Art. 40 national option	§ 256, § 284 (2) No. 4	Option of applying simplified methods of calculating stock values for inventory items (e.g. average cost method, LIFO, FIFO) – adopted.
Art. 41	§ 250 (3)	Debt redemption payment.
Art. 42	§§ 253 (1) sentence 2; §§ 285 No. 12	Valuation of provisions.
Art. 43 (1)		Additional disclosures in the notes on the accounts.
Art. 43 (1) No. 1	§ 284 (2) Nos 1 and 2	Valuation methods and currency translation methods.
Art. 43 (1) No. 2	§ 285 No. 11, § 286 (3) sentence 1 No. 1, § 286 (3) sentence 2	Information concerning affiliated enterprises.
Art. 43 (1) No. 3	AktG § 160 (1) No. 3	Number and nominal value of shares subscribed in the financial year.

Fourth Directive	*HGB (unless otherwise stated)*	*Content*
Art. 43 (1) No. 4	AktG § 160 (1) No. 3	Number and nominal value of shares of each kind.
Art. 43 (1) No. 5	AktG § 160 (1) Nos. 5 and 6	Number of convertible loans and similar securities, giving details of the rights which they incorporate; profit participation rights, rights from betterment certificates and similar rights, giving details of the nature and number of each type of rights.
Art. 43 (1) No. 6	§ 285 Nos 1 and 2	Total amount of liabilities with a remaining term of more than five years and of liabilities which are secured by mortgages or other rights.
Art. 43 (1) No. 7	§ 285 No. 3, EGHGB Art. 28 (2)	Information about financial commitments which do not appear in the balance sheet.
Art. 43 (1) No. 8	§ 285 No. 4	Analysis of sales by area of activity and by geographically defined markets.
Art. 43 (1) No. 9	§ 285 Nos 7 and 8 (b)	Average number of employees and personnel expenses, analysed by groups.
Art. 43 (1) No. 10	§ 285 No. 5	Extent to which the results have been influenced by depreciation of assets based on tax regulations.
Art. 43 (1) No. 11	§ 274	Information about deferred taxation.
Art. 43 (1) No. 12	§ 285 No. 9 (a) and (b)	Information about personnel expenses of the members of the management body, of a supervisory board, advisory board or similar body.
Art. 43 (1) No. 13	§ 285 No. 9	Information about advances and loans granted to members of the designated bodies.
Art. 43 (2)	Not adopted	Special regulation to be optionally applied to investment companies.
Art. 44 national option	§ 267 (1), § 288 sentence 1	Simplification of the notes dependent on the size of the enterprise – adopted.
Art. 45 (1) (a) national option	§ 287	Option to allow details of subsidiaries, associates, etc., to: Take the form of a statement (adopted).
Art. 45 (1) (b) sentences 1 and 3 national option	§ 286 (3) sentence 1 No. 2	Be omitted if they would materially harm one of the enterprises (adopted). This exception must be disclosed in the notes.
Art. 45 (1) (b) sentence 2 national option	Not adopted	National option to require the approval of a court if exercising the exception mentioned in art. 45 (1) (b) sentence 1.
Art. 45 (2) sentence 1	§ 286 (2)	Option of allowing non-disclosure of segment information if disclosure harmful to the enterprise.
Art. 45 (2) sentence 2 national option	§ 267 (2), § 288 sentence 2	Option of allowing non-disclosure of segment information for small companies – adopted.
Art. 46 (1)	§ 289 (1)	Minimum information standards for the management report.
Art. 46 (2) (a)	§ 289 (2) No. 1	Further content: post-balance sheet events.
Art. 46 (2) (b)	§ 289 (2) No. 2	Further content: expected development of the enterprise.
Art. 46 (2) (c)	§ 289 (2) No. 3	Further content: area of research and development.
Art. 46 (2) (d)	AktG 160 (1) No. 2	Further content: amount of own shares; in Germany this information is to be given in the notes.

Fourth Directive	*HGB (unless otherwise stated)*	*Content*
Art. 47 sentence 1	§ 325 (1) and (2)	Disclosure.
Art. 47 sentence 2 national option	Not adopted	Option of exempting the management report from disclosure.
Art. 47 (2) national option	§ 267 (1), § 326	Simplifications for small companies concerning disclosure.
Art. 47 (3) national option	§ 267 (2), § 327	Simplifications for medium-size companies concerning disclosure – adopted.
Art. 48	§ 328 (1) No. 1, § 328 (3)	Form and content of documents for disclosure, publication and duplication.
Art. 49	§ 328 (2)	If the financial statements are reproduced in publications, etc., which are not required by law, reference must be made in the title to the fact that it is not the legally required form of publication.
Art. 50	§§ 325 (1), 326	Proposal for and resolution of the appropriation of the profit.
Art. 51 (1) (a)	§ 316 (1) sentence 1	Audit requirement.
Art. 51 (1) (b)	§ 316 (1) sentence 1, § 317 (1) sentence 3	Scope of the audit.
Art. 51 (2) national option	§ 267 (1), § 316 (1) sentence 1	Option of exempting small corporations from the audit requirement – adopted.
Art. 51 (3)	§ 331 No. 1, § 334 (1) Nos 1 and 3	Sanction requirements.
Art. 55 (2) national option	Art. 23 (1) (3) EGHGB	Final provisions: date of first appliance of the rules.
Art. 56 (2)	§ 285 No. 14	Final provisions: name and seat of the company's parent which prepares consolidated statements for the largest number of enterprises and of its parent which prepares consolidated statements for the smallest number as well as the place where these statements can be obtained are to be disclosed.
Art. 57 national option	Not adopted	Final provisions.
Art. 58 national option	Not adopted	Final provisions.
Art. 59 national option	Not adopted	Final provisions.
Art. 60 national option	Not adopted	Final provisions.
Art. 61 national option	Not adopted	Final provisions.

THE SEVENTH DIRECTIVE

Seventh Directive	*HGB (unless otherwise stated)*	*Content*
Art. 1 (1) (a)	§ 290 (2) No. 1	Requirement to prepare group accounts and a group management report if the majority of voting rights is owned by a domestically based company.
Art. 1 (1) (b)	§ 290 (2) No. 2	Requirement to prepare group accounts and a group management report if a domestically based company enjoys the right to appoint or dismiss the majority of the members of the administrative, management or supervisory body and is a shareholder.
Art. 1 (1) (c) sentence 1	§ 290 (2) No. 3	Requirement to prepare group accounts and a group management report if a domestically based company exercises a dominant influence given either by contract or by the memorandum and articles of the company. National option that the controlling company need not be a shareholder – adopted.
Art. 1 (1) (c) sentence 2 national option	§ 290 (2) No. 3	National option to apply this even if the parent company is not a shareholder – adopted.
Art. 1 (1) (d) (aa) national option	Not adopted	Requirement to prepare group accounts and a group management report if a parent company is a shareholder, and actually does nominate the majority of board members over a two-year period, without any other shareholder exercising a dominant influence.
Art. 1 (1) (d) (bb)	§ 290 (3) sentence 2	Requirement to prepare group accounts and a group management report if a domestically based parent company exercises the majority of the votes as a result of an agreement with the other shareholders.
Art. 1 (2) (a)	Not adopted	National option to require the consolidation if the parent company exercises a dominant influence.
Art. 1 (2) (b)	§ 290 (1)	Requirement to prepare group accounts and a group management report if a domestically based company and the affiliated enterprise are under unified management.
Art. 2 (1)	§ 290 (3) sentences 1 and 2	Further definition of the rights accruing to a parent company.
Art. 2 (2) (a)	§ 290 (3) sentence 3 No. 1	Rights which are held for the account of other persons to be deducted.
Art. 2 (2) (b)	§ 290 (3) sentence 3 No. 2	Rights attached to shares which are held as collateral to be deducted.
Art. 2 (3)	§ 290 (4)	Voting rights to be deducted.
Art. 3 (1)	§ 294 (1)	Enterprises to be consolidated.
Art. 3 (2)	§ 290 (3)–(4), § 294 (1)	Enterprises to be consolidated.
Art. 4 (1) (a)	Definitions of the companies to which the directive is to be applied in the headline of the third book's second chapter	Definition of the companies which come within the purview of the adopted regulations.
Art. 4 (2)	§ 290 (1)–(2)	Exemption due to the business form.

Seventh Directive	*HGB (unless otherwise stated)*	*Content*
Art. 5 national option	Not adopted	Further exemption criteria.
Art. 6 (1) national option	§ 293 (1) No. 2	National option concerning exemptions dependent upon size – adopted.
Art. 6 (2) national option	§ 293 (1) No. 1	National option 'Offset of inter-company debtors, creditors, investment/share capital normally cancelled on consolidation may be not effected for the purposes of calculating size limits (but size limits increased by 20%)' – adopted.
Art. 6 (3)	§ 293 (4)	Regulation of size criteria.
Art. 6 (4)	§ 293 (5)	Art. 6 not to be applied if a subsidiary is itself listed on a community stock exchange.
Art. 6 (5) national option	§ 293 (1)	National option for the limits set out in art. 6 (1) to be increased during a transitional period of ten years by 150% (economic limits) and 100% (number of employees) – adopted.
Art. 7 (1)	§ 291 (1), § 291 (3) sentence 2	Exempting group accounts and group management reports.
Art. 7 (2) (a)	§ 291 (2) No. 1	Exempting group accounts and group management reports.
Art. 7(2) (b) (aa)	§ 291 (2) No. 2	Exempting group accounts and group management reports.
Art. 7 (2) (b) (bb)	§ 291 (1) sentence 1	Exempting group accounts and group management reports.
Art. 7 (2) (c)	§ 291 (2) No. 3	Exempting group accounts and group management reports.
Art. 7 (3) national option	Not adopted	Exempting group accounts and group management reports.
Art. 8 (1) sentence 1 national option	§ 291	A parent undertaking which is under the dominant influence of another EC undertaking does not consolidate.
Art. 8 (1) sentence 2	§ 291 (3) sentence 1	Unless more than 10% (20%) of the shareholders of an AG (GmbH) do not object – adopted.
Art. 9 national option	Not adopted	Option of making the exemption from consolidation of the subsidiary of a foreign parent company in the EC which heads a national sub-group dependent on the publication of certain data.
Art. 11	§ 292	Power to issue regulations concerning the exemption of group accounts and group management reports – adopted through the *Konzernbefreiungsverordnung* (KonBefrV).
Art. 12 national option	Not adopted	Requirement to prepare group accounts if there is a permanent link which contributes to the parent company's trading and results in a dominant influence or if both companies are managed on a unified basis – not adopted.
Art. 13 (1)	§ 296 (2) sentence 1	Voluntary exclusion if the subsidiary is not significant in relation to the requirement to present a true and fair view.

Seventh Directive	*HGB (unless otherwise stated)*	*Content*
Art. 13 (2)	§ 296 (2) sentence 2	The enterprises must be included if, taken together, they are not insignificant.
Art. 13 (3) (a) (aa)	§ 296 (1) No. 1	Voluntary exclusion due to significant and continuing limitations which inhibit the exercise of the parent's rights.
Art. 13 (3) (a) (bb)	Not adopted	Voluntary exclusion due to significant and continuing limitations which inhibit the exercise of unified management.
Art. 13 (3) (b)	§ 296 (1) No. 2	Voluntary exclusion if the necessary information cannot be obtained.
Art. 13 (3) (c)	§ 296 (1) No. 3	Voluntary exclusion if the shares are held for resale purpose only.
Art. 14 (1)	§ 295 (1)	Exclusion due to divergent activities.
Art. 14 (2)	§ 295 (2)	Definition of the term 'divergent activities'.
Art. 14 (3)	§ 295 (3)	Exclusion to be referred to in the notes.
Art. 15 national option	Not adopted	National option of excluding from consolidation a parent company which does not carry out industrial and commercial activities – not adopted.
Art. 16 (1)	§ 297 (1)	Components of the group accounts.
Art. 16 (2)	§ 297 (2) sentence 1	Group accounts must be prepared in a clear and comprehensible fashion.
Art. 16 (3)	§ 297 (2) sentence 2	Group accounts must present a true and fair view (in Germany: in compliance with required GoB).
Art. 16 (4)	§ 297 (2) sentence 3	To the extent that the adopted regulations do not provide a true and fair view explanations must be given in the notes.
Art. 16 (5)	Not adopted expressly	National option of exempting from and derogating the regulations in order to comply with the true and fair view – not adopted expressly.
Art. 17 (1)	§ 298 (1)	Applicable rules.
Art. 17 (2) national option	§ 298 (2)	National option to combine inventories if consolidation entails undue expenses – adopted.
Art. 18	§ 300 (2)	Assets and liabilities must be taken up in their entirety.
Art. 19 (1) (a)	§ 301 (1) sentence 2 No. 1, § 301 (1) sentence 3	The value of the shares owned by the parent company to be offset against equity on the basis of the book values of the assets and liabilities.
Art. 19 (1) (b)	§ 301 (1) No. 2, § 301 (1) sentence 4	National option of authorizing or requiring the value of the shares owned by the parent company to be offset against equity on the basis of the item values at the date of acquisition or of initial consolidation (the revaluation method) – adopted.
Art. 19 (1) (c) sentence 1	§ 301 (3) sentence 1	Consolidation difference must be shown separately in the balance sheet.
Art. 19 (1) (c) sentence 2	§ 301 (1) sentence 5, § 301 (3) sentences 2–3	Consolidation differences and the method applied must be explained in the notes.

Seventh Directive	*HGB (unless otherwise stated)*	*Content*
Art. 19 (2)	§ 301 (4)	Capital consolidation is not applicable to shares in the parent enterprise which belong to the parent or a subsidiary.
Art. 20 national option	§ 302	National option of using the pooling of interest method – adopted.
Art. 21	§ 307 (1)	Minority interests.
Art. 22	§ 300 (2) sentence 1	The income and expenses must be taken up in their entirety.
Art. 23	§ 307 (2)	The profit and loss applicable to minority interests to be disclosed separately in the profit and loss account.
Art. 25 (1)	§ 297 (3) sentence 2	Substantive consistency.
Art. 25 (2)	§ 297 (3) sentences 3–5	Permission of departure from the substantive consistency under exceptional circumstances. Disclosure and justification in the notes.
Art. 26 (1) sentence 1	§ 297 (3) sentence 1	Disclosure as if all group enterprises comprised a legal entity.
Art. 26 (1) (a)	§ 303 (1)	Consolidation of inter-company balances.
Art. 26 (1) (b)	§ 305 (1)	Consolidation of revenues and expenses.
Art. 26 (1) (c) sentence 1	§ 304 (1)	Treatment of inter-company profits.
Art. 26 (1) (c) sentence 2 national option	Not adopted	National option of partially eliminating unrealized profits or losses on the basis of the percentage of equity held.
Art. 26 (2) national option	§ 304 (2)	National option of permitting the non-elimination of unrealized profits or losses if elimination would entail undue cost and the transactions were on an arm's length basis – adopted.
Art. 26 (3)	§ 303 (2), § 304 (3), § 305 (2)	Exemption from the consolidation of inter-company balances, inter-company profits and of income and expenses if the amounts to be eliminated are not material to the presentation of a true and fair view.
Art. 27 (1)	§ 299 (1)	Date to which the group accounts are to be prepared.
Art. 27 (2) national option	§ 299 (1) and (3)	National option of requiring or permitting the group accounts to be as of a date different from that of the parent company's individual accounts – adopted.
Art. 27 (3)	§ 299 (2) sentence 2	Interim accounts.
Art. 28 national option	§ 294 (2)	Where the composition of the group has changed significantly during the year, information to be given to make comparisons meaningful. National option of requiring or permitting the preparation of an adjusted opening balance sheet – permitted.
Art. 29 (1)	§ 298 (1), § 308 (1) sentence 1	Valuation methods to be uniform and in accordance with the Fourth Directive.
Art. 29 (2) (a) national option	§ 308 (1) sentence 1	The group accounts to be drawn up following the same principles as those used by the parent company in its individual accounts, but: other methods may be required or permitted provided they conform to the Fourth Directive – not adopted.

Seventh Directive	*HGB (unless otherwise stated)*	*Content*
Art. 29 (2) (b)	§ 308 (1) sentence 3	Departure from the valuation methods to be explained in the notes.
Art. 29 (3) sentence 1	§ 308 (2) sentences 1 and 3	In the event of differing valuation methods the value of assets and liabilities is to be restated in accordance with the valuation principles of the parent company.
Art. 29 (3) sentence 2	§ 308 (2) sentence 4	Departures in exceptional circumstances.
Art. 29 (4)	§ 306	Deferred taxation to be accounted for.
Art. 29 (5) national option	§ 308 (3)	Elimination of value adjustments carried out for tax purposes but: assets may be required or permitted to be included in the annual accounts without prior elimination of tax value adjustments – permitted.
Art. 30 (1)	§ 309 (1) sentences 1 and 2	Goodwill arising on consolidation to be dealt with in the same way as goodwill identified in the Fourth Directive.
Art. 30 (2) national option	§ 309 (1) sentence 3	Goodwill may be deducted on the face of the balance sheet from reserves – adopted.
Art. 31	§ 309 (2)	Treatment of a negative consolidation difference.
Art. 32 national option	§ 310	Proportional consolidation – adopted.
Art. 33 (1)	§ 311 (2)	Definition of an associated enterprise.
Art. 33 (2) (a)	§ 312 (1) sentence 1 No. 1, § 312 (1) sentence 2	Investment to be shown at inception by book value in parent, with difference shown separately, or:
Art. 33 (2) (b)	§ 312 (1) sentence 1 No. 2, § 312 (1) sentence 3	Accounting value of the proportion of investee's equity.
Art. 33 (2) (c)	§ 312 (1) sentence 4	Method applied to be explained in the notes.
Art. 33 (2) (d)	§ 312 (3) sentence 1	Date at which difference calculated.
Art. 33 (3) national option	§ 312 (5)	Associate's accounting methods to be brought into line with those of parent but: valuation adjustments may be required – not adopted.
Art. 33 (4)	§ 312 (4) sentence 1	Annual adjustment of the carrying value of the investment in the parent's books.
Art. 33 (5)	§ 312 (2)	Allocation of the consolidation difference.
Art. 33 (6)	§ 312 (4) sentence 2	Profit or loss from the associated enterprises to be separately disclosed in the profit and loss account.
Art. 33 (7)	§ 312 (5) sentences 3–4	Intra-group transactions to be eliminated.
Art. 33 (8)	§ 312 (6)	Last available financial statements of the associated enterprise are to be used; where associate is a group, above provisions to apply to sub-consolidation.
Art. 33 (9)	§ 311 (2)	Materiality exemption.
Art. 34 No. 1	§ 313 (1) sentence 2 Nos. 1–2	Additional disclosures in the notes on the accounts: valuation, depreciation and foreign currency methods.
Art. 34 No. 2 (a)	§ 313 (2) No. 1	Name, seat and percentage of shares held in each company included in the consolidation.

Seventh Directive	*HGB (unless otherwise stated)*	*Content*
Art. 34 No. 2 (b)	§ 313 (2) No. 1 sentence 2, § 269 (3)	Same information where companies are excluded from consolidation under arts 13 or 14.
Art. 34 No. 3 (a)	§ 313 (2) No. 2	Same information as in art. 34 No. 2 (a) for associated enterprises.
Art. 34 No. 3 (b)	§ 313 (2) No. 2	Including any excluded as being immaterial.
Art. 34 No. 4	§ 313 (2) No. 3	Same information as in art. 34 No. 2 (a) for companies which have been included proportionally in the consolidation.
Art. 34 No. 5	§ 313 (2) No. 4	Significant trade investments.
Art. 34 No. 6	§ 314 (1) No. 1	Total amount of debt due in more than five years.
Art. 34 No. 7	§ 314 (1) No. 2	Details of financial commitments not included in the consolidation, pension commitments to be disclosed separately.
Art. 34 No. 8	§ 314 (1) No. 3	Disclosure of turnover in different product and geographical segments.
Art. 34 No. 9 (a)	§ 314 (1) No. 4, first half of the sentence	Average number of employees, by category and total remuneration.
Art. 34 No. 9 (b)	§ 314 (1) No. 4, second half of the sentence	Numbers for companies consolidated proportionately to be disclosed separately.
Art. 34 No. 10	§ 314 (1) No. 5	Extent to which profit measurement has been affected by valuations designed to maximize tax relief.
Art. 34 No. 11	§ 306	Deferred taxation.
Art. 34 No. 12 sentences 1 and 2	§ 314 (1) No. 6 a–b	Membership of the executive board, supervisory board, advisory board or similar body of the parent enterprise, including remuneration, etc.
Art. 34 No. 12 sentence 3 national option	Not adopted	Further information about the remuneration of the above-mentioned employees.
Art. 34 No. 13 sentence 1	§ 314 (1) No. 6 (c)	Advances and loans granted by the parent company and the subsidiary enterprises.
Art. 34 No. 13 sentence 2 national option	Not adopted	Further information about advances and loans granted by the parent company and the subsidiary enterprises.
Art. 35 (1) (a) national option	§ 313 (4)	Option of allowing details of subsidiaries, associates, etc. (art. 34 (2)–(5)) to: take the form of a statement – adopted.
Art. 35 (1) (b) sentences 1 and 3 national option	§ 313 (3) sentence 1	Be omitted if they would prejudice the interests of the group – adopted. This exception must be disclosed in the notes.
Art. 35 (1) (b) sentence 2 national option	Not adopted	Option of requiring the approval of the court if exercising the exception mentioned in art. 35 (1) (b) sentence 1.
Art. 35 (2)	§ 314 (2)	Option of allowing non-disclosure of segment information if materially harmful to group's interests.

Seventh Directive	*HGB (unless otherwise stated)*	*Content*
Art. 36 (1)	§ 315 (1)	Minimum information standards for the group management report.
Art. 36 (2) (a)	§ 315 (2) No. 1	Further content: post-balance sheet events.
Art. 36 (2) (b)	§ 315 (2) No. 2	Further content: anticipated development of the group.
Art. 36 (2) (c)	§ 315 (2) No. 3	Further content: areas of research and development.
Art. 36 (2) (d)	§ 314 (1) No. 7	Further content: amount of shares which are taken or held as securities; in Germany, this information to be given in the notes.
Art. 37 (1)	§ 316 (2)	Audit requirement of the group accounts.
Art. 37 (2)	§ 316 (2), § 317 (1) sentence 3	Audit requirement of the management report and the group management report.
Art. 38 (1)	§ 325 (3)	Disclosure requirements.
Art. 38 (2) national option	Not adopted	Option of exempting the group management report from disclosure.
Art. 38 (5)	§ 328 (1) No. 1, § 328 (2)–(3)	Form and contents of documents for disclosure, publication and duplication.
Art. 38 (6)	§ 335 No. 6	Sanctions against offending the disclosure requirements.
Art. 39	EGHGB art. 27	Transitional and final provisions: adoption of the regulations.
Art. 40 (1)	§ 298 (1), § 308 (2) sentence 2	Transitional and final provisions: adoption of the regulations.
Art. 40 (1) sentence 2	§ 293 (2) and (3)	Transitional and final provisions: exemptions for credit institutions.
Art. 41 (1)	§ 271 (2)	Transitional and final provisions: definition of affiliated enterprises.
Art. 41 (3) national option	Not adopted	Transitional and final provisions.
Art. 41 (5) national option	Not adopted	Transitional and final provisions.
Art. 49 (2)	EGHGB art. 23 (2)	Transitional and final provisions: date of first application of the adopted regulations.

Appendix D
Useful information

INFORMATION ON ACCOUNTING

Publications

Commercial publishers issue various technical publications ranging from annual handbooks to loose-leaf services, newsletters and magazines.

There are a number of periodicals in accounting and related areas. These include: *Der Betrieb* (weekly); *Der Betriebs-Berater* (weekly); *Deutsche Steuerzeitung* (twice a month); *Deutsches Steuerrecht* (twice a month); *Finanzrundschau* (twice a month); *GmbH-Rundschau* (monthly); *IdW-Fachnachrichten* (monthly); *Neue Wirtschaftsbriefe* (weekly); *Steuer und Wirtschaft* (quarterly); *Steuerliche Betriebsprüfung* (monthly); *Die Wirtschaftsprüfung* (twice a month).

The following list gives an overview of the principal reference books and commentaries on accounting law:

Reference books:

Castan, E., Heymann, G., Müller, E., Ordelheide, D. and Scheffler, E. (eds) (1987) *Beck'sches Handbuch der Rechnungslegung*, Munich: C.H. Beck.

von Wysocki, K. and Schulze-Osterloh, J. (eds) (1987) *Handbuch des Jahresabschlusses in Einzeldarstellungen*, Cologne: Otto Schmidt.

Commentaries:

Adler, H., Düring, W. and Schmaltz, K. (1987) *Rechnungslegung und Prüfung der Unternehmen. Kommentar zum HGB, AktG, GmbHG, PublG nach den Vorschriften des Bilanzrichtlinien-Gesetzes*, 5th edn, Stuttgart: C.E. Poeschel.

Budde, W.D., Clemm, H., Pankow, M. and Sarx, M. (1990) *Beck'scher Bilanzkommentar*, 2nd edn, Munich: C.H. Beck.

Küting, K. and Weber, C.P. (1989) *Handbuch der Konzernrechnungslegung*, Stuttgart: Schäffer.

Küting, K. and Weber, C.P. (1990) *Handbuch der Rechnungslegung. Kommentar zur Bilanzierung und Prüfung*, 3rd edn, Stuttgart: Schäffer.

The reference books give a systematic description of and comments on specific topics while the commentaries proceed according to the paragraphs of the law.

Every few years, the *Institut der Wirtschaftsprüfer* (IdW) issues the *Wirtschaftsprüfer-Handbuch* (2 volumes) which is designed as a reference book for auditors. Besides covering matters not dealing directly with financial reporting, it also describes the laws governing accountancy and comments on them. It covers those regulations that are often omitted, such as the special rules for banks, insurance companies, building societies and publicly owned businesses.

Information sources

There is a considerable amount of information available about accounting and financial reporting in Germany. The *Beck'sches Handbuch der Rechnungslegung* contains a literature service covering the up to date literature and jurisdiction on accounting regulations. This literature is organized according to the areas of financial reporting and is continually updated. In addition to this there are a number of databases (especially BLISS), covering the literature on accounting.

INFORMATION ON COMPANIES

Economic and firm data are offered by a wide range of databases. The *Handbuch der Wirtschaftsdatenbanken* 1992 published by Hoppenstedt & Co. describes the contents of the most important databases world-wide and the admission requirements of the suppliers. Examples for databases containing firm-level data of Germany corporations are FINN/COIN, FITT, HADOSS and HOPPENSTEDT.

In addition to this, the *'Saling'-Aktienführer* published by Hoppenstedt & Co. is available in book form. It lists in alphabetical order all 560 German and 248 foreign companies whose stock is traded on the German stock exchange. Reports contain the names of the members of the board of directors and the supervisory board, the major shareholders, the number of employees, the development of the capital, the development of the stock value and dividends paid during the last years and excerpts of the balance sheet and the profit and loss account.

LIBRARIES

Deutsche Bibliothek
Zeppelinallee 4-8
D-60325 Frankfurt am Main

IdW-Bibliothek
Tersteegenstraße 14
D-40474 Düsseldorf

In addition, the large university and especially the faculty libraries in Germany offer a wide range of literature on accountancy and auditing.

Glossary

In addition to this glossary, financial statement terminology may be found in the following tables in this book:

- Chapter 6, Table 6.6 (Simplified *Industriekontenrahmen*).
- Chapter 7, Table 7.3 (Layout of the balance sheet).
- Chapter 7, Table 7.5 (Appropriation of profit).

GERMAN–ENGLISH

A

Abhängigkeitsbericht	dependence report
Abschreibung	depreciation
Abschreibungs-Tabellen	depreciation tables
Absetzung für Abnutzung (AfA)	deduction for normal business wear and tear
Absetzung für Substanzverringerung (AfS)	deduction for material depletion
Aktien	shares
Aktienbörse	stock exchange
Aktiengesellschaft (AG)	joint stock corporation
Aktiengesetz (AktG)	Joint Stock Corporation Act
Aktionärsbrief	letter to shareholders (shareholders' letter)
Aktivierung	capitalization
aktivischer Unterschiedsbetrag	positive consolidation difference
Allgemeines Deutsches Handelsgesetzbuch (ADHGB)	General German Commercial Code
Anhang	notes (on the financial statements)
Anlagespiegel	schedule of fixed assets
Anlagevermögen	fixed assets
Anschaffungskosten	acquisition costs

Anschaffungskostenprinzip	historical cost principle
Anschaffungsnebenkosten	incidental costs of acquisition
Aufsichtsrat	supervisory board
Aufwands- und Ertragskonsolidierung	consolidation of revenues and expenses
Aufwandszuschüsse	expenditure subsidies
außerordentliche Aufwendungen	extraordinary expenses
außerordentliche Erträge	extraordinary revenues
außerplanmäßige Abschreibung	exceptional depreciation

B

Bankkredit	bank credit
bedingte Kapitalerhöhung	conditional capital increase
beizulegender Wert	attributed value
Bestätigungsvermerk	audit opinion
Beteiligung	participating interest (participation)
Betrieb	plant
Betriebsrat	workers' council
Betriebsstätte	(permanent) establishment
Betriebsverfassungsgesetz (BetrVG)	Industrial Constitution Act
Bewertung	valuation
Bewertungsgrundsätze	basic valuation principles
Bilanz	balance sheet
Bilanzansatz	recognition of assets and liabilities
Bilanzbündeltheorie	bundle theory
Bilanzgewinn	balance sheet profit
Bilanzierungshilfe	accounting convenience
Bilanzierungswahlrechte	accounting options
Bilanzkontinuität	balance sheet continuity
Bilanzrichtliniengesetz	Accounting Directives Act
Bilanzstichtag	balance sheet date
Bilanzverlust	balance sheet loss
Bodensatztheorie	theory of permanent average balances
Börsengesetz (BörsG)	Stock Exchange Act
börsennotierte Kapitalgesellschaft	quoted corporation
Börsenzulassungsverordnung (BörsZulV)	Stock Exchange Listing Requirements Order
Buchwertmethode	book value method
Bundesanzeiger	*Federal Official Gazette*
Bundesaufsichtsamt für das Kreditwesen	Federal Banking Supervisory Board
Bundesaufsichtsamt für das Versicherungswesen	Federal Supervisory Office for Insurance
Bundesbank	Federal Central Bank (the Bundesbank)
Bundesbankgesetz	Federal Bank Act
Bundesfinanzhof	Federal Fiscal Court

Bundesgerichtshof	Federal Supreme Court
Bundeskartellamt	Federal Monopolies Commission
Bundesverband Deutscher Banken eV	Confederation of German Banks

D

Dauerschuldverhältnisse	continuous obligations
Dauerschuldzinsen	interest on permanent debt
Depotstimmrecht	proxy voting
Deutsche Angestellten Gewerkschaft (DAG)	German Salaried Employee's Union
Deutsche Vereinigung für Finanzanalyse und Anlageberatung (DVFA)	German Association of Finance Analysts and Investment Consultants
Deutscher Beamtenbund	German Public Service Federation
Deutscher Genossenschafts- und Raiffeisenverband	German Association of Co-operatives
Deutscher Gewerkschaftsbund (DGB)	German Trade Union Federation
Deutscher Sparkassen- und Giroverband	German Savings Bank Association
Disagio	capitalized discount/disagio
Durchschnittssteuersatz	average tax rate
dynamische Bilanzlehre	dynamic balance sheet school

E

Eigenkapital	equity
Eigenkapitalquote	equity ratio
Einfuhrumsatzsteuer	import turnover tax
eingetragene Genossenschaft	registered co-operative
einheitliche Bewertung	uniform valuation
einheitliche Leitung	unified management
Einigungsstelle	conciliation board
Einkaufsgenossenschaft	purchasing co-operative
Einkommenskonzept	income concept
Einkommensteuer (ESt)	income tax
Einkommensteuer-Durchführungsverordnung (EStDV)	Ordinance Regulating the Income Tax Act
Einkommensteuer-Richtlinien (EStR)	Income Tax Regulations
Einkommensteuergesetz (EStG)	Income Tax Act
Einzelabschluß	accounts of the individual enterprise (individual accounts)
Einzelbewertung	item-by-item valuation
Einzelunternehmung	sole proprietorship
entgeltlicher Erwerb	acquisition for valuable consideration
Entwicklungskosten	development costs

Equitykonsolidierung (-bewertung)	equity method
Erbschaft-/Schenkungsteuer	inheritance tax/gift tax
Ergebnisverwendungsrechnung	appropriation account
Ermessensrücklagen	discretionary reserves
Ertragsteuern	earnings taxes
Erwerbsmethode	purchase method
Europäische Gemeinschaft	European Community

F

faktischer Konzern	*de facto* group
Fiktion der rechtlichen Einheit (Einheitsgrundsatz)	legal entity fiction
Finanzanlagen	financial assets
Finanzgericht	fiscal court
Folgekonsolidierung	subsequent consolidation
Forschungskosten	research costs
Fremdkapital	debt (loan capital)
Fremdkapitalzinsen	interest on debt capital
Fremdwährungsposition	foreign currency position
Fusion	legal merger in which one loses its separate identity

G

Gängigkeitsabschreibungen	write-off for non-marketability
Gemeinnützigkeitsrecht	Charities Act
Gemeinschaftskontenrahmen der Industrie (GKR)	Common Framework of Accounts for Industry
gemildertes Niederstwertprinzip	weaker principle of lower value
genehmigtes Kapital	authorized capital
Genossenschaftsregister	special register where co-operatives are recorded
geometrisch-degressive Abschreibung	reducing balance depreciation
geringwertige Wirtschaftsgüter	low-value business goods
Gesamtkostenverfahren	total cost method
Gesamtverband der Deutschen Versicherungswirtschaft	German Insurance Association
Geschäfts- oder Firmenwert	goodwill
Geschäftsbericht	annual report
Geschäftsjahr	financial year
Gesellschaft bürgerlichen Rechts (BGB-Gesellschaft)	civil law partnership

Gesellschaft mit beschränkter Haftung (GmbH)	limited liability company
gesetzliche Rücklage	legal reserve
Gewerbebetrieb	domestic business (business establishment)
Gewerbeertrag	business profit
Gewerbeertragsteuer (GewErtSt)	trade tax on earnings
Gewerbekapitalsteuer (GewKapSt)	trading capital tax
Gewerbesteuer	trade tax
Gewerkschaft	union
Gewinn- und Verlustrechnung	profit and loss account
Gewinn- und Verlustübernahme-Vertrag	profit and loss transfer agreement
Gewinnrücklagen	profit reserves
Gewinnverteilungsfunktion	profit distribution function
Gewinnverwendung	appropriation of profit
Gewinnvortrag	profit brought forward
gezeichnetes Kapital	subscribed capital
Gläubigerschutz	protection of creditors
Gleichordnungskonzern	equal ranking group
Gliederung	format
Grunderwerbsteuer (GrESt)	real property transfer tax
Grundkapital	subscribed capital of a joint stock corporation
Grundsätze ordnungsmäßiger Bilanzierung	principles of regular financial reporting
Grundsätze ordnungsmäßiger Buchführung (GoB)	principles of regular accounting
Grundsätze ordnungsmäßiger Inventur	principles of regular stocktaking
Grundsteuer (GrSt)	real property tax
Gruppenbewertung	group or collective valuation

H

Handelsgesetzbuch (HGB)	Commercial Code
Handelsregister	commercial register
Hauptversammlung	general meeting (stockholders' meeting)
Herstellungskosten	production costs
Hypothekenbank	mortgage bank

I

immaterielle Vermögensgegenstände	intangible fixed assets
Imparitätsprinzip	imparity principle
Industrieobligation	corporate bond
Informationsfunktion	information function
Inhaberaktie	bearer share

Institut der Wirtschaftsprüfer eV (*IdW*)	Institute of Certified Public Accountants
Interessenzusammenführungsmethode	pooling of interests method
Inventur	stocktaking
Investitionszulagen	investment allowances (non-taxable)
Investitionszuschüsse	investment subsidies (taxable)

J

Jahresfehlbetrag	loss for the year
Jahresüberschuß	profit for the year

K

Kapitalanteilsmethode	capital share method
Kapitalerhöhung aus Gesellschaftsmitteln	capital increase out of company funds
Kapitalerhöhung gegen Einlagen	capital increase for consideration
Kapitalgesellschaft	corporation
Kapitalgesellschaft & Co. KG	special form of limited partnership
Kapitalherabsetzung	reduction of subscribed capital
Kapitalherabsetzung durch Einziehung von Aktien	capital reduction through cancellation of stock
Kapitalkonsolidierung	capital consolidation
Kapitalmarkt	capital market
Kapitalrücklage	capital reserve
Kapitalverkehrsteuer (*KVSt*)	capital transfer tax
Kirchensteuer	church tax (tithes)
Kommanditgesellschaft (*KG*)	limited partnership
Kommanditgesellschaft auf Aktien (*KGaA*)	limited partnership with shares
Kommanditist	limited partner
Komplementär	personally liable general partner
Konsolidierungskreis	consolidation set
Kontenart	account type
Kontengruppe	account group
Kontenklasse	account class
Kontenplan	accounts plan
Kontenrahmen	accounts framework
Kontrollrechte	rights of control
Konzern	group (of affiliated companies)
Konzernabschluß	group accounts
Konzernabschlußbefreiungsverordnung (*KonBefr V*)	Group Accounts Exemption Order
Konzernlagebericht	group management report
Konzernverfassungsrecht	group governance law

konzertierte Aktion	concerted action
Körperschaftsteuer (KSt)	corporation tax
Kosten der Ingangsetzung und Erweiterung des Geschäftsbetriebs	expenditure on the start-up and expansion of the business
Kraftfahrzeugsteuer (KraftSt)	motor vehicle tax
Kreditanstalt für Wiederaufbau	Reconstruction Loan Corporation
Kreditwesengesetz (KWG)	Banking Act
Kulanzrückstellung	provision for liberal settlements of customers' complaints

L

Lagebericht	management report
Landeszentralbank	regional central bank
Landgericht	regional court
langfristige Auftragsfertigung	long-term made-to-order production
latente Steuern	deferred taxation
Leasinggeber	lessor
Leasingnehmer	lessee
leistungsabhängige Abschreibung	production unit depreciation method
lineare Abschreibung	straight-line depreciation
Lohnsteuer (LSt)	salary tax

M

Maßgeblichkeit	authoritativeness principle
Materialaufwand	cost of materials
Mehrstimmrechtsaktien	multiple-voting shares
Mehrwertsteuer (MWSt)	value-added tax
Minderheitenanteile	minority shareholders
Mitbestimmung	co-determination
Mitbestimmungsgesetz (MitbestG)	Co-determination Act
Mitunternehmer	joint proprietor
Montan-Mitbestimmung	*Montan* co-determination

N

nachträgliche Anschaffungskosten	subsequent acquisition costs
Namensaktie	registered share
Neubewertungsmethode	revaluation method
Niederstwertprinzip	principle of lower value
niedrigerer beizulegender Wert	lower attributable value
Nutzungsgenossenschaft	producer co-operative

O

Oberlandesgericht	intermediate court of appeal
offene Handelsgesellschaft (OHG)	general partnership
Offenlegung	disclosure
öffentliche Betriebe in privatrechtlicher Form	public-sector enterprises under private law
öffentliche Zuwendungen	government grants
ordentliche Kapitalherabsetzung	regular capital reduction
Organgesellschaft	dependent company
organische Tageswertbilanz	organic current value balance sheet
Organschaft	fiscal unit for corporation tax purposes (interlocking relationship)
Organträger	dominant company

P

pagatorisches Prinzip	pagatoric principle
Partenreederei	co-ownership of vessels
passivischer Unterschiedsbetrag	negative consolidation difference
Pensionskasse	pension fund
Pensionsrückstellung	provision for pension
Pensionssicherungsverein	Pension Guaranty Association
periodenfremde Aufwendungen	prior-year expenses
periodenfremde Erträge	prior-year revenues
Personalaufwand	employment costs
Personengesellschaft	partnership
Personenhandelsgesellschaft	commercial partnership
planmäßige Abschreibung	systematic depreciation
Privatbank	private banker
Produkthaftungsrückstellung	provision for product liability
Prüfungsbericht	audit report
Prüfungspflicht	audit requirement
Publikumsgesellschaften	public corporations
Publizitätsgesetz (PublG)	Disclosure Act

Q

Quartalsberichte	quarterly reports
Quellentheorie	source theory
Quotenkonsolidierung	proportional consolidation

R

Realisationsprinzip	realization principle

Rechnungslegung	financial reporting
Regionalbank	regional bank
Reichsfinanzhof (RFH)	former highest fiscal court
Reinvermögenszugangstheorie	net assets increase theory
Rücklage für eigene Aktien	reserve for own shares
Rückstellung	provision
Rückstellung für drohende Verluste aus schwebenden Geschäften	provision for losses on uncompleted transactions
Rückstellung für ungewisse Verbindlichkeiten	provision for uncertain liabilities

S

Sachanlagen	tangible assets
satzungsmäßige Rücklagen	statutory reserves
Schmalenbach-Gesellschaft/Deutsche Gesellschaft für Betriebswirtschaft (SG)	German Association for Business Economics
Schuldenkonsolidierung	consolidation of intra-group balances
Schuldscheindarlehen	(borrowers') note loan
Sonderbetriebsvermögen	special business property
Sonderposten mit Rücklageanteil	special item with a reserve component
sonstige betriebliche Aufwendungen	other operating expenses
sonstige betriebliche Erträge	other operating revenues
Sozialplanrückstellung	provision for a social plan
Spezialbank	special bank
Spezialleasing	special lease
Spitzensteuersatz	top tax rate
Stammaktien	ordinary shares
Stammkapital	subscribed capital of limited liability company
statische Bilanzlehre	static balance sheet school
Stetigkeit	consistency
Steuerabgrenzung	deferred taxation
Stichtagskursmethode	closing rate method
stille Anschaffungswertrücklagen	hidden historical cost reserves
stille Tageswertrücklagen	hidden current value reserves
strenges Niederstwertprinzip	strict lower value principle
Substanzsteuern	capital taxes

T

Tarifautonomie	principle of free collective bargaining
Teilamortisationsvertrag	non-full-pay-out lease

Teilwert	part-of-the-whole value
Teilwertabschreibung	part-of-the-whole-value depreciation
Teilwertvermutung	part-of-the-whole-value supposition
transitorische Aktiva	pre-paid expenses
transitorische Passiva	deferred income

U

umgekehrte Maßgeblichkeit	reverse authoritativeness principle
Umlaufvermögen	current assets
Umsatzkostenverfahren	cost of sales method
Universalbank	universal bank
Unterkonto	sub-account
Unternehmensfortführung	going concern
Unternehmensverträge	enterprise agreements
Unterordnungskonzern	group of subordinated affiliates

V

Verbindlichkeiten	liabilities
Verbindlichkeitsdisagio	redemption premium on loans
Verbrauchsteuern	consumption taxes
verdeckte Gewinnausschüttung	hidden distribution of profit
verdeckte Kapitaleinlage	hidden contribution of capital
vereidigter Buchprüfer	sworn auditor
vereinfachte Kapitalherabsetzung	simplified capital reduction
Verkehrsteuern	transaction taxes
Verlustvortrag	loss brought forward
Vermögensteuer (VSt)	assets tax
Verschmelzungsmehrwert	fusion surplus
Versicherungsaufsichtsgesetz	Supervision of Insurance Companies Act
Versicherungsgesellschaft	insurance company (enterprise)
Versicherungsteuer	insurance tax
Versicherungsverein auf Gegenseitigkeit	mutual insurance society
Vertragskonzern	contractual group
Verursachungsprinzip	accrual principle
Verwaltungskosten	administrative costs
Verwertungsgenossenschaft	commercial co-operative
Vetriebskosten	selling expenses
Vollamortisationsvertrag	full pay-out lease
Vollkonsolidierung	full consolidation
Vorräte	inventories, stocks
Vorsichtsprinzip	prudence principle
Vorstand	executive board
Vorzugsaktie	preference share

W

Währungsumrechnung	foreign currency translation
Wechselsteuer	tax on drafts and bills of exchange
Werbungskosten	income-related expenses
Wertaufhellungsprinzip	revealed value principle
Wertaufholung	writing back
Wertpapiere	investments
Willkürrücklagen	arbitrary reserves
Wirtschaftsausschuß	economic council
Wirtschaftsprüfer	auditor (*Wirtschaftsprüfer*)
Wirtschaftsprüferkammer	chamber of the *Wirtschaftsprüfer*
Wirtschaftsprüferordnung	Regulation governing the Profession of *Wirtschaftsprüfer*
Wirtschaftsprüfung	auditing

Z

Zeitbezugsmethode	temporal method
zu versteuerndes Einkommen	taxable income
Zulagen	allowances (non-taxable grants)
Zuschreibung	write-up
Zuschüsse	subsidies (taxable grants)
Zwangsrücklagen	mandatory reserves
Zwischenabschluß	interim accounts
Zwischengewinn/-verlust	intra-group profit/loss
Zwischengewinneliminierung	elimination of intra-group profits

ENGLISH–GERMAN

A

account class	*Kontenklasse*
account group	*Kontengruppe*
account type	*Kontenart*
accounting convenience	*Bilanzierungshilfe*
Accounting Directives Act	*Bilanzrichtliniengesetz*
accounting options	*Bilanzierungswahlrechte*
accounts framework	*Kontenrahmen*
accounts of the individual enterprise (individual accounts)	*Einzelabschluß*
accounts plan	*Kontenplan*
accrual principle	*Verursachungsprinzip*
acquisition costs	*Anschaffungskosten*
acquisition for valuable consideration	*entgeltlicher Erwerb*
administrative costs	*Verwaltungskosten*
allowances (non-taxable grants)	*Zulagen*
annual report	*Geschäftsbericht*
appropriation account	*Ergebnisverwendungsrechnung*
appropriation of profit	*Gewinnverwendung*
arbitrary reserves	*Willkürrücklagen*
assets tax	*Vermögensteuer (VSt)*
attributed value	*beizulegender Wert*
auditing	*Wirtschaftsprüfung*
audit opinion	*Bestätigungsvermerk*
audit report	*Prüfungsbericht*
audit requirement	*Prüfungspflicht*
auditor (*Wirtschaftsprüfer*)	*Wirtschaftsprüfer*
authoritativeness principle	*Maßgeblichkeit*
authorized capital	*genehmigtes Kapital*
average tax rate	*Durchschnittssteuersatz*

B

balance sheet	*Bilanz*
balance sheet continuity	*Bilanzkontinuität*
balance sheet date	*Bilanzstichtag*
balance sheet profit/loss	*Bilanzgewinn/-verlust*
bank credit	*Bankkredit*
basic valuation principles	*Bewertungsgrundsätze*
book value method	*Buchwertmethode*
borrowers' note loan	*Schuldscheindarlehen*
bundle theory	*Bilanzbündeltheorie*
business profit	*Gewerbeertrag*

C

capital consolidation	*Kapitalkonsolidierung*
capital increase for consideration	*Kapitalerhöhung gegen Einlagen*
capital increase out of company funds	*Kapitalerhöhung aus Gesellschaftsmitteln*
capital market	*Kapitalmarkt*
capital reduction through cancellation of stock	*Kapitalherabsetzung durch Einziehung von Aktien*
capital reserve	*Kapitalrücklage*
capital share method	*Kapitalanteilsmethode*
capital taxes	*Substanzsteuern*
capital transfer tax	*Kapitalverkehrsteuer* (*KVSt*)
capitalization	*Aktivierung*
chamber of the *Wirtschaftsprüfer*	*Wirtschaftsprüferkammer*
Charities Act	*Gemeinnützigkeitsrecht*
church tax (tithes)	*Kirchensteuer*
civil law partnership	*Gesellschaft bürgerlichen Rechts*
closing rate method	*Stichtagskursmethode*
co-determination	*Mitbestimmung*
Co-determination Act	*Mitbestimmungsgesetz* (*MitbestG*)
co-ownership of ships	*Partenreederei*
Commercial Code	*Handelsgesetzbuch* (*HGB*)
commercial co-operative	*Verwertungsgenossenschaft*
commercial partnership	*Personenhandelsgesellschaft*
commercial register	*Handelsregister*
Common Framework of Accounts for Industry	*Gemeinschaftskontenrahmen der Industrie* (GKR)
concerted action	*konzertierte Aktion*
conciliation board	*Einigungsstelle*
conditional capital increase	*bedingte Kapitalerhöhung*
Confederation of German Banks	*Bundesverband Deutscher Banken eV*
consistency	*Stetigkeit*
consolidation of intra-group balances	*Schuldenkonsolidierung*
consolidation of revenues and expenses	*Aufwands-und Ertragskonsolidierung*
consolidation set	*Konsolidierungskreis*
consumption taxes	*Verbrauchsteuern*
continuous obligations	*Dauerschuldverhältnisse*
contractual group	*Vertragskonzern*
corporate bond	*Industrieobligation*
corporation	*Kapitalgesellschaft*
corporation tax	*Körperschaftsteuer* (KSt)
cost of materials	*Materialaufwand*
cost of sales method	*Umsatzkostenverfahren*
current assets	*Umlaufvermögen*

D

de facto group	*faktischer Konzern*
debt (loan capital)	*Fremdkapital*
deduction for material depletion	*Absetzung für Substanzverringerung* (AfS)
deduction for normal business wear and tear	*Absetzung für Abnutzung* (AfA)
deferred income	*transitorische Passiva*
deferred taxation	*latente Steuern* (*Steuerabgrenzung*)
dependence report	*Abhängigkeitsbericht*
dependent company	*Organgesellschaft*
depreciation	*Abschreibung*
depreciation tables	*Abschreibungs-Tabellen*
development costs	*Entwicklungskosten*
disclosure	*Offenlegung*
Disclosure Act	*Publizitätsgesetz* (*PublG*)
discretionary reserves	*Ermessensrücklagen*
domestic business (business establishment)	*Gewerbebetrieb*
dominant company	*Organträger*
dynamic balance sheet school	*dynamische Bilanzlehre*

E

earnings taxes	*Ertragsteuern*
economic council	*Wirtschaftsausschuß*
elimination of intra-group profits	*Zwischengewinneliminierung*
employment costs	*Personalaufwand*
enterprise agreements	*Unternehmensverträge*
equal-ranking group	*Gleichordnungskonzern*
equity capital	*Eigenkapital*
equity method	*Equitykonsolidierung* (*-bewertung*)
equity ratio	*Eigenkapitalquote*
establishment (permanent)	*Betriebsstätte*
European Community	*Europäische Gemeinschaft*
exceptional depreciation	*außerplanmäßige Abschreibung*
executive board	*Vorstand*
expenditure on the start-up and expansion of the business	*Kosten der Ingangsetzung und Erweiterung des Geschäftsbetriebs*
expenditure subsidies	*Aufwandszuschüsse*
extraordinary expenses	*außerordentliche Aufwendungen*
extraordinary revenues	*außerordentliche Erträge*

F

Federal Bank Act	*Bundesbankgesetz*
Federal Banking Supervisory Board	Bundesaufsichtsamt für das Kreditwesen
Federal Central Bank (the Bundesbank)	Bundesbank
Federal Fiscal Court	Bundesfinanzhof
Federal Monopolies Commission	Bundeskartellamt
Federal Official Gazette	*Bundesanzeiger*
Federal Supervisory Office for Insurance	Bundesaufsichtsamt für das Versicherungswesen
Federal Supreme Court	Bundesgerichtshof
financial assets	*Finanzanlagen*
financial reporting	*Rechnungslegung*
financial year	*Geschäftsjahr*
fiscal court	*Finanzgericht*
fiscal unit for corporation tax purposes (interlocking relationship)	*Organschaft*
fixed assets	*Anlagevermögen*
foreign currency position	*Fremdwährungsposition*
foreign currency translation	*Währungsumrechnung*
format	*Gliederung*
former highest fiscal court	Reichsfinanzhof (RFH)
full consolidation	*Vollkonsolidierung*
full pay-out lease	*Vollamortisationsvertrag*
fusion surplus	*Verschmelzungsmehrwert*

G

General German Commercial Code	*Allgemeines Deutsches Handelsgesetzbuch* (ADHGB)
general meeting (stockholders' meeting)	*Hauptversammlung*
general partnership	*offene Handelsgesellschaft* (OHG)
German Association for Business Economics	Schmalenbach-Gesellschaft/Deutsche Gesellschaft für Betriebswirtschaft (SG)
German Association of Cooperatives	Deutscher Genossenschafts- und Raiffeisenverband
German Association of Finance Analysts and Investment Consultants	Deutsche Vereinigung für Finanzanalyse und Anlageberatung (DVFA)
German Banking Law	*Kreditwesengesetz* (KWG)
German Insurance Association	*Gesamtverband der Deutschen Versicherungswirtschaft*
German Public Service Federation	*Deutscher Beamtenbund*

German Salaried Employees' Union	Deutsche Angestellten Gewerkschaft (DAG)
German Savings Bank Association	Deutscher Sparkassen- und Giroverband
German Trade Union Federation	Deutscher Gewerkschaftsbund (DGB)
going concern	*Unternehmensfortführung*
goodwill	*Geschäfts- oder Firmenwert*
government grants	*öffentliche Zuwendungen*
group (of affiliated companies)	*Konzern*
group accounts	*Konzernabschluß*
Group Accounts Exemption Order	*Konzernabschlußbefreiungsverordnung* (KonBefrV)
group governance law	*Konzernverfassungsrecht*
group management report	*Konzernlagebericht*
group of subordinated affiliates	*Unterordnungskonzern*
group or collective valuation	*Gruppenbewertung*

H

hidden contribution of capital	*verdeckte Kapitaleinlage*
hidden current value reserves	*stille Tageswertrücklagen*
hidden distribution of profit	*verdeckte Gewinnausschüttung*
hidden historical cost reserves	*stille Anschaffungswertrücklagen*
historical cost principle	*Anschaffungskostenprinzip*

I

imparity principle	*Imparitätsprinzip*
import turnover tax	*Einfuhrumsatzsteuer*
incidental costs of acquisition	*Anschaffungsnebenkosten*
income concept	*Einkommenskonzept*
income tax	*Einkommensteuer* (ESt)
Income Tax Act	*Einkommensteuergesetz* (EStG)
Income Tax Regulations	*Einkommensteuer-Richtlinien* (EStR)
income-related expenses	*Werbungskosten*
Industrial Constitution Act	*Betriebsverfassungsgesetz* (BetrVG)
information function	*Informationsfunktion*
inheritance tax/gift tax	*Erbschaft-/Schenkungsteuer*
Institute of Certified Public Accountants	Institut der Wirtschaftsprüfer eV (IdW)
insurance company (enterprise)	*Versicherungsgesellschaft*
insurance tax	*Versicherungsteuer*
intangible fixed assets	*immaterielle Vermögensgegenstände*
interest on debt capital	*Fremdkapitalzinsen*
interest on permanent debt	*Dauerschuldzinsen*
interim accounts	*Zwischenabschluß*
intermediate court of appeal	*Oberlandesgericht*

intra-group profit/loss	*Zwischengewinn/-verlust*
inventories, stocks	*Vorräte*
investment allowances	*Investitionszulagen*
investment subsidies	*Investitionszuschüsse*
investments	*Wertpapiere*
item-by-item valuation	*Einzelbewertung*

J

joint proprietor	*Mitunternehmer*
joint stock corporation	*Aktiengesellschaft* (AG)
Joint Stock Corporation Act	*Aktiengesetz* (AktG)

L

legal entity fiction	*Fiktion der rechtlichen Einheit* (Einheitsgrundsatz)
legal mergers	*Fusionen*
legal reserve	*gesetzliche Rücklage*
lessee	*Leasingnehmer*
lessor	*Leasinggeber*
letter to shareholders (shareholders' letter)	*Aktionärsbrief*
liabilities	*Verbindlichkeiten*
limited liability company	*Gesellschaft mit beschränkter Haftung* (GmbH)
limited partner	*Kommanditist*
limited partnership	*Kommanditgesellschaft* (KG)
limited partnership with shares	*Kommanditgesellschaft auf Aktien* (KGaA)
long-term made-to-order production	*langfristige Auftragsfertigung*
loss brought forward	*Verlustvortrag*
loss for the year	*Jahresfehlbetrag*
low-value business goods	*geringwertige Wirtschaftsgüter*
lower attributable value	*niedrigerer beizulegender Wert*

M

management report	*Lagebericht*
mandatory reserves	*Zwangsrücklagen*
minority shareholders	*Minderheitenanteile*
Montan co-determination	*Montan-Mitbestimmung*
mortgage bank	*Hypothekenbank*
motor vehicle tax	*Kraftfahrzeugsteuer* (KraftSt)
multiple-voting shares	*Mehrstimmrechtsaktien*
mutual insurance society	*Versicherungsverein auf Gegenseitigkeit*

N

negative consolidation difference	*passivischer Unterschiedsbetrag*
net assets increase theory	*Reinvermögenszugangstheorie*
non-full-pay-out lease	*Teilamortisationsvertrag*
notes (on the financial statements)	*Anhang*

O

Ordinance Regulating the Income Tax Law	*Einkommensteuer-Durchführungsverordnung* (EStDV)
ordinary shares	Stammaktien
organic current value balance sheet	*organische Tageswertbilanz*
other operating expenses	*sonstige betriebliche Aufwendungen*
other operating revenues	*sonstige betriebliche Erträge*

P

pagatoric principle	*pagatorisches Prinzip*
part-of-the-whole value	*Teilwert*
part-of-the-whole-value depreciation	*Teilwertabschreibung*
part-of-the-whole-value supposition	*Teilwertvermutung*
participating interest (participation)	*Beteiligung*
partnership	*Personengesellschaft*
pension fund	*Pensionskasse*
Pension Guaranty Association	*Pensionssicherungsverein*
pension provision	*Pensionsrückstellung*
personally liable general partner	*Komplementär*
plant	*Betrieb*
pooling of interests method	*Interessenzusammenführungsmethode*
positive consolidation difference	*aktivischer Unterschiedsbetrtag*
preference share	*Vorzugsaktie*
pre-paid expenses	*transitorische Aktiva*
principle of free collective bargaining	*Tarifautonomie*
principle of lower value	*Niederstwertprinzip*
principles of regular accounting	*Grundsätze ordnungsmäßiger Buchführung* (GoB)
principles of regular financial reporting	*Grundsätze ordnungsmäßiger Bilanzierung*
principles of regular stocktaking	*Grundsätze ordnungsmäßiger Inventur*
prior-year expenses	*periodenfremde Aufwendungen*
prior-year revenues	*periodenfremde Erträge*
private banker	*Privatbank*
producer co-operative	*Nutzungsgenossenschaft*

production costs	*Herstellungskosten*
production unit depreciation method	*leistungsabhängige Abschreibung*
profit and loss account	*Gewinn-und Verlustrechnung*
profit and loss transfer agreement	*Gewinn-und Verlustübernahme-Vertrag*
profit brought forward	*Gewinnvortrag*
profit distribution function	*Gewinnverteilungsfunktion*
profit for the year	*Jahresüberschuß*
profit reserves	*Gewinnrücklagen*
proportional consolidation	*Quotenkonsolidierung*
protection of creditors	*Gläubigerschutz*
provision	*Rückstellung*
provision for a social plan	*Sozialplanrückstellung*
provision for liberal settlement of customers complaints	*Kulanzrückstellung*
provision for losses on uncompleted transactions	*Rückstellung für drohende Verluste aus schwebenden Geschäften*
provision for pension	*Pensionsrückstellung*
provision for product liability	*Produkthaftungsrückstellung*
provision for uncertain liabilities	*Rückstellung für ungewisse Verbindlichkeiten*
proxy voting	*Depotstimmrecht*
prudence principle	*Vorsichtsprinzip*
public corporations	*Publikumsgesellschaften*
public-sector enterprises	*öffentliche Betriebe in privatrechtlicher Form*
purchase method	Erwerbsmethode
purchasing co-operative	*Einkaufsgenossenschaft*

Q

quarterly reports	*Quartalsberichte*
quoted corporation	*börsennotierte Kapitalgesellschaft*

R

real property tax	*Grundsteuer* (GrSt)
real property transfer tax	*Grunderwerbsteuer* (GrESt)
realization principle	*Realisationsprinzip*
recognition of assets and liabilities	*Bilanzansatz*
Reconstruction Loan Corporation	Kreditanstalt für Wiederaufbau
redemption premium on loans	*Verbindlichkeitsdisagio*
reducing balance depreciation	*geometrisch-degressive Abschreibung*
reduction of subscribed capital	*Kapitalherabsetzung*
regional bank	*Regionalbank*

regional central bank	*Landeszentralbank*
regional court	*Landgericht*
registered co-operative	*eingetragene Genossenschaft*
registered share	*Namensaktie*
regular capital reduction	*ordentliche Kapitalherabsetzung*
Regulation concerning *Wirtschaftsprüfer*	*Wirtschaftsprüferordnung*
research costs	*Forschungskosten*
reserve for own shares	*Rücklage für eigene Aktien*
revaluation method	*Neubewertungsmethode*
revealed value principle	*Wertaufhellungsprinzip*
reverse authoritativeness principle	*umgekehrte Maßgeblichkeit*
rights of control	*Kontrollrechte*

S

salary tax	*Lohnsteuer* (LSt)
schedule of fixed assets	*Anlagespiegel*
selling expenses	*Vetriebskosten*
shares	*Aktien*
simplified capital reduction	*vereinfachte Kapitalherabsetzung*
sole proprietorship	*Einzelunternehmung*
source theory	*Quellentheorie*
special bank	*Spezialbank*
special business property	*Sonderbetriebsvermögen*
special form of the limited partnership	*Kapitalgesellschaft & Co. KG*
special item with a reserve component	*Sonderposten mit Rücklageanteil*
special lease	*Spezialleasing*
special register where cooperatives are recorded	*Genossenschaftsregister*
static balance sheet school	*statische Bilanzlehre*
statutory reserves	*satzungsmäßige Rücklagen*
stock exchange	*Aktienbörse*
Stock Exchange Act	*Börsengesetz* (BörsG)
Stock Exchange Listing Requirements Order	*Börsenzulassungsverordnung* (BörsZulV)
stocktaking	*Inventur*
straight-line depreciation	*lineare Abschreibung*
strict lower value principle	*strenges Niederstwertprinzip*
sub-account	*Unterkonto*
subscribed capital	*gezeichnetes Kapital*
subscribed capital of a limited liability company	*Stammkapital*
subscribed capital of a joint stock corporation	*Grundkapital*
subsequent aquisition costs	*nachträgliche Anschaffungskosten*

subsequent consolidation	*Folgekonsolidierung*
subsidies (taxable grants)	*Zuschüsse*
Supervision of Insurance Companies Act	*Versicherungsaufsichtsgesetz*
supervisory board	*Aufsichtsrat*
sworn auditor	*vereidigter Buchprüfer*
systematic depreciation	*planmäßige Abschreibung*

T

tangible assets	*Sachanlagen*
tax on drafts and bills of exchange	*Wechselsteuer*
taxable income	*zu versteuerndes Einkommen*
temporal method	*Zeitbezugsmethode*
theory of permanent average balances	*Bodensatztheorie*
top tax rate	*Spitzensteuersatz*
total cost method	*Gesamtkostenverfahren*
trade tax	*Gewerbesteuer*
trade tax on earnings	*Gewerbeertragsteuer* (GewErtSt)
trading capital tax	*Gewerbekapitalsteuer* (GewKapSt)
transactions taxes	*Verkehrsteuern*

U

unified management	*einheitliche Leitung*
uniform valuation	*einheitliche Bewertung*
union	*Gewerkschaft*
universal bank	*Universalbank*

V

valuation	*Bewertung*
value-added tax	*Mehrwertsteuer* (MWSt)

W

weaker principle of lower value	*gemildertes Niederstwertprinzip*
workers' council	*Betriebsrat*
write-off for non-marketability	*Gängigkeitsabschreibungen*
write-up	*Zuschreibung*
writing back	*Wertaufholung*

Bibliography

CHAPTER 1 GERMANY: THE COUNTRY

Hübner, E. and Rohlfs, H.-H. (1991) *Jahrbuch der Bundesrepublik Deutschland*, Munich: C.H. Beck.

Institut der deutschen Wirtschaft (ed.) (1991) *Zahlen zur wirtschaftlichen Entwicklung der Bundesrepublik Deutschland*, Cologne: Deutscher Instituts-Verlag.

Model, O., Creifelds, C. and Lichtenberger, G. (1991) *Staatsbürger-Taschenbuch*, 25th edn, Munich: C.H. Beck.

Reuter, K. (1985) *Föderalismus. Grundlagen und Wirkungen in der Bundesrepublik Deutschland*, 2nd edn, Heidelberg: R. von Decker's Verlag.

Statistisches Bundesamt (ed.) (1992) *Statistisches Jahrbuch 1992*, Wiesbaden: Metzler Poeschel.

CHAPTER 2 FORMS OF BUSINESS ORGANIZATION AND CORPORATE GOVERNANCE

Hansen, H. (1980) 'Die Gesellschafter größerer GmbH', *GmbH-Rundschau*, pp. 99–102.

Ordelheide, D. (1986) 'Der Konzern als Gegenstand der betriebswirtschaftlichen Forschung', *Betriebswirtschaftliche Forschung und Praxis*, pp. 293–312.

Theisen, M.R. (1991) *Der Konzern*, Stuttgart: Poeschel.

Wiedemann, H. (1980) *Gesellschaftsrecht* I. *Grundlagen*, Munich: Vahlen.

Wöhe, G. (1990) *Einführung in die Allgemeine Betriebswirtschaftslehre*, 17th edn, Munich: Vahlen, pp. 333–90.

CHAPTER 3 FINANCE AND CAPITAL MARKETS

Bundesbank (1992) 'Längerfristige Entwicklung der Finanzierungsstrukturen westdeutscher Unternehmen', *Monatsberichte der Deutschen Bundesbank* 10, pp. 25–39.

Bundesministerium der Finanzen (1979) *Bericht der Studienkommission 'Grundsatzfragen der Kreditwirtschaft'*, Bonn: Stollfuss-Verlag.

Commerzbank (ed.) (1988) *Eigenkapitalquoten der Unternehmen weltweit verbessert*, Bericht der Abteilung Volkswirtschaft D89, 22 July.

Institut der deutschen Wirtschaft (ed.) (1993) *Internationale Wirtschaftszahlen*, Cologne: Deutscher Instituts-Verlag.

Ordelheide, D. (1986) 'Der Konzern als Gegenstand der betriebswirtschaftlichen Forschung', *Betriebswirtschaftliche Forschung und Praxis*, pp. 293–312.

Perlitz, M., Küpper, H. and Löbler, H. (1985) 'Vergleich der Eigenkapitalausstattung deutscher, US-amerikanischer und britischer Unternehmen', *Zeitschrift für Unternehmens-und Gesellschaftsrecht*, pp. 16–49.

Schierenbeck, H. (1981) *Institutionelle Bankbetriebslehre. Eine Einführung in die institutionellen Grundlagen des Geld-, Finanz-und Bankwesens*, Stuttgart: Poeschel-Verlag.

Schneider, H., Hellwig, H. and Kingsman, D.J. (1986) *The German Banking System*, 4th edn, Frankfurt am Main: Fritz Knapp.

Süchting, J. (1989) *Finanzmanagement. Theorie und Politik der Unternehmensfinanzierung*, 5th edn, Wiesbaden: Gabler.

Wenger, E. (1990) 'Die Rolle der Banken in der Industriefinanzierung und in der Unternehmenskontrolle am Beispiel der Bundesrepublik Deutschland', *Wirtschaftspolitische Blätter* 2/3, pp. 155–68.

CHAPTER 4 CO-DETERMINATION AND THE LABOUR MARKET

Backhaus, J. and Nutzinger, H.G. (eds) (1986) *Codetermination*, Berlin, Heidelberg and New York: Springer.

Chmielewicz, K., Grossmann, A., Inhoffen, A.O. and Lutter, M. (1977) 'Die Mitbestimmung im Aufsichtsrat und Vorstand. Darstellung, Vergleich und Kritik der rechtlichen Regelungen aus juristischer und betriebswirtschaftlicher Sicht', *Die Betriebswirtschaft*, pp. 105–45.

Kittner, M. (1991) *Gewerkschaftsjahrbuch 1991. Daten - Fakten - Analysen*, Cologne: Bund.

Kurth, J. (1958) *Geschichte der Gewerkschaften in Deutschland*, 2nd edn, Hanover and Frankfurt am Main: Goedel-Verlag.

Nutzinger, H.G. (ed.) (1982) *Mitbestimmung und Arbeiterselbstverwaltung. Praxis und Programmatik*, Frankfurt am Main and New York: Campus-Verlag.

Summers, C.W. (1979) 'Worker participation in the United States and the Federal Republic: a comparative study from an American perspective', *Recht der Arbeit*, pp. 257–66.

Wächter, H. (1983) *Mitbestimmung*, Munich: Vahlen.

CHAPTER 5 TAXATION

Fuisting, B. (1902) *Grundsätze der Steuerlehre*.

Jacobs, O. (ed.) (1988) *Unternehmensbesteuerung und Rechtsform*, Munich: C.H. Beck.

Lanfenberger, H. (1956) 'Die Einkommensbesteuerung', in W. Gerhoff and F. Neumark (eds) *Handbuch der Finanzwissenschaft* II, Tübingen: J.C.B. Mohr, pp. 447–501.

Neumark, F. (1947) *Theorie und Praxis der modernen Einkommensbesteuerung*, Berne.
Rose, G. (1986) *Betrieb und Steuer* I. *Die Ertragsteuern*, 9th edn, Wiesbaden: Gabler.
Schanz, G. (1896) 'Der Einkommensteuerbegriff und die Einkommensteuergesetze', *Finanz-Archiv*, pp. 1–87.
Schneeloch, D. (1986) *Besteuerung und betriebliche Steuerpolitik* I. *Besteuerung*, Munich: Vahlen.
Wöhe, G. (1989) 'Überblick über die Konzernbesteuerung', in K. Küting and C. Weber (eds) *Handbuch der Konzernrechnungslegung*, Stuttgart: Schäffer, pp. 189–244.

CHAPTER 6 AN INTRODUCTION TO FINANCIAL REPORTING IN GERMANY

Section 1 The role of the financial statements

Baetge, J. (1976) 'Zu den Rechnungslegungszwecken des Jahresabschlusses', in J. Baetge, A. Moxter and D. Schneider (eds) *Bilanzfragen. Festschrift für Ulrich Leffson*, Düsseldorf: IdW-Verlag, pp. 11–30.
Ballwieser, W. (1990) 'Ist das Maßgeblichkeitsprinzip überholt?', *Betriebswirtschaftliche Forschung und Praxis*, pp. 477–498.
Castan, E. (1987) 'Zweck und Inhalt des Jahresabschlusses und Lageberichts', in E. Castan, G. Heymann, E. Müller, D. Ordelheide and E. Scheffler (eds) *Beck'sches Handbuch der Rechnungslegung*, Munich: C.H. Beck, B100.
Coenenberg, A.G. (1992) *Jahresabschluß und Jahresabschlußanalyse*, 13th edn, Landsberg am Lech: Moderne Industrie.
Döllerer, G. (1988) 'Handels- und Steuerbilanz nach dem Bilanzrichtlinien-Gesetz', in W. Mellwig, A. Moxter and D. Ordelheide (eds) *Einzel- und Konzernabschluß*, Wiesbaden: Gabler, pp. 91–104.
Dziadkowski, D. (1992) 'Verhältnis von Handels-und Steuerbilanz', in E. Castan, G. Heymann, E. Müller, D. Ordelheide and E. Scheffler (eds) *Beck'sches Handbuch der Rechnungslegung*, Munich: C.H. Beck, B120.
Fleischer, K. (1987) *Die aktienrechtliche Rechnungslegung als Informationsinstrument der finanziellen Lage der Unternehmung. Gegenwärtiger Stand und Weiterentwicklung unter Berücksichtigung des Bilanzrichtlinien-Gesetzes*, Frankfurt am Main, Berne and New York: Lang-Verlag.
Haeger, B. (1989) *Der Grundsatz der umgekehrten Maßgeblichkeit in der Praxis. Bilanzierungsprobleme unter besonderer Berücksichtigung des Sonderpostens mit Rücklageanteil*, Stuttgart: Schäffer-Verlag.
Haller, A. (1992) 'The Relationship of Financial and Tax Accounting in Germany: A Major Reason for Accounting Disharmony in Europe', *The International Journal of Accounting*, pp. 310–23.
Moxter, A. (1984) *Bilanzlehre* I. *Einführung in die Bilanztheorie*, 3rd edn, Wiesbaden: Gabler.
Moxter, A. (1987) 'Zum Sinn und Zweck des handelsrechtlichen Jahresabschlusses nach neuem Recht', in H. Havermann (ed.) *Bilanz-und Konzernrecht. Festschrift für R. Goerdeler*, Düsseldorf: IdW-Verlag, pp. 361–74.
Ordelheide, D. (1990) 'Soft transformations of accounting rules of the 4th Directive in Germany', *Les Cahiers Internationaux de la Comptabilité*, No. 3, pp. 1–15.

Raupach, A. (1989) 'Maßgeblichkeit und umgekehrte Maßgeblichkeit', in W. Mellwig, A. Moxter and D. Ordelheide (eds) *Handels- und Steuerbilanz 2*, Wiesbaden: Gabler, pp. 105–17.

Schildbach, T. (1989) 'Überlegungen zur Zukunft des Verhältnisses von Handels- und Steuerbilanz', *Betriebswirtschaftliche Forschung und Praxis*, pp. 123–40.

Schneider, D. (1983) 'Rechtsfindung durch Deduktion von Grundsätzen ordnungsmäßiger Buchführung aus gesetzlichen Jahresabschlußzwecken?', *Steuer und Wirtschaft*, pp. 141–60.

Schneider, D. (1991) 'Die Anfänge der "Steuerbilanz" und die Entstehung des Maßgeblichkeitsprinzips', in N. Herzig (ed.) *Betriebswirtschaftliche Steuerlehre und Steuerberatung. Festschrift Rose*, Wiesbaden: Gabler, pp. 175–90.

Stobbe, T. (1991) *Die Verknüpfung von handels- und steuerrechtlicher Rechnungslegung*, Berlin: Duncker & Humblot-Verlag.

Wagner, F.W. (1990) 'Die umgekehrte Maßgeblichkeit der Handels- für die Steuerbilanz. Eine Analyse ihrer ökonomischen Wirkungen', *Steuer und Wirtschaft*, pp. 3–14.

Wilhelmi, H. (1965) 'Das neue Aktiengesetz' 1, *Aktiengesellschaft*, pp. 153–5.

Section 2 A legalistic system

Barth, K. (1953) *Die Entwicklung des deutschen Bilanzrechts* I. *Handelsrecht*, Stuttgart: Selbstverlag Kuno Barth.

Barth, K. (1955) *Die Entwicklung des deutschen Bilanzrechts* II. *Steuerrecht*, Stuttgart: Selbstverlag Kuno Barth.

Biener, H. and Berneke, W. (1986) *Bilanzrichtlinien-Gesetz*, Düsseldorf: IDW-Verlag.

Busse von Colbe, W. and Reinhard, H. (eds) (1989) *Zwischenberichterstattung nach neuem Recht für börsennotierte Unternehmen. Empfehlungen des Arbeitskreises 'Externe Unternehmensrechnung' der Schmalenbach-Gesellschaft/Deutsche Gesellschaft für Betriebswirtschaft eV*, Stuttgart: Schäffer.

Busse von Colbe, W., Müller, E. and Reinhard, H. (eds) (1989) *Aufstellung von Konzernabschlüssen, Empfehlungen des Arbeitskreises 'Externe Unternehmensrechnung der Schmalenbach-Gesellschaft/Deutsche Gesellschaft für Betriebswirtschaft eV*, 2nd edn, Düsseldorf and Frankfurt am Main: Handelsblatt.

Busse von Colbe, W., Geiger, K., Haase, H., Reinhard, H. and Schmitt, G. (eds) (1991) *Earnings according to the DVFA/SG Method: Joint Recommendations of the DVFA Commission for Methodology of the Financial Analysis and of the Working Group 'External Company Accounting' of the Schmalenbach-Gesellschaft*, Stuttgart: Schäffer.

Helmrich, H. (1986) *Bilanzrichtlinien-Gesetz. Texte, Stellungnahmen, Protokolle*, Munich: C.H. Beck.

Schröer, T. (1993) 'Historical development of company law in Germany (1861–1900)', *The European Accounting Review*, No. 2 (forthcoming).

Section 3 Bookkeeping, charts of accounts and stocktaking

Betriebswirtschaftlicher Ausschuß des Bundesverbandes der deutschen Industrie (1986) *Industrie-Kontenrahmen – IKR*, 6th edn, Bergisch-Gladbach: Heider-Verlag.

Bieg, H. (1987) 'Buchführungspflichten und Buchführungsvorschriften', in E. Castan, G. Heymann, E. Müller, D. Ordelheide and E. Scheffler (eds) *Beck'sches Handbuch der Rechnungslegung*, Munich: C.H. Beck, A100.

Eisele, W. (1990) *Technik des betrieblichen Rechnungswesens*, 4th edn, Munich: C.H. Beck.

Korth, H.-M. (1990) *Industriekontenrahmen*, Munich: C.H. Beck.

Schär, J.F. (1932) *Buchhaltung und Bilanz auf wirtschaftlicher, rechtlicher und mathematischer Grundlage für Juristen, Ingenieure und Kaufleute und Studierende der Betriebswirtschaftslehre*, Berlin: Springer.

Schmalenbach, E. (1927) 'Der Kontenrahmen', *Zeitschrift für handelswissenschaftliche Forschung*, pp. 385–402.

Schmalenbach, E. (1939) *Der Kontenrahmen. Mit dem Anhang: Kontenpläne und Kontentabellen*, 6th edn, Leipzig: G.A. Gloeckner.

Uhlig, B. (1987) 'Inventur', in E. Castan, G. Heymann, E. Müller, D. Ordelheide and E. Scheffler (eds) *Beck'sches Handbuch der Rechnungslegung*, Munich: C.H. Beck, A20.

CHAPTER 7 THE ACCOUNTS OF INDIVIDUAL ENTERPRISES

Section 1 The obligation to prepare accounts

Castan, E. (1992) 'Aufstellung und Feststellung des Jahresabschlusses', in E. Castan, G. Heymann, E. Müller, D. Ordelheide and E. Scheffler (eds) *Beck'sches Handbuch der Rechnungslegung*, Munich: C.H. Beck, B101.

Section 2 GoB and the 'true and fair view'

Ballwieser, W. (1989) 'Grundsätze ordnungsmäßiger Bilanzierung', in E. Castan, G. Heymann, E. Müller, D. Ordelheide and E. Scheffler (eds) *Beck'sches Handbuch der Rechnungslegung*, Munich: C.H. Beck, B105.

Beisse, H. (1984) 'Zum Verhältnis von Bilanzrecht und Betriebswirtschaftslehre', *Steuer und Wirtschaft*, pp. 1–14.

Beisse, H. (1988) 'Die Generalnorm des neuen Bilanzrechts', in B. Knobbe-Keuk, F. Klein and A. Moxter (eds) *Handelsrecht und Steuerrecht. Festschrift für G. Döellerer*, Düsseldorf: IdW-Verlag, pp. 25–44.

Budde, W.D., and Förschle, G. (1988) 'Das Verhältnis des true and fair view zu den Grundsätzen ordnungsmäßiger Buchführung und zu den Einzelvorschriften', in W. Mellwig, A. Moxter and D. Ordelheide (eds) *Einzel- und Konzernabschluß*, Wiesbaden: Gabler, pp. 27–46.

Döllerer, G. (1959) 'Die Grundsätze ordnungsmäßiger Bilanzierung, deren Entstehung und Ermittlung', *Betriebs-Berater*, pp. 1217–21.

Leffson, U. (1987) *Die Grundsätze ordnungsmäßiger Buchführung*, 7th edn, Düsseldorf: IdW-Verlag.

Moxter, A. (1985) 'Das System der handelsrechtlichen Grundsätze ordnungsmäßiger Bilanzierung', in G. Gross (ed.) *Der Wirtschaftsprüfer im Schnittpunkt nationaler und internationaler Entwicklungen*, Festschrift für K.v. Wysocki, Düsseldorf: IdW-Verlag, pp. 17–28.

Müller, W. (1988) 'Die ordnungsmäßige Bilanzierung und ihre Kodifizierung nach neuem Bilanzrecht', in W. Mellwig, A. Moxter and D. Ordelheide (eds) *Einzel- und Konzernabschluß*, Wiesbaden: Gabler, pp. 3–26.

Ordelheide, D. (1993) 'Externes Rechnungswesen', in *Vahlens Kompendium der Betriebswirtschaftslehre 2*, 3rd edn, Munich: Vahlen, pp. 219–314.

Ordelheide, D. (1993) 'The true and fair view, a German and a European perspective', *European Accounting Review*, No. 1, pp. 81–90.

Schneider, D. (1983) 'Rechtsfindung durch Deduktion von Grundsätzen ordnungsmäßiger Buchführung aus gesetzlichen Jahresabschlußzwecken?', *Steuer und Wirtschaft*, pp. 141–60.

Section 3 Financial statement formats

Adler, H., Düring, W. and Schmaltz, K. (1989) *Rechnungslegung und Prüfung der Unternehmen* I–III, 5th edn, rev. K.-H. Forster, R. Goerdeler, J. Lanfermann, H.P. Müller, G. Siepe, K. Stollberg and S. Weirich, Stuttgart: Poeschel-Verlag.

Ballwieser, W., and Häger, R. (1991) *Jahresabschlüsse mittelgroßer Kapitalgesellschaften. Ausweis, Gestaltung, Berichterstattung. Ergebnisse einer Untersuchung von 150 mittelgroßen Kapitalgesellschaften*, Düsseldorf: IdW-Verlag.

Borchert, D. (1990) 'Gewinn- und Verlustrechnung. Gliederung', in K. Küting and C.P. Weber (eds) *Handbuch der Rechnungslegung*, 3rd edn, Stuttgart: Schäffer, pp. 1483–580.

Castan, E. (1987) 'Grundsätze der Gliederung', in E. Castan, G. Heymann, E. Müller, D. Ordelheide and E. Scheffler (eds) *Beck'sches Handbuch der Rechnungslegung*, Munich: C.H. Beck, B141, B146.

Castan, E. (1987) 'Gliederung der Bilanz', in E. Castan, G. Heymann, E. Müller, D. Ordelheide and E. Scheffler (eds) *Beck'sches Handbuch der Rechnungslegung*, Munich: C.H. Beck, B200.

Castan, E. (1991) 'Anlage zur Bilanz der publizitätspflichtigen Personenunternehmung', in E. Castan, G. Heymann, E. Müller, D. Ordelheide and E. Scheffler (eds) *Beck'sches Handbuch der Rechnungslegung*, Munich: C.H. Beck, B740.

Knop, W. (1990) 'Gliederung der Bilanz', in K. Küting and C.P. Weber (eds) *Handbuch der Rechnungslegung*, 3rd edn, Stuttgart: Schäffer, pp. 1153–207.

Ordelheide, D. (1992) 'Handelsbilanz', in K. Chmielewicz and M. Schweitzer (eds) *Handwörterbuch des Rechnungswesens*, 3rd edn, Stuttgart: Poeschel.

Ordelheide, D. (1993) 'Externes Rechnungswesen', *Vahlens Kompendium der Betriebswirtschaftslehre 2*, 3rd edn, Munich: Vahlen, pp. 219–314.

Schildbach, T. (1992) *Der handelsrechtliche Jahresabschluß*, 3rd edn, Herne and Berlin: Neue Wirtschafts-Briefe.

Treuarbeit (ed.) (1990) *Jahres- und Konzernabschlüsse '88. Ausweis, Gestaltung, Berichterstattung*, Düsseldorf: IdW-Verlag.

Section 4 Recognition of assets and liabilities

Section 4.1 Assets

Ballwieser, W. (1987) 'Grundsätze der Aktivierung und Passivierung', in E. Castan, G. Heymann, E. Müller, D. Ordelheide and E. Scheffler (eds) *Beck'sches Handbuch der Rechnungslegung*, Munich: C.H. Beck, B131, B134, B137.

Ballwieser, W. and Häger, R. (1991) *Jahresabschlüsse mittelgroßer Kapitalgesellschaften. Ausweis, Gestaltung, Berichterstattung. Ergebnisse einer Untersuchung von 150 mittelgroßen Kapitalgesellschaften*, Düsseldorf: IdW.

Brezing, K. (1985) 'Der Gegenstand der Bilanzierung und seine Zurechnung in Handels- und Steuerrecht', in K. von Wysocki and J. Schulze-Osterloh (eds) *Handbuch des Jahresabschlusses in Einzeldarstellungen* I/4, Cologne: Otto Schmidt-Verlag.

Eibelshäuser, M. (1983) *Immaterielle Anlagewerte in der höchstrichterlichen Finanzrechtsprechung*, Wiesbaden: Gabler.

Flume, W. (1973) 'Die Frage der bilanziellen Behandlung von Leasing-Verhältnissen', *Der Betrieb*, pp. 1661–7.

Glasel, L. (1991) 'Leasing', in E. Castan, G. Heymann, E. Müller, D. Ordelheide and E. Scheffler (eds) *Beck'sches Handbuch der Rechnungslegung*, Munich: C.H. Beck, B710.

Hauptfachausschuß des Instituts der Wirtschaftsprüfer (1989) 'Stellungnahme 1/1989. Zur Bilanzierung beim Leasinggeber', *Die Wirtschaftsprüfung*, pp. 625–7.

Havermann, H. (1986) 'Ansatzvorschriften für Kapitalgesellschaften', *Betriebswirtschaftliche Forschung und Praxis*, pp. 114–28.

Hüttemann, U. (1985) 'Posten der aktiven und passiven Rechnungsabgrenzung', in K. von Wysocki and J. Schulze-Osterloh (eds) *Handbuch des Jahresabschlusses in Einzeldarstellungen* II/8, Cologne: Otto Schmidt-Verlag.

Moxter, A. (1982) *Betriebswirtschaftliche Gewinnermittlung*, Tübingen: J.C.B. Mohr.

Moxter, A. (1985) *Bilanzrechtsprechung*, 2nd edn, Tübingen: J.C.B. Mohr.

Ordelheide, D. and Hartle, J. (1986) 'Rechnungslegung und Gewinnermittlung von Kapitalgesellschaften nach dem Bilanzrichtlinien-Gesetz', *GmbH-Rundschau*, pp. 9–19, 38–42.

Runge, B. (1990) 'Leasing im Steuerrecht des letzten Jahrzehnts', *Der Betrieb*, pp. 959–62.

Treuarbeit (ed.) (1990) *Jahres- und Konzernabschlüsse '88. Ausweis, Gestaltung, Berichterstattung*, Düsseldorf: IdW-Verlag.

Woerner, L. (1989) 'Der schwebende Vertrag im Gefüge der Grundsätze ordnungsmäßiger Bilanzierung. Vollständigkeitsgebot, Vorsichtsprinzip, Realisationsprinzip', in W. Mellwig, A. Moxter and D. Ordelheide (eds) *Handels- und Steuerbilanz 2*, Wiesbaden: Gabler, pp. 35–55.

Section 4.2 Liabilities

Biener, H. (1988) 'Rückstellungen für drohende Verluste aus schwebenden Geschäften bei Dauerrechtsverhältnissen', in B. Knobbe-Keuk, F. Klein and A. Moxter (eds) *Handelsrecht und Steuerrecht. Festschrift für G. Döllerer*, Düsseldorf: IdW-Verlag, pp. 45–64.

Clemm, H., and Nonnenmacher, R. (1990) 'Kommentierung von § 249 HGB Rückstellungen', in W.D. Budde, H. Clemm, M. Pankow and M. Sarx (eds), *Beck'scher Bilanzkommentar*, 2nd edn, Munich: C.H. Beck, pp. 297–358.

Coenenberg, A. (1986) 'Aufwandsrückstellungen für Substanzerhaltung', *Betriebs-Berater*, pp. 910–15.

Deutsche Treuhandgesellschaft (1987) *Betriebliche Altersversorgung und Jahresabschluß*, Düsseldorf: Eigenverlag.

Döllerer, G. (1987) 'Ansatz und Bewertung von Rückstellungen in der neueren Rechtsprechung des Bundesfinanzhofes', *Deutsches Steuerrecht*, pp. 67–72.

Groh, M. (1989) 'Abzinsung von Rückstellungen', in W. Mellwig, A. Moxter and D. Ordelheide (eds) *Handels- und Steuerbilanz 2*, Wiesbaden: Gabler, pp. 119–26.

Jacobs, O. (1988) 'Berechnung von Rückstellungen in der Steuerbilanz', *Deutsches Steuerrecht*, pp. 238–47.

Kupsch, P. (1989) 'Neuere Entwicklungen bei der Bilanzierung und Bewertung von Rückstellungen', *Der Betrieb*, pp. 53–62.

Moxter, A. (1989) 'Rückstellungen für ungewisse Verbindlichkeiten und Höchstwertprinzip', *Betriebs-Berater*, pp. 945–9.

Pankow, M., and Pieger, J. (1990) 'Kommentierung von § 249 HGB Rückstellungen für Pensionen und ähnliche Verpflichtungen', in W.D. Budde, H. Clemm, M. Pankow and M. Sarx (eds) *Beck'scher Bilanzkommentar*, 2nd edn, Munich: C.H. Beck, pp. 359–408.

Scheffler, E. (1989) 'Rückstellungen', in E. Castan, G. Heymann, E. Müller, D. Ordelheide and E. Scheffler (eds) *Beck'sches Handbuch der Rechnungslegung*, Munich: C.H. Beck, B233.

Section 5 Valuation rules

Section 5.1 Basic valuation principles

Forster, K.-H. (1985) 'Bewertungsstetigkeit – was sie ist und was sie nicht ist', in G. Gross (ed.) *Der Wirtschaftsprüfer im Schnittpunkt nationaler und internationaler Entwicklungen*, Festschrift für K.v. Wysocki, Düsseldorf: IdW-Verlag, pp. 29–43.

Hauptfachausschuß des Instituts der Wirtschaftsprüfer (1975) 'Stellungnahme 2/1975. Zur Berücksichtigung der Substanzerhaltung bei der Ermittlung des Jahresergebnisses', *Die Wirtschaftsprüfung*, p. 614.

Hauptfachausschuß des Instituts der Wirtschaftsprüfer (1976) 'Stellungnahme 3/1976. Zur Bilanzierung bei Personengesellschaften', *Die Wirtschaftsprüfung*, pp. 114–21.

Koch, H. (1957) 'Die Problematik des Niederstwertprinzips', *Die Wirtschaftsprüfung*, pp. 1–6, 31–5, 60–3.

Leffson, U. (1987) *Die Grundsätze ordnungsmäßiger Buchführung*, 7th edn, Düsseldorf: IdW-Verlag.

Mahlberg, W. (1923) *Bilanztechnik und Bewertung bei schwankender Währung*, Leipzig.

Schmalenbach, E. (1956) *Dynamische Bilanz*, 4th edn, Leipzig: G.A. Gloeckner.

Schmidt, F. (1929) *Die organische Tageswertbilanz*, 3rd edn, Leipzig: G.A. Gloeckner.

Schneider, D. (1976) 'Realisationsprinzip und Einkommensbegriff', in J. Baetge, A. Moxter and D. Schneider (eds) *Bilanzfragen. Festschrift für Ulrich Leffson*, Düsseldorf: IdW-Verlag, pp. 103–17.

Siegel, T. (1987) 'Allgemeine Bewertungsgrundsätze', in E. Castan, G. Heymann, E. Müller, D. Ordelheide and E. Scheffler (eds) *Beck'sches Handbuch der Rechnungslegung*, Munich: C.H. Beck, B161.

Section 5.2 Acquisition cost and production cost

Küting, K. (1989) 'Aktuelle Probleme bei der Ermittlung der handelsrechtlichen Herstellungskosten', *Betriebs-Berater*, pp. 587–96.

Moxter, A. (1988) 'Aktivierungspflichtige Herstellungskosten in Handels- und Steuerbilanz', *Betriebs-Berater*, pp. 937–45.

Ordelheide, D. (1989) 'Anschaffungskosten', in E. Castan, G. Heymann, E. Müller, D. Ordelheide and E. Scheffler (eds) *Beck'sches Handbuch der Rechnungslegung*, Munich: C.H. Beck, B162.

Ordelheide, D. (1992) 'Herstellungskosten', in E. Castan, G. Heymann, E. Müller, D. Ordelheide and E. Scheffler (eds) *Beck'sches Handbuch der Rechnungslegung*, Munich: C.H. Beck, B163.

Ordelheide, D. (1992) 'Zum Verbot der Aktivierung von Vertriebskosten in den Herstellungskosten gemäß § 255 Abs. 2 Satz 6 HGB', in A. Moxter, H.P. Müller, R. Windmöller and K. von Wysocki (eds) *Rechnungslegung*, Düsseldorf: IdW-Verlag, pp. 507–18.

Ordelheide, D. (1993) 'Externes Rechnungswesen', *Vahlens Kompendium der Betriebswirtschaftslehre 2*, 3rd edn, Munich: Vahlen, pp. 219–314.

Selchert, F.W. (1986) 'Probleme der Unter- und Obergrenze von Herstellungskosten', *Betriebs-Berater*, pp. 2298–306.

Wohlgemuth, M. (1985) 'Die Herstellungskosten in Handels- und Steuerbilanz', in K. von Wysocki and J. Schulze-Osterloh (eds) *Handbuch des Jahresabschlusses in Einzeldarstellungen* I/10, Cologne: Otto Schmidt-Verlag.

Sections 5.3–6 Depreciation, write-offs and write-backs

Bundesministerium für Finanzen/Finanzminister (Finanzsenatoren) der Länder (eds) (1990) AfA-Tabellen.

Coenenberg, A. (1992) *Jahresabschluß und Jahresabschlußanalyse*, 13th edn, Landsberg am Lech: Moderne Industrie, pp. 110–25.

Knobbe-Keuk, B. (1989) *Bilanz- und Unternehmenssteuerrecht*, 7th edn, Cologne: Otto Schmidt-Verlag.

Nordmeyer, A. (1987) 'Sachanlagen', in E. Castan, G. Heymann, E. Müller, D. Ordelheide and E. Scheffler (eds) *Beck'sches Handbuch der Rechnungslegung*, Munich: C.H. Beck, B212.

Siegel, T. (1987) 'Besondere Bewertungsgrundsätze für das Anlagevermögen, das Umlaufvermögen und die Verbindlichkeiten', in E. Castan, G. Heymann, E. Müller, D. Ordelheide and E. Scheffler (eds) *Beck'sches Handbuch der Rechnungslegung*, Munich: C.H. Beck, B165.

Siegel, T. (1987) 'Bewertungswahlrechte und Möglichkeiten der Abweichung von den Bewertungsgrundsätzen', in E. Castan, G. Heymann, E. Müller, D. Ordelheide and E.

Scheffler (eds) *Beck'sches Handbuch der Rechnungslegung*, Munich: C.H. Beck, B167.

Siegel, T. (1991) 'Wertaufholung (Zuschreibung)', in E. Castan, G. Heymann, E. Müller, D. Ordelheide and E. Scheffler (eds) *Beck'sches Handbuch der Rechnungslegung*, Munich: C.H. Beck, B169.

Streim, H. (1983) 'Das Wertaufholungsgebot. Eine zweckmäßige handelsrechtliche Schutzvorschrift', *Die Wirtschaftsprüfung*, pp. 671–83.

Section 5.7 Particular valuation rules

Bundesministerium für Finanzen (1992) 'Anwendung der Lifo-Methode. Beachtung des Niederstwertprinzips, BMF-Schreiben vom 21.2.1992 - IV B2 - S 2147 - 1/92', *Der Betrieb*, p. 554.

Burkardt, D. (1988) *Grundsätze ordnungsmäßiger Bilanzierung für Fremdwährungsgeschäfte*, Düsseldorf: IdW-Verlag.

Busse von Colbe, W. (1992) 'Langfristige Fertigung, Prüfung der Rechnungslegung', in K. von Wysocki and A. Coenenberg (eds) *Handwörterbuch der Revision*, 2nd edn, Stuttgart: Poeschel, pp. 1198–207.

Döll, B. (1984) *Bilanzierung langfristiger Fertigung*, Frankfurt am Main: Lang-Verlag.

Forster, M. (1988) 'Gewinnrealisierung bei langfristiger Fertigung', in E. Castan, G. Heymann, E. Müller, D. Ordelheide and E. Scheffler (eds) *Beck'sches Handbuch der Rechnungslegung*, Munich: C.H. Beck, B700.

Freidank, C.C. (1989) 'Erfolgsrealisierung bei langfristigen Fertigungsprozessen', *Der Betrieb*, pp. 1197–204.

Hauptfachausschuß des Instituts der Wirtschaftsprüfer (1984) 'Stellungnahme des HFA 1/1984. Bilanzierungsfragen bei Zuwendungen, dargestellt am Beispiel finanzieller Zuwendungen der öffentlichen Hand', *Die Wirtschaftsprüfung*, p. 612.

Hauptfachausschuß des Instituts der Wirtschaftsprüfer (1984) 'Geänderter Entwurf einer Verlautbarung des HFA zur Währungsumrechnung im Jahres- und Konzernabschluß', *Fachnachrichten*, pp. 443–7.

Hauptfachausschuß des Instituts der Wirtschaftsprüfer (1984) 'Entwurf einer Verlautbarung des Hauptfachausschusses (HFA). Zur Währungsumrechnung im Jahres- und Konzernabschluß', *Die Wirtschaftsprüfung*, pp. 585–8.

Herzig, N. (ed.) (1990) *Vorratsbewertung nach der Lifo-Methode*, Cologne: Otto Schmidt-Verlag.

Section 6 Equity

Coenenberg, A. (1992) *Jahresabschluß und Jahresabschlußanalyse*, 13th edn, Landsberg am Lech: Moderne Industrie.

Heymann, G. (1987) 'Eigenkapital', in E. Castan, G. Heymann, E. Müller, D. Ordelheide and E. Scheffler (eds) *Beck'sches Handbuch der Rechnungslegung*, Munich: C.H. Beck, B231.

Section 7 Deferred taxation

Hennig, B. (1986) *Bilanzierung latenter Steuern*, Bochum: Studienverlag Dr. N. Brockmeyer.

Hille, K. (1982) *Latente Steuern im Einzel- und Konzernabschluß*, Frankfurt am Main: Lang-Verlag.

Laser, H. (1987) 'Latente Steuern', in E. Castan, G. Heymann, E. Müller, D. Ordelheide and E. Scheffler (eds) *Beck'sches Handbuch der Rechnungslegung*, Munich: C.H. Beck, B235.

Section 8 Hidden reserves

Harris, T.S. and Lang, M. (1992) *The Value-Relevance of German Accounting Measures. An Empirical Analysis*, working paper, New York: Columbia University.

Section 9 The notes on the accounts

Schülen, W. (1992) 'Grundsätze für den Inhalt des Anhangs', in E. Castan, G. Heymann, E. Müller, D. Ordelheide and E. Scheffler (eds) *Beck'sches Handbuch der Rechnungslegung*, Munich: C.H. Beck, B410.

CHAPTER 8 GROUP ACCOUNTS

Sections 1–2 History, function and legal regulation of group accounts

Busse von Colbe, W. (1985) 'Der Konzernabschluß im Rahmen des Bilanzrichtlinien-Gesetzes', *Zeitschrift für betriebswirtschaftliche Forschung*, pp. 761–82.

Busse von Colbe, W. (1987) 'Der Konzernabschluß als Bemessungsgrundlage für die Gewinnverwendung', in H. Havermann (ed.) *Bilanz- und Konzernrecht. Festschrift für R. Goerdeler*, Düsseldorf: IdW-Verlag, pp. 61–77.

Busse von Colbe, W., and Ordelheide, D. (1993) *Konzernabschlüsse*, 6th edn, Wiesbaden: Gabler.

Hartle, J. (1987) 'Grundlagen und Grundsätze des Konzernabschlusses', in E. Castan, G. Heymann, E. Müller, D. Ordelheide and E. Scheffler (eds) *Beck'sches Handbuch der Rechnungslegung*, Munich: C.H. Beck, C10.

Müller, H. (1988) 'Konzernabschluß nach neuem Bilanzrecht aus der Sicht des Analysten', in W. Mellwig, A. Moxter and D. Ordelheide (eds) *Einzelabschluß und Konzernabschluß*, Wiesbaden: Gabler, pp. 141–52.

Ordelheide, D. (1986) 'Der Konzern als Gegenstand betriebswirtschaftlicher Forschung', *Betriebswirtschaftliche Forschung und Praxis*, pp. 293–312.

Sahner, F. (1981) 'Die Bedeutung des Einheitsgrundsatzes für den Konzernabschluß im Aktiengesetz und in der 7. EG-Richtlinie', *Zeitschrift für betriebswirtschaftliche Forschung*, pp. 711–36.

Wentland, N. (1979) *Die Konzernbilanz als Bilanz der wirtschaftlichen Einheit Konzern*, Frankfurt am Main: Lang-Verlag.

Section 3 The obligation to prepare group accounts

Busse von Colbe, W. and Ordelheide, D. (1993) *Konzernabschlüsse*, 6th edn, Wiesbaden: Gabler.

IdW-Sonderausschuß Bilanzrichtlinien-Gesetz (1988) 'Entwurf einer Verlautbarung. Zur Aufstellungspflicht für einen Konzernabschluß und zur Abgrenzung des Konsolidierungskreises', *Die Wirtschaftsprüfung*, pp. 81–4.

IdW-Sonderausschuß Bilanzrichtlinien-Gesetz (1988) 'Stellungnahme SABI 1/1988. Zur Aufstellungspflicht für einen Konzernabschluß und zur Abgrenzung des Konsolidierungskreises', *Die Wirtschaftsprüfung*, pp. 340–3.

Kommission der Europäischen Gemeinschaften (1991) *Stellungnahme zur Gleichwertigkeit von Abschlüssen von Unternehmen aus Drittländern*, Brussels, 15 March 1991, XV/109/90 DE (2nd rev.).

Maas, U., and Schruff, W. (1986) 'Der Konzernabschluß nach neuem Recht', *Die Wirtschaftsprüfung*, pp. 201–10, 237–46.

Maas, U., and Schruff, W. (1991) 'Befreiende Konzernrechnungslegung von Mutterunternehmen mit Sitz außerhalb der EG', *Die Wirtschaftsprüfung*, pp. 765–72.

Odenwald, O. (1992) 'Aufstellungspflichten des Konzernabschlusses', in E. Castan, G. Heymann, E. Müller, D. Ordelheide and E. Scheffler (eds) *Beck'sches Handbuch der Rechnungslegung*, Munich: C.H. Beck, C200.

von Wysocki, K. (1987) 'Konzernabschluß: Aufstellungs- und Einbeziehungspflichten nach neuem Recht', *Die Wirtschaftsprüfung*, pp. 277–81.

Section 4 The scope of consolidation

Busse von Colbe, W. (1986) 'Die Equitymethode zur Bewertung von Beteiligungen im Konzernabschluß', in E. Gaugler, H.G. Meissner and N. Thom (eds) *Zukunftsaspekte der anwendungsorientierten Betriebswirtschaftslehre. Festschrift für E. Grochla*, Stuttgart: Poeschel-Verlag.

Busse von Colbe, W., Müller, E., and Reinhard, H. (eds) (1989) *Aufstellung von Konzernabschlüssen. Empfehlungen des Arbeitskreises 'Externe Unternehmenstechnung' der Schmalenbach-Gesellschaft/Deutsche Gesellschaft für Betriebswirtschaft eV*, 2nd edn, Düsseldorf and Frankfurt am Main: Handelsblatt.

Busse von Colbe, W. and Ordelheide, D. (1993) *Konzernabschlüsse*, 6th edn, Wiesbaden: Gabler.

Harms, J.E., and Knischewski, G. (1985) 'Quotenkonsolidierung versus Equity-Methode im Konzernabschluß', *Der Betrieb*, pp. 1353–9.

IdW-Sonderausschuß Bilanzrichtlinien-Gesetz (1988) 'Entwurf einer Verlautbarung. Zur Aufstellungspflicht für einen Konzernabschluß und zur Abgrenzung des Konsolidierungskreises', *Die Wirtschaftsprüfung*, pp. 81–4.

IdW-Sonderausschuß Bilanzrichtlinien-Gesetz (1988) 'Stellungnahme SABI 1/1988. Zur Aufstellungspflicht für einen Konzernabschluß und zur Abgrenzung des Konsolidierungskreises', *Die Wirtschaftsprüfung*, pp. 340–3.

Odenwald, O. (1989) 'Konsolidierungskreis', in E. Castan, G. Heymann, E. Müller, D. Ordelheide and E. Scheffler (eds) *Beck'sches Handbuch der Rechnungslegung*, Munich: C.H. Beck, C210.

Ordelheide, D. (1986) 'Konzern und Konzernerfolg', *Wirtschaftswissenschaftliches Studium*, pp. 495–502.

Sahner, F., and Kammers, H. (1983) 'Die Abgrenzung des Konsolidierungskreises nach der 7. EG-Richtlinie im Vergleich zum Aktiengesetz 1965 – ein Fortschritt?', *Der Betrieb*, pp. 2149–53, 2209–12.

Strobel, W. (1987) 'Zum Begriff des Konsolidierungskonzerns nach neuem und altem Konzernbilanzrecht', *Der Betrieb*, pp. 237–45.

Treuarbeit (ed.) (1990) *Konzernabschlüsse '89. Ausweis, Gestaltung, Berichterstattung. Ergebnisse einer Untersuchung von 100 großen Konzernen*, Düsseldorf: IdW-Verlag.

Zündorf, H. (1987) 'Zur Abgrenzung des Konsolidierungskreises für Gemeinschaftsunternehmen', *Der Betrieb*, pp. 1852–3.

Section 5 Standardization of the accounts of individual enterprises

Busse von Colbe, W., and Ordelheide, D. (1993) *Konzernabschlusse*, 6th edn, Wiesbaden: Gabler.

Harms, J.E., and Küting, K. (1984) 'Zur Einheitlichkeit der Bewertung im Konzern nach künftigem Bilanzrecht', *Betriebs-Berater*, pp. 105–14.

Hauptfachausschuß des Instituts der Wirtschaftsprüfer (1988) 'Stellungnahme HFA 3/1988. Einheitliche Bewertung im Konzernabschluß', *Die Wirtschaftsprüfung*, pp. 483–5.

Hauptfachausschuß des Instituts der Wirtschaftsprüfer (1988) 'Stellungnahme HFA 4/1988. Konzernrechnungslegung bei unterschiedlichen Abschlußstichtagen', *Die Wirtschaftsprüfung*, pp. 682–3.

IdW-Sonderausschuß Bilanzrichtlinien-Gesetz (1988) 'Entwurf einer Verlautbarung. Einheitliche Bewertung im Konzernabschluß', *Die Wirtschaftsprüfung*, pp. 84–6.

Lange, S. (1992) 'Vereinheitlichung des Bilanzstichtags', in E. Castan, G. Heymann, E. Müller, D. Ordelheide and E. Scheffler (eds) *Beck'sches Handbuch der Rechnungslegung*, Munich: C.H. Beck, C320.

Lederle, H. (1987) 'Vereinheitlichung der Bilanzinhalte', in E. Castan, G. Heymann, E. Müller, D. Ordelheide and E. Scheffler (eds) *Beck'sches Handbuch der Rechnungslegung*, Munich: C.H. Beck, C300.

Ordelheide, D. (1985) 'Bilanzansatz und Bewertung im Konzernabschluß', *Die Wirtschaftsprüfung*, pp. 509–18.

Section 6 Foreign currency translation

Arbeitskreis Weltabschlüsse der Schmalenbach-Gesellschaft/Deutsche Gesellschaft für Betriebswirtschaft eV (1979) *Aufstellung internationaler Konzernabschlüsse*, special issue 9 of *Zeitschrift für betriebswirtschaftliche Forschung*, Düsseldorf and Frankfurt am Main: Handelsblatt.

Busse von Colbe, W. (1981) 'Umrechnung der Abschlüsse ausländischer Konzernunternehmen nach dem Zeitbezug oder zum Stichtagskurs?', in H. Bergner (ed.) *Planung und Rechnungswesen in der Betriebswirtschaftslehre. Festschrift für G. von Kortzfleisch*, Berlin: Duncker & Humblot-Verlag, pp. 311–29.

Busse von Colbe, W. and Ordelheide, D. (1993) *Konzernabschlüsse*, 6th edn, Wiesbaden: Gabler.

Busse von Colbe, W., Müller, E. and Reinhard, H. (eds) (1989) *Aufstellung von Konzernabschlüssen. Empfehlungen des Arbeitskreises 'Externe Unternehmensrechnung' der Schmalenbach-Gesellschaft/Deutsche Gesellschaft für Betriebswirtschaft eV*, 2nd edn, Düsseldorf and Frankfurt am Main: Handelsblatt.

Gebhardt, G. (1987) 'Vereinheitlichung der Recheneinheit durch Währungsumrechnung', in E. Castan, G. Heymann, E. Müller, D. Ordelheide and E. Scheffler (eds) *Beck'sches Handbuch der Rechnungslegung*, Munich: C.H. Beck, C310.

Hummel, W. (1987) *Probleme der Umrechnung von Jahresabschlüssen aus Hochinflationsländern*, Frankfurt am Main: Lang-Verlag.

Institut der Wirtschaftsprüfer in Deutschland eV (1984) 'Entwurf einer Verlautbarung zur Währungsumrechnung im Jahres- und Konzernabschluß' *Fachnachrichten*, pp. 364–7.

Institut der Wirtschaftsprüfer in Deutschland eV (1986) 'Geänderter Entwurf einer Verlautbarung zur Währungsumrechnung im Jahres- und Konzernabschluß', *Die Wirtschaftsprüfung*, pp. 664–7.

Treuarbeit (ed.) (1990) *Konzernabschlüsse '89. Ausweis, Gestaltung, Berichterstattung. Ergebnisse einer Untersuchung von 100 großen Konzernen*, Düsseldorf: IdW-Verlag.

Zillessen, W. (1982) 'Zur Praxis der Währungsumrechnung deutscher Konzerne', *Die Betriebswirtschaft*, pp. 533–52.

Section 7 Consolidation of capital

Busse von Colbe, W. (1985) 'Der Konzernabschluß im Rahmen des Bilanzrichtlinien-Gesetzes', *Zeitschrift für betriebswirtschaftliche Forschung*, pp. 761–82.

Busse von Colbe, W., and Ordelheide, D. (1993) *Konzernabschlüsse*, 6th edn, Wiesbaden: Gabler.

Dreger, K.-M. (1969) *Der Konzernabschluß*, Wiesbaden: Gabler.

IdW-Sonderausschuß Bilanzrichtlinien-Gesetz (1988) 'Stellungnahme SABI 2/1988. Behandlung des Unterschiedsbetrags aus der Kapitalkonsolidierung', *Die Wirtschaftsprüfung*, pp. 622–5; *Fachnachrichten*, pp. 376–80.

Küting, K., and Weber, C.-P. (1986) *Der Konzernabschluß nach neuem Recht*, Stuttgart: Schäffer-Verlag.

Maas, U., and Schruff, W. (1986) 'Der Konzernabschluß nach neuem Recht', *Die Wirtschaftsprüfung*, pp. 201–10, 237–46.

Ordelheide, D. (1986) 'Endkonsolidierung bei Ausscheiden eines Unternehmens aus dem Konsolidierungskreis', *Betriebs-Berater*, pp. 766–72.

Ordelheide, D. (1987) 'Kapitalkonsolidierung nach der Erwerbsmethode', in E. Castan, G. Heymann, E. Müller, D. Ordelheide and E. Scheffler (eds) *Beck'sches Handbuch der Rechnungslegung*, Munich: C.H. Beck, C401, C402, C403.

Ordelheide, D. (1987) 'Kapitalkonsolidierung und Konzernerfolg', *Zeitschrift für betriebswirtschaftliche Forschung*, pp. 292–301.

Pfaff, D. (1989) 'Kapitalkonsolidierung nach der Interessenzusammenführungsmethode', in E. Castan, G. Heymann, E. Müller, D. Ordelheide and E. Scheffler (eds) *Beck'sches Handbuch der Rechnungslegung,* Munich: C.H. Beck, C410.

Schindler, J. (1986) *Die Methoden der Kapitalkonsolidierung nach dem Bilanzrichtlinien-Gesetz,* Frankfurt am Main: Lang-Verlag.

Treuarbeit (ed.) (1990) *Konzernabschlüsse '89. Ausweis, Gestaltung, Berichterstattung. Ergebnisse einer Untersuchung von 100 großen Konzernen,* Düsseldorf: IdW-Verlag.

Weber, C.-P. (1991) *Praxis der Kapitalkonsolidierung im internationalen Vergleich,* Stuttgart: Schäffer-Verlag.

Wentland, N. (1979) *Die Konzernbilanz als Bilanz der wirtschaftlichen Einheit Konzern,* Frankfurt am Main: Lang-Verlag.

Section 8 Consolidation of intra-group balances

Arbeitskreis 'Weltabschlüsse' der Schmalenbach-Gesellschaft/Deutsche Gesellschaft für Betriebswirtschaft eV (1979) *Aufstellung internationaler Konzernabschlüsse,* special issue 9 of *Zeitschrift für betriebswirtschaftliche Forschung,* Düsseldorf and Frankfurt am Main: Handelsblatt.

Busse von Colbe, W. and Ordelheide, D. (1993) *Konzernabschlüsse,* 6th edn, Wiesbaden: Gabler.

Dreger, K.-M. (1968) 'Konzerninterne Forderungen und Verbindlichkeiten bei der Konsolidierung', *Zeitschrift für Betriebswirtschaft,* pp. 279–94.

Fischer, H. (1987) 'Schuldenkonsolidierung', in E. Castan, G. Heymann, E. Müller, D. Ordelheide and E. Scheffler (eds) *Beck'sches Handbuch der Rechnungslegung,* Munich: C.H. Beck, C420.

von Wysocki, K. (1970) 'Die Eliminierung von Zwischenverlusten und die erfolgswirksame Schuldenkonsolidierung im aktienrechtlichen Konzernabschluß', *Die Wirtschaftsprüfung,* pp. 590–4.

Section 9 Elimination of intra-group profits

Busse von Colbe, W., Müller, E. and Reinhard, H. (eds) (1989) Aufstellung von Konzernabschlüssen. Empfehlungen des Arbeitskreises 'Externe Unternehmensrechnung' der Schmalenbach-Gesellschaft/Deutsche Gesellschaft für Betriebswirtschaft eV, 2nd edn, Düsseldorf and Frankfurt am Main: Handelsblatt.

Busse von Colbe, W. and Ordelheide, D. (1993) *Konzernabschlüsse,* 6th edn, Wiesbaden: Gabler.

Klein, K.-G. (1989) 'Zwischenergebniseliminierung', in E. Castan, G. Heymann, E. Müller, D. Ordelheide and E. Scheffler (eds) *Beck'sches Handbuch der Rechnungslegung,* Munich: C.H. Beck, C430.

Treuarbeit (ed.) (1990) *Konzernabschlüsse '89. Ausweis, Gestaltung, Berichterstattung. Ergebnisse einer Untersuchung von 100 großen Konzernen,* Düsseldorf: IdW-Verlag.

Zündorf, H. (1987) 'Zur Problematik der Zwischenergebniseliminierung im Rahmen der Quotenkonsolidierung', *Betriebs-Berater,* pp. 2125–33.

Section 10 Consolidation of revenues and expenses

Busse von Colbe, W. and Ordelheide, D. (1993) *Konzernabschlüsse*, 6th edn, Wiesbaden: Gabler.

Riese, J. (1987) 'Aufwands- und Ertragskonsolidierung', in E. Castan, G. Heymann, E. Müller, D. Ordelheide and E. Scheffler (eds) *Beck'sches Handbuch der Rechnungslegung*, Munich: C.H. Beck, C470.

von Wysocki, K. (1987) 'Die Konsolidierung der Innenumsatzerlöse nach § 305 Abs. 1 Nr. 1 HGB', in H. Havermann (ed.) *Bilanz- und Konzernrecht. Festschrift für R. Goerdeler*, Düsseldorf: IdW-Verlag, pp. 723–49.

Section 11 Deferred taxation

Arbeitskreis 'Rechnungslegungsvorschriften der EG-Kommission' der GEFIU (1984) 'Latente Steuern im Einzel- und Konzernabschluß nach dem Bilanzrichtlinien-Gesetz', *Der Betrieb*, pp. 625–7.

Coenenberg, A.G., and Hille, K. (1979) 'Latente Steuern im Einzel- und Konzernabschluß', *Die Betriebswirtschaft*, pp. 601–21.

Debus, C. (1987) 'Latente Steuern', in E. Castan, G. Heymann, E. Müller, D. Ordelheide and E. Scheffler (eds) *Beck'sches Handbuch der Rechnungslegung*, Munich: C.H. Beck, C440.

Harms, J.E., and Küting, K. (1985) 'Probleme latenter Steuern im Entwurf des Bilanzrichtlinie-Gesetzes', *Betriebs-Berater*, pp. 94–101.

Hille, K. (1982) *Latente Steuern im Einzel- und Konzernabschluß*, Frankfurt am Main: Lang-Verlag.

Treuarbeit (ed.) (1990) *Konzernabschlüsse '89. Ausweis, Gestaltung, Berichterstattung. Ergebnisse einer Untersuchung von 100 großen Konzernen*, Düsseldorf: IdW-Verlag.

Section 12 Proportional consolidation and the equity method

Busse von Colbe, W. (1986) 'Die Equitymethode zur Bewertung von Beteiligungen im Konzernabschluß', in E. Gaugler, H.G. Meissner and N. Thom (eds) *Zukunftsaspekte der anwendungsorientierten Betriebswirtschaftslehre. E. Grochla zum 65. Geburtstag gewidmet*, Stuttgart: Poeschel-Verlag.

Busse von Colbe, W. and Ordelheide, D. (1993) *Konzernabschlüsse*, 6th edn, Wiesbaden: Gabler.

Harms, J.E. and Knischewski, G. (1985) 'Quotenkonsolidierung versus Equity-Methode im Konzernabschluß', *Der Betrieb*, pp. 1353–9.

Herrnberger, K. (1987) 'Quotenkonsolidierung von Gemeinschaftsunternehmen', in E. Castan, G. Heymann, E. Müller, D. Ordelheide and E. Scheffler (eds) *Beck'sches Handbuch der Rechnungslegung*, Munich: C.H. Beck, C500.

Küting, K. and Zündorf, H. (1988) 'Die Praxis des Equity-Accounting', *Betriebs-Berater*, pp. 872–81.

Küting, K., Weber, C.-P. and Zündorf, H. (1987) 'Die Equity-Methode im Übergang auf die neue Konzernrechnungslegung', *Betriebs-Berater*, pp. 1496–502.

Müller, E. with C. Lauer (1992) 'Konsolidierung im Rahmen der Equity-Methode', in E. Castan, G. Heymann, E. Müller, D. Ordelheide and E. Scheffler (eds) *Beck'sches Handbuch der Rechnungslegung*, Munich: C.H. Beck, C511.

Treuarbeit (ed.) (1990) *Konzernabschlüsse '89. Ausweis, Gestaltung, Berichterstattung. Ergebnisse einer Untersuchung von 100 großen Konzernen*, Düsseldorf: IdW-Verlag.

von Wysocki, K. (1990) 'Zur Equity-Methode nach §§311 und 312 HGB', in J. Baetge (ed.) *Konzernrechnungslegung und -prüfung*, Düsseldorf: IdW-Verlag, pp. 105–28.

Zündorf, H. (1987) *Quotenkonsolidierung versus Equity-Methode*, Stuttgart: Schäffer-Verlag.

Section 13 The notes on the group accounts

Gzuk, R. (1987) 'Konzernanhang', in E. Castan, G. Heymann, E. Müller, D. Ordelheide and E. Scheffler (eds) *Beck'sches Handbuch der Rechnungslegung*, Munich: C.H. Beck, C600.

Harms, J.E. and Küting, K. (1984) 'Der Konzernanhang nach künftigem Recht', *Betriebs-Berater*, pp. 1977–84.

Schulte, W. (1986) 'Inhalt und Gliederung des Anhangs', *Betriebs-Berater*, pp. 1468–80.

Selchert, F. and Karsten, J. (1986) 'Inhalt und Gliederung des Konzernanhangs', *Betriebs-Berater*, pp. 1258–64.

CHAPTER 9 SUPPLEMENTARY REPORTS

Bridts, C. (1990) *Zwischenberichtspublizität*, Düsseldorf: IdW-Verlag.

Busse von Colbe, W. and Reinhard, H. (eds) (1989) *Zwischenberichterstattung nach neuem Recht für börsennotierte Unternehmen. Empfehlungen des Arbeitskreises 'Externe Unternehmensrechnung' der Schmalenbach-Gesellschaft/Deutsche Gesellschaft für Betriebswirtschaft eV*, Stuttgart: Schäffer.

Busse von Colbe, W., Geiger, K., Haase, H., Reinhard, H. and Schmitt, G. (eds) (1991) *Earnings according to the DVFA/SG method. Joint Recommendation of the DVFA Commission for Methodology of the Financial Analysis and of the Working Group 'External Company Accounting' of the Schmalenbach-Gesellschaft*, Stuttgart: Schäffer.

Gzuk, R. (1987) 'Konzernlagebericht', in E. Castan, G. Heymann, E. Müller, D. Ordelheide and E. Scheffler (eds) *Beck'sches Handbuch der Rechnungslegung*, Munich: C.H. Beck, C610.

Scheffler, E. (1991) 'Zwischenbericht der börsennotierten AG/KGaA', in E. Castan, G. Heymann, E. Müller, D. Ordelheide and E. Scheffler (eds) *Beck'sches Handbuch der Rechnungslegung*, Munich: C.H. Beck, B750.

Semler, J. (1980) 'Erläuterungs- und Lagebericht, Quartalsberichte sowie Formen der Publizität', *Zeitschrift für betriebswirtschaftliche Forschung*, pp. 177–210.

CHAPTER 10 AUDIT AND DISCLOSURE

Section 1 The auditing profession and the audit of the financial statements

Baetge, J. (1988) *Abschlußprüfung nach neuem Recht*, Stuttgart: Schäffer-Verlag.

Baetge, J. (1990) 'Prüfung des Konzernabschlusses', in J. Baetge (ed.), *Konzernrechnungslegung und -prüfung*, Düsseldorf: IdW-Verlag, pp. 175–200.

Baetge, J. (ed.) (1990) *Konzernrechnungslegung und -prüfung. Vorträge und Diskussionen zum neuen Recht*, Düsseldorf: IdW-Verlag.

Egner, H. (1980) *Betriebswirtschaftliche Prüfungslehre*, Berlin and New York: de Gruyter-Verlag.

IdW-Fachausschuß für moderne Abrechnungssysteme (1988) 'Grundsätze ordnungsmäßiger Buchführung bei computergestützten Verfahren und deren Prüfung', *Die Wirtschaftsprüfung*, pp. 1–35.

Institut der Wirtschaftsprüfer (1992) *Wirtschaftsprüfer-Handbuch 1992* 1, 10th edn, Düsseldorf: IdW-Verlag.

Leffson, U. (1988) *Wirtschaftsprüfung*, 4th edn, Wiesbaden: Gabler.

Schnicke, C. (1988) 'Organisation der Erstellung und Prüfung des Konzernabschlusses', in W. Mellwig, A. Moxter and D. Ordelheide (eds) *Einzelabschluß und Konzernabschluß*, Wiesbaden: Gabler, pp. 153–75.

Selchert, F.W. (1988) *Jahresabschlußprüfung der Kapitalgesellschaften*, Wiesbaden: Gabler.

Section 2 Disclosure

Apelt, B. (1991) *Die Publizität der GmbH*, Berlin: Duncker & Humblot-Verlag.

Ballwieser, W., and Häger, R. (1991) 'Das Bilanzierungsverhalten mittelgroßer Kapitalgesellschaften', in K. Chmielewicz and K.-H. Forster (eds) *Unternehmensverfassung und Rechnungslegung in der EG*, special issue 29 of *Zeitschrift für betriebswirtschaftliche Forschung*, Düsseldorf and Frankfurt am Main: Handelsblatt, pp. 107–22.

Biener, H. (1989) 'Die Publizität der Rechnungslegung im Wandel', in *Betriebswirtschaftliche Forschung und Praxis*, pp. 213–30.

Index